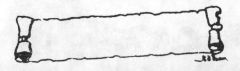

JEAN RENOIR

◆

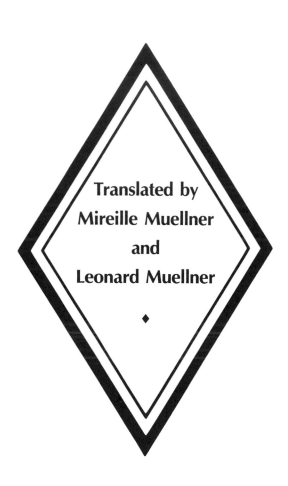

Translated by
Mireille Muellner
and
Leonard Muellner

♦

CÉLIA
BERTIN

JEAN RENOIR

A LIFE IN PICTURES

◆

THE JOHN HOPKINS UNIVERSITY PRESS

BALTIMORE AND LONDON

Originally published as *Jean Renoir*
© Librarie Académique Perrin, 1986

© 1991 The John Hopkins University Press
All rights reserved
Printed in the United States of America
96 95 94 93 92 91   5 4 3 2 1

The John Hopkins University Press
701 West 40th Street
Baltimore, Maryland 21211
The John Hopkins Press Ltd., London

∞   The paper used in this book meets the minimum requirements of
American National Standard for Information Sciences—Permanence
of Paper for Printed Library Materials, ANSI Z39.48-1984.

Library of Congress Cataloging-in-Publication Data

Bertin, Célia, 1921–
[Jean Renoir. English]
Jean Renoir : a life in pictures / by Célia Bertin ; translated by
Mireille Muellner and Leonard Muellner.
p.   cm.
Includes bibliographical references and index.
ISBN 0-8018-4184-4
1. Renoir, Jean, 1894–   . 2. Motion picture producers and
directors—France—Biography. I. Title.
PN1998.3.R46B4713   1991
791.43'0233'092—dc20   [B]   90-23138

Uncredited photographs are from the Jean Renoir Archives.

CONTENTS

♦

"The spectacle of real life is a thousand times richer than the most beguiling inventions of our imagination."
Jean Renoir
Ma vie et mes films, 121

"Reality is always magical."
Jean Renoir
Cahiers du cinéma 78, Christmas 1957, 27

ACKNOWLEDGMENTS

◆

This biography could not have been written without the help of Alain Renoir, Henri Cartier-Bresson, Anne de Saint-Phalle, François Truffaut, and Dido Renoir. I also wish to thank Danielle Hunebelle, a supportive friend who was kind enough to read and reread my manuscript, pencil in hand.

My thanks are now too late for Dido, Anne, and François. With unequalled generosity and understanding, they shared with me their memories and their letters. Videotapes that they provided made it possible for me to see some films that are no longer accessible. Jean-Paul Le Chanois also reminisced for me.

I was fortunate to have the help of Roland Stragliati and also of Claude Gauteur, who generously put at my disposal his knowledge of Jean Renoir's art and his own work in progress. Professor Alexander Sesonske also let me consult several documents in his possession.

In addition, I wish to thank all those who so willingly provided me with information: Janine André Bazin, Françoise Arnoul, Jean-Pierre Aumont, Jean-Louis Barrault, Paul Barzman, Sylvia Bataille, Loleh Bellon, Claude Beylie, Pierre Braunberger, Leslie Caron, André Cerf, Marjorie and Philippe Cézanne, Aline Cézanne, Yvonne Dornès, Nicholas Frangakis, William H. Gilcher, Claude Heymann, Norman Lloyd, Madame Eugène Lourié, Giulio Macchi, Marc Maurette, Frédéric Mitterrand, Claude and Evangèle Renoir, Jean Rouch, Catherine Rouvel, Ruta Sadoul, Jean Serge, Jean Slade, Serge Tubiana, Alexandre Trauner, Denise and Christian Tual, Jeanne Weymers, André Zwobada, and the Archives of the French National Cinematography Center in Bois-d'Arcy, where I was allowed to review some materials. I also wish to express my gratitude to my husband for his interest in my work and his support.

JEAN RENOIR

◆

THE MAN WHO

PAINTED WOMEN AND

JOIE DE VIVRE

♦

At the end of his life, Jean Renoir confided to a friend, "My problem is, I'm a nineteenth-century man." A tongue in cheek remark, and a surprising admission from a man who was to die in 1979 with an international reputation as the most progressive filmmaker of his day. But in fact it is neither incongruous nor unnatural. There is a real truth in it. The further I have gone in my discovery of Jean Renoir and his work, the more I have thought "portrait of the artist's son." The man who painted women and *joie de vivre* made an unavoidable, indelible mark on his son in all aspects of his life.

In the Renoir household, the children were never told that their father was a "great artist"—Renoir forbade such terms—nor were they permitted to put on airs because of his fame. On the contrary, a kind of well-groomed modesty and ebullience had to be maintained at all times. An extraordinary family, it tried to convince itself that it was actually the same as any other, and it clung to the peasant values that both parents had been born into.

Pierre-Auguste Renoir, the painter, was born near the end of the first half of the nineteenth century, on February 25, 1841, in Limoges, the same town in which his father had been born. Four years later, Léonard, a tailor, set out for Paris with his young family to seek his fortune. Auguste was the youngest of his four children at the time. In

1

those days the trip to Paris by stagecoach lasted more than two weeks. On arriving, Léonard found his family an apartment between the Louvre and the Tuileries, a *quartier* of winding streets and sixteenth-century houses that was looked down upon by the middle class. Some of the houses had been ransacked during the Revolution [of 1830]. By settling down amid this decay, working-class families were actually reviving an old tradition: with a new king installed in the Tuileries, simple people found themselves once more their sovereign's next-door neighbors. Auguste Renoir and the youngsters in his neighborhood played cops and robbers, yelling and screaming, right under the royal apartments. Once in a while, a woman sitting in the window with her knitting would open it and throw handfuls of candy to the children; she would ask them—the brats never obeyed—if they wouldn't go and play a little further on. She was Queen Marie-Amélie, wife of King Louis-Philippe.

Auguste Renoir loved these anecdotes. He had a historian's gift for the telling detail. His observations, which gave him a heightened sense of the changes he had witnessed during his lifetime, in fact drew him to history. And his reminiscences were far from forgotten. They played a part in forming the interests and mental cast of his son. Renoir also loved recalling the old tale that his grandfather François was of noble descent. A foundling, he had been adopted by a clog-maker who gave him his name and taught him his trade. In 1815, this François went from Limoges to Paris in the hope that Louis XVIII would help him discover his high birth. Léonard the tailor betrayed little sympathy for these fantasies; his children laughed even harder at their grandpa's silly dreams. There were five children in all, only one a girl, Lisa. She was the second oldest, a born rebel who went on to become a disciple of Fourier and Saint-Simon.

As for Jean Renoir, he forgot nothing. He remembered this royalist fantasy when he dreamed up the exiled aristocrats of *La Marseillaise*. Some relatives, as a joke, used to call his father "monsieur le marquis." In *The Rules of the Game*, Jean gave this same title to the character played by Dalio as a way of putting him at the mercy of the people and the nobility at once. In fact, those two constituencies are a recurrent obsession in Jean's life and work.

After the fall of Louis-Philippe, establishment types took over the palace, and a decision was made to demolish the surrounding *quartier* in order to make room for the court of the Louvre. On the lookout for cheap housing (the tailor did not, of course, strike it rich), the Renoir family moved to the Marais, a pretty part of the city peopled by artisans living over their shops or next to their studios. Auguste slept on the workbench at which his father squatted all day long. At thirteen, it was time for him to be apprenticed. His two older brothers and his sister already had trades that insured their survival: one brother was a silversmith, the other a tailor like his father, working for a master-tailor in a shop on the *grands boulevards* downtown. Lisa was a seamstress. Her contempt for convention notwithstanding, she was about to marry an engraver, Charles Leray, who had illustrated several books and was working for the Parish fashion magazines.

Like Henri, the oldest of the brothers, Leray had not failed to observe Auguste's gifts as a draughtsman. Even as a child, he was making decent likenesses of neighbors and relations. He used to draw, the story goes, on whatever came his way, in his schoolbooks or on the floor with bits of his father's chalk. No one thought he would ever become a painter, but why not point him toward an occupation in which he could use his gifts, such as sketching fashion designs? Léonard, born in Limoges, preferred to imagine his son painting porcelains. He knew a manufacturer in the neighborhood. But another, different opportunity presented itself first.

At the parochial school he was attending, it had been noticed that Auguste had a truly beautiful voice. He was accepted into the choir of St. Eustache's, a famous one that was led by a still unknown composer named Charles Gounod. The young choirmaster took a liking to Auguste and trained him in harmony and composition as well as singing. His ambition was to make an accomplished musician of him. Gounod's first goal was to get the young fellow into the chorus of the Paris Opéra, whence he predicted a great career for him as a tenor. Auguste was inspired by what Gounod was teaching him and never missed a lesson, but the theater did not tempt him. Rather than be listened to and looked at, he preferred to listen and look at others; that was the pleasure he was constitutionally unable to forgo. As Jean Renoir put it, he had "a passion for the beings and things of this world." When eventually he said his farewell to Gounod, the latter was full of regrets. Auguste shared his sadness, but he was convinced he should become an apprentice in the studio of a porcelain factory. Later, he often told his son not to force his character or destiny. "Let your life float downstream like a cork," he was fond of saying.

Auguste Renoir did not put this "cork theory" into words until later, but he lived by it instinctively from the start. He advanced quickly during the five years he spent in the porcelain factory studio. Since the historical portraits he painted on plates sold so well, particularly the profile of Marie-Antoinette on dessert dishes, his sister Lisa, with her concern for social justice, arranged with his employers to have him paid by the piece instead of at apprentice's wages. The young man wanted to learn as much as he could of his trade, so he also took up throwing pots and firing them. He loved the way the colors of the glazes changed and fused; he would fuss over the temperature in the wood-fired kiln for twelve hours at a stretch. But in 1858, the porcelain factory on the rue Vieille-du-Temple closed its doors: machines were now reproducing earthenware and porcelain plates with the same design by the thousands.

That was a big change from the way of life he grew up with. The age of machines had arrived. Renoir sensed its significance and was curious to know more. But first things first: he had to find himself another job. He applied for one with a manufacturer of waterproof canvas awnings, assuring the man that he knew all about painting them. He was so clever at it, in fact, that he earned a good living, though he did not pass up the chance to decorate a café now and then. His first was a hole-in-the-wall at Les Halles, where he painted a Venus rising from the sea. Its success brought more commissions, and he eventually decorated the walls of about twenty cafés in Paris. Moreover, he began painting for himself, not in secret, but not announcing to everyone that he had found his calling, either. After three or four years, he quit painting awnings and decorating cafés and joined the Gleyre studio, one of the most famous in Paris, at the urging of Charles Leray and some other painters who dined on his mother's pot-au-feu every Saturday night. The tailor and his family got along well with the artists in their neighborhood. It was as though they lived in the same village. They were loyal and always ready to help each other. They all thought of themselves as belonging to the class of people who work with their hands and exploit no one.

All his life, Pierre-Auguste clung to the notion of not wanting to exploit anyone. For instance, he refused to invest in industrial stocks, which he considered a faceless form of exploitation. And the feeling that there are clearly defined social classes was to inspire in Jean Renoir the idea that the horizontal divisions of society are more important than what he called its vertical ones—nationalities. In *Grand Illusion,* for instance, the aristocratic French captain played by Pierre Fresnay has closer ties to Erich von Stroheim, the German aristocrat who is a career officer like himself, than to Maréchal (Jean Gabin), who had been a mechanic before the war.

But genius is isolating, even before it has come to the surface.

4

The painters who were his parents' friends encouraged young Auguste and gave him worthy advice: go to the Louvre, copy the masters. Auguste listened, though he already knew what he was looking for and no one else did. In Gleyre's studio, he wanted above all to learn to draw the human figure. His other goals were obscure to his friends also.

It isn't easy now to imagine Renoir as a young man. Most of the portraits and photographs of him have accustomed us to an elderly man with an emaciated face and a body wracked by rheumatism. But there once was a tall, slender youth with light brown hair, light brown eyes ("verging on yellow," according to his son) and a rather thin, elongated face. A few years later, Cézanne said of him: "He is a bit girlish, a bit fickle, easily moved by his feelings, first one way, then another; unsure of himself, always ready to give way to circumstances or influences, appearing indecisive." What Cézanne noticed might also be called "playing the cork"; actually, Renoir did not give way, nor was he indecisive. He simply wanted to get at what others could teach him, and a negative or even a positive stand entailed the risk of losing the chance to do so. As a result, he was a slave to his unquenchable desire to extract what he could from everyday events, from human beings as well as art. He was insatiably curious, but he hated to put himself on display, as he hated people who appeared to take themselves seriously. He knew he was different and that he had to accept the difference. His need to paint took precedence over everything, even his taste for women's beauty. Women were pleased by this young, ardent man, and for him, painting them was his way of loving them. But he had no time to lose and did not wish to lose much of it with them. He said as much more than once. Yet he knew how to paint a female body that was as delectable as it looked to him.

At Gleyre's, he made friends with Bazille and so finally had someone to talk with about his work. Gleyre and even Fantin-Latour, who sometimes visited the studio, recognized his exceptional gifts, though they cautioned him about his love for color. Using such bright tonalities just wasn't done. Renoir knew how to achieve their dusky highlights, but that was not what he had in mind. Thanks to Bazille, he met first Sisley, then Monet, Frank Lamy, and Pissarro. At the Closerie des Lilas, they drank bock beer together and spoke intensely of their artistic ideals. Studying past masters was not for them; painting was not just transposing, it was capturing a moment, revealing what struck the eye: the cast of light over an unstudied fragment of a landscape, its contours marked only by color changes. Renoir agreed with them about taking the direct route to what he saw. The old school of painting was dying, and it was time to break away, to be free, and to express what the senses perceived, what one person's gaze would choose to view. Won over by the enthusiasm of his friends, he was as ready as they were to throw off conventions. Yet he could not keep himself from asking questions: did Fragonard, in his portraits, paint only what he saw, or had he melded the remembered vision of other painters' work into his own? Renoir's friends weren't interested in Fragonard, however; in that he was once more alone, but no matter. He knew how to survive. In 1864, he sent a painting to the Salon. It was accepted, so he submitted another in 1865. But it was rejected, as were his friends'. All of them were convinced that the only way to prove they were right was to exhibit their work. But the art dealers and the organizers of the Salon would have none of it. In the meantime, Renoir had to take up decorating cafés again. All his savings were spent, and he could no longer attend Gleyre's studio. Still, he did not give up the gatherings at the Closerie, any more than he gave up his dream of painting for pleasure.

That was also the dream of his son, Jean: making a movie for the fun of it. One can sense the sheer delight they took in their work. The pleasure generated by a love of one's calling is rare enough to be remarked, since artistic creation does not often also provide happiness.

As soon as he was once again able to give up painting murals in bars, Auguste joined forces with Claude Monet. They shared everything: the rent for a studio, the coal bills, food, the model. They even shared portrait commissions. Monet exacted some commissions from shopkeepers, who, if they were grocers, paid in kind. He pretended to be a dandy to impress his clients. This was when Renoir first met Cézanne; they were to be close friends. Thanks to Bazille, a loyal friend, he also met admirers like the young Prince Bibesco, who was close to Napoleon III and the Empress. Apart from these contacts that "scraped the mud off his boots," as he put it, he and Monet had a hard time making headway with the middle class of the Second Empire, which at that time was transforming the capital, crisscrossing it with boulevards, and lining them with buildings whose façades were as imposing as they were repetitive. Auguste missed the lovely old architecture, its lightness and elegance, and he disliked the new style as well as the mercantilism that had inspired it—only a century later does it begin to seem interesting. He was never dazzled by wealth, and his idea of luxury had nothing to do with market value. He was proud to have been born among artisans. They had taught him to love the traces of a human hand in an art object, a piece of furniture, or the harmonious lines of a building. (This sort of affinity for refinement and simplicity was inherited by his son.) To arouse his interest, rich admirers had to have something more to offer than money. He did not try to impress them, because his mind was set on painting and living his own way.

◆

Renoir's sense of history did not lead to involvement in politics. Wars preoccupied him even less than society. Before 1870 he had not spent a day as a soldier. A lucky number in the military lottery had saved him from the seven years of active duty that awaited those less fortunate. But during the [Franco-German] war, he was drafted into the tenth cavalry regiment and stationed at Tarbes. It was the first time he saw a horse close up. Yet in six months, he became an accomplished horseman, as comfortable with horses as he had been with models, people said. Moreover, he gave painting lessons to the captain's daughter, whose tastes quickly became as revolutionary as his own. For starters, she would have liked to burn all of Winterhalter's paintings! But he was soon to lose sight of this young person, and he never had a chance to hear the sound of cannon, which would have startled him. Demobilized and sent back to Paris at the beginning of the commune, Renoir learned that his friend Bazille had been killed in that disastrous war. A group of painters he knew well aligned themselves with the revolutionary camp, but Renoir was careful to keep his distance. During the commune, his parents, his sister Lisa, and her husband Charles Leray were living at Louveciennes. Equipped with two passes, one from the Communards and another from the Versaillais (obtained through the good offices of Prince Bibesco), he crossed the lines often to paint there, oblivious to the risks he was taking.

Jean could easily imagine the life Auguste led during this period. His father spoke of it often, though he himself was never to know its rigors. He never knew poverty first hand, nor did he have to experience his father's lonely struggle to remain faithful to his vision of the world after the age of thirty. Fortunately for him, Auguste Renoir didn't have a personality like Cézanne's. Above and beyond what others perceived as a kind of adaptiveness, he had ferocious determination. He accepted his money woes and even found a way to laugh at them. Even though Jean Renoir never saw lean years, he had learned as a very young boy what it meant to be devoted to one's craft just by watching the way his father lived. He also learned that good humor can continue to flourish despite suffering and anxiety. He had seen his father in the grip of terrible pains caused by arthritis; but once he got the better of them, they seemed to go away. These ills, which had begun in 1888 with a local facial paralysis, became more and more excruciating and unremitting until his death. (Jean, who always said he himself was a true coward, in fact owed a certain type of physical courage to his father's example.) Renoir had a deep concern for others that is not always an attribute of genius. He knew how to live well and also how to make the lives of others pleasant. Apparently, his parents had the same knack. Aside from his brother Edmond, six years his junior, who went to school and became a journalist, Renoir's family didn't know who he really was, but it made no difference in the closeness they all felt toward him.

All of Renoir's painter friends except Monet had different backgrounds than his. But their lot was the same: though the middle class, which Renoir really distrusted, had spawned the others, they were no more successful than he at selling their canvases. In 1874, tired of being barred from regular exhibition of their work by the jury of the Salon, they organized a group show at a gallery owned by the photographer Nadar. A reporter for *Charivari* was the first to call them impressionists, taking the name from the title of one of Monet's paintings in the exhibition. What happened next is well known. The next year, at the Hôtel Drouot, Berthe Morisot, Sisley, Renoir, and Claude Monet sold sixty paintings at auction, but the prices were so low that some paintings had to be withdrawn; the whole sale netted a mere 10,449 francs. That was when Georges Charpentier bought a Renoir for 180 francs and invited the artist home to dinner.

In 1869, Renoir painted the portrait of Charpentier's mother, but he decided to keep his distance, since he did not wish to seem to profit from his friendship with the famous publisher, whose wife presided over the most brilliant literary and political salon in Paris. After a second meeting, Renoir became a frequent visitor. He got along well with Mme. Charpentier, who helped him with a project that reveals what kind of person he was. After the war and the commune, there was a lot of misery in Paris; Renoir had become aware of the terrible neglect suffered by the children in his own neighborhood, Montmartre. His idea was to organize a dance to benefit them at the Moulin de la Galette. With Mme. Charpentier's support, the benefit resulted in the creation of "Le Pouponat," an institution that founded the first day care center for the many illegitimate children in the district. At the Charpentiers', Renoir met Gambetta and Clemenceau, Maupassant, Zola, the Goncourt brothers, Flaubert, the inventor/poet Charles Cros, the musician Cabaner, who was a great lover of Cézanne's paintings, Alphonse Daudet, whom he admired, and Ivan Turgenev. He also came to know Mallarmé there, who was to become a close friend.

Little by little, Renoir acquired the habit of getting out into the fashionable world. According to his son, for a long time he owned just three articles of clothing (more would have been encumbering): "two of them were gray and striped, and the older one was to paint in; plus a dinner jacket."[1] Apparently the homes he visited were inhabited by sophisticated people who were tolerant of such eccentricities. Renoir enjoyed attractive surroundings and the company of elegant young women and polite children; they, in turn, were ready to pose for him, since he told good stories and sang during sittings. This was how he came to know the lights of Parisian society.

He kept getting more portrait commissions, and, moreover, he was allowed to treat his subjects as he wished. Soon he was able to make a living more easily than his friends could. Some of the paintings were masterpieces. Apart from their pictorial merits, they are portraits that could be read by a novelist. Renoir knew how to take the face of a worldly woman or an actress, a model or a gallery owner, or even Richard Wagner, and give it the arresting complexity that can be discovered in people if one takes the trouble to observe them well. Collectors soon became his friends. He would visit them in their country homes, which is how he came to paint so much at Wargemont, near Dieppe, at the house of Paul Bérard, or how he came to know Paul Gallimard, the father of the publisher, who was a great collector of impressionist art and especially appreciated Renoir. The two of them became such good friends that they traveled together to Spain, and Renoir eventually spent two summers with the Gallimard family at their country estate in Bénerville, where Gaston and his two younger brothers, Raymond and Jacques, posed for him. Renoir had great affection for Choquet, whom he called "the greatest French collector since the kings, maybe even the greatest in the world since the popes!" Jean Renoir, who reports the remark, adds: "By popes, my father meant Julius II, who knew how to get Michelangelo and Raphaël to paint: leave them well enough alone" (ibid., 187).

Renoir loved to talk; in the social circles that valued his painting, he was even "a brilliant conversationalist," a prized attribute. "In tails, Renoir became an aristocrat," wrote Jeanne Baudot, a student of his who was part of that world and who was later to be Jean's godmother.

---

[1] *Renoir par Jean Renoir* (Paris, 1962), 205 (= *Renoir, My Father*, trans. Randolph and Dorothy Weaver [Boston, 1962], 212).

A painter herself, Jeanne observed him in many contexts: in high society, in his studio talking with professional models or other painters or even his next-door neighbors. "Because of his sensitivity and intensity, he changed himself to suit the interlocutor."[2] The remark shows that Renoir applied the theory of the cork to all situations.

Yet it was not an infallible theory in painting, the field dearest to his heart. For a long time, Renoir kept his ties to the impressionists, though he was sure he could not follow them in every respect. Still, he agreed with them more than with anyone else. In 1876 they found an enthusiastic art dealer who began exhibiting their work jointly in the rue Le Peletier. These avant-garde painters who were often looked upon as former Communards were, ironically, championed by a devout Catholic who did not conceal his loyalty toward the Count of Chambord, pretender to the throne. In the elections of 1877, this man, Paul Durand-Ruel, was personally and financially hurt by the result, a victory for the Republican party. There was nothing at all revolutionary about the artistic preferences of the victorious middle class, who agreed to make July 14 the national holiday. Their bourgeois taste in painting ran to Carolus-Duran, Bouguereau, and Meissonier.

The impressionists exhibited as a group until 1886. That was the year Durand-Ruel showed their work successfully at the American Art Association on Madison Square in New York. He sold $18,000 worth of paintings there. Three years before, he had organized exhibitions in London, Rotterdam, and Boston. In 1879, Renoir's work began to appear in the Salon again. From 1880 on, it became clear that he was distancing himself from impressionism. He still felt loyal to his friends, however, so when he met dealers like Choquet, Vollard, or Père Tanguy, he immediately introduced them to the impressionists. He never dreamed of breaking with them personally.

Reading what others have written and what he said or wrote about himself, it is difficult to imagine Auguste Renoir ever being in crisis. There is such an abundance of sanity and vigor in him, and so much balance. He appears no more tortured than his models. In fact, we know that he suffered terrible physical agony, though he withstood it and always looked the epitome of harmony and happiness. But he agonized over his desire to escape from the impasse in which he had put himself by following the theories of his friends. Light colors, pink or purple shadows, the play of light through leaves, a bright yellow stream—these were things never before represented that he, too, longed to make acceptable to the public, but he wondered if they

Jeanne Baudot, *Renoir: Ses amis, ses modèles* (Paris, 1949), 80.

shouldn't be presented in a more structured format. People kept saying that he and his friends rejected the conventions only because they were unable to stick to them. Did they know how to draw at all? The press was openly hostile and never treated them fairly. Renoir was practical and perceptive, and he understood the public's questions. He had no desire to teach it a lesson, but he did wish to master his craft, to make it more profound and able to express what he felt when he looked at poppies or little girls at the seashore or a rowboat at Chatou or the dazzling body of a model. He wanted to create his own pictorial language to express his love for life, for the festival of color that life always celebrates. The naive offer of sumptuous flesh is a compelling sign of his intelligence and love. Jean Renoir inherited this unselfconscious naivete along with the ease of address that is everywhere apparent in his father's work. And changeable as he was, Auguste Renoir's work remains a creative unity. Despite technical variations, there is the same observant eye, the same passion for the same things, along with a gentle force trembling with love in the presence of beauty. That unity was readily apparent in the huge retrospective that traveled to London, Paris, and Boston in 1985, drawing record-breaking crowds in each city.

♦

The same moment that Renoir's painting changed, so did his life. In 1880, he met a seamstress just under twenty years old (he was almost forty) who, like him, used to visit the little restaurant on the rue Saint-Georges across from his studio. Aline Charigot lived with her mother. Both of them were born in Essoyes, a village in Le Barrois on the border between Champagne and Burgundy near Troyes. They moved to Paris when Aline's father abandoned them, repelled by his wife's inordinate zeal for housework. He fled her as far as North Dakota, from which he returned in 1870 to fight in the war; after the defeat, he wasted no time going back to the new family he had started. The story of this grandfather intrigued Jean and was ultimately the inspiration for a sketch called "The Electric Floor Polisher" in his last movie, *Le Petit Théâtre de Jean Renoir*. But by the time Jean knew Grandma Charigot, the sun had set on her days as a parquet virtuoso.

Renoir was not the catch she had dreamed of for her daughter—he was too old (almost as old as she, in fact), too poor, and his painting was not real art. But judgments like that never dissuade daughters in love. The owner of the restaurant where they met had a wider perspective. She found Renoir passable but too thin. Aline had nothing against thinness. The inevitable happened, although they did not actually begin living together until 1882. Returning from a trip, they discovered how hard it was to live without one another.

For Auguste Renoir, living with a woman meant having more time to paint. He soon gave up his excursions into the outside world—they took up too many long evenings. He lost some of his more elegant models but kept others, "that *internationale* of girls whose skin takes the light."[3] From the beginning, Aline let him have his way. She was the wife he needed: there, and not demanding. She did not understand the questions that preoccupied him, and she did not try to answer them for herself. She was not wild about his painting, though she enjoyed seeing him paint and posing for him. Like him, she was good-natured and loved to laugh. She had blond hair, blue eyes, and a face like a well-fed cat's. She can be seen in the famous painting called *The Luncheon of the Boating Party*: there she sits on the left, in a blue dress, wearing a hat with poppies on it, playing with a little dog.

The painting dates from the time when Auguste thought he had reached the limits of impressionism.[4] He was beginning various experiments, ranging from painting with a palette knife to coloring drawings with washes. Jean Renoir also faced problems of technique, but he resolved them more easily, since a filmmaker's issues are not the same as a painter's. For one thing, a film is not just an individual's reflections on the world. It is a group endeavor. Jean Renoir telling a journalist, "Art working to change nature is an old story,"[5] sounds like something he learned by listening to his father and analyzing his paintings. He, too, must have pondered the questions raised by impressionism: the father's inner struggles were not unknown to the son. Each picture is a different adventure, whether in a painting, a film, or a book. At the same time, there is the continuity of the life one has chosen to live.

In 1885, Aline gave birth to a son, Pierre, who eventually became an actor. So as not to disturb the painter when the baby cried, Aline's idea was to move from the studio on the rue Saint-Georges into a new apartment at the same time as Renoir would move into a separate studio. Renoir agreed; this kind of homespun practicality was typical of her. She did not know his friends and visited no one, not even other painters. The only one she knew was Cézanne, who showed up un-

---

[3] *Renoir par Jean Renoir*, 153 (= *Renoir, My Father*, 147.)
[4] Claude-Roger Marx, *Renoir* (Paris, 1937), 108.
[5] Ole Vinding, *Pour vous*, 13 October 1932, 294, cited by Claude Gauteur in *Jean Renoir, ou La double méprise* (Paris, 1980), 92.

expectedly one day three months after Pierre was born and moved in with them. He brought along his friend Hortense Fiquet, whom he married the following year, and their son, Paul, whom the Renoirs treated as one of their own. But Berthe Morisot, whom Renoir liked very much and visited often, did not meet Aline until the summer of 1891. Degas, who caught sight of Aline once at a show, said to Renoir of her, "Your wife looks like a queen surrounded by mountebanks." Since Degas was a misogynist, that was a compliment. For Renoir, she was what a woman should be: a housekeeper. In their household, she created a serenity that hardly changed when wealth and fame arrived. She let him travel alone and did not object if he went out by himself. She was not tempted by some lifestyle she had never known and did not even care to imagine. It was not social ambition that drove her into the arms of the man whom she always called "Renoir." They were not actually married until April 14, 1890; but the fact of marriage brought about no change in their already settled habits. That was the year the great portrait of *Mesdemoiselles Catulle Mendès* was exhibited at the Salon.

In April 1887, Renoir and Aline moved again, to another section of Montmartre. Living at the Château des Brouillards was like being in the countryside. On a slope of the Butte Montmartre, high above the city's gray—people knew nothing about pollution then—on the site of an eighteenth-century summer house that had disappeared during the Revolution, a cluster of buildings had been constructed and a garden, all surrounded by hedgerows. A few ruined outbuildings still existed, as well as some beautiful trees from what had been the park. The main building had a rectangular foundation and was three stories high. It had been subdivided into several dwellings. Though it was called a château, in fact it was an unpretentious place that had nothing to do with what had been there before. Like the others, the Renoirs' home had a small garden of lilacs and rosebushes. Not far off was the "maquis," an overgrowth of hawthorns and tumbledown shacks. The avenue Junot, at that time just "a confused jumble of rosebushes,"[6] was eventually built over a part of it. Aline loved it there, since it reminded her of her childhood home. She had not even tried to lose her country accent and never thought of herself as a Parisian. Her neighbors in this little urban village were a picturesque lot, but she had too much to do at home to care. In any case, neighborhood gossip interested her much less than it did her husband, who passed on his taste for it to his son Jean.

[6] *Renoir par Jean Renoir*, 289 (= *Renoir, My Father*, 290).

FIRST NAME: JEAN

◆

Renoir was not really sure he wanted the baby that was born a little after midnight on September 15, 1894. He wrote his friend Berthe Morisot: "I have something really ridiculous to tell you . . . the arrival of a second son, named Jean. Mother and child are doing well."[1] Thirteen years had passed since *The Luncheon of the Boating Party.* Aline was a little plump, and at thirty-five her beauty was that of a mature woman. She was soon to gain a lot of weight and become the image of the protective and nurturing mother. Actually, she was more devoted to Renoir than to her children. Before the birth of her second child, she sent for a fifteen-year-old cousin in Essoyes, Gabrielle Renard, so as not to be overly burdened by the new arrival.

Times had changed since Pierre was born. There was a cook in the house, and some of Renoir's models were lending a hand with the housework. Neither middle-class tendencies nor slovenliness was tolerated. The point was to be free, and a way of life prevailed that was both simple and refined. The impetus for it came from Aline's humble origins. Most people in that section of Paris kept to their peasant values, and the young women in the Renoir household, who were part servant and part model, felt completely at ease there. The warm understanding between husband and wife was contagious. Both knew how to create a lighthearted atmosphere at home, and both hated pretension. Their home was a place of laughter, where people did not take life too seriously. Though Renoir worked like a madman, he was not difficult to live with. A hard early life and modest origins had taught

[1] Henry Perruchot, *Renoir* (Paris, 1966), 259.

him restraint and discretion: the problems he faced in painting were his own concern, and he did not inflict them on the young women who depended on him and who gave him, in return, their hearts.

As the years went by, the number of women he presided over grew. Renoir's whole personality inspired affection in those around him. He was an avid listener, especially if the subject was not painting. He had a genuine interest in others, in what befell them, in what was told them, what they observed, their family stories, even their complaints. He loved to be with amusing people, and his neighborhood had an abundant supply. His thirst for gossip endeared him to those who shared it. He certainly had another side, but people loved him precisely for his unwillingness to inflict his own preoccupations on those around him. His son Jean learned this principle by observation and example—it was all the more impressive for being unsaid. Never referring to his own experience, Renoir relayed what he heard from his friends in the neighborhood or what his fellow painters and art dealers told him about others. He would only comment and enjoy; he had that rare gift of knowing how to create harmony around himself.

Aline had the same disposition. She was happy and lively and always seemed in charge of any situation. Renoir was not her idol; she was his outspoken partner. The house and family life were her domain. When Jean was born, Pierre, who was nine years old, went to the Sainte-Croix boarding school in Neuilly. It was a school that pleased Renoir, not because of its high intellectual standards, but because it had big gardens. Pierre liked it there, too. He was a secretive child who knew what he wanted. Big for his age, and swarthy, he resembled his father physically.

Jean, on the other hand, resembled his mother, though her response when she first laid eyes on him was, "My god, he's ugly," and Renoir said, "That mouth! What an oven! He's going to be a pig!" Gabrielle grabbed him and said, "Well, *I* think he's beautiful," and everyone laughed.[2] Not only did she find him beautiful, but according to her, he had all the virtues. She would never let him go.

The young girl and her baby were a strange pair. Over the years, they became the kind of friends whom only death could part. But such thoughts were far from the mind of Gabrielle in those early days in Montmartre at the Château des Brouillards, though there was an

---

[2] *Renoir par Jean Renoir* (Paris, 1962), 271 (= *Renoir, My Father,* trans. Randolph and Dorothy Weaver [Boston, 1962], 275).

occasion on which death did threaten the baby. In the beginning of the winter of 1895, Renoir had gone south with Jeanne Baudot to stay with her parents, either to paint or to visit Paul Cézanne, probably both. Renoir was an anxious father, always frightened that something bad would happen to his children. That was why he forbade them to have haircuts (to prevent them from getting bumped on the head); he wanted the floors to be washed with lots of water to get rid of the wax that might make his children slip and fall. He even had the sharp corners of their tables rounded off. This time the bad weather was to blame, and nothing could have been done to prevent what happened: Jean got a bad case of bronchitis, and by week's end, Aline and Gabrielle were worn out from staying up to take care of the sick child. They decided to wire the father; Renoir returned immediately to relieve them, himself more dead than alive, and the baby was eventually saved.

As babies go, this one was a little monster. He cried without stopping and became enraged when he realized he was no longer in the arms of his beloved Gabrielle, whose name he somehow deformed into "Bibon." Aline would laugh at his shrieking and his tears. She was pleased to see such a vigorous child, and she enjoyed him, nor was she worried about his fits of rage that could only be stilled by stern scolding. He wanted to stay curled up like a puppy in Gabrielle's warm embrace. But his mother was always intervening, trying to teach him what he had no desire to learn: to be clean, to be quiet, and a few other artifacts of civilization, even if it took a slap or two.

Jean was baptized before winter came. Georges Durand-Ruel, the art dealer's youngest son, was his godfather, and Jeanne Baudot his godmother. She was a painter in her own right, and a person totally devoted to the family and to Renoir himself, whom she revered. The ceremony was at Saint-Pierre de Montmartre, and, naturally, Jean cried the whole time. Jeanne, who was carrying the baby, found that he grew heavier and heavier. It was a beautiful day, and the party afterwards, held in the yard at the Château des Brouillards, was long remembered. There was an abundance of Jordan almonds and sweet wine, the latter served by Gabrielle from barrels purchased for the occasion. Friends and neighbors forgathered.

◆

The year Jean was born was marked by two events that are revealing about the personality of Auguste Renoir: the death of Gustave Caillebotte and the conviction of Captain Dreyfus. Caillebotte was a painter and a great collector. Auguste's friend and Pierre's godfather, he had made Renoir the executor of his will. This meant it was his duty to persuade the Luxembourg museum to accept canvases that Caillebotte had bought from his friends since the beginnings of impressionism—not an easy job. Renoir had a long battle on his hands. He gave it his all. Busy as he was, Renoir wrote letters, made visits, tried every avenue to convince the bureaucrats to do the impossible: change their minds. Finally, part of the bequest was accepted. For the first time, impressionist paintings hung from walls belonging to the French Republic.

At the same time the legal system of that republic was condemning Captain Dreyfus on charges of treason, stripping him of his military rank, and deporting him to Devil's Island for life. An affair that would deeply divide the people of France was only just beginning. As each episode unfolded, Renoir always refused to get involved, saying, "I am for Watteau against Bouguereau"; he was determined to remain apolitical. For Renoir, human justice did not exist, but painting did and had to be defended. As a painter, he never let himself get caught up in discussions of the Dreyfus affair, however painful or serious they were. He only saw in them "always the same two camps, with just the names changing from one century to the next: Protestants vs. Catholics, Republicans vs. Royalists, Communards vs. Versaillais. . . . As for me, I just want to be French" (ibid., 250). On the pretext that it was a matter of politics, he would not acknowledge that an injustice was committed and an innocent man condemned. A staunch individualist, Renoir would say that politics is for second-raters and refuse to listen further.

But the Dreyfus affair did have great repercussions, and most of the Renoir family friends were liberals who sided with Dreyfus. So it was impossible for Jean not to be impressed by the remarks of Gabrielle or his father on the subject. He was soon to learn the overriding importance of painting in the life of his whole family and to hear lengthy discussions of Caillebotte's legacy, which, according to Renoir, was far more significant than the Dreyfus affair. All this came back to Jean later on: echoes of his father's attitude toward politics can be found in a play called *Carola* that Jean wrote in 1960.

The children were not permitted to disturb Renoir in his studio. Aline was especially strict on the subject of crying, since he had always hated hearing babies cry, which is why he had not wanted to have any children of his own. He often wanted to paint the new child, whom he loved tenderly and anxiously. Painting was his way of expressing his affection for it. There are numerous portraits of Gabrielle and her little friend—it was too difficult to have one without the other, and not worth the trouble! Once in a while the child appears by himself, but Gabrielle was always in the background, getting him to pose. In the famous portrait, *Jean Sewing,* Jean is sewing a dress for his camel. Renoir wanted to paint the boy, but he would not stop crying, so Gabrielle had the idea of telling him that his little tin toy was chilly and needed a dress. (This time, at least, Renoir's desire to paint the child won out over his fear that he might hurt himself with the needle.) Later on, to keep him from fidgeting while posing, Gabrielle would read Andersen or Perrault fairy tales aloud, to the delight of all three of them. Jean remembered those moments well.

According to Renoir, a model should not be reduced to rigid immobility. But Jean moved a little too much and cried a little more often than he was entitled to. He could not stand not getting what he wanted. To hear what he himself says about his childhood, one would think he had been raised according to Dr. Spock. In fact, Jean is a good advertisement for the success of that method! With Gabrielle overprotecting him, Jean flourished. He had beautiful golden curls and an appealing round face. She would take him shopping or exploring the neighborhood, carrying him everywhere. The country girl was fascinated by what she came across, and Parisians, always talkative, were even more so for a pretty thing who seemed to enjoy listening so much. There was plenty of local color. The husband of the concierge at 13, rue Girardon, a delivery man at Dufayel's furniture store, was a real marquis. Clovis Hugues, the deputy from Montmartre and an anticleric, was Renoir's best source for gossip, even though his own wife and daughters were more talked about than anyone else in the neighborhood. The newspaper dealer, the upholsterer, and the launderer were all characters. The latter, always tipsy, "made my mother and Gabrielle melt with his accent (of the Nièvre), which resembled that of Essoyes." Toulouse-Lautrec, a visitor at the Renoirs', once invited the girl and her charge to sit with him at a café, where he sipped mulled wine in the company of his models, "a couple of whores from the boulevard de Clichy dressed up as Arabs." There were also the denizens of the "maquis," who had built themselves wretched shacks—dreamhouses to them—from old boards. Gabrielle knew an elderly gentleman wearing academic ribbons who worked indefatigably at a fair booth featuring Roman chariot races with rats for horses and mice as charioteers. Then there was Josephine, the fishwife, who raised rabbits, chickens, and goats around a

shack that had "bits of waxed canvas plugging holes in the roof."
Josephine had two daughters, one of whom was a dancer at the
Opéra; the other, who "went astray," "would visit her mother in a
two-horse victoria with a coachman in livery."

Along with Madame Renoir, Gabrielle and Jean used to gather
snails in the "maquis." Aline led the quiet life that she preferred. To
her, it was not so important that her husband's paintings were beginning to sell at high prices. She was not certain that his success would
last, but she was ready to do what was necessary so that all benefited
from it. Renoir had always loved to paint in the countryside; she always wanted to live there. For two years, they spent several months
in the house that Oscar Wilde wintered in at Berneval in Normandy. It
was near Wargemont, where the Bérard family lived, and there is a
painting called *The Luncheon at Berneval* in which Jean appears. The
whole family also began traveling to the south of France, to a town
near Grasse called Magagnosc. In 1898, Renoir painted the portrait of
Jean sewing the dress for his camel there. Aline did not like staying in
hotels. She would put up with traveling only if she could bring her
whole world along with her. She especially longed to go back to Essoyes. Finally she bought a house there. It was a real winegrower's
house, and she had it enlarged so that there was enough room to put
up models, friends, and young painters passing through. Renoir had
a studio built in the rear of the backyard where no one would disturb
him. It was paradise on earth, a real godsend for these young city
dwellers to return to their beginnings. Their stays at Essoyes gave
Jean a real love and understanding of country life. He also made
friends with some distant cousins to whom he remained loyal all
his life.

That was where he met his first poacher. This one was a kid his
own age who had never worn shoes and knew how to catch pike and
steal chickens. Jean never forgot Godefer, and from then on he was
fascinated by poachers. That countryside, on the border of Champagne and Burgundy, always had a special appeal. Auguste Renoir
loved it, too, despite the bicycle accident in the summer of 1897 "that
changed my father's life into a martyrdom." The townspeople soon
adopted the painter even though he was not one of their own: he ate
little, did not drink to excess, and worked nonstop. Though Aline
would go fishing with her boys and Gabrielle, he was rarely to be
seen, except when sketching or painting a landscape. Otherwise he
stayed shut up in his studio.

For Jean, the house at Essoyes was important. When he was three years old, the family moved out of the Château des Brouillards into an apartment at 64, rue La Rochefoucauld (there was a studio nearby). It was still in Montmartre, but at the base of the butte instead of at its heights. For a child, even a large apartment with a big balcony and lots of plants is not the same thing as a house with a yard and a back door. But the family did not stay very long at that address. The apartment was on the fifth floor, and Renoir was beginning to have such pains in his legs that he could not climb the stairs. So they moved once again, in the same neighborhood to be sure, to the rue Caulaincourt. Renoir found a studio at street level a few houses down.

These days Gabrielle was his model, more or less by chance. One day when he had no one, Aline suggested that she help him out. They were all at Magagnosc, and all the local girls were busy picking jasmine. Gabrielle was unaware of her beauty, and posing did not frighten her. She was used to it. The models had been her friends. Where was the evil in undressing for a painting? Besides, evil was not a preoccupation in the Renoir household; everyone knew that nothing was simple, and everyone believed in redemption. Jean was the only one not in favor. But under the circumstances, no one even asked his opinion. During the sittings, he simply had to do without his beloved Bibon.

Jean knew how to enjoy himself on his own. There was no shortage of toys. He had a whole collection of tin soldiers that his godfather, Georges Durand-Ruel, kept adding to since he knew the boy loved them. They were in Napoleonic uniform and made at Nuremberg, but Jean thought they were French. "I was especially fond of the grenadier guards, with their big bearskin hats. I was always imagining myself as a grenadier guard, on sentry duty in front of a building, in a guard box, with a very big bearskin hat, no, not just a hat, also an apron, an axe, and a great beard. Actually, I was a sapper—that was my dream, to be one of the sappers in the Napoleonic Guard. There I was, on campaign, and a fantastic campaign it was. For me, war with all its misery and misfortune did not exist in the era of the beautiful uniforms. Real war goes on in dirty uniforms, for instance, in the paintings of Alphonse de Neuville, with his scenes from 1870, like *The Last Cartridges*, which really bothered me terribly and made me afraid. I hated that war, because it was a war where there was blood, where people really killed each other, where the people really seemed to suffer. I liked the Napoleonic wars. You didn't die in them. You only pretended to be dead. There were grand gestures, like putting both your hands on your heart. There wasn't any blood, you just swooned into the arms of the woman who ran the canteen, and she gave you a drink from a barrel. For me, it was all a bit like the opera."[3] While Jean was playing with his soldiers, he forgot about Gabrielle and stayed quietly with his mother, the serving girls, and the cook, Madame Mathieu, who was amazed that the lad hadn't yet been sent to school.

◆

School was a subject it was better not to bring up. Jean dreamed of having a uniform like his brother, and if he went to school, he would also get a haircut. Another fantasy! His father insisted it was not necessary to teach children anything or to send them to school before their tenth birthday. He did not believe in the things they taught before that age, and in this, too, he professed to be apolitical. At the time, there was a division of opinion between those in favor of parochial schools and those who preferred secular ones. He dismissed these adversaries equally, and yet he sent Pierre to a religious college and made the same choice for Jean. After a younger brother, Claude, was born at Essoyes on August 4, 1901, Jean was sent off sooner than had been planned to Catholic boarding school, a scant four years before the separation of church and state was approved.

The education Jean got at home before going to boarding school was as his father wished it. There was nothing normal about it. The child took part in grown-up activities to an unusual extent because of Gabrielle, who although young was not a nanny like any other. The little tike felt secure with her and in the bosom of an extended family that included friends as well as models. He did not distinguish among them. There was love, support, and fun. The important thing was that Gabrielle should be there. Without her, things fell apart. Renoir, who had them pose together often, knew it only too well. The reciprocal love between these two young creatures nourished them both. Jean had no idea that Gabrielle was still almost a child herself. She protected him, and that's all he felt. What's more, she carried him around with her everywhere. Shopping trips in Montmartre were only a small portion of their activities together, of the things she helped him discover.

Once Madame Renoir decided to buy a white wooden dresser for her young cousin's bedroom. She sent Gabrielle along with Jean, who was two at the time, to Dufayel's, a large furniture store specializing

[3]From the transcript of a radio program, "Bureau des rêves perdus," August 1954.

in Henri II and Louis XIII sideboards, then in fashion. The store was offering a rare diversion at no cost to its customers: a movie. Gabrielle was delighted, but Jean began screaming in terror as soon as the room became dark and the first images appeared on the screen. The young woman hurried to the exits, baby in arms, hardly suspecting that moviemaking would one day become the passion of her little hero. She had more success with Punch and Judy in the park, so it was some time before she tried that novelty again. . . . Also, Renoir had recommended the puppet show in the Jardin des Tuileries for his son, because it stuck to the traditions of Lyons more faithfully than its competition on the Champs-Elysées. "The most exquisite moment was right before the curtain rose. The cloth quivered to the sound of the accordion coming from the wings. Then there were three loud pops, as at the Comédie Française. According to Gabrielle, I was so excited that at times I peed in my pants when the curtain actually rose."[4]

This incident, a token of Jean's lively and delightful emotionality, was repeated; "for me, the first work of diuretic art that comes to mind is Stravinsky's *Petrushka*." Jean saw the ballet in its debut performances in 1911, with his parents and Gabrielle. They watched it from the Edwards' stall. Edwards, owner of *Le Matin*, was married at the time to Misia Sert, as she would later be called. Renoir really enjoyed painting this woman. She was friends with everyone who was anyone in music, painting, and poetry—and at the time that meant many people of extraordinary merit. When Edwards' wife dragged him along to see an exhibit, he would slip out to play cards with his chauffeur in the bar next door. Even so, he became great friends with Renoir. They enjoyed each other's company, even though they had little to say to one another. In fact they had no interests in common, since Renoir could not have cared less for business, nor Edwards for painting. However, the press magnate did appreciate the good food served at Madame Renoir's, and during his wife's portrait sittings, he would play cards with Gabrielle. Then they would stay for dinner, as on the night of the *Petrushka* performance.

◆

Guests praised Aline Renoir's cooking to the skies, but she only supervised in the kitchen. Her main source of inspiration was a woman named Marie Corot, who had been the painter's cook for many years. Marie Corot's recipes were truly precious. Jean declared this a fact,

---

[4]Jean Renoir, *Ma vie et mes films* (Paris, 1974), 26.

and the subject was important to him, since as far back as he could recall he had appreciated good food.

Vollard reports that Martial Caillebotte, a banker who was the collector's brother, would say: "It's amazing, I've never had a bouillabaise at my house like the ones we have at the Renoirs'. And I have a real cook, while they just have those maids whose sole qualification is 'a skin that takes the light well.'"[5] Jean speaks of his mother's bouillabaise, too. But he also tells us that thanks to his parents, he would have been able to survive food shortages. In the Renoir household, the children were brought up to eat all kinds of food and to clean their plates. It's a common rule, to be sure, but it seems inconsistent with the Dr. Spock side of their upbringing.

Martial Caillebotte and Maurice Gangnat were businessmen, like Edwards. Gangnat had excellent taste in painting and loved Renoir's work, which he collected. All three were frequent visitors, as was Vollard—he first came to the Château des Brouillards when Berthe Morisot died. It was she who had sent Renoir this exotic merchant with an unerring eye.

Naturally, Jean Renoir got to know the greatest painters. Of Berthe Morisot, who died a year after he was born, he had no memory, but he knew that his father spoke about her often and missed her a great deal. Jean remembered the visits he paid Cézanne with his father. They would go to Cézanne's house near the place Pigalle in the late afternoon, when the light was fading and painters stopped working. There was a large stove in the studio, so hot that it glowed bright red. The tea in the pot sitting on it was black, and Cézanne would drink cup after cup of it and offer it to his guests, who always refused.[6] Artist friends were always welcome at the Renoirs': Monet; Degas, of whom Renoir said, "Since Chartres, I know of only one sculptor—Degas"; Pissarro, who was born in the Antilles, like Vollard. Also among the family friends were Abel Faivre and Forain, writers like Lestringuez, whose son, Pierre, became a great friend and collaborator of Jean's; and Georges Rivière, a widower with two daughters whom Aline thought of as her own. Aline had similar feelings for the children they called "the Manet girls," Berthe Morisot's daughter, Julie Manet (Berthe had married the painter's brother) and her two cousins, the daughters of one of Berthe Morisot's sisters. One of them eventually married Paul Valéry.

[5] Ambroise Vollard, *La vie et l'oeuvre de Pierre-Auguste Renoir* (Paris, 1919), 165.
[6] Jean Renoir, *Ecrits, 1927–1971*, ed. Claude Gauteur (Paris, 1976), 27.

"The Manet girls" and the daughters of Georges Rivière were much older than Jean, as was Cézanne's son. His name was also Paul, and later on he married Renée Rivière. Renée's sister, Hélène, married Edmond, the son of Renoir's youngest brother, a writer and journalist. In this group of intimates there was a mixture of generations that favored understanding between young and old. Jean's older friends were a link between himself and the generations of his parents and their friends.

This kind of extended family consisting of friends as well as models was a source of pleasure to Jean's father. Because of it, the child learned to observe others in his home. He was interested in what grown-ups said among themselves, and it opened his mind to all sorts of subjects. He listened and remembered all kinds of stories that struck a chord in him for whatever reason. The house was always full of different sorts of people. Besides friends, models, and their boyfriends, there were others who came to pose, women of the world or actresses wrapped in sable coats and bedecked with pearls, as beautiful as fairy tales. Auguste Renoir appreciated their luxury and elegance, and their talk raised his spirits.

The little boy was dazzled and devoured them with his eyes. For him, they were all part of the mythical world of show business. He loved to hear his father talk about the theater, about Jeanne Granier, his favorite actress, or even better, the prettiest theater in Paris, les Variétés, where the painter had often gone with his neighbor Offenbach and seen Hortense Schneider in her stall, "the queen of the place . . . a fine woman!"[7] The child mixed up past and present. His view of reality was that of Gabrielle and his father. The anecdotes he tells about his father give a sense of the freedom of his discourse and the type of subjects it comprised. Renoir had a real talent for talk that his son, by all appearances, inherited.

As though this school of life were in need of being completed, the painter's oldest brother, Henri, wanted to make his contribution as well. He and his wife were devotees of the "caf'conc'," as the café concert, a kind of cabaret, was called, and he found out to his horror that Jean, aged five, was totally ignorant of this typical Parisian institution. Renoir saw nothing wrong with the idea, so the retired engraver and his wife took the child with them to the shows that were their delight in life. The only thing Jean drank was grenadine, but he soaked up all the off-color stories (later he called them "wonderfully obscene") in repertoire at "The Ant," "La Scala," or "The Eldorado."

[7] *Renoir par Jean Renoir*, 184 (= *Renoir, My Father*, 190).

Given the success of these Thursday afternoon jaunts, the tireless Gabrielle offered to take the boy on Sundays to the Théâtre Montmartre, where they were still playing "just about all the melodramas of the golden age." Renoir was unhappy with the genre: "The local middle-class man goes there and weeps over the misery of the poor orphan girl. He returns to his domicile, his eyes still red, and fires the maid because she's gotten pregnant." Still, he thought it appropriate that his son find out about a popular art form that made such effective use of the average person's emotional responses. But he disapproved of his son attending matinées at the Comédie-Française with the scions of the middle class. He believed that if Jean had a taste for the classics, he would have no trouble discovering them, or any other form of literature, for himself. From his own experience, Renoir felt that people broaden their knowledge and attain culture simply by living and meeting other people from all sectors of society, each dedicated to his own art or trade. His sons were to receive an eclectic education given them by people who were not pedagogues. If he needed an example to confirm his belief in these principles, he had only to consider Gabrielle. This young peasant girl was changing on the spot, nourishing herself happily on all that an exceptionally rich environment could offer.

The province of education was one in which Madame Renoir did not intervene. She put her trust in her husband. It often appears that she let things go, but she knew exactly what was happening, nor would she have kept silent if mistakes were being made. Jean was born rebellious, and she was not worried. To her it was reasonable to delegate the responsibility of mastering him to Gabrielle. Jean knew very well that his mother was there. Displeasing her was neither necessary nor desirable. He avoided her, because she was the one who scolded him.

Renoir and his wife complemented one another. Each had a strong character, and neither was caught up in the cult of appearances. These were qualities that they admired in others. They also shared strong though unspoken religious feelings. Renoir's faith was sincere, but he had no desire to create conflict with others, so he "played the cork" and went along with the atheistic views held by his friends. His tolerance was boundless. "It seemed to him impossible to suppose that 250 million Hindus had been wrong for four thousand years" (ibid., 147). He never set foot in a church. Aline went to mass at 11 A.M., which gave her time to run her household, start Sunday lunch before the service, and afterwards oversee its final preparation.

As a child, Jean had no notion of how unbelieving Gabrielle actually was. He never asked her about such things, and it never occurred to him that people could doubt the existence of God. Gabrielle respected the restraint of the Renoirs, whose faith reminded her of her own mother's. In matters of religion, Jean was strongly influenced by his father, and he was equally secretive about it.

◆

As a small child, Jean was convinced that his father knew everything. He was always ready to listen to whatever Renoir would say, probably because everyone else was, too. No one discussed "the boss," as Gabrielle and the models called him. Madame Renoir always did as she pleased, but she was rarely in conflict with him. Among the members of the household, it was axiomatic that Renoir was right. Yet he did not pontificate. On the contrary, throughout his life he maintained a way of expressing himself that was marked by a kind of merry irony, as though he himself was unsure of what he was saying and did not know that his opinion would prevail. His laugh and this pretended lack of assurance were part of his modesty. Even when remarking on his art, he evinced lightheartedness. Jean soon learned to respect his father's painting; appreciating it came later. His father refused to help him with that. Emotions cannot be made to order. People acquire judgment in proportion to interest, through observation and comparison. Renoir only taught Jean that what looks simple is not always. He made clear to him the importance of a craft. Genius and good sense are often incompatible, but they were harmonious in Auguste Renoir. His senses were informed, and his mind was as astute as his technique was nimble. The beauty of his painting at its best impresses for the way it transcends the quotidian.

To the boy, artwork was for a long time just part of family life. It was natural to have paintings around, and he did not understand that they were the product of long hours during which his father closed himself up in the studio and demanded silence—not an easy demand to comply with! When a painting disappeared from the walls of the apartment and reappeared at the house of some friend, Jean felt uncomfortable. He felt despoiled, "robbed" is the term he uses. Nor was he aware that his father's paintings were fetching higher and higher prices. Money talk was not allowed at home, not because it was improper, but because some people have money—some have a lot, others even too much—and some do not. Whatever the case, it had nothing to do with what they were really worth. His parents indeed drew no distinctions between rich and poor friends. They did teach their children that money was hard to earn and should not be wasted. It was not an easy lesson to learn, since Madame Renoir, who was so generous, gave it out like manna from heaven, right and left, even to those whom she knew would take it from her hand to the bar next door. The prospect made her laugh. She taught her children that it was not embarrassing to give or receive charity, and she spent money on others with joy. There was no more fear in her that her husband's ability to provide would falter.

Vollard reports that "at the Doria sale in 1899, *La Pensée* went for 22,100 francs; less than twenty years earlier, Renoir had sold it for 150 francs."[8] This was a far cry from the Drouot auction at which paintings were withdrawn for lack of bidders. The following year, Renoir was awarded the Legion of Honor. He felt bad for his friends who had not yet received such honors. To Monet he wrote that he hoped "this bit of ribbon will not come between our friendship." Later, on reflection, he wrote: "Today I realize that I wrote you a stupid letter. I now wonder what difference it could make to you whether I have some medal or not."[9]

Medals no more changed Renoir than wealth did. In any case, he remained marginal for a long time to come. Undersecretary of State for Fine Arts Dujardin-Beaumetz, infamous for forbidding state museums to purchase paintings by Cézanne, held his post from 1905 to 1910. Renoir was used to the loneliness that goes with genius. He evolved in his own way, never burdening those around him with the joys or the setbacks of his inner struggles. Neither the man nor his work suggests a person who suffered. The departure from impressionism and the "return to classical traditions" that are spoken of by Jean Leymarie were not noticed by the general public.[10] Its tastes were those of Dujardin-Beaumetz. Still, in 1904, a Renoir retrospective was organized by the Salon d'Automne, new at the time, with such success that the painter was happy about it for several days.

In this period before radio and television, when the cinema hardly existed, an artist's reputation was made by word of mouth. Renoir had his staunch defenders among those opposed to the bathetic official art. Women were especially enthusiastic about his work, and those who commissioned portraits by him often became his friends. Through such connections he managed to buy, on sale, some outfits

---

[8] Vollard, *Pierre-Auguste Renoir,* 86.

[9] *Renoir par Jean Renoir,* 420 (= *Renoir, My Father,* 421).

[10] Jean Leymarie, *Impressionism: A Biographical and Critical Study,* trans. James Emmons (Geneva, 1955).

from the high fashion house Callot Soeurs. They were from prior seasons, but that bothered neither the models nor the painter. All had superb lines and were extremely well made. Gabrielle, who did not care about fashion, even wore them to go out, which was why Vollard, when he first laid eyes on her, said she looked like a bohemian.

Gabrielle soon became Renoir's favorite model, dividing her time between him and the child, who at long last got used to those hours of separation. Without being the least bit self-conscious about her behavior toward him, she had succeeded in making him feel secure. Thanks to her as well, the birth of his little brother does not seem to have disturbed Jean, who was almost seven at the time. Gabrielle was twenty-two, and more than ever she was his mother image. The newborn had his own mother, who treated him more tenderly than she had her other sons. Renoir made many drawings of the baby. It has often been written that this late-born child revived his father. The birth certainly gave some added drive to his work, and the love in his portraits of Coco, as little Claude was called, is evident. But Renoir was too wise and too attentive to the feelings of others to deprive Jean of the share of affection and tenderness needed to defuse his jealousy. There were, to be sure, typical but apparently rare acts of aggression toward his little brother. Madame Renoir responded with a good spanking. Jean always remembered the one he got at Essoyes the day he perched his brother, then just learning to walk, on the edge of the roof; though the reason for his behavior seems to have escaped him.

Looking back on this time through books and eyewitnesses, it is clear that no damage was done despite an explosive potential for it. The parents seem to have been born well adjusted, just like Gabrielle. It is easy to imagine the neuroses that these three boys could have acquired, and under the circumstances their parents' success is worth commending. Having a genius for a father is no easier than being a genius oneself.

It was soon time to send Jean off to school in order to give his little brother some room and to let Gabrielle really fulfill her function as model. The short hair, sportcoat, and cap of a boarding school student appealed to Jean, but once inside he found that the place lacked charm, though it was among the most elegant in Paris. Gabrielle did not try to change his mind since she did not care one way or the other. Madame Renoir had no prejudices on the subject either. Pierre was always a model pupil, and she could have bet that Jean would not be. From the start, he hated school. Compared to the little peasants at Es-

soyes or the son of the café owner in Grasse, whom he thought was a
real Rockefeller, the little Parisian boys were boringly nice. Jean was
too independent and too pigheaded; he had Gabrielle and needed no
one else.

There he was, aged nine, at Sainte-Marie de Monceau boarding
school; fortunately, there were Sunday afternoons to compensate for
all the horrors of the week before. For some reason that he never
understood, there was a picture show every Sunday in the parlor. The
panic fear of that day at the furniture store was long forgotten; the
silver screen fascinated Jean, and of all the short subjects he saw during those afternoons, he especially loved "The Adventures of Automaboul." In their choice of programs the fathers "showed a taste that
anticipated the surrealists by thirty years," Jean later reported.[11] Wearing a goatskin coat with starched fur, outsized goggles, and the obblig-
atory driver's helmet, Automaboul was a burlesque character. His car
never did what he expected it to. It would go backward instead of forward, and then stop dead; after a few frenzied jolts, it would spit fire
and disappear in a cloud of smoke; or again, it would start up all by
itself once Automaboul had made it clear that he would have nothing
more to do with it. For Jean these short films were all the more magical for their muteness. The explosions of the recalcitrant engine were
inaudible, as were the indignant shrieks and stubborn resolves of
Automaboul himself. Apparently the child enjoyed this even more
than Punch and Judy. The magic of the darkened room and the mysterious purring of the projector made such an impression that his love
of film soon surpassed that of all other entertainment. Automaboul
also gave him a lifelong taste for cars.

In those days, films were still a novelty to which the small child
had no access except on Sunday afternoons. When Jean ran away
from school, the place he ran to was home. His mother did not appreciate such behavior, and Gabrielle also showed her disapproval. Yet
Jean continued it, since his father laughed when he saw him appear at
home on school days. His opinion of schooling for children had not
changed. To Renoir, the only annoying part of Jean's escapades was
the obligatory note excusing his absence.

Jean was not long for this Paris boarding school. After several
trips to the south of France, his parents took up residence at Cagnes-
sur-Mer in 1903. They had rented part of the local post office overlooking the route to Vence. In 1907, they bought a little farm called

---

[11] Renoir, *Ma vie et mes films*, 27.

"Les Collettes." Its olive trees are well known from Renoir's paintings and also Jean's pictures of them in *Picnic on the Grass*. They intended to build a house there that would be large enough for the whole family and the models and would include a large studio opening onto the backyard.

♦

Every year, the pain became more intense and the paralysis grew. Renoir went off to take the cure at Aix, in Bourbonne-les-Bains, where Madame de Sévigné had also treated her "rheumatism." But nothing stopped the progress of the disease. To keep his hands working, Renoir had gotten into the habit of juggling with three balls. He was very skillful at it and seemed to enjoy himself. At Essoyes, to keep his arms and legs moving, he played pool with his wife; she became a real champion. Soon the time came for him to quit pool and even *boules* [lawn bowling]. He then began playing with a *bilboquet* [cup and ball], "like Henri III in the Dumas novels." Next he took up tossing and catching a little, well-polished stick; but it, too, had to be abandoned. By 1902, the paralysis on the left side of his face became visible, and he had to walk with a cane. With total paralysis in the offing, the family trips to the south lasted longer and longer, in the hope they would slow the disease. But Renoir had no desire to abandon Paris completely. There were his friends, old and new, including Espagnat, Bonnard, Vuillard, Albert André, Claude's godfather, and his wife Maleck. Between acute phases, when the pains were excruciating, he worked more and more, hounded by the slipping of time. His body became emaciated. In the spring of 1904, before the useless cure at Bourbonne-les-Bains and the retrospective at the Salon d'Automne, he scarcely weighed 110 pounds.

Jean had no regrets about leaving his school. He had only one friend there, Jacques Mortier, whom he later came across in Nice. At the time he was too young to be aware of his father's disputes with the partisans of official art, but it seems clear that his fellow pupils were the children of the middle class that knew nothing of Renoir. He got into trouble with several of them, and his father laughed to hear of it as heartily as when he played hooky. The boy was well aware that his father did not look like the other fathers he saw in the school visiting room. He had already found out that for Renoir "the great dividing line was between those who perceive and those who reason. Mistrusting the *folle du logis*, or imagination, he allied himself with the world of instinct as opposed to the world of imagination."[12] What he had to say was the fruit of his experience as "a journeyman painter," as he called himself. He never tired of saying how glad he was that he was not born to intellectuals. A shoemaker, a tailor, hand laborers, that was what pleased him. Jean never forgot his father's lessons, which covered every phase of life. For instance, he said it was bad to cut your fingernails too short, since you had to protect the tips of your fingers, their most sensitive parts: "if you expose them you run the risk of blunting your sense of touch and depriving yourself of much pleasure" (ibid., 43). His father also taught him that "a Parisian is a marvelous creature behind his workbench in the Faubourg Saint-Antoine, but outside of Paris, he wrecks everything" (ibid., 427).

On the other hand, the lessons learned at the Masséna elementary school or at high school in Nice had much less staying power. Jean showed no more bent for study in the south of France than he had in the north. Life at home was so much more interesting! As he grew older, he began to realize how lucky he was, and the importance of his father's work filled him with pride. His friend Paul had the same feelings toward his father, who died in 1906. The loss was deeply disturbing. The friendship between Cézanne and Renoir was old, profound, and a part of everyday life in both households.

Without sacrificing any of her genuineness, Gabrielle had also discovered the world of painting. She always shared her impressions with Jean, her wild ecstasies and inspired joys, but she kept from him the grief she felt for the sufferings of "the boss." She was horrified by the anxiety that would come across his face when he felt the pain intensify, depriving him more and more of the use of his legs and his deformed arms. Renoir lived in dread of not being able to work, but he forgot the dread when the pain subsided. As if worries over her husband's health were not enough, Aline Renoir had found out that she was diabetic. Insulin had not yet been discovered, and she knew that her life was threatened. Despite all this, she kept up the high spirits that the painter cherished and needed to keep working. The serving girls and the models needed no coaxing to please her and respond to the boss's good humor.

Jean, shielded by Gabrielle, was ready to believe that their day-to-day life was as brilliant, harmonious, and beautiful as his father's canvases. Living at Cagnes was even more fun than living in Mont-

---

[12] *Renoir par Jean Renoir*, 143 (= *Renoir, My Father*, 147.)

martre. There were all sorts of new people whom they had grown to know and love, people who came to see his father and who made him laugh. The house "Les Collettes" pleased him almost as much as Essoyes, and he realized that his father felt better there. But Jean could not even contemplate what life would be like without Gabrielle. Because of her, school always seemed dull, and he made no friends.

As a child and an adolescent, Jean had hardly any ties to his brother Pierre. He had no reason to warm up to a boy who spouted poetry and who could not care less about him anyway. Pierre's only love was the theater. Jean loved it as well, but only as a spectator. The sight of his brother declaiming before an imaginary audience or for the neighborhood girls did nothing for Jean, and Renoir himself showed no enthusiasm for it. According to him, the theater was an ideal occupation for women, but it was not suited to men. Pierre was undeterred by this notion and went to the Conservatoire, where his talents were noted. His father relented, and in 1907 Pierre entered the Odéon, where he began his acting career under the direction of Antoine. In 1911, he landed his first movie role in *La Digue,* in which Abel Gance made his debut as a director.

In 1910, Pierre spent his summer vacation with his parents. They all went to Bavaria to stay with the Thurneyssen family, friends of Renoir who had rented a house at Wessling right on the lake. Renoir walked with two canes now, but he did walk, which was something of a victory. He painted a great deal, and, as always, with abandon. Feeling liberated by the change of scene, he was so happy he hummed to himself while working. He did portraits of the Thurneyssens and their son, Alexander, aged twelve and as beautiful as his mother; Claude was only nine at the time. Renée Rivière accompanied them on the trip; Muhlfeld, a famous conductor of the day, was giving her voice lessons. Jean played trumpet and was also being instructed by Muhlfeld (ibid., 424). The trip was a great success, a happy occasion. A crowd of young people, friends of Thurneyssen, visited them from Munich, and they all took walks through the forest, went swimming in the lake, joined in picnics, country teas, and blueberry picking.

Back in Cagnes, Renoir suddenly could walk no more. Madame Renoir had to buy him a wheelchair. On the tram ride to Nice to order it, she wept the whole way. Jean went with her, and he remembered the tears rolling down her cheeks; yet his mother "was not a sentimental person." Renoir was never to use his legs again.

The next day, Madame Renoir found another apartment in Paris on the Boulevard Rouchechouart. It was on the second floor, with a studio on the street floor. The staircase between was easy for carrying Renoir up and down on a litter. But after a while Renoir noticed that the building was right on the corner of the rue Viollet-le-Duc. Since Viollet-le-Duc was "the architect he hated most of all," Renoir could not stand being close to his name and wanted to move out (ibid., 44). Clearly, Renoir had lost none of his bite or passion. But none of the women around him were eager to move again, and neither was Baptistin, their chauffeur.

In any case, Renoir's goal in life was still to work and express himself. Though he spent very little time in Paris, he was concerned not to lose his ties to it altogether. Aside from his physical ailments, Jean was on his mind, since he wanted him at least to pass his baccalaureat. The lad's scholastic career had been severely compromised by frequent changes of school and his stubborn desire to have as much fun as he had had with Gabrielle as a child. And nonchalance was fashionable at the time, despite the rumors of war that made the rounds now and then. There was a close call in Agadir in July of 1911, just when Jean was celebrating passing the first part of his baccalaureat. He took a correspondence course in philosophy for that section of the examination, and Gabrielle immersed herself in the textbooks as much as he did in order to ask him questions. Thanks to her help, he passed. But then what? He took some mathematics courses, but halfheartedly. His father was discouraged by his apparent lack of seriousness and knew that his studies would not last long. He imagined him as a smithy, a musician (Aline made Jean learn to play piano), a gamekeeper, or a nurseryman.

The law making three years of military service compulsory had just been passed, and the army was popular. Jean decided to become an officer. The cavalry, his father's branch, was tempting. He loved horses, but was incapable of submitting to discipline. He thought that in the context of army life, he would rediscover the security he had with Gabrielle. In the meantime, she had left the household. She was soon to marry Conrad Slade, an American painter who greatly admired Renoir. The story goes that Aline Renoir took offense at the role her young cousin was playing in the life of her aging husband, who was suffering more and more. Gabrielle was protecting him as she had little Jean. Aline, who had never been jealous of the affection between Gabrielle and her son, couldn't stand the idea of some other woman watching over her husband, although she was already ill herself and having trouble getting around.

On January 4, 1914, glory came for Renoir. That was the day

on which Raymond Poincaré, president of the Republic of France, opened galleries in the Louvre where the work of three living painters was hung: Degas, Monet, and Renoir. It was an unprecedented event. Without seeking to do so, Jean benefited from the possibilities that this event created for him. To be sure, he was a little rich boy, and he felt it even in the army, when for the first time in his life he left familiar surroundings. There he discovered another world: garrison life, and whorehouses, strange and disturbing places for him. The year he passed in the army was an important one that would reappear much later in his literary works.

WAR AND DEATH

◆

Life looked promising to this young man who would reach twenty a week before the beginning of autumn in 1914. Tall and slender, his large mouth, bright eyes, and reddish hair gave him a certain appeal. He could have been a character in *Voyageurs de l'impériale*, which Aragon had yet to write. The reality he lived was enough to make one dream: he was the son of one of the greatest painters alive, he had friends of all ages to whom art was important, and every day was a holiday; as for money, there was enough around to make it irrelevant. He and his friends were neither cursed nor trapped by it. And all of them knew how to have a good time, to laugh, and to love beauty in all its forms.

It must have been a good summer. Jean Renoir did not know what to want or whom to love, and there was still time to decide and no need to hurry. Being in the army would not hurt. According to a tradition that his family still subscribed to, army life made boys into men. Having become a first-class horseman, though he appreciated the discipline less than the horses, he stood for the entrance examination for the Cavalry School at Saumur, and passed. Was it a good career choice for him? A soldier's day seemed monotonous. Fortunately, he was good humored. He had been brought up to get along with people easily and was never snobbish or condescending.

Renoir and his friends and family did not see the war coming, and neither did Jean and his army buddies. Officers and soldiers did not even have the right to vote. Few of the men even knew that the Socialist party won votes and seats in the May legislative elections. Jean knew about the income tax that had been under discussion and was voted in by the new Chamber of Deputies, but only because his father's friend, Georges Rivière, was its author. Jean also knew that the three-year law was upheld, so that even if he had not beaten the draft by enlisting, he would have had to do three years of military service.

People had become accustomed to international tensions, and no one was especially upset when Archduke Ferdinand, heir to the Austro-Hungarian throne, was assassinated at Sarajevo on June 28. It was just another Balkan crisis. On July 15, as had been planned, President Poincaré and his prime minister, Viviani, left for Russia. Their trip does not seem to have changed the czar's attitude, nor did it solve any of the economic problems between the two countries. But once they returned to Paris on July 29, Austria-Hungary declared war on Serbia. On July 30, Russia began mobilizing. That upset the apple cart. In France, general mobilization was decreed on August 1. On August 3, after invading Belgium, Germany declared war on France.

The old painter, cloaked in glory but paralyzed by terrible pains, was still working hard. His wife knew that she was sick but refused to let it get the better of her. Then they saw two of their three sons go to war. The surprising news reached them at Cagnes, in the house called Les Collettes that they loved so much. Aline decided to leave for Paris immediately. She wanted to see her eldest, Pierre, before he was sent to the front. She took the train, while Renoir himself, scarcely able to move, left by car for the same destination. A young Italian chauffeur, Bistolfi, Baptistin's replacement, was to take care of him and carry him from one place to another.

When Aline reached Paris, Pierre had already left to join his unit. Instead of him she found her daughter-in-law, the actress Véra Sergine, and a baby just a few months old, her first grandson, Claude, whom she had never seen before. She took them both to Les Collettes, where she also wanted to make them stay. Renoir for his part succeeded in locating Jean, who was a sergeant in the first regiment of dragoons. He went to visit him at Lagny, where the colonel gave a luncheon in his honor; Jean was permitted to attend. Seeing his son in combat dress amid the other soldiers was comforting to the old man. Some situations are less awful in reality than when imagined in advance. A few days later, Jean the dragoon took part in combat, armed with a lance.

No one seems to have foreseen the length, the extent, and the horror of that war. The memories of Paris under siege in 1870 had not faded. It was unimaginable that this time could be worse. Aline Renoir only knew of those days from the tales Renoir told; she was a little girl at the time, younger than her son Coco, who turned thirteen the day after Germany declared war on France. Claude-Coco and baby Claude, his nephew, brightened the atmosphere at Les Collettes. Their mere presence was a comfort to Aline, who was consumed with anxiety.

In mid-September, Aline managed to get a pass to go to Amiens, where Jean was hospitalized. People have written that he was kicked by a horse, but his family members never heard of such a thing. He was treated at the hospital in Amiens, then sent to convalesce at Luçon, in the Vendée. According to his son, Alain, the "injury" might have been a "Venus's kick," cavalry slang for gonorrhea. When his mother came to visit him at Amiens, he announced his intention of leaving the cavalry, which was doing nothing, to join the Alpine infantry operating in the Vosges. Aline did not object, but she was terrified. So was Renoir. He had not forgotten his friend Bazille, the painter, killed "stupidly" during the retreat of 1870: along a muddy path in Beaune-la-Rolande, he had been hit by German cannon fire. After the victory of the Marne, which miraculously halted the enemy advance, the Germans began digging trenches and getting in them. The Allies did the same, and this war, which people at first said would be a short one, settled in for the long haul.

In the beginning of 1915, Jean, then a second lieutenant, was transferred at his own request to the sixth battalion of Alpine infantry and sent to the front. He saw the terrible carnage from the first German offensives in the north. There and then he decided that he would never make a career of the army. He often told people he was "born chicken," but somehow he became a hawk when he felt it was necessary. There was always that ambivalence in him: he called himself weak, but at the same time he had a chivalrous side that kept him from joining the cowards. He had given his word, and he had been brought up to think that was important. He had not read the novels of Alexandre Dumas, his father's favorite, in vain. Nor had he forgotten the fantasies he used to indulge in with his tin soldiers. There were the beautiful uniforms and pretty canteen workers with their consoling bosoms. All of that had nothing to do with reality, but Jean's code of honor arose from it nonetheless. He wanted to be like everyone else and not escape the slaughter as a person of privilege. He did not appreciate shirkers.

At about the same period, his brother Pierre got his right arm smashed to bits, and the boys' mother set off for Carcassonne, where he was operated on. His life was not in danger, but the seriousness of his wound really upset Pierre. As a cripple, he thought he would never again act on stage, which was his life's ambition. He did not complain, but his mother knew very well what he was thinking. Her role had always been to buck him up, and she did it this time, too. Pierre, taciturn, was a courageous fellow. He was discharged after being wounded and operated on several times. He had bone grafts so that eventually he could use his arm with the help of a prosthesis. His dedication was such that he eventually succeeded in resuming his craft. In fact he learned to move so skillfully that his infirmity was utterly unknown to both theater and movie audiences.

◆

In April of 1915, when the Renoirs were just beginning to worry about what had happened to Jean, who had spent the winter amid the mud and cold of the trenches, a letter reached Les Collettes announcing that he was in the hospital at Gérardmer with the neck of his femur fractured by a bullet. He described the wound as slight, but Madame Renoir would have none of that and made straight for his bedside. In fact, the wounded man was in much worse health than he had admitted. He had been hit one morning during patrols between the lines, and he had had to wait for nightfall before being evacuated by mule. At the hospital he was diagnosed as suffering from gangrene, and the issue was whether his life could be saved by amputation. Perhaps the gangrene had already spread above the joint. Madame Renor begged them to try the impossible and not to operate. It turned out that her pleas were heeded: by a miraculous stroke of good fortune, the chief physician of the hospital, who wanted to operate on Jean, was suddenly replaced by a military nurse, a certain Professor Laroyenne of Lyon. A decree by Clémenceau had just obliged all professors of medicine to become chiefs of the hospitals that they were working in. And Laroyenne had just invented a procedure to cure gaseous gangrene. Jean's wound was drained with a rubber catheter and irrigated with water. Little by little, the gangrene subsided, and Madame Renoir was able to return home, reassured.

This trip to Jean's bedside and its swirling emotions exhausted Aline. She was only fifty-six, but the diabetes of which she never spoke made her seriously ill. In general, she went out or even moved as little as possible. When she had to put herself to bed soon after her return to Cagnes, she knew that she would never get up again. She didn't want to bother anyone, and she was especially anxious that Renoir not know the gravity of her physical state: he ought to paint, not worry about her. The physical agony he had endured for so long was enough for one person; no need for another object of concern. She had herself discreetly taken to the hospital in Nice, where she died on June 28, 1915. Renoir was desolate. He felt very old, except with a canvas in front of him and a paintbrush in his crippled hand.

At that moment Jean was in the hospital at Besançon, where he was supposed to stay for several more weeks. His sister-in-law, Véra Sergine, had the job of telling him the news. Her arrival created a sensation among the patients: "The door opened, and we officers, all fifty of us, were confronted by a woman with short hair and a short skirt. The last women we had seen had hair down to their knees and long skirts, so long in fact that little brooms were sewn into the hems to sweep the sidewalks. I really had the feeling that I was witnessing a historic change in the condition of women."[1] Jean did not take this idea very far; all he says is that this new fashion was "symbolic of the working woman." He says nothing of what he felt while listening to her message. Like his father, he still did not willingly express inner feelings.

For him as for his fellow soldiers, death had become an everyday reality. Yet he was not ready to accept that it would overtake his own mother. She seemed so strong to him, despite her illness, and so much depended on her, as he well knew. Still, between them there had been no real intimacy. Gabrielle was the object of all his affection and tenderness. He and his mother loved one another without ever trying to understand each other. She found him funny, though he never knew why. He had sometimes exasperated her in the past. Now it was too late to change all that. It is impossible to predict the reaction that the death of a loved one will produce. Nor can one foresee what memories will well up. Every time he speaks of her in his writings, Jean gives her her due. It took a grown man to appreciate the special qualities of this woman, who may not have been as simple as she seemed.

◆

A few weeks after his mother died, Jean was sent to Paris to convalesce. His father returned there to the apartment on the Boulevard Rochechouart in order to be with him. "The Bakerwoman" and "Big Louise" kept house and modeled for him. Models and servants often

[1]Jean Renoir, *Ecrits, 1926–1971*, ed. Claude Gauteur (Paris, 1974), 16.

had nicknames in the Renoir household. It was a way to mark their closeness to the family. But despite the dedication of these two women and the trouble they took, Renoir always felt lost in his studio. The voice of "The Mistress" would never again resound there, and all the drawers and cubbyholes were empty. No one had lived in the apartment since the war started, and Madame Renoir had had all the canvases and drawings sent down to Cagnes. She had managed all his materials as easily and knowingly as she had arranged flowers and set them out around the house.

Renoir had not imagined what it might be like to live without her. The daily delights that she thought up so inconspicuously were now gone forever. The good will of others could not fill the void she left, and Gabrielle, too, was gone. She lived in Montparnasse, on the other side of the Seine, with her husband, Conrad Slade. Renoir knew him well; in fact they were friends. But friends, no matter how close they are, can do little when life has lost its meaning. Once again, the only thing left for him was to work, as much as the physical suffering permitted, and it allowed itself to be forgotten less and less. But painting was the great cure that allowed him to forget everything and withstand anything.

When he was not painting, Renoir was prey to the kind of phobias that obsessed him when his sons were little. He would think of the risks that they were running or the catastrophes that might overtake them. Walking with crutches, Jean might slip on the staircase or on a well-waxed floor. Renoir gave orders to wash everything with plenty of water.

Jean also had a hard time getting used to the empty, deserted apartment. He said nothing, though he understood how lost his father felt. There they were, the two of them, stricken with grief, and one no better than the other at getting around. Being alone together was new to them. They observed each other carefully, a pair of cripples. But for the first time in his life, Jean felt up to conversing with his father. His experiences of the past few months had been the hard way to grow up.

The two of them still had such a taste for life that without even being aware of it, they were about to rescue each other and restore a world that they had sincerely thought was gone forever. The father was in shock from the death of his wife, the son from the experience of war. But with their kind of inner vitality, anything can be overcome, though they themselves did not know it. Neither of them was introspective, and that surely increased their ability to survive.

On the Boulevard Rochechouart and throughout the neighborhood, there was a strange fever on the streets. When he arrived, Jean recognized the flower seller on the street corner, but the street itself was completely changed. It was crowded with soldiers on leave or from allied countries. Although the front had moved away from Paris, the cafés and all the other pleasure domes were crammed with men in uniform. Profiteers flaunted their riches shamelessly; ladies of the night were energetically and unabashedly at work, distracting their ephemeral friends. It all seemed to prove that the home front deserved its bad reputation: the shirkers were flushed with success. Yet it was impossible to forget that soldiers were dying every day, that the trenches were hell on earth, and that no one knew where the hell would end. The only sure thing was that in the spring there would be more battles, probably more murderous than those before.

The Renoirs, father and sons, tried not to think about it. Pierre and Véra Sergine came to lunch often with their little boy, Claude, who was two. Pierre had been honorably discharged because of his crippled arm, and he was worried that he would not be able to resume his career as an actor. But even if the war lasted a very long time, the other Claude would still be too young to take part in it. For the moment, Jean was going to the doctors and the hospital at the Invalides for treatment. His leg was mending very slowly, and they began to wonder if it would ever mend completely. No one said anything, but it was unlikely that he could return to the front.

Jean spent a lot of time with his father, watching him work for hours on end, happy to be useful to him in his studio. He would clean the brushes and palette, and sometimes he was even permitted to squeeze paint from the tubes, a privilege heretofore reserved for Madame Renoir or Gabrielle. In the book he wrote about his father, Jean describes these activities in detail, and he explains the way his father mixed his colors on the canvas itself. "He was obsessed with keeping a transparent effect on the surface of his painting during all phases of its completion. As I said before, he worked on the whole surface at once, and the subject matter would emerge from the welter of brushstrokes like a photographic image on a plate." Jean learned to appreciate the painter's work, and he was fascinated by the amount of thought as well as talent that went into a painter's choices. There was a kind of total self-abnegation that the painter underwent before his subject that Jean was just discovering, since he had not yet really understood his father's genius. He spent so much time watching and also listening to his father, who finally was talking to him, that in the end he understood painting from within, as a painter does. He could have devoted his life to writing about art or becoming a connoisseur.

The thought of doing so never entered his mind. Nor had he been tempted to become a painter—perhaps he had not dared. He preferred telling people that he had no talent and evincing deep humility with respect to his father. After having spent his childhood admiring him, he began to admire painting itself. He loved hearing his father reminisce aimlessly or talk about the problems he was having with a work in progress.

This was the time when Jean gathered most of the material for his book. Renoir needed the attention that his son was paying him, and their intimacy was a consolation to him. Never before had he felt so close to the exuberant boy, the outsized puppy dog who had always been more interested in horses, car engines, and women than in art.

◆

Whatever time he did not devote to painting, Jean spent on movies. He was just as entranced as on those Sunday afternoons in Sainte-Marie de Monceau that he spent gaping at *Automaboul*. But *Automaboul* had disappeared. The movies he went to see were American. It did not take him long to choose them, since they were the only ones he liked. French films weren't fun. They were farfetched and "intellectual," a pejorative term in the Renoir household, where instinct was appreciated and intellect distrusted. *The Perils of Pauline*, a serial, was one of his favorites. Each episode dramatized an installment appearing that week in Hearst's *Chicago American*. In 1915, Pathé published twelve of these installments in *Le Matin* under the title *The New York Mysteries*. A combination of *The Perils of Pauline* and *The Grasping Hand*, they were a huge success. Pearl White, the heroine of those fantastic adventures, was an inspiration to Aragon, Breton, and Louis Delluc. But Jean knew none of these young men, who were soon to become the poets and filmmakers of his generation. He had not yet gone beyond his father's circle of friends. And his infatuation with American film was all his own. Typically, he raised it to fever pitch: Jean would see, on average, not less than twenty-five movies a week. Some theaters, like the Parisiana and the Grand Royal, showed double features, while the Pigalle showed one only "with extra added attractions."

When he came home from the movies, Jean would talk enthusiastically about what he had just seen. His father, who was too disabled to get himself taken to any movie theater—though there were some close by—was nevertheless very curious about these people who could transport him to a world he had never imagined. Coco also became as fanatic a moviegoer as his brother. So they decided to buy a projector. Coco quickly learned how to operate it, and they rented movies that were as much fun for Renoir as for his sons. High spirits had returned to the household.

The movie camera and its miracles could not make them forget the war. As his leg got better, Jean longed to return to active duty. He couldn't stand the slackers on the home front. Long afterwards, he wrote this about his combat buddies: "If you could put a label on the men who fought in the Great War, it would read 'perfect anarchists.' They didn't give a damn about anything. They didn't believe in big ideas. They didn't mind destroying cathedrals. They didn't believe in 'the war for freedom.' They didn't even give a damn about dying, since they thought life wasn't worth living. They had come down to the dregs of existence. The strangest thing was that, despite their total skepticism, they were terrific fighters. They were caught in a system that they had no idea how to get out of."[2] Jean wanted to be involved again, since he felt close to these "perfect anarchists" and could not stand people at home talking about the *Boches,* and the *poilus,* and heroism.[3] Later he said he was "annoyed" by the way war was presented in the movies, too.

Jean knew that he would always have a limp, but he refused to get himself discharged. He thought aviation was the solution, since in the sky his bad leg would not get in the way. His father was sad but not surprised to see him go. He would never have allowed Jean to sacrifice himself for his sake. Renoir did not want to be protector or protected, and he had always believed in independence. The love that he felt for his son, to whom he now felt closer than ever, actually prevented him from interfering. He understood the reasons that this young, vigorous fellow had for returning to battle. Yet it is impossible to get used to having people one loves in danger, and Renoir once again lived in dread of what might happen to this son, who had now become his right hand. Still, nothing got in the way of his work, not the physical pain or the fear or the loss of those long hours of intimate talk. He was painting more and more freely.

◆

The blossoming of Renoir's painting, in stark contrast to the cruelty of the war going on at the time, bespeaks an astounding concentration of energy and spirit from a person whose own physical suffering was

---

[2] Jean Renoir, *Ma vie et mes films* (Paris, 1974), 133.

[3] *Boches* and *poilus:* derogatory French slang for German and French soldiers, respectively [*Trans.*].

so great. To Jean it was a miracle, and detaching himself from his father and his deep quest for beauty was no small sacrifice on Jean's part. Worse, his debut in aviation was a disappointment. His job was reconnaissance. "I didn't have any fun at all. I was nuts about the way [the plane] worked, and tagging along in the sky while someone else was at the controls made me feel like someone had put a toy in front of me and told me not to touch it. Toys are only interesting when you can take them apart."[4]

After a few months, he was sent to the flight school at Ambérieu. Getting a pilot's license turned out to be not so simple. They flunked him the first time, not for his lack of skills, but because he was ten pounds overweight! He got down to regulation weight in a week; but then he gained back several pounds in the wild party celebrating his successful diet. He was finally assigned to squadron C64 anyway. According to Jean, it was "an army squadron ready for anything." They flew reconnaissance flights, took photographs of enemy positions for strategic maps, and carried out machine-gunning runs that were both bloody and useless. Behind the bemused irony in his reminiscences of this period, one can sense the joy he felt. He "adored" his plane, an old Caudron. Caudrons were made entirely of wood and had rotary engines, while Jean thought that "planes with normal four-stroke engines" were "only good for short hops." The rotary engine was for him "the symbol of aviation." He even loved the castor oil trickling down his jumpsuit when he hopped off the plane after a flight; the smell of it was "intoxicating." ("This expensive oil was what they used to lubricate rotating engines" [ibid., 137].) He "admired to distraction" one of the pilots of the fighter squadron in his sector, Warrant Officer Pinsard, a renegade cavalryman who had served in the dragoon guards and would not give up his uniform, "a black tunic over crimson pants" (ibid., 138). Jean loved manly bravura and control, and he confesses to "a kind of affection" for the German fighters, while he "couldn't stand" the "penpushers in staff headquarters," "the shirkers." Jean was easily carried away. Aviators knew they were a privileged group: they slept in beds and ate at tables—a far cry from what Jean had known in the trenches. It was all a big change from the first few weeks of the war, when Jean, too, had had a uniform with crimson pants and fought on horseback armed with a lance. It was now 1916.

Bursting with health, Jean felt no different from the other "boys,"

[4]Renoir, *Ma vie et mes films*, 37.

as they called themselves. He had extraordinary ease in adapting himself. Without any deliberate effort on his part, he made other people think he was just like them, and at the time he also believed it himself. In the company of his friends, he had the same feelings as they and expressed them in the same ways, only with a bit more flair. They took him for a soldier like themselves, and Jean played along with the idea, since he felt good when he was with them. He never was homesick for his other life on boulevard Rochechouart or at Les Collettes, and his buddies in turn forgot that he was the son of a painter whose name, at least, they all knew.

Around this period, Jean heard of Charlot for the first time.[5] One of his friends in the squadron told him that his father, Professor Richet, a Nobel prize winner in medicine, thought Charlot was a genius. On his next leave, Jean found out that his brother Pierre already knew about Charlot and shared Richet's opinion of him. So he went to see for himself and was immediately won over, without imagining that "Charlot," whose real name he had no inkling of, would become one of his best friends one day.

Like everyone, Jean lived a day at a time. His squadron was stationed in Champagne, not far from Essoyes. Yet he had hardly any news of his father, for whom writing was sheer torture. But Jean remembered getting an envelope written by Big Louise. It contained the three words, "For you, Renoir," and included a violet picked at Les Collettes under the olive trees near the fountain used for washing clothes.[6] The affection that his father conveyed in this way meant a lot to Jean. He was still part of their life, and they kept him informed— Big Louise and his brother Claude wrote him as much as he needed to know, and hearing that his father was busy was a big relief.

In the year 1916, at the urging of Maillol, Auguste Renoir began sculpting "through an intermediary," as Jean Leymarie put it. Richard Guino, a Catalan who was one of Maillol's pupils, sculpted what Renoir's crippled hands could no longer create. According to Paul Hasaerts, "This sculpture is above all and incontestably Renoir's. The choice of subjects is Renoir's; the type of person and gestures are Renoir's. The volumes and their opulence are his as well, as is the way they interlace and fit together. And the technique itself, isn't it also his—supple, vibrant, at once simple and contrived without appear-

---

[5] Charlot is Charlie Chaplin's stage name in France [*Trans.*].

[6] The poignance of this message in French arises from the juxtaposition of a respectful surname address with the intimate second person singular word for *you* [*Trans.*].

ing so?"[7] During that year, the French government organized a big Renoir show at La Haye. In the following spring, another of the same proportions was held at Barcelona, and in the fall, Zurich was host to Renoir's triumphs. The painter himself was too old to travel, but the homage moved him; at the same time, he found it "funny." He had achieved the kind of recognition that he never hoped for; his country was even exhibiting his work in neutral countries as propaganda. Better still, Renoir had the comfort of seeing his son's career as an aviator come to a safe conclusion after an unfortunate incident involving a missed landing.

"French aviation was undiminished as a result: I was not a very good pilot," wrote Jean.[8] What he gained from it was experience as a photographer. Both the mechanics and the technique of it had become familiar to him. In order to take pictures behind the German lines, the usual purpose of his missions, he had the idea of putting a wide-angle camera in the other seat. It used plates that were half a meter square. Jean took the controls in the rear of the plane, while his co-pilot, Neyret, who was a good photographer, sat in front. The shots, which turned out to be successful, awakened Jean's interest in photography.

Sent back from the front with a wound that was much less serious than his earlier one, Jean was posted to Paris and soon began going to movies again. He saw all the Chaplin films he could, over and over again, as well as other American movies. In those days, the programs in the theaters changed twice a week, and Jean would see as many as forty films a week. He discussed them with his brother Pierre, who had a real affection for American popular films. Soon Jean began to realize that behind the actors he so admired was the director, whose job Pierre had explained to him. That was how he came to know of D. W. Griffith, at his height in those days. One day Griffith would become another friend of Jean's.

The young man's years of apprenticeship continued. He followed events unfolding at the various fronts from a safe distance. Like all those who took part in the war, he was deeply scarred by the experience, but he could not imagine himself as a career officer and decided to quit the army. Before his final discharge, he served as head newspaper censor in Nice, a stint that allowed him to spend a lot of time at

[7] Paul Hasaerts, *Renoir sculpteur*, reprinted in *La maison de Renoir: Catalogue du Musée Renoir du souvenir* ("Les Collettes," Cagnes-sur-Mer, 1976).

[8] Renoir, *Ma vie et mes films*, 38.

Cagnes with his father, now residing there permanently and unable to travel. Renoir's legs were now completely paralyzed. His driver, Bistolfi, had been drafted into the Italian army, and he could not find anyone else to do the job.

When Jean went back to Les Collettes, the orange trees and the vineyard that his mother had planted had not been touched since her death. The house itself had come back to life, though. Everything had been rearranged to allow the old painter to keep on working. Big Louise, who was as strong as a horse, carried him to his wheelchair every morning. There was also a sedan chair used to carry him to the studio in the garden. Renoir was so thin that he really had nothing more than skin on his bones, and the skin itself was so thin that almost anything irritated it. Simple cuts produced an unbearable burning sensation; still he kept on painting, and with irrepressible joy.

Starting in 1915, a new model had restored his good humor. Andrée Heuschling, a seventeen-year-old Alsatian girl who had fled to Nice with her mother and sister, was a redhead. Her skin glowed more than all the models Renoir had known previously. She would come by tram, humming some popular song loudly but out of tune. She loved to dance and had the quintessential Renoir face, round yet somehow pointy, with a small nose. She soon became his main model. Jean used to say that Madame Renoir, who had asked about models at the Nice painting academy, had discovered Andrée and "given her to my father as a final gift before her death" (ibid., 42). Dédée, as they called her, posed for *The Chiffon Dress* the first year, and for *The Pink Bedjacket* the following year, 1918; then for *Woman with the Guitar* and *The Large Bather* in 1919. She became attached to the old painter and had fun making him laugh with elaborate tales of the adventures of her girlfriends. Her imagination and devil-may-care attitude answered to the qualities Renoir had admired all his life.

Inevitably, Jean fell hopelessly in love with this Dédée. Like many young men of his class, he had only known women trained in lovemaking: those of the demimonde, of whom Colette writes so well, or the ones whom his father called "frogs," or prostitutes. Dédée fit none of these categories. Thanks to her, Jean let go of the war. Back in his father's home, he was caught up in the Mediterranean tints, the perfumed herbs, the aromatic shrubs and flowers. The scents were overwhelming, more bewitching than he remembered. In such a place it is hard to believe that your buddies are still fighting where there is no beauty, and you can hardly believe that yourself experienced such hardships. "The great olive trees with their silver highlights" and the roses in the garden were as magnificent as Renoir painted them, and Andrée herself was as radiant in person as on canvas. Her beauty was irresistible, and Jean could not distinguish the paintings from the model: their sparkle only added to hers. Many years later, he wrote of her: "Andrée was one of the vital elements which helped Renoir to interpret on his canvas the tremendous cry of love he uttered at the end of his life."[9] The remark attests to the affection and respect in which he held both his father and the young woman.

Jean was twenty-four years old when the armistice was signed. Once discharged, he had no idea what to do. His father, who had not forgotten painting porcelain plates and throwing pots as a young man, had the idea of setting up a studio and a kiln for Claude, who had to learn a trade at age seventeen. Jean decided to become a potter as well. He had no desire to get away from Les Collettes. If he had, he would have lost his Dédée, for it was unthinkable that she abandon Renoir. She was needed there, and the thought that someone else might take her place was intolerable; she wanted to think of herself as unique. It was comforting to recognize herself in Renoir's works. That was the way she wanted to see herself, and she was sensitive to the importance she had assumed in the life of the old artist whom she so admired. She was sure he was a genius, since he did not paint like anyone else. The simplest of his still lifes reflected his mixture of sensuality and mysticism. Everyone around him sensed it, and the result was an elation that Dédée herself came to need. Jean's love for her was part of it. As in the early days, which she herself had not known but which had made Jean what he was, everything was set up so that Renoir could keep painting. And he did. Yet little by little, his force dwindled, his suffering grew worse. On December 3, 1919, the morning of his death, he was painting a bouquet of anemones; Dédée was there, and so was Jean.

A few weeks later, on January 24, Jean and Dédée were married, as had been planned.

---

[9] *Renoir par Jean Renoir* (Paris, 1958), 451 (= *Renoir, My Father*, 452.)

A CHAPLIN

IN PETTICOATS

◆

There was laughter, there were tears. "Joy always came after sorrow," wrote Guillaume Apollinaire, a poet who died on the day of the armistice. Grief for the death of the painter was still fresh. So were memories of the funeral mass in the little church at Cagnes and the burial at Essoyes, where Auguste lay beside Aline. It wasn't really possible to celebrate at Jean and Andrée's wedding. But joy still ruled, with sadness alongside. His father's death grieved Jean and his bride alike. In a household that was always so hospitable, the newcomer had easily found her niche. She had long since become part of the family, and no one found it unnatural that she shared their sorrow. Dédée was sincere and genuine, and Renoir had loved her spontaneity even more than her spectacular beauty.

Renoir had included Dédée in the project of setting up the pottery studio. According to Jean, his father found her "very gifted," and all three of them, Dédée, Jean, and Claude, the youngest of the brothers, were supposed to learn the craft. He "wanted to see us work together at shaping and decorating useful objects. He had no confidence in trades in which the hand of man played no part."[1] In accord with Renoir's wish, they did everything with their hands, going to get the clay themselves in the fields and mixing it with sand from a nearby brook. The wheel was an old one, and the kiln burned wood.

---

[1] Jean Renoir, *Ma vie et mes films* (Paris, 1974), 43.

They charged it up by night. Whole faggots had to go into the firebox to keep it going. During firing, which lasted about ten hours, they listened to records—phonographs were still a rarity, since both the equipment and the disks were very expensive. They would drink wine from their vineyard and eat dark bread with olives and anchovies. Such mixtures of luxury and simplicity were typical of Jean. Without thinking about it, he had always lived that way.

On the death of their father, the three Renoir sons divided among themselves his paintings and other possessions. They had the help of Jacques Mortier, a school friend of Jean's who had become a lawyer. But as there was no pettiness in them, so there was no dispute among them either. The three ended up financially independent and could live as they wished. Pierre, despite his war wound, had resumed a career in the theater. He eventually did brilliantly in movies and on stage, a success that owed nothing to his inherited wealth. He played an unforgettable Siegfried in Giraudoux's play of the same name, and he was associated with Louis Jouvet during his whole career. As for Jean and Claude, they had no idea when or what the production of plates and pots would add to their incomes. Nor were they worried about it. Most of their friends were also living on annuities.

The switch from streetcars to sports cars was a big one for Dédée. Jean loved high-performance cars, and he drove around in a Napier. Dédée, in the habit of asking herself each month if ends would meet, now had nothing to worry about and could even support her sister and mother. She was living out a kind of fairy tale. Not yet twenty, she was in love with a tall, elegant, well-turned-out young man. A slight limp did not detract in the least from his bearing: in fact, she thought they made a remarkable couple. Both had red hair, and both had Renoir faces—small nose, eyes far apart, full mouth. He kept on telling her that she was beautiful, and God knows she was that, an unusual beauty who had been painted into immortality. Furthermore, she knew how to live for the here and now, for a wondrous present that also brought unexpected joys.

Living at Les Collettes was part of the dream: olive trees in the moonlight, starry nights curled up in each other's arms, the smell of the wood fire and the way the flames licked out when the door of the kiln was opened. They lived out their hearts' desires and were beholden to no one. War faded from their minds. Only the memory of Renoir remained, brought back by the light through the olive branches. There were roses in the garden all year round. Nearby were friends, like the painter Albert André, Claude's godfather, whom

Renoir thought of as his "other son," his wife, Maleck, and Pierre Lestringuez, now a writer. New friends appeared, like Basset, another writer who lived in Nice and introduced Jean to Dostoyevsky. In fact, Basset was so taken with the author of *The Brothers Karamazov* that he nicknamed himself Dmitri, called his dog Grushenka, and quoted Raskolnikov at the least provocation. There was also Pierre Champagne, a strapping fellow, straight as an arrow, who was wild about movies and fast cars; he looked like Don Quixote, and quickly became a devoted friend. Like his father, Jean had a knack for making friends, and he also really needed to have a little circle of intimates around him. Wherever he was, he always managed to create one. These days, however, Jean had no sense of the impression he made on others. Like his wife, he lived for the moment. Swept away by their immediate surroundings, neither of them sensed how marginal they had actually become. The news of the day did not concern them. National disillusionment assuredly did not reach Les Collettes. Nor were they aware of the free fall of the franc. With the wealth in their own kingdom, with the paintings of Renoir and the little world that had been created for them, they lived a wild life without ever being aware that these were, in fact, the Roaring Twenties.

On October 21, 1919, a baby was born at Les Collettes: Alain, spitting image of his father. His godmother was young Aline Cézanne, daughter of Jean's close friends, Renée and Paul; his godfather was Philippe Gangnat, the art collector's son. Claude was away doing his military service. Shortly after the birth of his son, Jean decided to leave Cagnes as well. But his departure did not mean he had abandoned either the potter's craft or his father's memory, since he moved to Marlotte, on the banks of the Loing, where Renoir had often painted. He bought a house and grounds right at the edge of the forest of Fontainebleau. The young couple were bewitched by their natural surroundings, which also offered another advantage: it was just a short trip from Marlotte to Paris and all its movie theaters.

At first, the two of them were preoccupied with pottery. Jean wanted to set up a factory, and he sent for a potter from Cagnes named Baude to work with him. Jean threw some lovely pots that were quickly snatched up by collectors (some of his work can actually still be seen at the Barnes Foundation in Merion, Pennsylvania). But such demanding manual labor did not really suit his temperament. He was absentminded and always curious about something. Working on his own did not suit him, nor did he enjoy staying in the same place for long. Like his father, he would ask others questions and listen carefully to their answers, but he was also in the habit of asking himself questions. He was a voracious reader, and as a result his learning grew broader and broader. Yet he would never be a "learned man," since he was at once too subtle and too bright. Like the people with whom he surrounded himself, Jean also had a sense of the good life that was reflected in all his activities. Gabrielle and her husband became regular visitors. The mutual affection between her and Jean had never waned. Only the distance from Paris to Cagnes had come between them.

Gabrielle had had a son a year before Alain was born. He was named Jean. Just as with the Jean of old, she devoted herself passionately to him. Her vivaciousness was undiminished. Like Jean and Dédée, she and Conrad Slade led a bohemian existence, but one that still had a place in it for their child. They lived in Montparnasse, a neighborhood where they knew and were known to everyone. During the war, shortly after they were married, they dined regularly at Rosalie's, a little restaurant that also catered to Picasso, Braque, Modigliani, Apollinaire, and two Russians who often shared a table with them— Lenin and Trotsky. Jean reports to us this detail about the Slades, but it has no parallel at all in his life with Dédée. Outside their small circle, they met hardly anyone. Nor did they try to.

Soon after they arrived in Marlotte, the Cézannes joined them there. They bought "a superb old house" called la Nicotière because Jean Nicot had lived in it. "Paul Cézanne, on the threshold of old age, still looked like the portrait his father had painted of him as a harlequin. He was as blind as a bat but amazingly strong physically. He looked a little like a circus strongman performing in a Paris park," as Jean puts it (ibid., 81). Renée Cézanne called Jean her brother. In fact their intimacy was based on shared habits, understanding, indulgence, tenderness, and long conversations. It was really a kind of love, with the bonds between Jean and the Cézannes just as strong as those between true relatives.

At Marlotte, the Cézannes' door was always open, and the hospitality they offered was as simple and generous as Madame Renoir's had been in the old days. "At day's end at the Cézannes' in Marlotte, total freedom reigned. As I remember them, those evenings were occupied with the wanton pleasures of the more cultivated bourgeoisie." Parties usually happened on Sunday, but the Cézannes and the Renoirs saw each other every day. With the Cézannes as their neighbors, the little circle was closed once more, and daily life was as it had been at Cagnes. The newborn was an addition, but Marie, a stocky nanny from Artois, took over his upbringing. She was nothing like Gabrielle, but neither was Dédée like Aline Renoir. Dédée was too young and inexperienced and did not know what to do with her infant. She refused to accept the constraints that come with motherhood, and she thought of the child as a hindrance to her full enjoyment of life. She loved dressing up like her favorite film stars, wearing extravagant clothes, stunning makeup, and fancy hairdos. People would stop her in the street to ask her what movie they had seen her in. They not only took her for an actress, but for an American one to boot. Like Jean, she loved Charlie Chaplin, and she also loved American movies to the exclusion of all others. As for her young husband, he enjoyed her being noticed as much as she did. They were truly mad about movies, but the thought never occurred to them that they could make their own. Her beauty in full flower, Dédée was a child playing grown-up games. Jean admired her, and her eccentricities did not displease him in the least. Actually, he spent more time taking care of her than worrying about making clay pots.

Their favorite pastime was setting out at top speed in the car for Paris to see movies. They would go to cheap little theaters where the program changed twice a week and there were always two features and sometimes three. Sometimes they went to three or four shows on a single trip, as Jean had done by himself during the war. On the way home to Marlotte, they prolonged their pleasure with talk about their favorite sequences, criticizing the acting or the close-ups of Mary Pickford in *Pollyanna* or *The Sparrows* or of Lilian Gish in *Orphans of the Storm* or in other films not directed by D. W. Griffith. They talked and talked without realizing that they were actually learning a trade in the process. As they spoke, ideas came to Jean. They were both equally intoxicated with the movies, but they never gave a thought to getting involved with French filmmaking. They thought it was vulgar or pretentious or both at once. Yet through Pierre and Véra Sergine, they could have had easy access to it.

Véra and Pierre had both shot films for the production company called Films d'Art, but Pierre had no illusions about their work and confided to Jean: "Movies," he told him, "aren't for us. Our literary and artistic baggage is too heavy and slows us down. We should leave it to the Americans." His conclusion was that "French dramatic art is bourgeois art" (ibid., 40). Even so, there were theater professionals in France interested in what the critic Canudo had called "the seventh art." There was a group of directors and critics—one easily turned into the other—who wanted to make avant-garde movies or great popular spectacles with artistic merit. This was the era when Louis Delluc, a screenwriter, started the so-called ciné-clubs. He invented their name and became the guiding light of the French avant-garde, which was inspired by Griffith, De Mille, Ince, Chaplin, and the Swedes and Germans. He founded the review *Cinéa* and aggressively recruited as spectators people who still thought of films as vulgar distractions. Germaine Dulac and Marcel L'Herbier were avant-garde directors in the process of creating French Impressionist cinema with the most sophisticated production techniques. Jean Epstein had published *Bonjour cinéma* in October of 1921 after meeting Blaise Cendrars the previous year in Nice during the shooting of Abel Gance's *La Roue* (*The Wheel*). In Paris everyone interested in technical fireworks was awaiting that film impatiently. It was due to come out in 1923, four years after the first *J'accuse* (*I Accuse*), also directed by Gance.

A war movie, it was the exact opposite of what Jean Renoir liked. *La Roue*, which was equally grandiose in style, was hailed as a masterpiece because of its pacing. Actually, Gance had systematized the technique of montage sequences he had borrowed from Griffith, as Georges Sadoul has said.[2] Jean had learned from his father to distrust theories and intellectuals, and what he heard people saying about French filmmaking was enough to alienate him from it completely. Dédée instinctively shared his opinion in this regard, and, like him, she was bewitched by the imagination, outrageousness, and technical skill of American films, which both of them were beginning to know very well indeed.

◆

Apart from parties with friends that went on into the night or constant moviegoing in Paris, they did not adopt the way of life of elegant young marrieds, spending their evenings at the Boeuf sur le Toit or the Bal Nègre on the rue Blomet. They were not fans of the surrealist poets and painters, though their wealth and connections would have made them welcome if they had wished it. But they heeded Renoir's dictum: live life as you understand it, and pay no heed to fashion. The painter's son had too strong an identity of his own for that sort of thing.

Jean was aware of a variety of feelings that his wife's beauty gave rise to. He wanted others to admire and be jealous of the woman he loved, who was even more lovely and extraordinary than she seemed

---

[2] Georges Sadoul, *Histoire d'un art, le cinéma des origines à nos jours* (Paris, 1949), 161.

at first. His father's paintings reveal her in all her splendor. He did not wish to describe her in words, but to project her image across the screen. Her marvelous body would be unveiled, at least as much as it could be, just as his father had done in *The Large Bathers.* And then she would dance—she already danced very well, but she would take lessons and dance even better. That was how Jean Renoir decided to make movies. He had no intention of becoming a director. He only wished to be the *deus ex machina* who would transform his wife into a movie star. It was to be an act of homage to her beauty as well as the realization of a desire so secret that neither of them admitted it to the other.

As if by chance, suddenly everything changed. One day in 1923, Jean and Dédée found themselves in a movie theater on the Champs-Elysées where *Le Brasier ardent* (*The Blazing Inferno*) was playing. The star and director of this film was one Ivan Mosjukin, a Russian refugee actor who had been in France since 1920 and who happened to be making movies with the help of his friend, Alexander Kamenka, the founder of the Albatross studio in Montreuil-sur-Seine. The audience went wild, and its whistling and shrieking only excited the Renoirs even more. They were delighted to see a good movie that was not, for once, made on the other side of the Atlantic. Until then, Jean thought there was no hope outside of America, which was why he had never tried making a movie. How could he even think of challenging Hollywood? Besides, there was a bevy of actresses there whose craft would have left Dédée in the shade. If, as Mosjukin's movie implied, one could make movies in France, everything was once again possible. Jean immediately spoke to Dédée about it, and despite what she told a journalist many years later,[3] she had indeed dreamed of becoming a star and playing a femme fatale, a coquette, or an ingenue. She craved adulation, and Jean was eager that she let herself be adored. Their fantasies had gotten as far as inventing a stage name for her, Catherine Hessling. Its Anglo-Saxon ring was no coincidence.

Albert Dieudonné, co-starring at the time with Véra Sergine in a play called *Un lâche* (*A Coward*), wanted to make his mark in movies. A few years later, he would land the great role of Napoleon in Abel Gance's film, but he was also interested in directing. He had already made a few films for Gaumont and Auber from his own screenplays. Being ready for a new partner, he thought he would have more freedom with Jean Renoir. So he agreed to film Jean's screenplay and to

[3]Specifically, Pierre Philippe, *Cinéma 61*, 8, 57.

co-star with Dédée. Jean needed to feel affection for the people he worked with, and he was not especially attracted to Dieudonné. In his eagerness to see Catherine Hessling on the screen, he decided to take a chance. However, he asked Pierre Lestringuez to help with the screenplay. Jean tells us that he and Pierre were friends "before they were born," since their fathers had been close.[4] Pierre was an established literary personality with ties to Cocteau and Giraudoux, and he was enthusiastic about any project that interested Jean. This time he even tried acting to accommodate his friend—Pierre was just the trusty accomplice that Jean needed. It was always important to have fun, even in a project with as weighty a title as this one: *Catherine, ou Une vie sans joie* (*Catherine, or A Life without Joy*).

The story recalls the *Diary of a Chambermaid*, a book Jean read when he was very young because its author, Mirbeau, was a friend of his father's and had made a strong impression on him. People have said more than once that the themes of this story were near and dear to him: love affairs with servants, the poor oppressed by the rich, a ferocious critique of bourgeois corruption. Jean finally got the screen rights to Mirbeau's novel twenty-two years later, in 1946. This first time, however, the maid falls in love with her employers' consumptive son. The boy's father is a courageous deputy whose political rivals exploit his son's idyllic romance with the young girl. Hounded, Catherine runs away, and a string of misfortunes ensues, her carriage is hurled from a cliff, a vicious pimp enslaves her, and she is victimized by a lecherous policeman played by Jean himself. The soap opera ends on a high note—which is more than can be said of Jean's relationship with Dieudonné.

That ended up with Jean contradicting Dieudonné, who went around telling the newspapers that he was "the only director" and that he had collaborated in the story development. "Besides, Monsieur Renoir was my partner and pupil. Time alone will tell if his future productions justify my confidence."[5] The film was completed in 1924 but not shown until 1927. Then Dieudonné revised it after a succession of edits. Jean wanted the film to be free of realism; Dieudonné did not know what he wanted. Impressed by the weight of his own experience, he believed he was in charge of his producer and the young fellow's untrained wife, who for some reason preferred to follow her husband's instructions rather than to learn at the feet of a

[4] Jean Renoir, *Ma vie et mes films*, 65.
[5] *Cinéma-Ciné*, January 5, 1926.

56

master, that is, himself. Jean extracted everything he could from Catherine's body language, her gestures, and her facial expressions. André Bazin hit the mark when he wrote that she combined "in a disturbing way the mechanical and the living, the fantastic and the sensual, with the result a strange, striking expression of femininity."[6] From her very first film, it was clear that she was an extraordinary person. Jean's eyes never left her during the filming, and it is unthinkable that he said nothing. With all due respect for Dieudonné, who claimed to have collaborated on the script, the movie bears Jean's seal in another way as well—it was filmed outdoors at Cagnes and Saint-Paul-de-Vence.

◆

Jean's disagreement with Dieudonné was a disappointment that might have soured him on moviemaking, but at that moment Jean discovered, again by accident, *Folies de femmes* (*Foolish Wives*). He was "astounded" by it and went back to see it ten times. The film brought him back to a sort of realism, at least temporarily. Stroheim, with his Viennese sensibility, had found a way to recreate the ambience of Europe immediately after the war—the movie, which was filmed in Hollywood, took place in Monaco in 1919—and it drove Jean to try to profit from the French tradition that he had, in fact, inherited. "I started looking around and was amazed to discover plenty of things that were purely and simply French and that I could easily transpose onto film. I began to realize that the way a washerwoman moves her arms, the way a lady combs her hair before a mirror, even a farmer selling his produce from a truck, each has its own sculptural value. From my father's paintings and those of others of his generation, I made a kind of study of gesture and attitude."[7] Apparently, he never forgot what he learned, since the gestures in Renoir's film are always remarkably appropriate and expressive.

The persona of Catherine Hessling restricted Jean to a certain kind of subject. The boundary between fantasy and reality became indistinct where she was concerned. It was impossible to predict what she would do or how she would feel, an attribute that delighted Jean. To his mind, the first film they had made did not do her justice, however irrepressible they both may have been. Something else had to be done, and quickly. Emboldened by Stroheim's film and egged on by

[6] André Bazin, *Jean Renoir* (Paris, 1971), 78.
[7] Jean Renoir, *Ecrits, 1926–1971*, ed. Claude Gauteur (Paris, 1974), 40.

their friend Lestringuez, that same year (1924) they started a new project, *La Fille de l'eau* (*The Water Girl*), from a screenplay by Lestringuez that Jean Renoir reworked. Afterwards, Jean said that he had wished to exhibit Catherine's sculptural virtues in a fantastic setting, the forest of Fontainebleau near Marlotte. The film juxtaposes great beech trees with the masts of shipwrecks on the sea floor. The sets were his invention. Exterior shots were done at La Nicotière, the Cézannes' estate, and at the café Au Bon Coin on the banks of the Loing. Jean did the special effects—Catherine on a white horse galloping through clouds and falling through the sky—in the old Gaumont studios in Paris.

In those days, double exposures were shot at the same time as the rest of the film. Taking them was a two-step process. For *La Fille de l'eau* they had to build a canvas cylinder sixty feet in diameter that was painted black on the inside and the base. Catherine galloped on her white horse inside it; then, on the same, as yet undeveloped roll of film, they photographed the cloud background. The camera was mounted on a platform placed along the cylinder's central axis, so that it was possible to photograph a "perfect panorama." Special effects like this fascinated Jean and his friends. After all, they were just as interested in having fun as in revitalizing the French cinema. They believed in Jean and trusted him as well. The star of the film, Catherine, took care of the costumes along with Mimi Champagne, Pierre's wife. Pierre had been promoted to assistant director. He also acted and was in charge of transporting the photographic equipment. Lestringuez was not just the scriptwriter. He also played the villain. Pierre Renoir had a diabolical walk-on role, and the painter André Derain played the owner of the café Au Bon Coin; the flower of local manhood was played by a young American, Van Doren, on vacation in Marlotte. In these enchanting surroundings, all of Jean's attention was focused on Catherine, whom he instructed to play her part in jerky, stop-and-start movements, echoing the movement of the projector's wheel. After all, this was the movies, and the audience shouldn't forget it for a moment.

Except for its dream sequence, the film is Jean Renoir's version of realism: stress on the details of daily life, everyday objects and gestures, a dog following Catherine around during the first half of the movie; for an instant, little Alain appears. It is all a reflection of Jean's universe, and this is the surprising part. For an hour and ten minutes we get a glimpse of a man, a beginner whose awkwardness does not prevent him from expressing a vision. This is no longer the aspiring producer of *Une vie sans joie*. In addition to directing his actors, so important to him later on, Jean discovered a real passion in himself for technique. He soon became familiar with the photo lab, where he learned the stages of film development. They reminded him of how clay changes while cooking in the kiln. In fact, everything about this new trade intrigued him. He became a devotee of fast cutting, and in *La Fille de l'eau*, some of the shots have no more than five frames. Moreover, he admits to a penchant for shooting from "bizarre" angles: one might also call it practicing scales. His were certainly up-tempo.

La Fille de l'eau was ready for distribution the following April (1925), but not a single distributor picked it up. Disappointed by this setback, which meant a serious loss of money, Jean and Catherine would have to suffer the consequences. Working freelance is harder in movies than in other professions, since the commercial side of film-making can never be underestimated. Jean thought it was impossible to go on and that the wisest course was to return to pottery. That is what his father had done after spending all his savings at the Gleyre studio—he went back to painting cafés. Did Jean remember? He opened a shop near the Place de la Madeleine, and he and Catherine moved into an apartment at 30, rue de Miromesnil, in a building where the Cézannes and Pierre Renoir lived. Jean had forgotten that business was not for him. They had pots to sell and fabrics painted by Maleck, Albert André's wife, but Jean was hopeless as a salesman, and Catherine was no better. Moreover, she had seriously devoted herself to acting and dancing. In fact, she was champing at the bit, even though she knew only too well that they and their friends were all amateurs, with the exception of the technicians and Pierre Renoir. The leading position of French cinema before 1914 had vanished, and what remained was simply trying to stay on its feet after Pathé had sold all of its studios. Even so, Louis Delluc and others still had faith in the future. By 1925, the French public was hooked on movies. There were 184 theaters in Paris. Couldn't they get their film shown in just a few of them?

When they first started shooting *La Fille de l'eau*, Pierre Lestringuez invited Jean to lunch with a friend of his, Pierre Braunberger, who had just come back from the United States. Braunberger had, as he put it, contributed "after a fashion" to Rudolph Valentino's *Monsieur Beaucaire*. He was also an assistant to the famous Irving Thalberg, who had not yet become Scott Fitzgerald's *Last Tycoon*. Braunberger had actually lived in Hollywood, Jean and Catherine's unreachable promised land. He brought back hundreds of anecdotes about this strange world, and Jean was overjoyed. The conversation begun at lunch did not conclude until three the next morning. "I always had a weakness, if not a real affection, for this charming eccentric who had stepped right out of the pages of Courteline's *Les Linottes* (*The Linnets*)," Jean said.[8] For his part, Braunberger, the American movie fanatic, was an enthusiastic, intelligent, curious, and imaginative person who was completely won over by Jean. He understood immediately that Jean Renoir was a filmmaker unlike the rest. Getting him the chance to keep making films was worth fighting for. But his first attempt to do so was not a success, for he, too, was unable to find a distributor for *La Fille de l'eau*.

Jean needed the encouragement he received from such friends, but down deep he had no intention of giving up filmmaking however much he pretended the opposite. Pottery was not a credible alternative. Industrial production did not interest him, and he understood that the reason his work sometimes sold was his name: people would buy "a vase by Renoir." So while minding the store, he wrote some synopses: one called *Alice,* three pages long, dated 22 November 1925, and, probably the same year, a *Don Juan,* fourteen pages long.[9]

In 1925 the first surrealist exhibition took place. It impressed Jean and Catherine much less than *Potemkin* and *The Goldrush,* also shot that year, and Fritz Lang's adaptation, *Die Nibelungen,* or von Stroheim's *Greed.* They became friendly with some movie people, among them Jean Tedesco. Tedesco had transformed the Vieux-Colombier theater, where Jacques Copeau and his company had made their debut in 1913, into an avant-garde movie house. It had become the meeting place of real movie lovers. Jean and Catherine ran into him one day in Montparnasse, and Tedesco told them that he had included the dream sequence from *La Fille de l'eau* in one of his shows. At first, Jean was angry. It wasn't legal to cut a work into pieces and let the public sample them without the auteur's consent. But they were intrigued by Tedesco's reaction—he was not at all dismayed by such reproaches—and so they went to the theater that same evening. They duly noted that *Extracts from La Fille de l'eau* was enthusiastically applauded. When the house lights came up, Catherine received a standing ovation. "For the first time in my life," Jean notes, "I experi-

[8] Jean Renoir, *Lettres d'Amérique* (Paris, 1984), 232.

[9] Resumés of them can be found in Jean Renoir, *Oeuvres de cinéma inédites,* ed. Claude Gauteur (Paris, 1981), 18.

enced the intoxication of success."[10] After an evening like that, giving up filmmaking was unthinkable.

◆

The production group was joyously reassembled. Undiminished in his admiration for *Foolish Wives,* Jean decided to make a film of one of the most famous works of French realism/naturalism, Zola's *Nana.* His accomplices, Lestringuez and Braunberger, shared his taste and egged him on. Lestringuez wrote the screenplay, Renoir revised it, and Denise Leblond-Zola wrote the captions. "The Leblond-Zola family gave us the rights and was more cooperative than we could have hoped," Jean later recalled (ibid., p. 72). But the production of the film turned out to be very costly. Braunberger, as devoted to the project as Renoir himself, began making inquiries about a German co-producer. Catherine was ecstatic. Every day she came up with new ideas about playing Nana, and she would mime them for Jean and Lestringuez, already hard at work themselves. In the end, he and Jean were the only financial partners in the project, but that did not worry her a bit. Like Jean, she had no doubts about their success. Everything looked great.

For the role of Count Muffat, Jean wanted Werner Krauss, whom he had seen in *The Cabinet of Dr. Caligari* and on stage in Ibsen's *Wild Duck.* Along with Emil Jannings, Krauss was a leading light in German cinema, which at the time was strongly influenced by expressionism. Jean says that Krauss taught him a great deal about the craft of acting. "What impressed me about him was first of all his technical skills, his knowledge of makeup and the mileage he got from his minor physical idiosyncrasies. After a few tries, he had invented a Count Muffat who was and yet wasn't Werner Krauss" (ibid., p. 71). Krauss seems to have been more clearheaded than actors usually are. Valesksa Gert, also from the German theater, played Zoe, Nana's chambermaid. Braumberger got the approval of a German production company, and *Nana* was the first French film shot in Germany after the war.

Shooting started in October 1925, at the same time as the Locarno Conference, whose goal was to relax international tensions and accelerate the process of disarmament foreseen by the League of Nations. There were fledgling attempts at reconciliation with Germany, for

[10]Jean Renoir, *Ma vie et mes films,* 71.

instance, the joint French-German Committee on Information and Documentation that was created with Briand's encouragement by the Mayrisch family (Mayrisch was a steel magnate from Luxemburg) and the ACJF (French Catholic Youth Action Committee) that had been revived by Marc Sangnier. On January 26, 1926, the French government accepted the anticipated evacuation of the Cologne region. It was the first stage in an evacuation of the whole Rhineland that the Germans were clamoring for. On September 8, 1926, France sponsored the acceptance of Germany into the League of Nations, "seat of reconciliation, arbitration, and peace," in the words of Aristide Briand.

Relations between France and Germany were not simple. There had been the defeat of 1870, Alsace-Lorraine, and World War I; but there were also Madame de Staël and the German philosophers, musicians, and romantics. Like other sophisticated Frenchmen, Jean Renoir made it a point of honor to speak and read German, and he knew his way around German literature. He had not forgotten the vacations in Bavaria with his father and the Thurneyssen family. He felt at home in Berlin. Many years later, speaking about Ernst Lubitsch—he knew every one of his films—he wrote:

> To preserve nature's remarkable equilibrium, God grants conquered nations the gift of art. At least, that is what happened to Germany after its defeat in 1918. Before Hitler, Berlin was overflowing with talented people. During that short renascence, the Jews, not just the German Jews but those of neighboring countries as well, brought a kind of imagination to the city that was probably the best thing to come out of the period. Lubitsch offers the perfect example of that era's ironical way of approaching the great problems of life. His spirited movies were a distillation of Berlin intellectual life at the time. He was such a generously gifted person that when Hollywood invited him to work there, he not only did not lose his Berlin style, he actually converted the Hollywood film industry to it. In fact Hollywood is still under Lubitsch's influence, which means that it is still influenced by the Berlin I knew as a young man.[11]

Catherine and Jean enjoyed Berlin so much and were so readily accepted by the German filmmakers that they subsequently returned there to act in other films. Jean had some German friends. One of them, the philosopher Karl Koch, was the husband of Lotte Reiniger, creator of a miniature shadow theater. She had made some short films

---

[11] Herman G. Weinberg, *The Lubitsch Touch* (New York, 1971), from an extract of a letter to the author dated July 22, 1967.

of it, one of which, a masterpiece called *Prince Achmed*, was much admired by Jean and Catherine. The friendship between Jean and Koch arose from the fact that in 1916, Koch was an artillery captain in the German army. He had commanded an antiaircraft battery in the region of Reims, where Jean was a pilot in a reconnaissance squadron. Koch used to speak of the ceaseless attacks of the squadron across from them, and Jean remembered that his squadron "was the target of a German battery that caused it much grief. Koch and I came to the conclusion that it was his battery and my squadron. So we had fought together. Things like that bring people closer together." [12] This is the theory of a world classified horizontally, as dear to Jean as the theory of the cork was to his father.

◆

Jean Renoir made friends everywhere. In that, he never changed. One of his buddies from those days, André Cerf, a portly little fellow, now a very old man still full of life and memories that he serves up at will, was his assistant and played the role of "Tiger," Nana's groom. He told me: "Jean had a big mouth. He was a smooth talker, who could persuade you that black was white or vice versa There was never a dull moment when he was around, we were never bored." A ceaseless patter of droll remarks streamed forth from him. Even so, he never forgot what he was about.

The sumptuous, baroque backdrops for the film were designed by Claude Autant-Lara and built in Germany. The interiors they shot in Paris (Gaumont Studios) and Berlin (Grünewald); the exteriors in and around Paris. Cerf remembers them filming in the Paris Zoo. According to Jean himself, *Nana* was the first movie he made "worth talking about." [13] He criticizes the film's awkwardness, but is sure that it retains some interest nevertheless, not as a curiosity but because it constructs a timeless fantasy and exudes a strange eroticism. The combination of Catherine Hessling and Werner Krauss is amazing. Clearly, Jean set them free to interpret their roles as they wished, and Catherine as Nana is more surprising than Krauss as Muffat. The other actors are neatly distributed between the two extremes they constitute, which gives a kind of unity to their variety. One can sense Jean and Catherine's fascination with Charlie Chaplin in the way she plays her character, with conviction and a kind of offhand naiveté. It

---

[12] Jean Renoir, *Ma vie et mes films*, 146.
[13] *Le Point*, December 18, 1938.

gives the poor girl, a victim of her own narcissistic delusion, a really seductive charm.

Nana was a reaction against the sluggishness of French cinema at the time. The pace of the film is swift. Lestringuez and Renoir had learned their lessons well from the Americans. They boiled down the story by suppressing characters and making the action nonstop. Jean knew exactly what he was trying to do. When the film came out, he said, "To be sure, we were concerned to recreate the real atmosphere of the book, and at times we pushed things to the limit, but it also seemed to us that it isn't wrong to smile a little in the cruellest of worlds, amid the saddest kinds of human drama, even as one witnesses, in the story of a single woman, the collapse of a whole way of life."[14]

Jean was in total control of the formal aspects of this production, down to the smallest detail of technique or decor. He had two first-class cameramen, Alphonse Gibory and Charles Ralleigh, with whom he was working for the first time. The actors give the impression of being completely free to express themselves as they wish, but each gesture was approved in advance. As with the other films he was to make and everything else he took part in, Jean had made the film with intense passion. He did the work with friends, and he felt satisfied with the results. Nor did he neglect any opportunity to publicize the film before its release. The walls of Paris were covered with posters of Catherine Hessling as Nana. There were also advertisements and leaflets. For the film's premiere, Jean and Pierre Braunberger rented the Moulin Rouge, and the house orchestra played tunes by Offenbach.

"The film professionals," as Jean Renoir called them, did not appreciate it. Pierre Braunberger showed me the scar he received from a blow with an umbrella administered to his skull by the wife of the director, Léonce Perret. When the show came to an end, this large, strong, and very angry woman cried out, "It's a kraut movie." Jean, a disabled veteran, was not about to take the trouble to defend himself. The only thing he could do was laugh. Actually, it was not the German actors that bothered Madame Perret. It was Catherine, with her unusual and surprising interpretation of the role of Nana.

For several weeks, the film was shown exclusively at the Aubert Palace, a rarity in those days. It was being rented to theaters at "very good" prices, and its selling prices abroad were still amazing to Jean twelve years later. It won a measure of fame in Germany, where

[14] *Ciné-Miroir*, no. 100, June 15, 1926, reprinted in Jean Renoir, *Ecrits*, 233–35.

Catherine Hessling was especially appreciated. She had rave reviews and was compared to Asta Nielsen and Greta Garbo, then at the beginning of her career (Garbo had already been the star of *The Legend of Gösta Berling* and *The Street without Joy,* G. W. Pabst's great contribution to the revitalization of German cinema).

The bold style that permeated everything in the movie, from Catherine's acting to the framing of the shots and the set design, might have seduced the critics; the film's dramatic intensity might have aroused the interest of the Parisian public; but in the end, it was not a commercial success. Not including the production costs in Germany, it took one million francs to make, a huge bill that Jean alone had to pay. He thought he was ruined and was forced to sell some paintings, a very painful outcome. "It was as if a conversation I was having with my father was cut short forever," he wrote later.[15] He felt that being separated from those canvases was a kind of treason, and at Marlotte he kept the frames from which they had been removed empty in order to "rub his nose in the shame" of it. Catherine was also upset, since she, too, revered his father. But by this time they were too smitten ever to give up moviemaking.

◆

After being "ruined," their interests changed from what they had been when they first arrived at Marlotte. In the evening, they went out to listen to jazz with a new friend whom they had met at the Cézannes', Jacques Becker. Like them he loved jazz, American movies, and sports cars. At the age of eighteen, Jacques had gotten a job as a porter on a transatlantic liner and gone to visit New York in order to listen to jazz and see movies. When he met Jean and Catherine, he was twenty years old and not very eager to go into his father's business manufacturing batteries. He adored Jean, who was everything he wished to become. Apart from his war experiences and his responsibilities as a producer and director, Jacques recognized in Jean the same spoiled child as himself, someone who had always had an easy time of it, at least on the level of material possessions. There was a "horizontal" link between them; they shared the same education and bourgeois habits. Catherine Hessling was a star, the girl who loved dancing and was just as carried away by the music as the men were. They spent their evenings in clubs entertained by members of the Negro Review, starring Josephine Baker. Improvisational jazz espe-

---

[15] Jean Renoir, *Ma vie et mes films,* 77.

cially fascinated them. When the clubs closed, Catherine and Jean brought Jacques back to their house to listen to recordings of Louis Armstrong, Duke Ellington, and Red Nichols.

◆

That happened to be the moment when Armstrong made his first tour of France with a small ensemble. The three fans were disappointed that the large hall of the Champs-Elysées theater wasn't filled, so they decided to go hear him in Marseille and see how things went down there. In the Crystal Palace, a cavernous hall, the audience was a lot more receptive than in Paris. Every night they went wild and gave Armstrong ovations. The theater was filled to bursting.

This trip, as Jean himself recalls it, says a lot about the kind of life he and Catherine were leading. They were still members of the leisure class and could afford to travel for several days like groupies in pursuit of their idol. And that was a time when travel was a lot less simple than nowadays. Since Marseille is a port like New Orleans, its people, according to Jean, welcomed the music. People who live in ports have something in common, he thought. In Chicago, there were also some amazing jazz musicians, the Mount City Bluebirds, whose album Becker gave to the Renoirs. He himself had borrowed the records from Clément Doucet, a pianist who, along with Jean Wiener, was trying to invent a French form of jazz. "Jazz was a religion that calls for converts," and the religion was starting to catch on in France (ibid., p. 84).

Again thanks to Jacques Becker, Catherine and Jean met a black dancer from New York who had come to France with the Negro Review. His name was Johnny Huggins, and he wanted to live in Paris. The love they all shared for jazz inspired Jean to hire him to make a movie with Catherine and use up the large supply of fresh film leftover from the production of *Nana*. Pierre Lestringuez wrote a screenplay for them from an idea by André Cerf, and they shot the movie in the fall of 1926 in the courtyard of the studios at Epinay-sur-Seine. "Apparently, Doucet had written some marvellous music as accompaniment," according to François Truffaut.[16] Alexander Sesonske has written that Doucet's score remained in the same state as the project as a whole.[17] One thing is certain: after three days of shooting, production was interrupted because Johnny Huggins dropped out of

---

[16] In André Bazin, *Jean Renoir*, 206.
[17] Alexander Sesonske, *Jean Renoir, the French Films* (Cambridge, MA, 1980), 39.

sight, and 1200 meters of film were never exposed. Called *Charleston* or *Sur un air de Charleston* or even *Charleston Parade*, the film is a piece of comic science fiction in which Catherine Hessling, as a "savage" wearing practically nothing, uses all her charm and talent as a dancer to seduce Huggins, a scholar who has come by balloon from another planet to study the remains of our civilization, freshly devastated by a catastrophic glacier. The style is not far from Mack Sennett's, nor from the surrealists', whom Lestringuez knew better than Jean Renoir. Hessling and Huggins dance a frenzied Charleston that is phenomenal. The film was shocking for its eroticism and disturbing for its uninhibited fantasies. It had no success whatever when it was shown in March of the following year. Jean saw it as an homage to jazz and to Catherine Hessling, whom he had finally managed to lay bare, or almost bare, to the camera.

Toward the end of 1926, Claude Monet died. He had been Auguste Renoir's friend since they were young and just starting out. Monet was living at Giverny, where Jean seldom saw him, though he remained a kind of distant parent. When father and son were living together on the boulevard Rochechouart, the old painter had relived touching memories of his times with Monet. Being reminded of his father brought back a grief that was still fresh.

The failure of *Nana* and its consequences were not obscured by *Charleston*, which was just a short-lived diversion. Jean vowed once more to abandon moviemaking, unless, that is, someone offered him the job of making a commercial film of which he himself was not also the producer. Unless, in other words, a miracle happened. But the miracle did happen. Pierre Renoir had divorced Véra Sergine and married Marie Louise Iribe. The niece of the set designer Paul Iribe, who was a friend of Chanel, she had started a production studio with her husband and wanted to shoot a film in which she would be the star. She had a big distributor at her disposal as well as several theaters. What she lacked was a director. So she thought of Jean. He really needed the salary she was offering, but he wavered: this would be his first film without Catherine. Apparently Marie Louise Iribe had a strong sense of family. Since she was also Pierre Lestringuez's sister-in-law, she asked him to write the screenplay. According to Jean, he laid on "the clichés and the platitudes with a good will only slightly tempered by sarcasm."[18] In order to pander to the public, they named the film *Marquitta*, the title of a popular song that was then the rage.

[18]Jean Renoir, *Ma vie et mes films*, 77.

Only one print of the film survives. François Truffaut has given three different versions of its plot. Apparently it is a comedy à la Lubitsch, based on the song, which tells the tale of a street singer and a Slavic prince. He loses his crown and his fortune but is ultimately saved by his ex-girlfriend, who has become a star. It features a car chase along ocean cliffs and, to Jean's great joy, a special effects scene: a miniaturization of the Barbès-Rochechouart intersection and el station that was photographed using a mirror. The actors stood in front of parts of the mirror where the silvering had been scraped off. Behind them was a life-sized piece of the backdrop that matched the portion projected on the mirror by miniature. This bit of trick photography was the high point of the movie for Jean.

He later found out, to his delight, that the German cameraman Carl Freund had thought up a similar system and that Abel Gance was looking for something of the kind as well. Jean had also used a system whereby a camera dolly was placed on cushions (instead of wheels) so that it would slide along a plywood path that could easily be widened. This made it possible to move the camera sideways, backwards, and forwards as well, or even for it to turn on itself. His cameraman, Jean Bachelet, was wild about it, but most movie technicians wanted nothing to do with it. Such technical novelties amused Jean a great deal, and it did not bother him a bit if no one else tried them. His friends enjoyed them as much as he did.

Among the latter was Pierre Champagne, who was playing a taxi driver. A short time after the filming of *Marquitta*, Jean lost this dear friend in a car accident that almost cost him his own life, too. Champagne had just bought a Bugatti Brescia, a car that he had dreamed of owning for a long, long time. He immediately picked up Jean to take him for a ride in it, and they were driving at top speed on a hillside in the forest of Fontainebleau when the car skidded on an oil slick. Pierre Champagne was killed instantly. Jean, unconscious, was picked up by some poachers who were en route to sell their game at Les Halles. They did not hesitate to go out of their way to leave him at a hospital even though they could have been arrested with their contraband.

Pierre Champagne had been the ideal companion. They used to go fishing for shad together on the Garonne in May, and Jean knew he could be with him and not say a word, though silence was not typical of the man—far from it! Pierre's death made Jean forget the film that was so contrary to his ideals, and it also made him forget the acting of Marie Louise Iribe in a role that Catherine would have made something of.

Marquitta, which was shot in the winter of 1926, was shown in public for the first time on September 13, 1927. It was the expected success. So Jean proved to himself that he could make a commercial film; it was not something of which he needed proof. Despite the film's success, those whom he wished to convince of his ability remained unconvinced. No contracts were forthcoming, so he returned to being an amateur.

Three weeks after *Marquitta* another film came out, *La P'tite Lili* (*Little Lili*), with Catherine Hessling in the title role and Jean playing her pimp. Alberto Cavalcanti, a Brazilian three years younger than Jean who had studied law in his native country, directed the film. He had worked for a short time in the diplomatic corps and had gone on to study architecture in Geneva. Then he began designing sets for films in Paris in the early twenties, working for Marcel L'Herbier and Louis Delluc and hanging out with the avant-garde. Convinced that movies were the real language of the twentieth century, he was eager to devote his life to them. He was talented and imaginative, and a little unstable, though he remained faithful to his own nonconformist principles. Over the course of a long professional lifetime, he served the art of the film in a broad range of genres. After his beginnings with "the men of French impressionism," as Henri Langlois calls them, he found himself drawn to Jean Renoir's work.[19] He was intelligent, sensitive, and very sophisticated. Moreover, he was devoted to liberal social principles that he wished to express in film. Nothing more was required to become an intimate friend of Jean Renoir.

◆

During 1927, Cavalcanti shot not less than three films, all of them produced by Pierre Braunberger and starring Catherine Hessling: *Yvette,* from a Maupassant story; a feature film, *En rade* (*In the Lurch*); and *La P'tite Lili,* which, like *Marquitta,* was based on a popular song. In this case, the song dated from the Gay Nineties. It was one of those tunes that Catherine loved to hum about a poor girl of the streets who is exploited by her man. Cavalcanti knew how to use Catherine's body and her gift for mime. The movie was shown at the avant-garde Studio des Ursulines in the Quartier Latin, a fact that speaks for its quality. The avowed intention of the actors who opened this cinema, Tallier and Myrga, was to "show on their screen everything that epito-

---

[19] The first avant-garde or the impressionists of French films were Abel Gance, Marcel L'Herbier, Louis Delluc, Germaine Dulac, and Jean Epstein. Their impressionist films appeared from 1919 to 1924 [*Trans.*].

mizes originality, value, and effort. [20] After being featured on two successive programs there, the film was given a soundtrack and then distributed internationally by Tobis.

By an amazing coincidence, in this film, in which Jean is only an actor, he is surrounded by people destined to play major roles in his life: Catherine, who still fascinated him; their son Alain, barely six years old and playing a little fisherman; and a young Brazilian girl, Dido Freire, a friend of Cavalcanti's, who, like Alain, plays an extra. One day, she would become the second Madame Renoir, his companion for forty years and the woman whom Alain thought of as his real mother. There also appears for the first time the name, if not the face, of another woman, the film's editor. She was twenty years old at the time, a year older than Dido Freire. At fifteen she had started working at Pathé in Joinville-le-Pont coloring movies, a painstaking job that led nowhere. Jean Renoir had taught her to edit, a trade in which she excelled. Her name was Marguerite Houllé. Later, when she became part of his life, Jean allowed her to take the name Renoir, which she kept after they broke up because she was known by that name in the profession. The films of Jean, who was a born amateur, always involved everyone important to him, with just a few exceptions: for instance, Gabrielle and the Cézannes never appeared in his movies.

◆

In *La P'tite Lili*, as mentioned, Jean played a teasing, cynical pimp. He had already had a small role in *Catherine*, the film Dieudonné had directed, not because he thought of himself as an actor, but so that he could take part in the activity at that level of the production (his presence certainly did have an effect on Cavalcanti). A real desire to act only came later. For the moment, Jean longed to direct his own film. What had happened with *Nana* had cured him of grandiose financial exploits, but since his childhood he had loved Andersen's fairy tales. He thought that *The Little Matchgirl* would be a marvellous vehicle for Catherine, who loved the story as much as he did. To produce and direct the film, he got together with Jean Tedesco, who turned out to be the ideal partner.

From the start the two Jeans wanted to do everything themselves. They transformed the attic of the Vieux-Colombier theater into a studio with the help of another friend, Charles Ralleigh, an Englishman who was a cinema veteran. He had developed the first Mary Pickford

---

[20] Alexander Sesonske, *The French Films of Jean Renoir* (Cambridge, MA, 1980), 39.

and Douglas Fairbanks films in Hollywood and had been a cameraman in *Nana*. In his first films, Jean had Catherine's face made up with a thick white mask; her lips and the outlines of her eyes and eyebrows were painted black. Once he discovered panchromatic film, he gave up such violent contrasts. That was the film he wanted to use for interior scenes in *The Little Matchgirl*, but studio lighting was not suited to it, so he reverted to orthochromatic film, which provides only stark blacks and whites without gradations. In outdoor shots he did use panchromatic film and eliminated such contrasts in favor of a lovely range of grays.

The time had come for Jean to try something new. He'd never been interested in redoing things, and his father had impressed upon him the need for new experiments. He knew it was important to avoid becoming a prisoner of himself by always resorting to the same formulas. Panchromatic film needs more elaborate lighting, so Jean and his friends set to work to come up with it. They cut reflectors out of tin and used rheostats fed by a generator attached to an old automobile engine that they cooled with water from the faucet! A jerrybuilt rig like this made film professionals laugh, but it worked, as Jean and his friends found out when they developed the film. They did that themselves, too, in a lab they cooked up in Neuilly, in Ralleigh's kitchen, with wooden vats and black curtains on the windows. They made the first prints with an old camera. They felt like pioneers. Much later, in an interview with Jacques Rivette and François Truffaut, Jean says, "In my whole life, that was my only attempt at true craftsmanship, and we were a group of technicians who thought the problem was fun. We were very enthusiastic and very happy, too. . . . Oh! It was wonderful, it was exciting, it was even more exciting since the results were actually very beautiful."[21]

Fairy tales call for special effects, and Jean was utterly delighted with the task. The poetic quality he achieved is truly moving. In fact, he was restored to the world of his childhood: tin soldiers, dogs and cats, wind-up toys, dolls that also happen to be painter's models. Moreover, he was bewitched by the amazing, lost little girl who dreams and dies. He presents her as he saw her, heartrending and heartrent, shut out of the world that she yearns for and that destroys her even as she dreams she has forced her way inside it.

The Little Matchgirl was the last film Jean Renoir made with Catherine Hessling. He did not realize that at the time, and without

[21] Jean Renoir, *Entretiens et propos* (Paris, 1979), 49.

wanting to or knowing he was doing so, he made it into a portrait of her, the great love of his youth. Catherine was both troublesome and troubled; she was not strong enough for the life they were leading, and she no longer knew who she was. She had not become the actress she longed to be, and somehow she understood that she never would. This last film of hers is blatantly Chaplinesque. That was as they both wished, but she knew only too well that she could not compare to Chaplin. Moreover, she was unable to enjoy herself with the others as Jean was.

Which is not to say that she lacked admirers. Georges Simenon found her "deeply moving" in the film. She and Jean spent some evenings with him and his wife Tigy, a painter, in their ravishing Art Deco apartment on the Place des Vosges. It had an "American bar" lit in a way that Simenon was especially proud of. "People from Montparnasse, from Foujita to Vertès . . . but why list them all? Sometimes Josephine (Baker) herself was there, in all her glory, and there were Russian dancers and the daughter of an ambassador from Asia; at three in the morning, you'd find a certain number of naked bodies alongside others spread out on black velvet pillows where they would spend the night; still, at six in the morning, I would sit down in front of the typewriter for my daily ration of eighty pages." So Simenon tells it.[22] The Renoirs themselves had nothing to do. If they got to bed in the wee hours, they could sleep the next day through and begin again where they had left off. Though dancing and listening to jazz still pleased Catherine, the endless parties with their various intoxications were no longer what she needed. Loving, ripping apart, then loving again—it all happened too quickly for her. No one ever asked her if she was happy, but everyone thought she was since Jean adored her so. She lacked his curiosity, and he was too complicated for her to understand. She still followed him around, got excited, talked, and listened. In fact, she did everything that she thought was expected of her, but the spontaneity was gone. Since their salad days at Les Collettes, she had not changed or grown up. She was a pathetic child full of contradictions, a frozen little girl lighting matches to keep warm.

Shortly after the film came out in Paris (June 8, 1928), it had to be withdrawn. Rosemonde Gérard, widow of the author of *Cyrano de Bergerac*, and her son Maurice Rostand, brought a lawsuit against Renoir and Tedesco, accusing them of plagiarism. The Rostands, mother

[22] Georges Simenon, *Mémoires intimes* (Paris, 1981), 24–25.

and son, had written a comic opera several years before based on the same Andersen fairy tale, and an organ-grinder appeared in both the film and the opera. The trial lasted for two years. Ultimately, the Rostands' suit was vacated, but in the meantime, talkies were born. When the film was reissued, it had been cut by the distributor, who had also demanded a musical soundtrack and captions. Jean hated both of them. Sylvia Bataille remembered seeing the original version in the Vieux-Colombier theater. She was fifteen at the time. After the screening she was so impressed that she stopped Jean Renoir in the street and told him she wanted to be in movies. "You should wait," he replied, without suspecting that one day she would become one of his most powerful heroines, Henriette in *A Day in the Country.*

The Little Matchgirl marks an important moment in Jean Renoir's life: 1928 was the year in which sounds were first recorded on magnetic tape, Chiang Kai-Shek became president of the Republic of China, Stalin first came to power, Kurt Weil and Bertolt Brecht (who became one of Jean's friends) wrote *The Threepenny Opera,* and Pierre Renoir played *Siegfried,* Giraudoux's first play (those who were lucky enough to see it cannot forget his extraordinary interpretation of the amnesiac hero). Also in that year, Dreyer made *The Passion of Joan of Arc,* a film Jean admired greatly, and Bunuel and Dali made *Un chien andalou* (*An Andalusian Dog*), which belonged to an entirely different world from Renoir's.

Jean was as adamantly apolitical as his father had been before him, and a "manifesto" like the two Spaniards' film repelled him. He rejected its cruel violence. Moreover, this was a time when he distanced himself from any and all popular movements of whatever sort. There is no trace in his work of two events that distinguished the previous year and to which he could not have been insensitive: the demonstrations brought on by the executions of Sacco and Vanzetti, and Lindbergh's arrival at Le Bourget. Jean, who otherwise wrote so much, was too busy living and too little given to self-analysis to keep a diary. In the year 1928, he wrote a huge amount, including articles, more or less detailed synopses like *Puss-in-Boots,*[23] and interviews ostensibly by others but recognizably his own. At the end of his life, Truffaut was amazed at his ease in writing of all kinds, autobiography, novels, news, and stories.

When making his first movies, he was married to Catherine and preoccupied only with what directly concerned them. The priority

[23] This is its date according to Claude Beylie, Jean Renoir, *Oeuvres inédites,* 18.

was film. In those days they still had long stretches of free time during which they led a life of leisure in one or the other of their two residences, the apartment near the Faubourg Saint-Honoré or the house at Marlotte. Little Alain spent most of his time at Marlotte with his nanny and his grandmother, Madame Heuschling. Jean's ideas about the education of children came from his father and from his mother's and Gabrielle's love of nature. Alain went through a "little savage" phase, during which he adored animals, especially snakes and frogs, which he would brandish in the faces of his parents' terrified guests. Alain's place in his mother's life was small. Catherine had difficulty accepting the fact that she was actually his parent. All this was a far cry from the devoted care of Gabrielle and the loving atmosphere in which Jean had grown up. Aline Renoir did not spare the rod, but her sons knew her affection, her sense of balance, and the understanding that prevailed between her and their father. Alain, on the other hand, noticed greater and greater differences between his parents. When he was not completely ignored, he suffered from being torn between the two. His father, who loved him, was not always there; his mother was usually away. At least that was how it seemed to him. She was certainly not an ordinary mother, and she was fascinating to a little boy who could not understand that her emotional age was the same as his—whence their difficulties.

In the world of adults, which was often dangerous for him, beside his grandmother, his aunt Jeanne, and his nanny, Alain had a friend, Dido Freire. With or without Alberto Cavalcanti, his young coworker from *La P'tite Lili* came to Marlotte to visit him. She soon got into the habit of taking him to the zoo and local carnivals. She would let him have a turn at the shooting gallery, and he was proud of her because she was a good shot herself. They became so attached to one another that she took him with her on vacation to her mother's house in England. Her father had been the Brazilian consul general in Liverpool, where he had died in 1925. Dido had two sisters, one older, one younger than herself. They had been brought up in England, while she had gone to the Dupanloup boarding school in the rue de l'Assomption. Cavalcanti and his mother, friends of the family, were her guardians. Dido spent every Sunday with them near Sens, where they were living in the hermitage of Saint-Bon. A brunette with a dark complexion, big black eyes, and a fine, narrow face, it was impossible to mistake Dido for Alain's older sister. He was a redhead right out of his grandfather's paintings, with light-colored eyes, a round mug, and freckles. He was growing so fast that he would soon be taller than she. But he was only seven years old, and in order to cross the Channel with him she needed written authorization from Jean, a person whom she found intimidating. In fact she had known Catherine and Jean for a long time, and she admired them both, but neither of them paid any real attention to this young woman fresh out of a fancy boarding school.

Dido had just reached her majority when she took Alain to England for the first time (in those days, you had to be twenty-one, not eighteen). Alain, a secretive child, adopted her and trusted her. Their affection for each other did not arouse the jealousy one might expect in his mother, who was happy that someone was taking care of her son. To her, he was an encumbrance. The focus of Catherine's life was her relationship to Jean, who represented her career in film. Without him, she hardly stood a chance. At times, he seemed more interested in his projects and his friends than in her. It was no easy job to keep this devil of a man to herself, and she had no desire to lose him.

◆

Jean took up the idea of commercial filmmaking once more. The checkered career of *The Little Matchgirl* was no incentive to finance his own movies. Just before *Marquitta,* he had agreed to make some erotic films for Madame Régina, a highly sophisticated woman who owned some brothels in the south of France and who was much taken with excerpts from *La Fille de l'Eau* that she had seen at Tedesco's Vieux-Colombier theater. Her proposal was relayed to Jean by Pierre Lestringuez. Both of them thought it would be fun to collaborate on such a project. Their idea was to do an adaptation of the Marquis de Sade, which was much less known then than now. Madame Régina had read him and approved the idea. Was she a woman with taste? On the contrary, Jean and Lestringuez realized that the films that she had produced for her establishments were the stalest sort of pornography. After *Marquitta* was finished, the project was not resumed. Yet eroticism was in fashion. Nineteen twenty-eight was the year in which Georges Bataille published *Histoire de l'oeil* (*A History of the Eye*) and Louis Aragon *Le Con d'Irène* (*Irene's Cunt*), undercover, of course, since the year before, Aragon had joined the Communist party and respectability was obligatory among members of the proletariat.

Jean Renoir had been used to being around naked women since he was a small child, and he was no stranger to racy conversation—what went on between painter and model was hardly inhibited—nor had the company of soldiers done anything to tone down his language. Like his words, the images he made on film evoke a disturbing mystery in which sex, dream, and poetry intertwine. Renoir's vision of the world is not lacking in perversity, and it is too intelligent to be really innocent. Puritanical repression is completely alien to it. But Jean remembered his father's teaching; it is all right to be daring, but never at the expense of one's dignity. He always stayed within the limits imposed by elegance. Nor was his healthy outlook incompatible with complex feelings or the quest for multiple sensations.

Jean's next few films were to put some space between his work and his own taste and preoccupations. André Cerf knew from experience that Jean Renoir needed silent partners who would not make a nuisance of themselves. Cerf himself was an aspiring actor. He was a walk-on in Jacques Feyder's *Carmen* starring Raquel Meller (Buñuel had a small role, and he was also its assistant director, screenwriter, and producer), and all his life Cerf considered himself a movie gadfly. He had belonged to Renoir's team and would continue to for some time, but he also got around in French film circles, unlike Jean and most of his gang. It was Cerf's idea to put Jean in touch with Henry Dupuy-Mazuel, a producer whose company had gone bankrupt, which was not an uncommon event in those days. The film industry was unraveling. Dupuy-Mazuel had just been "recycled": he was now director of the Historical Film Society, an organization that was supported by the Poincaré government. He commissioned two films from Jean.

The first one, *Le Tournoi dans la cité* (*The Tournament in the City*), to a screenplay by Dupuy-Mazuel, takes place in the time of Catherine de' Medici and Charles IX. It was produced to commemorate the two thousandth anniversary of Carcassonne. Jean had at his disposal hundreds of horses, North African animals and others from the Cadre Noir de Saumur, neither of which even remotely resembled those of the sixteenth century. So despite its minute attention to historical accuracy in other respects, the film looks unrealistic because of them. A champion fencer, Aldo Nadi, directed its spectacular duels. Mallet-Stevens was the set designer; much of the movie was shot outdoors in Carcassonne—Carcassonne as restored, to be sure, by Violet-le-Duc, an architect whom Renoir used to abhor. But Jean was very happy to be working. Being in Carcassonne made him think of his father's mobilization there during the war of 1870. At the same time, all those horses brought back memories of his own stint in the cavalry. Jean had fun inventing and perfecting photographic techniques that might possibly generate a degree of interest that the pathetic screenplay was unlikely to arouse. He got the crew to build a wagon mounted on four bicycle wheels and to have it straddle the long, narrow table used in the banquet scene. By placing the camera on this wagon, Jean had a true traveling crane that went right over the heads of the guests. This way he could avoid photographing people from behind or having to shoot a long sequence of close-ups. The movie is also saved from boredom by its pacing and the general accuracy of its historical details. Not long ago the Film Archives Service of Bois-D'Arcy did an excellent job of reconstructing it, the master print having been destroyed in the Cinemathèque fire of 1959.

Jean made the second film commissioned by the Historical Film Society in the following year, again with a screenplay by Henry Dupuy-Mazuel. *Le Bled (Inside Algeria)* was intended to celebrate the one hundredth anniversary of France's arrival in Algeria. It was the first time Jean had crossed the Mediterranean, and he was struck by the beauty of the countryside. He remembered his father saying, "In Algeria I discovered two things: white, and getting drunk with your eyes. Everything there is white—burnooses, walls, minarets, streets. Over it there's the green of the orange tree and the gray of the fig." [24] Nor had Jean forgotten the Westerns that he loved so much: he staged his somewhat naïve screenplay like an old-style American movie. There's a gazelle hunt, chase scenes in the desert, a trained falcon ordered to peck out a traitor's eyeballs—no shortage of movie clichés. Most of the exteriors were shot in Algiers or Biskra. Jean's photographic technique is interesting. He used fast lenses, which are only a partial success, since the backgrounds are fuzzy. Like *Le Tournoi dans la cité*, it was an expensive movie to produce. They had to lay special train tracks to shoot in the desert, and the production team was forced to prolong its stay in Algeria for a long time. Marguerite (still Marguerite Houllé) did the editing. According to André Cerf, who was assistant director, she went with them and stayed until the shooting was complete.

In between these two long films produced by the Historical Film Society, Jean got the chance to make a commercial film, *Tire au flanc (Shirker)*, based on a vaudeville show that had been famous twenty years before. Jean had met Michel Simon through Alberto Cavalcanti, who was set designer for *Feu Mathias Pascal* by Marcel L'Herbier, Simon's first movie. Jean sensed his extraordinary personality right away. Full of enthusiasm for him, he decided to add a character to the play he was filming: Michel Simon became the male lead's manservant, with the starring role played by the dancer Georges Pomiès, an-

---

[24] *Renoir par Jean Renoir* (Paris, 1958), 228 (= *Renoir, My Father,* 236).

other of Jean's discoveries. In the play, all the jokes come from the dialogue, so Renoir's silent version is full of absurd situations, hamming, and sight gags.

Tire au flanc was produced by Pierre Baunberger on a low budget, and it did not win the success hoped for by the team that made it. Nowadays, this movie, which consists of a series of skits each containing from seven to ten shots, is still of interest to film buffs because of its technical innovations. "The camera movements in *Tire au flanc* are unbelievably bold," according to François Truffaut.[25] There is a tangible, breathless daring in Jean's use of improvisational techniques. Claude Heymann, who co-authored the screenplay with Renoir and Cavalcanti, had volunteered for military service at age eighteen during World War I. His memories of three months of basic training at Mont-Valérien were the inspiration for a series of gags and harebrained situations that kept Jean in stitches. In fact, Jean could not stop thinking of more skits to add. Heymann told me that at the time, Catherine Hessling and Jean were Pomiès fans, and André Cerf said the same. His skills as a dancer and their passion for pantomime were a perfect match. The movie is certainly closer to Charlie Chaplin and Mack Sennett than the vaudeville show whose title and theme it borrowed. Catherine Hessling was still an important presence at the time of *Tire au flanc*. According to Claude Heymann, when he was working on the screenplay, Catherine would pick him up to bring him to Marlotte in her blue Bugatti; she also has two walk-ons in the film. It was first shown in December 1928, though only for a short run.

♦

"In 1929, a monster appeared that drastically changed the profession—the talkie. I greeted it enthusiastically. I understood immediately everything that could be gained by the use of sound. Isn't understanding man the goal of every artistic creation, and isn't the voice the most direct expression of a human being's personality?" wrote Jean Renoir.[26] In June 1928, Jesse L. Lasky, a vice president of Paramount, came to Paris to announce the death of the silent film. *The Jazz Singer*, the first talkie, had been shot in 1927 and was shown in the United States that same year, but it did not come out in Paris until January of 1929. According to Jean, "At first with distrust, but soon with enthusiasm, the French began making talkies. I would have

[25] André Bazin, *Jean Renoir*, 213.
[26] Jean Renoir, *Ma vie et mes films*, 95.

liked to do as the others did, but I had been pigeonholed once and for all as a maker of dramatic silent films, as a kind of enemy of the theater, and no one in this new profession wanted to have anything to do with me: after all, the first uses of the talkie in France were for filming word-for-word plays that had been commercial successes."[27] At the end of the year, French film studios equipped themselves for sound. At Courbevoie, Jacques Haik, the producer who had introduced the man he dubbed "Charlot" to the French public, had a big studio built with two soundstages and two projection rooms wired for sound. Studios were converted to sound at Billancourt and the rue Francoeur. In 1930, Pathé-Nathan produced the first French newsreels "with sound and speech," *Pathé Journal;* soon after there was another, *Eclair Journal.*

Jean also tells us how he tried in those days to convince several producers to let him make *La Chienne* (*The Bitch*) based on a novel by La Fouchardière. He was thinking of using Michel Simon and casting Catherine Hessling as the heroine, but no one would accept his project. Yet he was sure that the subject suited his talents, and he was ready to fight to get it made. In the meantime, so as not to lose touch with their trade, his own and Catherine's, they took roles in a variety of movies. The roles they were offered, however, were not substantial. They reminded him of dressing up as a kid. One had to laugh and not take things too seriously, and there were plenty of funny things to laugh at.

Then Alberto Cavalcanti and Jean got the idea of filming a fairy tale of which they had always been fond: *Le Petit Chaperon rouge* (*Little Red Riding Hood*). Alberto was to be the director and Jean the producer. They did most of the shooting at the Renoirs', in Marlotte, during the summer of 1929. André Cerf tells of their trips to Beauce, where they traveled around for miles and miles looking for a windmill. The idea was to tie up Catherine on one of its arms.

Once more conditions were ideal. A crew of old friends, they worked hard together during the day and spent the evenings together as well; they drank, they gossiped, they sang and ate together, they loved each other. They felt free and happy. Marguerite was the editor; Pierre Prévert played a little girl with cropped hair and was assistant director; William Aguet played an elderly Englishwoman; André Cerf was another assistant and also played a notary with a big beard; and Jean himself played the wolf, and a rather scary wolf at that: in fact he

[27]Jean Renoir, *Écrits,* 43.

resembled nothing more than the sleazy pimp in *La P'tite Lili.* The result of it all was a fairy tale as told by the Marquis de Sade.

Another very short movie, *Vous verrez la semaine prochaine* (*And Next Week*) was shot on the fringes of *Le Petit Chaperon rouge.* It parodied the previews shown in movie theaters. Directed by Cavalcanti, it featured three Renoirs, Catherine, Jean, and Alain. Sadly, not a single copy of it has survived. The original, silent version of *Le Petit Chaperon rouge* was first shown at Les Agriculteurs. In May 1930, they made a version with sound. It had music by Maurice Jaubert, another of Jean's friends, and a song, "La Java du loup," with words by Claude-André Puget. It was first shown on May 14, 1930, at La Tribune du Cinéma.

Jean and his friend Pierre Braunberger were walk-ons in *Das Tagebuch einer Verlorenen* (*Diary of a Lost Soul*), a movie with the unforgettable Louise Brooks made by G. W. Pabst in Berlin in 1929. They play background drinkers in a nightclub, but according to what they both told Claude Beylie, that was the only thing they remembered about the film.[28] Jean and Catherine Hessling played in another German film whose exteriors were actually shot at Toulon. It was called *Die Jagd nach dem Glück* (*Hunting for Luck*) and was never shown in France. Jean's friend Karl Koch, with whom he shared war memories, and his wife Lotte Reiniger, the shadow-theater artist, wrote the screenplay. Catherine starred, and the film contained a little shadow play by Reiniger with the same title as the film. The director of the piece, Rochus Gliese, had been set designer for a film by F. W. Murnau called *Sunrise,* a masterpiece based on Sudermann's novella, *Die Reise nach Tilsit* (*A Trip to Tilsit*). Renoir played a gigolo; Aimée Tedesco, dancer and wife of Jean Tedesco, also had a role in the film along with a Russian actor named Alexander Mirsky. Jean loved the cosmopolitan atmosphere and the bohemian lifestyle in Berlin, but the film, shown there in May 1930, was a flop. Catherine Hessling's acting style was repellent to German audiences, and Jean's part did not impress them either. Only the shadow theater scenes have survived (at the Royal Belgian Cinemathèque). The whole thing was insignificant; like the others, the movie was just a way to pass the time. Jean was waiting impatiently to have his chance.

[28] "Spécial Renoir," *L'Avant-Scène Cinéma,* no. 251–52, 1 July 1980, 143.

TALKIE FOR

A CHATTERBOX

◆

For a long time, people thought he was only a dilettante, but Jean Renoir knew that for him, movies were more than a hobby. He was getting ready to devote his life to them. From observing his father, Jean had learned the difference between a pastime and a passion, but would he ever be as passionate as his father had been? Making movies is both simpler and more complex than painting. You never work alone, and the team carries you along and excites you. That is an advantage with disadvantages: you depend on others, and they are not necessarily teammates whom you have chosen: they can be producers, distributors, or, ultimately, the public, which either accepts or rejects you. Without a public, you can make paintings, but not films.

During the years that followed the late release of *The Little Match Girl*, shown in a cut version in London on December 29, 1929, and then during the following month in Paris, there was no clear sense of what the public thought of the films of Jean Renoir, and producers interpreted this uncertainty as they wished. None of Renoir's films was a hit, and aside from two feature-length films that he made for the Society of Historical Films, they are overly influenced by Charlie Chaplin and American filmmakers. Producers wanted to pigeonhole Renoir in silent films; they had not yet understood that the days of the silent film were numbered.

Jean was champing at the bit. He was certainly not a person who gave up easily. But he could not take on the role of producer himself, as he had done once more with *Le Petit Chaperon rouge*. His business agent, a certain Mr. Guillaume, had not forgotten the *Nana* disaster, and had in fact laid down the law to him. He knew Jean for a soft touch, and he considered it his solemn duty to protect him as best he could. The relationship between Jean Renoir and this man, whom he always called, precisely, "Mr. Guillaume," reflects how his circumstances had changed.

A painting called *Mardi Gras* that Cézanne painted in 1888 and that hangs in the Pushkin Museum in Leningrad represents two young boys: the younger Paul Cézanne as Arlequin, and Louis Guillaume as his Pierrot. Louis Guillaume and Paul, Jr., were boyhood friends. In the Renoir household it was said that Mr. Guillaume studied architecture but quickly gave it up in order to manage the finances of Paul Cézanne and Jean Renoir: both had turned everything over to him. He was their common sense and their conscience rolled up in one. Jean's friends knew him well and did not forget him, even if he was unprepossessing physically, a chubby little man with a pince-nez. "Mr. Guillaume, the eternal Mr. Guillaume! Jean never did a thing without first asking him his advice, but he didn't always take it!" so they all say. Mr. Guillaume lived on the rue Etex, near the Montmartre cemetery. He was a bachelor. The Cézannes and the Renoirs were more time consuming and doubtless more amusing than a wife would have been. He did have a mistress, who was said to be quite content. That was the way a lot of "bachelors" carried on. Their mistress stayed in the shadows, keeping house. Another peculiarity was that no one addressed him as "tu," as an intimate family member—the man's name with Mr. in front of it was already intimate enough. Alain Renoir cannot recall a single person ever calling Mr. Guillaume "Louis," though the man was no stranger in the Renoir household—he actually worked there three days a week! Such memories of Alain's go back to a relatively late period, since at Marlotte and when they lived on the rue de Miromesnil, Jean and Catherine were doing nothing in particular, so Mr. Guillaume's presence was unnecessary and rare.

While trying to find some silent partners for *La Chienne*, starring Catherine Hessling and Michel Simon, Jean wrote a synopsis called *Madame Bovary à rebours I et II* (*Madame Bovary in Reverse, Parts I and II*). Kept in the archives of the Compagnie Jean Renoir and ultimately published by Claude Gauteur,[1] it is the story of a cabaret singer sur-

---

[1] Jean Renoir, *Oeuvres de cinéma inédites*, ed. C. Gauteur (Paris, 1981), 413–27.

rounded by rich men who ultimately become her downfall. Is it the life of Catherine? Although the heroine's men friends in *Madame Bovary à rebours* have nothing in common with Jean Renoir and his gang, the story has a moral: money corrupts. The singer is the victim of men who have given her the means to reach the pinnacle of success; but despite her talent, Catherine was to know no more success. Couples like them do not come apart in a single day. Even though Catherine was becoming more and more suspicious, even if she ranted and raved about having no chance to act, even if Jean was eyeing other women and going out more and more often without her (to woo producers, he would say), and even though his nights out with the guys were becoming more and more frequent and lasting longer and longer, they still thought of themselves as a couple.

Children know sooner than adults what is happening beneath the surface, and they can tell when the problems are hopeless. Jean doted on his son and spoiled him a lot in a vain effort to make up for the child's mother's inability to be tender and loving. But that did not prevent Alain from being marked by the conflicts between his parents. When he was old enough to attend school, his father refused to let him go. He provided two tutors for the boy: the local priest from Marlotte, and, just to balance things out, a teacher from the public school who was a member of the PC (the French Communist party). Jean remembered that his own father, in his hostility to the idea of school, had sent him to snob boarding schools that Jean had a passion for running away from—the real object had been to get him out of the way when his baby brother was born. So Alain, who had no siblings at all, was to remain at home. He is sure that the priest had no idea that the boy had another teacher, but Jean took a fiendish pleasure in warning the Communist of it. In those days, for a cell leader, religion was still the opiate of the masses. Alain just learned to keep quiet.

The Cézanne kids, Jean-Pierre and Aline, his godmother, were older than he was. It was not until several years later that the age difference stopped being important. There was only a year's difference between Alain and Jeannot Slade, and he was an ideal companion for Alain. But he was not always available, since he traveled a lot with his parents. Then a case of osseous tuberculosis meant a lengthy cure for him in Berck on the North Sea. Jean Renoir visited Jeannot there from time to time, and his friend Koch camped out on the beach there, a beautiful one that seemed to go on forever.

A beach of such beauty belongs on film. Jean remembered the trip; either that or Koch, who was always around, reminded him of it when he was preparing *The Crime of M. Lange*. The last frame of the film, pregnant with optimism and good humor, was shot there. Whether he wished it so or not, from now on everything in Jean's life revolved around movies. No matter how far from the set, he still thought like a director. Film would become his family life, as painting had been for his father. The time was coming when a movie would be something more to him than an act of homage to Catherine's beauty. Like painting, it would become a way of expressing his feeling, what he saw, how he understood people. Beauty and the joy of life burst from Auguste's canvases. He had forgotten his personal agony by getting himself completely absorbed in the process of painting. Jean thought most often of that final period in his father's life, not as an example to follow, but because memories of the old man at once wracked by disease and exalted by life's gifts never ceased to haunt him.

◆

What the producers thought of Jean had no effect on his friends' confidence in his ability. Pierre Braunberger was not like other producers, with his safe containing only a dustpan and brush, a similarly empty refrigerator, his surrealist friends, his nervousness, and his imagination. Yet he made his mark, eventually becoming co-director of the Billancourt Studios. His colleague, Roger Richebé, was not, as he was, the son, grandson, and great-grandson of physicians, but his father did own a lot of movie theaters. Their silent partner was an industrialist whom Braunberger had brought in, a certain Mr. Monteux. What Braunberger had in mind was to make it possible for Jean Renoir to direct *La Chienne*, a project that he truly believed in. But to convince his partners to join in, Jean had to prove himself in commercial terms, in other words, he had to make a feature film very quickly on a short budget. A play by Feydeau, *On purge bébé* (*Baby Takes a Laxative*), was chosen. It took Jean six days to write the screenplay and less than a week to shoot it; by the end of the third week, the film had been edited. It was put on at the Roxy in June 1931, and money began clinking in the producers' coffers: they got back their 200,000 francs in production costs, and the profits soon exceeded a million francs.

Despite these promising beginnings, Pierre Braunberger knew that better things were forthcoming from Jean Renoir. The closeness of the film version to its original surprised both of them a bit. Jean had almost resigned himself, at least temporarily, to the slavery of someone else's words. He did allow himself two flights of fancy: he recorded the actual sounds of a toilet flushing and a chamber pot being smashed to bits. In those days, when talkies were really plays on film, everyone else used the same phony sound effects as in the theater. Jean Renoir made this movie with real stage actors as well, all of them top notch, including Michel Simon and Fernandel (his debut). It was a strange test Jean had to pass, especially when one remembers that the previous year had seen the release of Jean Cocteau's *Le Sang d'un poète* (*Blood of a Poet*), and December of 1930, of a second film by Buñuel and Dali, *l'Age d'or* (*The Golden Age*). "A poem on revolution and mad love," as Jean Mitry calls it,[2] *The Golden Age* was soon banned by the authorities. The same year as *On purge bébé* (*Baby Takes a Laxative*), you could see *M. le Maudit* (*M*) by Fritz Lang or Murnau and Flaherty's *Taboo*. But Jean wasn't worried about what other people were doing, and when the decision was made to go ahead with *La Chienne*, he felt he had gotten what he wanted. But Roger Richebé turned down Catherine Hessling in favor of an actress under contract with Billancourt: Janie Marèze had to be the star of all the movies made in their studios. Jean had no problem with this either. His goal was to make the film no matter what.

Changing the female lead actually meant a lot more than Jean had anticipated. Until then, the films he made without Catherine (*Marquitta, Tire au flanc,* the two historical movies, and *On purge bébé*, his "test" film) meant very little to him. *La Chienne* was a novel by Georges de La Fouchardière from which André Mouézy-Eon, author of *Tire au flanc*, had extracted a play produced in December 1930 in the Théâtre de la Renaissance. In choosing it, Jean for the first time chose a work that was at once popular *and* personal. The actress he was obliged to use was a professional, and Jean quickly understood what she had to offer in the role of the middle-class prostitute. The film that he was about to make would be something very different from the one he had imagined making with Catherine. There would still be marionettes—Punch giving the cop a thrashing—but they would only serve to introduce the film's flesh-and-blood characters. Janie Marèze, who played the heroine, Lulu, was, unlike Catherine, neither a mime nor a dancer.

The only thing Jean had against her was her accent, which was too upper-class. She had been brought up by nuns.[3] He had her practice speaking like a streetwalker, and it didn't take her long to learn how. Catherine would have taken on a very different persona, even

[2] Jean Mitry, *Dictionnaire du cinéma* (Paris, 1963), §4.10.
[3] Jean Renoir, *Ma vie et mes films* (Paris, 1974), 100.

with Michel Simon as her partner. She was dying to play the role, and Jean had promised her she would. In fact, this unkept promise meant the end of their life together. She needed to make movies as much as he did. Her face once more painted white, her lips as black as the kohl around her eyes, she longed to express the joys and woes of others and to be adored for it, as Charlie Chaplin had been before her.

When together, she and Jean still behaved as they had soon after the death of Auguste Renoir. Oblivious to what was going on around them, sheltered by their wealth from material concerns, they lived apart in a little world of their own devising. Making movies had simply been a new version of those kids' games in which the grown-ups' roles have more to do with fairy tales than real life. Catherine did not want to escape from that world, and she had never tried to adapt herself to the demands of Richebé and his colleagues. She was still the flower girl playing an American vamp from the era of the silent film. She refused to become the mother of her ten-year-old son.

Once separated from Jean, Catherine soon distanced herself from the world of movies where he, on the contrary, was more and more at home. Their mutual friends took Jean's side. He also took care of Alain, with the help of Madame Heuschling and Marie, the peasant girl from Picardy. This big change in Jean's life was a kind of farewell to the adolescence that his relationship to Catherine had artificially prolonged. Once the bond between them was cut, Jean could never go back. Nostalgia was not a feeling he recognized in himself. Madly in love with a childlike woman, he had wasted many years and a lot of money on the fantasies they had dreamed up together. Now he was more sober, though still unrepentant. He was determind not to forfeit his privileges, to finally try to capitalize on them. Nor did he abandon Catherine or her mother and sister. They all depended upon him. The legal separation was not actually declared until July 1935.

Jean's intention was to marry the so-called commercial element in his craft to the kind of movies he wanted to make. It would not always be easy to do that, but he also wanted to stop being labeled an amateur, now that he realized there was some justification for it. At his side there was another young woman, Marguerite Houllé, whom he had known for a long time. He had watched her transform herself little by little. "She, too, looked like a Renoir, and was close to nature," Françoise Giroud told me. Jean liked the way she would show him a tree, a flower, or a bird. "A working-class girl, a peasant," recalled André Zwobada, "her father was a worker." "She came from Montreuil," according to Henri Cartier-Bresson, and they called her "the little lion" because of her curls. Françoise Giroud, André Zwobada, and Henri Cartier-Bresson met her a little later on. When she moved in with Jean, she was just twenty-five years old. Jean did not take up with her as he had with Catherine: he was not about to play Pygmalion again, since he was the rare sort of person who tried to learn the lessons that life taught him. Marguerite did not stop working as a film editor. She became, as he put it, "my editor and my friend."

At age thirty-six, Jean was beginning to put on weight. His limp ruled out exercise, and the drinking never stopped at those endless nights out with the boys. But he was as charming and funny as ever. He had a knack with women, though he always gave the impression of being unsure of himself with them, which only made him more attractive. His manners were elegant, like those of a nobleman affecting street talk. Though he bought his clothes in department stores, everyone knew him for a gentleman. He had always been surrounded by a crowd of women as a child; as an adult, he was skillful enough in his relations with them to have friendships with several who were not, in fact, his lovers. Having grown up in the care of Gabrielle, he respected women for their intelligence. The female characters in his films are complex and well aware that society was set up to guarantee men their power. In taking the woman's standpoint, Jean was going against his father. In an era when men were expected to be macho about everything, he seemed ready to listen to what women had to say and to consider their point of view.

With Marguerite, Jean, who never took an interest in politics, had fallen into a family of activists. Her father and brother-in-law were trade unionists, and the younger of the two was a militant in the PC. Women still had no vote, but Marguerite recognized her own right to think. She was a leftist, and she told Jean why; he listened and understood. Heir to his father's skepticism, Jean wasn't sure that he shared her hopes for the future, but he said nothing. The worldwide economic crisis was beginning to make itself felt in France in ways that could not be ignored. Yet the PC was at a disadvantage. It used up all its energy in attacks on the Socialist party; in so doing, it willingly isolated itelf, pursuing a policy of denunciation and invective that cost it dearly in the following year's (1932) legislative elections. Jean did not feel ready to get involved. Yet he had never liked regular middle-class society—a good example is the character played by Michel Simon in *La Chienne*, a man being suffocated by bourgeois values. His only relief from poverty and his wife, who is as dull as his job in retail, is painting pictures nights and Sundays and being in love with Lulu; but she teases him and is actually no more moved by him and his dreams than is his wife. The only man Lulu is capable of loving is a man from her own dim world who is as false as she. The plot has a fatalistic quality that Jean found congenial. Born under a bad sign, such persons bring on themselves inevitable misfortune.

Life, films, and fiction were always mixed up for Jean Renoir. Violent death lurks in the background; tragedy is real. He knew them in wartime and in the accident that cost him his friend Pierre Champagne: he had come very close to being killed himself. These are things he would know more than once, being a person who did not hide from reality. Because of his brilliance, people came to him just as he went to them. On that occasion, chance brought him someone to play the pimp Dédé, the film's male supporting actor. In reality, Georges Flamant seemed more at home in that world than in movies, and he played the role of the pimp so naturally that he actually seduced Janie Marèze. He also boasted of his conquest, confiding his book of tricks for mastering women to his director and the rest of the production team. In those days, such talk was indeed appreciated by men, who were always on the lookout for new ways to be macho, a quality that no one was decrying as yet. The women listened as well. Not all of them were ecstatic about the joyous prospect of losing their will to a seducer, but they still would say nothing. Janie Marèze, subjugated and happy to be so, seems to have also lost any sense of what was going on around her, and seems not to have had even an inkling of the passionate feelings she had in fact aroused in Michel Simon. He, on the other hand, had not lost hope of getting lucky one day. Tragically, two weeks after the shooting was over, Georges Flamant bought himself a big American car with the money he had made for his role and went off with Janie Marèze to the south of France; they had an accident, and she was killed. At the cemetery, Michel Simon fainted, just as his character, Legrand, fainted on hearing the court sentence Dédé to death for the murder of Lulu, whom he, Legrand, had actually killed.

Jean let his actors play their roles the way they saw them. Michel Simon is unforgettable, Janie Marèze is perfection itself, and Georges Flamant is utterly comfortable in his character. The other parts were equally well cast, mostly with professional actors. Among them were also a few friends, including Jean Gehret, a Swiss musicologist who was a cousin of Ernest Ansermet and the first husband of the opera singer Irène Joachim. Gehret had done some theater in Geneva with the Pitoeffs and knew Michel Simon. He was administrator of the Poulet concerts and one of the founders of the Paris Symphony. His passions were divided between music and film. He became the producer of *Boudu*, played in several of Renoir's films, and eventually directed *Café du Cadran* (*Dial Café*) and then *Crime des justes* (*A Just Crime*), which was based on a novel by André Chamson. Jean Gehret was six years younger than Jean and completely devoted to him. The role he played—Dugodet, the lusty, brutish painter—was not in the original novel. Jean created the part for him.

After watching all those American movies and with the experience gained from making silent ones, Jean Renoir now knew how to make what he considered a decent movie. As usual, he made sure he was surrounded by friends: Claude Heymann, with whose help he had shot *Little Match Girl*, *Tire au flanc*, and *On purge bébé*, shared the duties of assistant director of *La Chienne* with Pierre Prévert. Suzanne de Troye, Marguerite's inseparable companion and likewise an editor, was responsible for continuity. Such working conditions were themselves a source of happiness.

From a technical standpoint, Renoir had acquired an admirable mastery of the means at his disposal. His combination of instinct and intelligence was not unhelpful in this regard either. He often used two or three cameras to avoid cutting off shots. Way before any other filmmaker, he began experimenting with depth of field. He was also interested in sounds, which were at that time recorded live since mixing did not exist. With an ear for street noises and voices, and given his love for popular songs (having been sung to sleep with them, or heard them hummed by his father's models or even his father himself), Jean had a feel for the way to use all these elements. The images that linger from his films also comprise sounds, whether they are actors' intonations or music or city noises or even an eerie silence. It would not be correct to say that Catherine Hessling's presence in the silent films was an impediment to Jean's creativity, but it is no less certain that in the talkies, right from the start, Jean had more drive, freedom, and originality. The dimension that sound added seems essential to his work, even a necessity. Making films is not painting, nor is it an art of movement and gesture alone. It appeals to the ear as well as the eye, like the life that it reflects.

Jean Renoir's films have been the subject of countless commentaries. They have been studied and analyzed in detail by numerous competent specialists. It is not my intention here to synthesize what others have written in this vein. I have seen the films again, and I have again been delighted by them even as I have sought to understand and portray my sense of Jean Renoir himself at the time that he made each of them.

One film that I have not seen is *Mam'zelle Nitouche*. It was another Braunberger-Richebé production, directed by Marc Allégret and based on a famous operetta by a contemporary of Offenbach. The film was made right before *La Chienne,* and Jean had a small role in it, that of the chief adjutant with a single scene opposite the star, Janie Marèze. It is not hard to imagine him playing his part with the same gusto he lent the part of the wolf in Cavalcanti's version of *Le Petit Chaperon rouge.* For him, it was just a short-lived distraction from the shooting of his own film. *Mam'zelle Nitouche* was released in September 1931, and *La Chienne* came out in Paris in mid-November of the same year.

It did not do so without mishap. The lawsuit brought by Rosemonde Gérard and her son against the *Little Match Girl* was nothing compared to the brawls that went on between Jean Renoir and the associates of his friend Braunberger. Up until the last day of shooting, he let the others see nothing of what he had done—Richebé was still under the impression that it was a musical comedy. His curiosity about the work did not extend to looking at the novel. La Fouchadière was considered a light writer, and that was enough for him. When they discovered the truth, it was a real scandal. The producers were under the impression that the only way they could avert a disaster was to keep Jean Renoir from editing the film. They gave the job to Paul Fejos, a Hungarian director who had worked in the United States and whom Braunberger had brought to Paris to shoot *Fantomas.* They went so far as to deny Jean entry to the studio at Billancourt; he was furious and convinced that they had stolen his film from him. Every day he tried to get into the studio to edit the film. There were altercations, threats on both sides, and once the producers even called the police. Finally Fejos turned down the job, and the task fell to the studio's editor, Denise Tual, whose name at the time was Denise Batcheff. Jean was convinced that someone not from his production team, someone who had not participated in the shooting of the film, could not edit his film without compromising his intentions. "For three days and three nights, I wandered from bar to bar in Montmartre, a romantic trying to find oblivion in alcohol," he tells us (ibid., p. 102). With the help of Yves Allégret, whom he happened to come across in his hazy peregrinations, he succeeded in gaining an audience with Monsieur Monteux, the silent partner, to whom he told his tale of woe. Monteux, in turn, was sympathetic, and thanks especially to his mistress's insistence, he demanded that Jean be allowed to edit his own movie.

La Chienne was very well received in its private showing for the producers' friends, among them Pierre Renoir and Jacques Becker, who were deeply moved by it, and Valentine Tessier, the actress, who "sobbed unrestrainedly." Still, Richebé had his doubts and decided to send the film to the boondocks for tryouts. He picked the Eastern city of Nancy, which was a disaster. The Croix de Feu and other far right groups denounced the movie as seditious, and Jean fell into despair: his projects for the future were once again foundering, and he saw himself rejected once more by the film world, whose acceptance he longed for.

A picaresque character who had once been a quartermaster in the Turkish navy and who, after sundry occupations, had managed to become the owner of several movie halls, including an especially luxurious one at Biarritz, decided to show the film there. Renoir had met this man, Siritzky, at the home of Marcel Pagnol. Alexander Korda had just finished producing *Marius* with Pagnol's help—Pagnol having made the movie script from his play and chosen the cast. It was a film that pleased Jean Renoir, who had always loved the south of France, but it was not a little different from his, and certainly more accessible to the general public, who could easily identify with the feelings, dilemmas, and limitations of its characters. Siritzky understood that it would not be so easy to make the public accept *La Chienne*. He decided to go all out. It was a tremendous publicity campaign—posters, press releases, newspaper articles advising families to stay away from *La Chienne*, a horrifying spectacle. The strategy worked like a dream: the theater was full at every showing, and it ran for several weeks. That gave the director of the Colisée some courage, and the film was finally booked for Paris, where it was a great success "for a record-breaking stretch" (ibid., p. 104).

The scandal at Nancy and the fights over who would edit were not, however, forgotten. Jean Renoir himself said that he had gotten the reputation of being a tough customer. Film producers were even more demanding than gallery owners: they liked meek directors. Producing films is risky business, and these people did not want to increase the odds against themselves by taking on headstrong people. They had their ideas about the nature of the marketplace, and they also had their taste. Jean Renoir was to find a few who had confidence in him, but most had a lot of trouble believing that such a muddle-headed, well-spoken, irascible, charming, and creative person would contrive to put together the kind of tidy success that would be guaranteed to fill their theaters. Jean Renoir had forgotten the anguish he felt when he could find no one to distribute *La Chienne*. Carried away by his work with Michel Simon, he was overflowing with optimism. "We understand each other perfectly: he hates the extravagant complications of life as a filmmaker as much as I do," he said in an interview with Nino Frank.[4] Their plan was to shoot two films a year: one a comedy, the other a drama. In the following year there was to be *Boudu sauvé des eaux* (*Boudu Saved from Drowning*)—but then the complications of life as a filmmaker were to separate the two men for a long time.

◆

In the beginning of 1932, Jean Renoir directed *La Nuit du carrefour* (*Maigret at the Crossroads*), based on a Georges Simenon novel. It was a project that had started up before the shooting of *La Chienne*. "When he came to ask me for the movie rights to *La Nuit du carrefour*, I was on the Normandy coast at Ouistreham, and I saw him arrive at 125 mph in a racing Bugatti. There was nothing phony about him, as a man or a moviemaker. He was always so natural when I saw him that I want to call him 'childish'—not a complimentary term, but to my mind it explains much about him and his life. Didn't he get that from his father? I am almost sure of it." These are the words of Simenon.[5] In the same letter, he writes: "What I want to bring out is his spontaneous side. Should I call him an innocent? That he would share with almost all creative artists.

"Without appearing to, in his affable and unpretentious way, he stuck stubbornly to his own guns, and he was certainly the least conventional of artists, especially of filmmakers." These two sides of the character of Renoir, whom Simenon called his brother, are complementary. He had a personality that drove people nuts if they happened to be less perceptive than Simenon. It is certainly true that sticking to his guns without seeming to was a key to Jean's behavior, and it is indeed an aspect of his nature that goes back to the world of his childhood, as Simenon guessed.

The two of them had known and respected each other since 1923. Jean admired his friend's literary output, and *La Nuit du carrefour* was one of the first novels in which Simenon's famous detective, Superintendent Maigret, appeared. He imagined his brother Pierre playing the role. None of Simenon's work had yet appeared on film, and the

---

[4] *Pour vous*, 19 November 1931, 157.
[5] In a letter to the author dated 12 March 1984.

two friends had little trouble agreeing on a deal. As Simenon says again: "Jean Renoir's independence often prevented him from working with the great producers of his day, since for them the director was only a cog, in no way the most important person making a film." Simenon always followed his friend's career, even from afar, and he also knew intimately the world of the producers.

For *La Nuit du carrefour,* they decided to do the editing of the script and the dialogue together. To guarantee that they wouldn't be disturbed, they rented a villa at cap d'Antibes, not far from the Renoir family home, Les Collettes, which had gone to Claude Renoir when the estate was divided. (Claude was the youngest of the brothers, but they all got together there when they could.) With this film, there was no question of involving Braunberger-Richebé productions. The idea was to make do with the money they could raise among friends. It was the old way of doing things for Jean—everything by the seat of his pants. Jacques Becker, who had just finished his military service, was dubbed the producer, and he was also assistant director. Claude Renoir, Jean's not yet nineteen-year-old nephew (son of Pierre), made his debut as well, as assistant cameraman. Jean was back in his element, making a movie with a bunch of friends who stuck together night and day. Twenty miles north of Paris, in Bouffemont, he had found a crossroads that corresponded to the place described in Simenon's novel. There were also a few forlorn buildings and a sort of abandoned farmhouse or inn where they all camped during the shooting. Pierre was the only one who had to shuttle back and forth to Paris, since he had a part in *Domino,* a play by Marcel Achard.

It was winter. It rained all the time. They would go out in the rain and fog to shoot at all hours of the day and night. Rain, fog, and darkness suited Simenon's tale, and he himself was in attendance for some of the filming. Jean had found "a funny creature, a strange little seventeen-year-old kid with a very pale face named Winna Winfried. I don't really believe in the word 'photogenic,' but in her case it fit. All you had to do was put her in front of the camera, and everything was perfect, including her voice. The sound engineer adored her, and so did I."[6] Winna and her partner, also a Dane, were about the only ones who had not belonged to the group before the film. The others were Jean Gehret, the painter Dignimont, and another painter, a Catalan, Jean Castanier. The latter quickly became a close friend, and he did the set design with William Aguet. Also taking part were a journalist, Michel Duran; Marguerite Renoir and Suzanne de Troye, the film's

[6]Jean Renoir, *Entretiens et propos* (Paris, 1979), 137–49.

editors; and Mimi Champagne, Pierre's widow (he had died in a car accident), in charge of continuity. The life of this community was not always simple, nor was Jean disturbed by the sentimental knots being tied and untied. In fact, he enjoyed them a good deal. There wasn't enough money to pay the people who were doing the work, but it didn't matter. They believed in what they were doing, and they had a good time. "When I go through that intersection, I see myself in that hot, wet fog: it was wet because the rain never stopped falling, and hot from our passion for our craft, which we longed to extricate from the marketplace," as Jean wrote later on.[7]

The film came out at the end of April 1932 at the Théâtre Pigalle, and it was not a success. Jean Mitry, who had a small role in the film and later on became director of the IDHEC (Institute for Advanced Studies in Cinematography) once told William Gilcher, the film historian, that at the end of the shooting, he had ruined three reels. He used the same film twice and only realized it when he saw it was double-exposed. That same year, two other Simenon novels were brought to the screen: *La Tête d'un homme* (*A Man's Head*), directed by Julien Duvivier, and *Le Chien jaune* (*The Yellow Dog*), by Jean Taride. Neither of them compares to Jean Renoir's work, which is so much richer and more creative. Nor did he betray Simenon, whose spirit is alive in the atmosphere, the lighting, the decor, and the images themselves, which have nothing to do with merely illustrating a novel.

Many years later, this film, with its brilliant poetic quality, got the praise it deserves. It was conceived in a delightful offhand, free spirit. Though darkly amusing, it is never violent or heavy. The voices, the sounds, the music—from a phonograph, there was nothing else—are bewitching and exactly appropriate. The French New Wave was enthusiastic about it: "*La Nuit du carrefour,* the only great French mystery movie, maybe even the greatest French adventure film," is the judgment of Jean-Luc Godard, a person not known for being generous with praise and who also knew what he was talking about.[8]

♦

Nineteen thirty-two is still, in retrospect, an important date: the first television programs were shown in Paris, and they offered a new, albeit distant threat to a movie industry that was already in crisis. Since

[7] *Cahiers du cinéma*, April 1960, 106, cited in J. Renoir, *Ecrits, 1926–1971*, ed. Claude Gauteur (Paris, 1974), 205.
[8] André Bazin, *Jean Renoir* (Paris, 1971), 224.

the advent of the talkie, the number of films that came out each year in France had doubled. Yet they were much more expensive to make, and installing sound systems in theaters and studios was not cheap either. Moreover, France, which had no patents of its own, had to pay the United States or Germany huge license fees to use their processes. Mergers didn't help, and the big companies were being liquidated, first Pathé-Nathan and then Gaumont-Franco-Films-Aubert. Independent companies took up the slack. In order to protect this branch of French industry, the Minister of National Education, one Anatole de Monzie, issued a decree on July 21, 1932, that defined a French film as "any film produced by a French company on French territory using exclusively French artists and technicians." Jean did not feel targeted by these defensives. He was too marginal. He was an artisan, not a manufacturer. Since the day he had chosen filmmaking as his craft, what others were doing did not engage his passionate interest as it had before. The year 1932 was also the year of *Que viva Mexico* by Sergei Eisenstein, of *Scarface* [Howard Hawks], and *I Am a Fugitive from a Chain Gang* [Mervyn LeRoy]. In France, *Le Million* (*The Million*) and *A nous la liberté* (*Freedom for Us*) had come out the year before, but René Clair's sensibility was so remote from Jean's that it had not engaged his interest even in the silent era.

When *La Nuit du carrefour* was just coming out, Jean Renoir was working up *Boudu sauvé des eaux* (*Boudu Saved from Drowning*), and that was all he had on his mind. At the time, Michel Simon had returned to the theater and was playing the role of Boudu created by Marcel Vallée five years earlier. The epilogue of *La Chienne* reminded him of his part as a tramp, and he suggested René Fauchois's comedy to Jean, who immediately got excited about the idea. A faithful translation of the play to film was out of the question from the start. "The role of the incorrigible tramp seemed to have been invented for this genius of an actor," Jean wrote.[9] He shot Michel Simon the way documentary filmmakers shoot lions and tigers. He used a very big lens and filmed him from a distance, walking the streets, in the midst of crowds, and along the river banks. In Fauchois's play, Boudu is reintegrated into society at the end, but in the movie, Michel Simon falls into the water again. As he escapes, he throws away his fancy wedding suit and regains his *joie de vivre*, once more a tramp in an idyllic landscape.

Many years later, while watching *Boudu*, Jean began laughing at

[9]Jean Renoir, *Ma vie et mes films*, 105.

the thought of a dog he had at the time named Jerry. Catherine Hessling had named him Jerry from the Jack London story, "Jerry on the Island." At Marlotte, Jerry used to sit outside, in front of Jean's window, while he worked. One day, the dog vanished. He got caught by the local dogcatcher, but on the way to the pound got wind of a slaughterhouse. Slipping away somehow or other, he treated himself to a dinner of raw meat. It was not the last time he attempted this escapade. Boudu was like Jerry, and Jean claimed that he owed to the dog what he had added to the character of Boudu.

Boudu Saved from Drowning is a comedy that uses none of the old tricks. Jean Renoir and Michel Simon had a lot of fun; they enjoyed incongruity and wanted to shock, so the result was a far cry from "boulevard" comedy, so far, in fact, that René Fauchois felt he had been betrayed and protested. *Boudu* is a film glorifying Michel Simon. It was thought up by a peer who knew all his capabilities and had movies in his blood. Without wanting to or knowing he was doing so, Jean Renoir was thirty years ahead of his time. He did not claim to belong to the avant-garde. He thought his innovations were as simple as could be. They are part of the pleasure that he got from making movies. He was no more carried away by technique than his father had been. Nor did he develop any theory to go with his filmmaking. The only thing that was important for him was to direct films the way he wanted to.

Michel Simon put up the money for the movie, and his friend Gehret was the producer. The film's success and its reviews were both qualified. Between *Feu Mathias Pascal* (*The Late Mathias Pascal*) and *Boudu*, Simon had shot twelve movies, and he had no regrets about *Boudu*. Of all the directors he worked with, Jean Renoir was best at bringing out his complex talents. Jean said of him: "His face is as gripping as an ancient tragic mask."[10] Yet their dream of shooting two films a year remained but a dream, since they didn't have the money to make it come true. They had talked about a *Hamlet* by Shakespeare and Jules Laforgue, and a screenplay by Jacques Deval, a famous comic writer, as well as film versions of André Derain's *N'Bongo* and Cami's *Jugement dernier* (*Last Judgment*).[11]

In this profession more than others, there is a lot of talk. There is discussion, there are conspiratorial airs. People are sworn to secrecy, and then, that evening, it turns out that everyone knows the secret.

---

[10] Cited by François Truffaut, *Les films de ma vie* (Paris, 1975), 55.
[11] Jean Renoir, *Oeuvres inédites*, 18–20.

Actually everyone knows what everyone else is up to, in work and in private life as well. None of the talk is important until a contract gets signed, and even then, the wind can shift.

◆

Boudu Saved from Drowning was not yet in the theaters when Jean signed a contract to bring yet another play to the screen. This time, the play's author, Roger Ferdinand, was the producer. It was an unconventional arrangement inspired by the huge success of the Pagnol plays that were turned into films, first *Marius*, directed by Alexander Korda in 1931, and then, in this same year (1932), *Fanny*, by Marc Allégret. Pagnol had been their producer.

> Marcel Pagnol is a great writer because he has remained a man from Marseille. When he speaks, he does not just speak for himself but for several million members of the middle class and for the southern French shopkeepers who speak through him. A single man by himself doesn't amount to much, but a person who has become the mouthpiece for a mob or a whole population, that's much more interesting; strange as it may seem, inept attempts at such universality only lead to a kind of frenzied and phony individualism. From seeing too much of the world, you stop being able to see anyone; and on this earth, only one thing counts, and that's being in touch with people.[12]

Although he appreciated Pagnol, Jean Renoir had no desire to film a play; but since he needed to revive his finances once again, he was ready to submit to another ordeal like *On purge bébé*.

At the time, Jean had a lot of expenses to cover. His separation from Catherine Hessling had not come cheap. Renoir canvases and drawings disappeared from his walls, and he himself had to move. Catherine kept the apartment on the rue de Miromesnil, while he moved to Meudon, into an old house on the rue Alexandre-Guilmant that was "built over the remains of an ancient convent that had been destroyed during the Revolution."[13] The backyard overlooked a path to the Observatory. He managed to keep the house at Marlotte and would soon get an apartment in Montmartre, at 9, rue des Saules, in the same building as his brother Pierre and his nephew Claude. Nearby was the Eglise Saint-Pierre, where he had been baptized. Jean was a bohemian who enjoyed houses, even if he scarcely lived in

---

[12] From a lecture given by Jean Renoir in January 1939, in England, cited in Jean Renoir, *Ecrits*, 47.

[13] Jean Renoir, *Ma vie et mes films*, 148.

them. He liked entertaining simply, sharing a bottle of wine and a decent meal, as his parents had done. All the friends who worked with him at one time or another remember this place or one of the others he lived in: each had his mother's piano in it and a bust of her in bronze (Jean really resembled her), a clock, and some dressers. Jean was still attached to the furnishings of his childhood. He carried them around with him like those precious drawings and paintings that he had to give up, brokenheartedly, one by one.

Chotard et Cie (*Chotard and Co.*) was not about to make a fortune. Roger Ferdinand's play was not much to speak of. Ferdinand worked for two months with Jean on the screenplay and got credit for the dialogue. It took twenty-three days (November–December 1932) to shoot in the Joinville studios, where Jean had succeeded in getting together at least part of his gang: Jacques Becker was his assistant, Jean Castanier the set designer, Charles Ralleigh, his old buddy from *The Little Match Girl*, the technical director, and Claude Renoir assistant cameraman. Suzanne de Troye took care of continuity and shared the editing work with Marguerite Renoir. Among the actors were Georges Pomiès, whom Jean had dug up again, Dignimont, and Fabien Loris, a friend of Castanier's and a member of the "October Group" (soon to become a source of actors and friends), as well as Georges Darnoux, who made his debut in *Boudu* and whom Jean liked very much. Darnoux was a real aristocrat, though a slightly wayward one. He raced cars and loved horses and women. He was also something of an alcoholic, though not the only one: there was a lot of drinking going on in this line of work at that time. Jean found him amusing.

Shoulder to shoulder with these more or less amateur actors were several theatrical professionals brought in by Roger Ferdinand, including Fernand Charpin, who had been in the Pagnol trilogy, and Jeanne Boitel. Using the ingenuity at his disposal to extricate himself from a job he didn't like (in this case, filming a play), Jean Renoir used the two groups of actors in such a way that his own group, although limited by Ferdinand's text, provides a different dimension. Pomiès especially offers a poetic interpretation of the role of the novelist lost in his dreams who finds himself marooned in his father-in-law's (Chotard, played by Charpin) grocery store. There's a lot more Renoir than Ferdinand in his character. He has a way of putting a twist on what he says that lightens up the action. This work was no great success, but one can still sense the hand of a truly creative temperament in it. Jean Renoir found new problems to resolve in each experience, and each readied the way for the next one.

After *Chotard et Cie* and the financial setback of *Boudu*, which was not an enticement for producers at a time when other French directors were contemplating exile to find work, Pierre Braunberger agreed to try to find some silent partners in Germany, where both men had some friends: Karl Koch and Lotte Reiniger had introduced him to Bertolt Brecht at the time of the great success of his *Threepenny Opera*. They became good friends. Brecht visited Renoir often at Meudon, along with Hans Eisler, Kurt Weill, and Lotte Lenya. Jean amused him by singing old French songs to the tune of a concertina that Brecht's secretary would always bring wrapped up in newspaper. Koch and Brecht were opposite types physically: Koch, a Rhinelander, "a fat German, who loved comfort, was a gourmand or even a gourmet," while Brecht, born and raised in Augsburg, "a city supposedly of Celtic origin," was "a thin German with tendencies to asceticism" (ibid., 149). Jean found that he resembled a medieval German monk from well before the Reformation. He was struck by his modesty. As he described him to Penelope Gilliat: "Perhaps he was, like many modest men, proud inside. He was a child. It's not so easy to remain a child. And he was sarcastic, which people never understand. He was romantic but also very sharp, and sharp people are not well understood."[14] These are strange remarks, since, on the one hand, Jean himself was a sharp child, and, on the other hand, he hardly ever described his friends. It was easy to get him to tell stories, but he was not given to character analysis. As he said, psychology didn't interest him. He also told Penelope Gilliat that he tried to raise money to make movies with Brecht.

◆

This trip to Berlin took place at the time of Hitler's election. Jean Renoir recalled it several times, and Pierre Braunberger also told me about it. It was not the first time Jean and Pierre were in Berlin together. They had even done some acting there, in G. W. Pabst's *Diary of a Lost Girl*. At the time of this trip, Pabst, who had made *Threepenny Opera* in 1931, was staying in France. Aside from Brecht and the Kochs, Jean wanted to see Alfred Flechtheim, an art dealer whom he had never met before. It was a good idea, since Flechtheim was a contributor to *Querschnitt*, a famous satiric review, and was able to initiate him into the disturbing nightlife of the German capital: its decadence was as multifaceted as the people whose disarray and moral

---

[14] *New Yorker*, August 23, 1969, 34–61.

decay it reflected, and Jean had never seen its like. Flechtheim also introduced him to Paul Klee: "Meeting him in itself justified my trip to Berlin."[15] In the meantime, Pierre Braunberger took responsibility for contacting producers and distributors. He also told me that he wanted to kill Hitler. In those early days of Nazism, the two of them witnessed the humiliating cruelties perpetrated by Brown Shirts on Jews in the streets. Jean never forgot it, and his only desire at the time was to put Pierre then and there on a train for Paris, which he managed to do after some difficulty. He feared for Braunberger, who liked to strike back and began to get provocative. "I saw him stand himself right in front of a big Nazi in uniform and give the Nazi salute with one hand while covering up his nose with the other" (ibid.). Jean was not reassured for his sake until he got a phone call from Paris that Braunberger was home, where he himself went a few days later.

So the trip to Berlin had not fulfilled its original purpose. On his return, Jean had to go through one of those awful stretches when he had to keep asking himself what door to knock on to find some cash. In matters of creativity, he did not dare to compare himself to his father, but the elder Renoir had suffered for a long time from an uncomprehending press and public; art dealers were no better. Renoir courageously kept on painting, with the support of his friends. Jean had friends as well, but in his profession, they were not enough. It was no help, their repeating to him that no one was finding work and that there was a crisis. Things were looking very bad. Starting a new jerry-built production was out of the question. No one said a word about the three films that he had directed and that were not worthless, even in his own eyes.

All of a sudden, Jean Renoir received the most tempting offer anyone could have made him: to shoot *Madame Bovary* for the New Films Society (NSF). The NSF was a production house that belonged to Gaston Gallimard, publisher of the *NRF* (*New French Review*) and son of the collector who had been a friend of Auguste Renoir and whom Jean, too, had known well. According to Robert Aron, director of the society, Flaubert was soon to be in the public domain, and his publisher, Charles Fasquelle, had surrendered the rights. Until then, the NSF had made only short, uninteresting, but profitable, films. The time had come for it to attempt something more honorable. Gaston Gallimard was enthusiastic about the idea. They thought of Jacques Feyder, who had just come back from the United States and

---

[15]Jean Renoir, *Ma vie et mes films*, 86.

whose film version of *Thérèse Raquin* for the silent screen had not been forgotten. The novelist Roger Martin du Gard, a close friend of "Gaston" (as they called Gallimard at rue Sébastien-Bottin, headquarters of the publishing business), agreed to write the screenplay and the dialogue. Gaston's notion was to give the role of Emma Bovary to Valentine Tessier, a famous actress who had acted for Copeau; when Copeau went into retirement and his theater was sold to Jean Tedesco, she had joined Jouvet's company and was giving masterly performances of Giraudoux. Gaston Gallimard was in love with her.

Robert Aron tells the story of a disastrous lunch at Larue's. Gaston Gallimard had invited Valentine and Mr. and Mrs. Feyder; Mrs. Feyder was none other than her rival, the actress Françoise Rosay. Valentine Tessier was not pleasing to Mr. Feyder and was less than that to his wife. The day after this lunch, Feyder said that he could not see Valentine Tessier in the part, and Gaston Gallimard gave up on him. Since Roger Martin du Gard had already begun working with Feyder, he decided to withdraw from the project.[16]

Jean was more than happy to be given full responsibility for the screenplay and the dialogue. He got Karl Koch to help him with parts of the book adaptation. To Jean, Valentine Tessier was the ideal Emma Bovary. Because of her, he decided to give the other roles to stage actors as well. He cast his brother Pierre in the role of Charles Bovary and Max Dearly as Homais. Dearly was an actor who had made his debut in Marseille playing the fairy Carabosse. "So he played her wearing a very big dress and on his knees; at the ends of his knees he put large pointed shoes that stuck out from under the dress, and the parts of the dress that dragged on the ground behind him hid his feet. He walked on his knees and looked like a dwarf fairy. A man who plays dwarf fairies is certainly someone who can play the pharmacist Homais, and he played him very well indeed."[17] Renoir also got Robert Le Vigan, Romain Bouquet, and Pierre Larquey, all distinguished actors. Jean had in mind a play more stylized than movie actors would provide. To compensate for the deliberately affected style that he asked the theater performers to provide, Jean was determined to shoot the film in natural surroundings, in real farms with real cows and a real barnyard. The objects in the film were the real thing, too, heavy doors and furniture, and the windows were also the actual windows of the houses. He paid closer attention to these de-

[16]Robert Aron, *Fragments d'une vie*, (Paris, 1981), 57–60.
[17]Jean Renoir, *Entretiens et propos*, 141.

tails than usual because he wanted to bring out the contrast between the reality of the decor and the emphatic gestures and expressions of the professional actors.

Despite her forty years, Valentine Tessier is Emma Bovary. From one end of the film to the other, the viewer has the feeling that there is a transparent veil between her and the others, between her and the backdrops. Set apart by her bearing and her acting style, she is not a real woman in the midst of all that reality. She is the image that Emma Bovary has of herself; in this, Renoir echoes Flaubert. Flaubert's world and that of Jean Renoir are far apart from each other, but the way that Jean loyally transforms a work that he would not himself have chosen to film constitutes a major point of interest in the film. He knew how to use Flaubert's extremely studied text for dialogue and how to coach the actors according to his desires. There is a very personal vision behind the film's images, and Jean's familiarity with the era is also apparent. *Madame Bovary* also reflects Jean's broad education and the interest he held in expressions of social difference.

Robert Aron, who saw him working at close range, was very impressed, but he also deplored the problems Jean Renoir's demands caused him in professional terms—the film went way over budget. At the time, Aron let himself be convinced, as when Jean told him he wished to extend the time for exterior shots because a hare had appeared between the legs of Valentine Tessier's horse and they had failed to capture it on film. The next day had to be spent on the lookout in front of the hare's burrow until it reappeared. They spent a whole day at it, but finally, since the hare was not in the mood for an appearance, they had to cancel its scene.

The film was shot in Normandy, at Lyons-la-Forêt, Rys, and Rouen, and then in the studios at Billancourt outside Paris. The shooting took six weeks and left the director with many happy memories. He recalled festive dinners in the inn at Lyons with Jacques Becker, his assistant, Claude Renoir, assistant cameraman, Joseph de Bretagne, sound engineer, and Marguerite, who did the editing. The "family," as Jean himself called it, was together again. After each day's intense activity, they could take their minds off things and laugh and then, tirelessly, plan the next day's work.

Evenings were happy and relaxing for everyone. Jean Renoir was no prude.

Our main diversion was a game inspired by the *Gaietés de l'escadron* (*High Times with the Squadron*) of Courteline. It was called "lefoutro," and here's how it was played: during dinner, when everyone was seated around the table, a napkin twisted into the shape of a penis was placed in the middle of the table. The rule was that everyone had to keep a respectful silence in the presence of this symbol. The first one to break it was punished by three whacks with "lefoutro" on the fingers, and the punishment was accompanied by the following formula: "I saw you making gestures to your neighbor. You insulted Mr. Lefoutro. You've paid, you're pardoned." The guilty one had to protest: "I protest, I couldn't have insulted Mr. Lefoutro because I was busy cutting up my chicken." The merit of this appeal was then put to a vote, and the punishment was doubled if the verdict was confirmed. Silly games like this got us ready for the next day's work better than boring disquisitions.[18]

An old friend, Roland Stragliati, told me about these evenings at Lyons-la-Forêt, which resembled a country wedding. Everyone knew everyone else, everyone had fun, nothing mattered. Roland, who had just gotten out of school, was a prop man. It was his first job. He saw Jean Renoir for the first time in the "authors' room" of the *NRF*. "For me, it was as though Hoot Gibson, one of the movie cowboys of my youth, had made an entrance into the big hall at a ranch in Arizona. In some strange way he looked like him."[19] Stragliati was won over, and the weeks he spent with them shooting *Madame Bovary* were an extraordinary, unforgettable experience. In Paris, Stragliati was still living with his parents, and the shooting went on so late that the last metro was long gone by the time he got out of the studios at Billancourt. It meant walking home, a long walk after a long day. Early one morning when he was in an especially bad way, Jean Renoir offered him a pick-me-up at the studio bar. "He said, 'Take it easy for a minute, my boy, I'll meet you there.' And he came and had a drink with me." Roland tells this story unprompted, and it is true that directors don't usually notice when a prop man is wiped out. So the human warmth so tangible in Renoir's films was not confined to them.

In a few reliable and high-spirited "Portraits of Jean Renoir," Stragliati gives an idea of the way the director of *Madame Bovary* handled his actors (ibid.). "On the set, Renoir was truly great. No one was ever better than he at directing the actors and getting the most out of them. But he had the touch, and it went something like this. An actor had just done a scene or, more often, a shot, and done it poorly. So Renoir went up to him, obviously delighted: "Well old man," he would cry out, "you were brilliant! It was really very good . . . only,"—there was always an "only"—"if you put your hat

---

[18] Jean Renoir, *Ma vie et mes films*, 107.
[19] *Positif*, September 1975, 173.

over your ear, sort of unselfconsciously, it would be totally perfect." The actor, delighted, was enthused and would start again. Then Renoir would intervene again: "This time, I have nothing to say: it was perfection itself. You see, we were right to do it one more time. Still, we could maybe try something . . . you come in on the right, put your hat on the night table, and answer back as though you were a little bit miffed. Here! Like this." And then he himself would play the scene just the right way. Then, always going from one superlative to the next, they would keep at it until he was completely satisfied, when he would still say: "Hey, the first time it was great, too. Maybe that's the one we'll take when we cut the film."

And Stragliati adds: "With this tact, his cunning, his feeling for actors' vulnerability and quickness to anger, Renoir was always able to get them to act in a way that is true to life. It's one of the most precious things that his assistants learned from him." He already knew how to do this during the filming of *Madame Bovary*, but only the people who saw him work seem to have noticed. Is this because he had for so long heard his father speak of the pleasure and the pain, the pleasure of painting and the pain of not being understood? Jean Renoir seems to have been resigned to it, or rather, he mentions nowhere, nor does anyone say it for him, that he was waiting for success. The only thing he wanted was the opportunity to keep on making films. Still, a success would have made a lot of things a lot easier.

Until the end of the editing, everything went smoothly. Then there were five or six showings in the theater at the Billancourt studio, and Jean Renoir was happy because Bertolt Brecht liked the film a lot. So did the fifty or so other people who were invited to see it. But *Madame Bovary* lasted for three hours. In those days, a movie show consisted of a double feature, with newsreels, intermission, etc. It was impossible to sell a film that was three hours long. It had to be cut, and they massacred it. Seventy minutes were cut from the film itself and the copy, and the outtakes were destroyed. Despite the fact that the film was constructed as a series of fully developed scenes, there are holes. Some scenes are lost that must have contained needed linkage. When Jean took the job, he knew that Flaubert had refused to have his books illustrated. As it is now, the film sticks in the mind as a passionate interpretation of a great novel, not an illustration of one.

According to Jean, *Madame Bovary* had already caused a stir in the rue Sébastian-Bottin. In a generous gesture that is a credit to him, while the film was being made, Gaston Gallimard gave it his personal backing. But when at the end it was discovered that they had gone way over budget, he refused to pay. The creditors threatened him, brandishing his signature. The whole company was on tenterhooks. Gaston did not give in, and in the end, he was not the one who lost money. He made a deal according to which the debts would be paid off from the film's receipts, and it was already clear that they would not be fat. Another matter not unrelated to *Madame Bovary* was making the rounds at the Gallimard publishing house: during the shooting, relations between Gaston and Valentine Tessier had deteriorated. In the rural surroundings of Lyons-la-Forêt, the fair actress had succumbed to the charms of Pierre Renoir. As usual, everyone in the company knew it before the one most concerned, and when he found out and got angry, the letters that his faithless lover sent back were collected by an employee from the wastebasket and circulated throughout the firm.

Jean Renoir did not know the story about the letters, which would have made him laugh; he needed a good laugh. He was the first one to learn that the public, the distributors, and the newspapers could make nothing of his film. As foreseen, the mutilated film version of *Madame Bovary* was a flop. When it was presented later on (November 1934) in New York at the Acme Theater, it was well appreciated. In Paris, the public premiere was at the Ciné-Opéra on January 4, 1934, but political events of the moment were not favorable to its opening. Five days after its brief career began, the Stavisky affair came to a close with the supposed suicide of the financier. He wasn't much of a swindler, at least compared to Madame Haneau and Oustric, who had been the talk of the town and had brought down ministers and ministries a few years before. But the public was growing weary of scandals that implicated so many politicians. The Stavisky affair only compromised a few obscure radical deputies, but radicals were in power in the government, so it immediately sparked demonstrations in Paris. This unleashed the press and brought to light another scandal that resulted in the resignation of the minister of justice, and that, in turn, brought down Chautemps, the prime minister. On January 29, a new government was formed with Daladier in charge, and on February 6, when the minister was presenting himself to the Chamber of Deputies, the demonstrations that had not stopped for a month degenerated into serious disturbances. The target was the Palais-Bourbon. There were fifteen dead and more than two thousand wounded. Daladier, who had been appointed by the chamber, was forced to resign. Even so, the parliamentary regime that the right wanted to bring down survived, and the parties of the left decided to regroup and prepare for an attempted fascist takeover.

Jean Renoir's friends felt personally threatened by the bloody events of February 6. In their responses, their extreme anger is apparent. Jacques Becker, with whom Jean felt no little affinity, was as hostile as Marguerite. Being wealthy by birth, as Jean was, made him feel guilty, and he was not the only one of the bunch to respond this way. Jean understood why they were upset, but he did not share their feelings. Nor was he ready, as they were, to get involved in the struggle on behalf of the working class, although he readily approved of the generous sentiments of his friends and of Marguerite. A kind of disenchantment came over him based on what his father had taught him about people and politics and what he himself had lived through in wartime. Thanks to Gabrielle, he always felt he was the same as everyone else, and he had no trouble being accepted anywhere. He supposed that he understood the problems of people whose principles were very different from his own, and his actual experience tended to validate that supposition.

◆

It was time for him to shoot a story that had been told to him ten years before by Jacques Mortier, his classmate at Sainte-Croix whom he had run across again at the lycée in Nice, a figure who cropped up now and then in the course of his life. Having become a police superintendent, Jacques Mortier was writing under the pseudonym of Jacques Levert. At his job in Martigues, he had learned a tale that Jean Renoir wanted to film and call *Toni*.

> The drama that I wish to bring to the screen takes place in a growing metropolitan area, at a construction site that is supposed to become one of the largest in France. Its actors are immigrants, gypsies, men whose life has yet to become fixed. These people are threatened with expulsion for the slightest lapse, they brood over their feelings for a long time in silence, but when they explode, they consume everything in sight.
>
> This mixture of repression and cruelty, of violence and severe timidity, has probably been the cause of the success of some American films without real artistic value; they are very powerful because they take place among pioneers, builders of towns, and the like.[20]

This is the way Jean announced his latest film. He was still thinking about American movies, and he wanted to bring to life men and women who were not usually presented on film.

First he went to the place in question, in the company of Jacques

---

[20] *L'effort cinématographique*, 20, 1 November 1934, communicated by Claude Gauteur in *Les Cahiers du film*, 5, November 1934.

Mortier, who reenacted the original investigation; Jean interrogated the people one at a time. The project was only filmed because of Pierre Gaut, one of the independent producers who came in during the crisis and as a result of the breakdown of the big monopolies. Pierre Gaut was a friend of Jean's, and he succeeded in getting together 500,000 francs, half of the sum needed. At Jean's suggestion, he went to see Marcel Pagnol, who said he would come up with the other half. Pagnol had started his own production company in Marseille. "He had his own distribution system and even a theater on the Canebière in Marseille. This was after *Marius* and *Fanny*. He had a terrific reputation, and that allowed him to win his independence. Pagnol's commercial success was based on his talent. It all worked very well."[21] He had just directed *Angèle*, with Fernandel and Orane Demazis, based on Jean Giono's novel, *Un de Beaumugnes* (*A Man from Beaumugnes*). Like him, Jean Renoir was ready to shoot his film on location, in real exteriors and interiors, but he did not want to use experienced actors. Pagnol directed him to Charles Blavette, who became Toni. Most of the other actors were not professionals.

Pierre Gaut took responsibility for producing the film, and Jean wrote the screenplay and dialogue with Carl Einstein, a friend of his and Pierre's. Marcel Pagnol was an adviser during the shooting; his notion of dialogue was the complete opposite of Jean's, who used words as little as possible. In *Toni*, because of the accent and a somewhat different use of language in general, Pagnol's abilities were vital. The documentary aspect of the subject demanded them.

Both Pagnol and Renoir were great talkers, they were the same age, and they got along well. Pagnol was a true Southerner, born in Aubagne. Even though he "came up" to Paris and was a tutor at the Lycée Condorcet, he never lost his accent or his ties to Provence and Marseille.[22] They were equally passionate about their occupations, but their lives were very different indeed, as were their experiences and their ways of expressing them. In order to make known his ideas about talkies in 1933, Pagnol had founded a "teaching review," as he called *Les Cahiers du film;* as he wrote, "first we will put literature into movies, and then we will put movies into literature." He carried on a crusade against a class of movies that were still unable to extricate themselves from the silent era and hardly spoke, at least to his ears. Before shooting a film, Pagnol had his actors rehearse, he prepared

---

[21] Jean Renoir, *Ma vie et mes films,* 109.
[22] Filmography of Marcel Pagnol by Patrice Brion in *Cahiers du cinéma*, December 1965, 173.

the scene, and he picked his takes right from the sound truck. From the sound of their voices he could tell what was happening on the set and whether they had to cut or keep going. He was able to detect an actor's mistake from his or her intonation.

Like Jean Renoir, Pagnol had a lot of power over those who worked for him. "In his country house, he put up technicians, actors, and workers, as a master carpenter might have done in the fifteenth century," says Jean.[23] This Southerner full of imagination and stories was even more fond than Jean of seat-of-the-pants, homemade machinery. Jean noted, not without pride, that Pagnol "used for his own films my electric equipment from the Vieux-Colombier" (ibid.).

For *Toni*, Claude Renoir was chief cameraman for the first time, and Jean used several panoramic shots. He said that he was interested in angle shots. "We shot the film on the spot, with the people from the place, breathing their air, eating their food, and living in every way the life of these workers."[24] Jean felt at home everywhere, and in the most natural way, without condescension. The proof is the films themselves, especially *Toni*, where he was intent on putting the characters in their social context. He was very careful and precise about it, going so far as to carry out an investigation of his own among the people of that harsh and wild countryside. They were so different from the people of Cagnes, whose life was a lot more gentle.

The movie was shot during the summer of 1934, during which Chancellor Dollfuss was assassinated in Vienna. On September 20 of that year, Jean Vigo's magnificent film, *L'Atalante*, came out; it was cut to ribbons and its title changed to *Le Chaland qui passe* (*Passing barge*) because that was the name of a popular song at that time. Its showing at the Colisée lasted only two weeks, but Jean Vigo never knew that. He died on October 4, never able to champion his work. That was the day Badoglio's army invaded Ethiopia. Five days later, in Marseille, Croatian terrorists assassinated King Alexander I of Yugoslavia and Louis Barthou, the French foreign affairs minister. A tumultuous time was beginning in the West. The first public showing of *Toni* took place on February 22, 1935, one month after the referendum in which the Saar voted to become part of the Reich. The film appeared in two theaters, the Ciné-Opéra and the Bonaparte. It was not more successful than *Madame Bovary* or, for that matter, the other films by its director, who was definitely not understood. The social concerns of *Toni*

---

[23] Jean Renoir, *Ma vie et mes films*, 109.
[24] Jean Renoir, *Entretiens et propos*, 134.

passed unnoticed, and it was rejected by *Regards*, the PC's weekly movie magazine,[25] which was as unreceptive as the public in general.

◆

After *Toni*, Roland Stragliati remembers a lunch at Meudon at which Jean Renoir spoke of a film project on the life of Lapp fishermen that was received without enthusiasm by the producers. "If they're not interested, too bad!" was Jean's melancholic remark. "I'm not about to keep on shooting mechanical films like *Le Tournoi*. . . . I'd rather switch jobs: I'll become a writer." "Before, during lunch, he was talking about Egon Erwin Kisch's *China geheim*, a book that he loved, and he repeated the same idea."[26] In the end he did become a writer, but despite the great difficulties that he was about to encounter, a body of movies by him kept growing. Renoir read a lot, which did not surprise Stragliati, who also was a great reader, although it was not such a common habit in the profession.

He wrote pages and pages of film projects. So, for example, on May 29, 1935, shortly after this conversation that took place "in the big studio where Renoir usually worked on his screenplays standing at a drawing table," he took notes for a contemporary version of *Romeo and Juliet*. It was situated in and around Paris, "in one of those overgrown housing developments that suit the real estate agents but not the buyers."[27] It was an idea that he took up several times over the years. He changed the title and the place where the story would unfold: once it was in Burgundy, another time in Algeria. He longed to go back to Algeria. Claude Gauteur accomplished the forbidding task of going through these papers to publish the *Oeuvres de cinéma inédites* ("Unpublished Film Works"), which are of great value, since they provide a picture of the extent of this "amateur's" work and also of the way in which the subject of his films changed and evolved as he took them up over and over again in the course of his life. It becomes clear that Jean Renoir carried around inside him a novelist's universe with an amazing diversity of characters in it, and he had the talent to bring them to life with a name and a few lines of text. For example: "Jeanne Lalande . . . a flirt, she isn't nasty but she needs to shine, and she practises flirtation as though it were a natural function. She is now no longer a young woman, but she has kept her charm, a prewar

[25] Claude Gauteur, *Jean Renoir, la double méprise* (Paris, 1980), 39.
[26] Roland Stragliati, "Portraits de Jean Renoir," *Positif*, September 1975, 1973.
[27] Jean Renoir, *Oeuvres inédites*, 63.

sort of charm." All kinds of places and times and moments in the development of society interested this extraordinary man.

◆

In his daily life, his curiosity made Renoir disconcerting company. Before going off to film the Corsican coalmen at Martigues and the Piedmontese laborers who worked the nearby quarries, he had taken on a young trainee named Luchino Visconti on the recommendation of Gabrielle Chanel. He knew the great fashion designer through Paul Iribe. He used to see her with Misia Sert, whose beauty and energy had left a strong impression on him when he was a little boy. Her name then was Misia Edwards, and she sat for a portrait by Renoir. Jean was just as comfortable with Chanel and Misia as with the immigrant peasants and laborers, and he had as much fun in their company and in that of their more or less reactionary friends as with the members of the October Group who were about to shoot his next film.

Jean Renoir had become friends with Jean Castanier, the Catalan painter who behaved like a poet and who had become part of his gang since *La Nuit du carrefour*, the first talkie Jean had made the way he liked to make films, that is, freely, without the supervision of a villainous producer who pins back your ears with his budget and has the nerve to insinuate himself into the cutting room with a pair of scissors in his hand. Castanier, who had a strong sense of communal life, fitted in quickly. He soon substantially increased the size of the group by bringing in other members of the October Group, whose existence his moviemaking friend did not yet know about.

◆

The October Group had been founded in 1932 by Jean-Paul Dreyfus (later to take the name Le Chanois). It consisted of Jacques Prévert and a group of young actors, painters, musicians, and writers who were fascinated by his wit and eloquence. I knew Jacques Prévert later on. I can see him walking along, a cigarette butt glued to his lip, holding forth at the head of a single file of friends who drank up his every word. What did he have to say? What his poems have to say: one word unexpectedly evoking the next, building phrases linked by a strange inner logic that defies common sense. He rhapsodized with incredible deftness: words never bounced back on him. The endless string of witticisms made you burst out laughing. Taking on clichés and accepted ideas, he delighted in turning them upside down. He also knew how to get angry and start fights, not from malice, but in a noisy war against stupidity and conformity. Along with his brother Pierre, the perfect partner, they were an act always ready to perform something new. Listening to them converse was sheer joy. Pierre would laugh in his charming, soundless way, his eyes half closed, his big nose pointing up, and his head cocked to one side. They were warm and often touching, those "frères Prévert."

Pierre had acted in Cavalcanti's *Le Petite Chaperon rouge* with Jean Renoir, and he was his assistant in *La Chienne*. "The delightful Pierre Prévert, a character who seemed to have stepped out of *A Midsummer Night's Dream*," was the way Jean described him.[28] He was thin and tall, and was always, like his brother, dressed to the nines, even when they were complete bohemians and hadn't two cents between them. When I knew them in 1946, Jacques looked like a big, well-fed cat. In any case, only Jacques Prévert or a cat could fall from a fifth-story window on the Champs-Elysées and not break its neck. Which is what happened to him one day, inadvertently, while he was talking. . . . He was still talking in a totally Prévertian delirium when he woke up in the hospital and said to the nurse: "You pretty thing, you, you banged me on the head with a silver hammer in the shape of a heart!" He recovered from the accident as a cat would have, and began walking again in short, staccato steps along the streets of Montmartre or St. Paul de Vence or Antibes, telling stories and keeping you awake till four in the morning. Those scenes on the street with the brothers Prévert were like images from his poems.

Sylvia Bataille met him for the first time at the Cyrano, a café on the rue Fontaine in Montmartre where the surrealists used to meet and where she had gone to ask André Breton to inscribe a book. "On my way out, Jacques began talking to me, and we wandered around until four in the morning. Jacques never stopped talking. . . . It was dazzling." She became a member of the October Group. Also part of it were Maurice Baquet, Jacques B. Brunius, Pierre Unik, Jean Dasté, Marcel Duhamel, Paul Grimault, Joseph Kosma, and many others. All members of the far left, they put on plays that we would call "relevant" and went off to factories to perform them. The group belonged to the French Worker's Theater Federation. Lou Bonin, who called himself Tchimoukoff—which really confused the cops who nabbed him one day after some royalists attacked him for tearing down one of their posters—directed the play by Jacques Prévert called *La Bataille de*

---

[28] Jean Renoir, *Ma vie et mes films*, 103.

Fontenoy (*The Battle of Fontenoy*), which they put on in Moscow in 1933 at the World Congress of Workers' Theater.

Two years later, during the winter of 1935–36, Jean Renoir also went to Moscow. He had been invited to show *Toni* at a festival. He went with Marguerite, Claude Renoir, who was his cameraman, and Georges Darnoux, the assistant director. Jean liked bringing Georges along, since he made him laugh. They didn't have much opportunity to laugh, though. Their stay was very tiring, and they didn't have a chance to see much of anything. They were in the USSR for only ten days, and during that time they attended screenings from eight in the morning until late in the evening. Claude Renoir told me that the Russians didn't understand a thing about *Toni*. They had switched reels, and Jean didn't say anything since he didn't want to embarrass them and because he undertook the trip to learn something as a director, not to get applause.

It was the great period in Soviet film, and Jean Renoir really admired the ones he saw as well as the photographs. His small troupe witnessed an attempt at color film, probably *Nightingale, Little Nightingale* by Nicolai Ekk, who had directed a fine film, *Poutievska* (*Road of Life*). But the color would bleed and was sometimes a bit out of sync, so that it did not always follow the contours of the people. In an article he wrote several months afterward, Jean tells how they partied all night long, celebrating the anniversary of the Jewish theater and its gifted actors and so almost missed the showing of *The Youth of Maxim*, the first film of a trilogy by Gregori Kozintsev and Leonid Trauberg. He was very impressed by this film, which marked a big change in acting technique away from the usual theatrical style.[29]

◆

Before leaving for Moscow, Jean Renoir had finished *Le Crime de Monsieur Lange* (*The Crime of Mr. Lange*), shot in twenty-eight days between October and November in 1935. Jacques Becker was hoping to make this film himself. It started from an idea by Jean Castanier, and Becker began looking for a producer. Since he had not yet won his wings as a filmmaker (aside from his functions as Jean's assistant, he had only made two short subjects), André Halley des Fontaines preferred Castanier's other director friend, and Jacques Becker was really hurt. He did not understand why Jean had accepted. In that regard, he did not understand his friend, who more than anything else

---

[29]Jean Renoir, *Ecrits*, 88–90, an article that appeared in *L'Humanité*, July 24, 1936.

just wanted to make movies. Castanier himself did not approve of Becker's bitterness. For him, it was a film by the October Group, and who cares what name was signed on it.

All the members of the group were going to work together. It was to be their second film. In 1932 they had shot a little masterpiece of Prévertian fantasy, *L'affaire est dans le sac* (*It's in the Bag*), directed by Pierre Prévert with screenplay and dialogue by Jacques. *The Crime of M. Lange* was to be made in an atmosphere of harmony and joy. Years later, Jean Renoir, who had forgotten his falling out with Jacques Becker (Becker, in turn, resumed his job as Jean's faithful assistant in *La Vie est à nous* [*It's Our Life*] the following year), wrote that the film reminded him of his house at Meudon and the visits of his friends Koch and Bertolt Brecht. The Germans did not take part in this project, but he had talked it over with them in long walks along the Seine, and their reactions were stimulating. The same goes for his jaunts with Castanier in the forests of Meudon, where on Sunday families forgot their weekday woes and picnicked under the trees; it was their story that they wished to tell. Then Jean Renoir and Castanier would go back to Meudon to write in the studio described by Roland Stragliati, where Jean wrote standing at a drawing table. The house at Meudon was also where Joseph Kosma presented him with the song "Au jour le jour, à la nuit la nuit" ("Let Day Be Day and Night be Night"). He had written the music to words by Jacques Prévert.

Jacques Prévert and Jean collaborated on the screenplay and the dialogue. Jean had known him for a long time. They saw each other often during the shooting of *La Chienne*. Then they lost track of one another a bit, but once Jean became a regular with the October Group, he saw him more often. Until that time, they did not go to the same cafés. Prévert and his group went to Aux Deux Magots, while Jean was a Montmartre loyalist. But he would also move around from time to time, followed by his own gang. The two men appreciated each other but never became close friends. Each was the leader of his own group, and Jacques was a product of surrealism while Jean kept his distance from the movement. As always, he rejected systematic doctrines. The two men never thought of working together. Jean Renoir called Jacques Prévert to the rescue because "the kind of undeveloped hash" that they had thought up, he and Castanier, was much too long. It was a stroke of genius on Jean's part to approach him, and it's a sign of Jean's clearheadedness that he did so. He understood what Prévert could provide. According to André Halley des Fontaines, his participation was not unproblematic. Jacques was always ready to run away and pound the pavements, so they had to shut him up in a study. He would slip finished pages under the door, and they only let him out for meals.

A look at the first version of the screenplay by Jean Renoir and Jean Castanier, entitled *L'Ascension de Monsieur Lange* (*The Ascent of M. Lange*), gives an idea of the extent of Prévert's contribution.[30] He tightened up the story elements and transformed the characters by changing their occupations. For instance, he was responsible for the neat idea of making Florelle a laundress. Jean made good use of the idea, and the women ironing in the shop remind one of Degas. In general, their collaboration was very positive. Prévert knew how to bend to Jean's desire not to be held to the outline and to finalize the dialogue while they were shooting the film. Stimulated by Prévert's inventiveness, Jean was strong and subtle enough to manage it and not let it go beyond the limits of a certain realism.

The Crime of M. Lange is assuredly a Renoir film. Prévert's participation is especially apparent in the dialogue; to understand his contribution to the screenplay you have to compare it to the original version. When sometime later Prévert collaborated with Marcel Carné, the whole film, in form and content, has his mark on it, and it is as though he directed it himself. In *The Crime of M. Lange*, Jean Renoir used a technique of his own devising, and no one was more inventive in that regard than he. His daring means that this film, like *Toni* and *La Chienne* and his other films, was ahead of its time.

One more time, Renoir indulged in the pleasure of shooting a movie for and with his buddies. You can sense how much fun they had, above all, Jean himself, who made Jules Berry, a big star, into a profiteering boss, a swindler, and a gigolo. He is so funny that even though he is the villain you cannot hate him. André Bazin has it right: "Renoir loved this kind of theatrical actor; they are never better than with him. He knew both how to direct them and how to make them completely relaxed" (ibid., p. 43). In *The Crime of M. Lange*, the viewer always has the feeling that Jules Berry is inventing his part, that the words are coming out of him. He is the perfect foil to the others, the "good guys," of the cooperative. The film reflects the hopes of the collective group that took part in its making. Good feelings and social justice triumph in the end. There is also, as in every Renoir film, a profound human dimension. François Truffaut put it well: "*Monsieur*

---

[30] André Bazin, *Jean Renoir*, 154–68.

Lange is the most spontaneous of Renoir's films, the one most crowded with acting and technical miracles, the one most full of pure truth and beauty; one might even say it was touched with grace" (ibid., pp. 233–34).

Many years later, Jean was asked about the way this film was received. He replied: "It was good. I don't think that *The Crime of M. Lange* was a commercial triumph—I'd be surprised to hear it—but it was a successful venture."[31] That was in 1957, and he was embellishing, partly because of the happy memories he had of making it and partly because, at the time that the film came out, on January 24, 1936, at the Auber Palace, he had something else in mind.

[31] Jean Renoir, *Entretiens et propos*, 60.

THE RIGHT TO DREAM

◆

"In my opinion, originality and success are strangers to one another," wrote Jean Renoir.[1] Experience had taught him not to count on the public. Jean-Paul Le Chanois told me that, at the end of 1935, just after the shooting of *The Crime of M. Lange* and before the trip to Moscow, he had gotten a phone call from Louis Aragon. He told him that Jean Renoir had agreed to direct a propaganda film for the PC (the French Communist party) for the legislative elections that were to take place at the end of April 1936. "I am happy to inform you that you will be the film's political supervisor," Aragon added.

A party member could not refuse such a commission, so Le Chanois was going to have to watch over Jean Renoir in order to ensure that he committed no doctrinal errors and didn't stray from the party line. In the film's credits, which, like all those of this period, were added afterwards, Le Chanois and André Zwobada were his co-writers and co-directors, with help from Paul Vaillant-Couturier, editor-in-chief of *L'Humanité,* for the screenplay and Jacques Becker for the direction. In principle, it was a team project, and Jean Renoir did nothing on his own.

Aragon set out to win over Jean Renoir, and he knew how to go about seducing people. He had a lot of class and great charm. After participating in the congress of revolutionary writers in Kharkov in 1930, he had split from the surrealists. As a party official, Aragon was director of the cultural center on the rue Navarin, and his goals were to develop and deploy his skills as a leader. They would come to the

[1] Jean Renoir, *Ma vie et mes films* (Paris, 1974), 119.

fore as soon as he was put in charge of the newspaper. His cultural center was a real meeting place. Jean-Richard Bloch and Pierre Daix were in charge of contacting writers, and Roger Désormières took care of music and musicians. Jean Renoir was invited there and was very well received by open-minded people who understood and loved his work. What's more, the rue Navarin is in Montmartre, not far from the apartment that Jean had at 9, rue des Saules. Jean-Paul Le Chanois also lived nearby, at 108, rue Lepic. He was an actor who had toyed with surrealism, had written his first play with Jacques Prévert, wanted to make movies, and had a small role in *La Chienne*. Unfortunately, his role was part of a sequence that was eventually cut. Jean Renoir knew all of this but had not yet been introduced to the man.

When he went to rue Lepic for the first time, the filmmaker asked him, "So, what are we going to do?" He had been assigned to this young man who had done such a great job of organizing his friends into the October Group, and they had to see how they could work together. "We took a lot of trouble writing the screenplay," Le Chanois told me, "and we showed it to Jacques Duclos, who gave us some advice." Jean Renoir had no desire to feel pushed around, even by a member of the political bureau. He demanded the extensive freedom that he had been promised. His "political superintendent" was a twenty-five-year-old who found the task burdensome. His responsibility was to get this temperamental person, a man who knew what he wanted but didn't appear to, to respect the party orthodoxy. It wasn't going to be easy.

Jean Renoir had accepted the proposition from his Communist friends at the encouragement of Pierre Braunberger. "You don't have a public following; do this and you'll have one overnight. All the militants will follow you hereafter." Braunberger confirmed for me that despite the proof he had already provided of his talent and his extraordinary inventions in the technical realm, in the guild of moviemakers Jean Renoir was still taken for an amateur. The purgatory that lasted no more than two years for New Wave directors lasted for more than ten for the director of *La Nuit du carrefour* and *Boudu Saved from Drowning*.

Success and money were not what motivated Jean to take on this job. Since the municipal elections in May, which had been a clear victory for the Socialists and Communists, the country was moving. The proof was that a film like *The Crime of M. Lange* actually existed and that there was activity in the rue Navarin. Expressions like "the wall of money" and "the two hundred families" had become part of the vocabulary of barroom conversation. People were indignant about the aggression in Ethiopia perpetrated by Mussolini's troops, and there was heated discussion of the confrontations between the rightist Croix de Feu and leftist militants like those of Limoges. They forced the government to take steps and, in December of 1935, to dissolve paramilitary factions. Jean Renoir was unable to forget what he had seen in Berlin with Pierre Braunberger when Hitler came to power. Later on he said: "The Communists were the people most active in the struggle against Hitler in those days, and I thought I should help them a bit."[2]

So despite his basic skepticism, Jean let himself be carried along by the political stance of his friends: Marguerite, who had long ago decided on her religion; Suzanne de Troye, her friend, and Jean Wiener, a pianist from the Boeuf sur le Toit nightclub whom she would soon marry—all of them were party members. Jacques Becker and Pierre Lestringuez were "fellow travelers." All Jean's new friends were either fellow travelers or party militants. Jean liked their enthusiasm, their broad hopes, their Communism dyed in patriotism, and their materialism, which was more sentimental than dialectical. They did not accept the myth of the ogre with a knife in his teeth; they wanted freedom and justice and thought that they prevailed on earth in the land where the October Revolution had taken place. Jean knew them so well that he had expressed their hopes and dreams in *The Crime of M. Lange.* But he also retained his admiration for the author of *Diary of a Chambermaid.* Although Mirbeau had denounced the unbearable egotism of the middle class, whom he blamed for corrupting their servants, he himself had remained fiercely individualistic and identified politically only with the anarchists. Mirbeau's novel, so full of human misery and mediocrity, dogged Renoir all his life. He did not respond in the same way as Mirbeau to the spectacle of society, but he did understand his point of view, a point of view that he presented in masterly fashion when he finally directed *Diary of a Chambermaid* twenty years later.

◆

Early in 1936, Jean Renoir read and got excited about an essay that was not overtly political: a scandal exposed by André Gide in a collection he had edited called *Ne jugez pas . . . (Judge Not . . .).* Renoir wrote three versions of *La Sequestrée,* which was based on the true

---

[2] Léo Braudy, *Jean Renoir: The World of His Films* (Garden City, 1972), 205.

story of a sequestered woman in Poitiers, and he had even chosen a lead for the film: a noted personality of the day, the pale-faced, red-haired, black-sheathed Marianne Oswald, a German-Jewish singer discovered by Jean Cocteau. But without a silent partner to put up some money, he had given up on the project.[3] He had thought of old friends like the Cézannes, with whom he remained close even if, without wanting to, they saw each other less often: "there wasn't enough time." Renée and Paul had not changed. They were mildly aware of the danger but were not directly concerned by it, and since they were not actually prevented from living as they had before, they did so as long as they could. It was their choice to keep their distance and not ask too many questions about what was coming. Jean was sensitive to such feelings, and he understood very well what was happening even in places that he did not often visit. That curiosity of his, which Gabrielle had taught him to use, was always on the alert for the slightest signs. It was rare that he was mistaken about someone's behavior, even that of people who were very unlike him in one way or another.

The movie that the PC wanted to produce for the election campaign was a series of sketches about various segments of society. Jean was not opposed to this formula. It had always been part of his technique to build each scene as a narrative unit, with beginning, middle, and end. Since this was a team project, in addition to his co-writers and co-directors, he had many assistant directors: Jacques Becker, Marc Maurette, Henri Cartier-Bresson, Maurice Lime, Jacques B. Brunius, Pierre Unik, and also six cameramen, including Claude Renoir, Jean-Serge Bourgoin, and Alain Douarinou. Marguerite did the editing.

The understanding was that no one would be paid. Money was collected during meetings. One morning, two men arrived at Le Chanois's place with two potato sacks full of coins. It took a long time to count the money because there was so much of it, about 60,000 francs in all. While they were shooting the film, Jean often invited the whole team to dinner at La Mascotte, a restaurant on the rue des Abbesses. When it came time to pay the bill, he would say with a smile, "The rich should pay." Everyone was won over by this graciousness and good humor. As had been foreseen, he himself had only one episode to direct. There were three in all, aside from the introduction and those parts that were a mixture of news and made-up scenes.

---

[3]Jean Renoir, *Oeuvres de cinéma inédites*, ed. C. Gauteur (Paris, 1981), 21–36.

François Truffaut said this of it: "Even if you see *La Vie est à nous* ("It's Our Life") without knowing it is a Renoir film, it is easy to recognize his manner in the smallest movement of the camera."[4] Marc Maurette told me that Jean supervised the editing of the whole film, which is still of interest today even if its political content seems naive and out of date. Besides the newsreel shots chosen by Jacques Brunius and the speeches of Duclos, Cachin, and Thorez, there are also places where the party directors make statements about the film and the people in it. There is even a sequence in which members of the Croix de Feu are marching past their leader, Colonel de la Rocque, who is dancing all the while. It is a trick shot that Jean Renoir enjoyed as much as Brunius, who thought it up.

They didn't even try to get a censor to pass on *La Vie est à nous* so that it could be shown in theaters. It was only intended as party propaganda. Like *The Crime of M. Lange,* it was a film made in high spirits by a team of technicians and actors who got along well. The list of actors includes almost the whole Renoir gang, amateurs and professionals alike. There they were, ready, like Jean himself, to take part in this new venture that made them no money but defended what they believed in: Pierre Unik, a poet who had gone from surrealism to Communism, played the role of Marcel Cachin's secretary; Charles Blavette, who had had the title role in *Toni,* Jean Dasté, Nadia Sibirskaia, who is so moving in *The Crime of M. Lange,* O'Brady, Marcel Duhamel, Jacques Becker, Jean-Paul Le Chanois, Jacques B. Brunius, and Jean Renoir himself, who plays the boss of the café, a role that he must have enjoyed, since he played it again in *Partie de campagne (A Day in the Country).* At the end of the movie, the whole group takes part in a marching procession and sings the *Internationale.* "A final apotheosis, inspired by shots in workers' films," as Bazin notes (ibid., p. 44); but it is also, like the rest, in Renoir's style. The whole film lasts a little more than an hour.

> Shooting *La Vie est à nous* put me in touch with people who were inspired by a sincere love for the working class. I believed then and still believe in the working class. To me, their rise to power was a possible antidote to our destructive egoism. Now, in the hemisphere in which chance has put me, among the overdeveloped countries, there is no more working class. Along with material prosperity has come spiritual impoverishment. One nail drives out the other; the worker who benefits from middle-class life becomes middle class himself. Nowadays, the real

[4] André Bazin, *Jean Renoir* (Paris, 1971), 234.

proletariat is in the underdeveloped countries. The Brazilian peasant is a member of the proletariat. A General Motors worker is not.

Militant leftists at the time of *La Vie est à nous* were sincerely disinterested people. They were French, with all that means in terms of failings and good points. They had no Russian mysticism or Mediterranean bombast. They were open-minded realists of various leanings, but they were still French. I felt comfortable with them, and we all loved the same popular songs and the same red wine.[5]

These words express the state of mind in which Jean Renoir offered his participation to the PC, and they reflect his views of society at the time.

To be shown at the meetings and fairs organized by the French PC, a film had to get the seal of approval of the Central Committee. That was no small matter, and the film's young political superintendent, Le Chanois, was very worried about the ordeal. At the committee meeting, several members began to express well-founded reservations, as Le Chanois still admitted fifty years later, "but Thorez interrupted them: 'No critiques,' he said, and the film passed." Without taking the trouble to explain them to his colleagues, Thorez knew of the promises Jean had been made, and asking for changes or cuts would have cost them his valued participation. He knew well that Renoir was not about to recite the Stalinist catechism. Moreover, *La Vie est à nous* is, as Georges Sadoul has said, "the first great militant film made in France, and also, incontestably, a work of art."[6]

There was no charge for admission, but the viewers had to subscribe to a new periodical, *Ciné-Liberté*, that had been started by Germaine Dulac, Henri Jeanson, Léon Moussinac, and Jean Renoir. Only a few issues of it were ever published. In the first one, which appeared on May 20, 1936, Renoir had an article on Chaplin's *Modern Times*, which had just come out; for the second, published a month later, he wrote up his ideas about the nationalization of the film industry. He was hostile to the idea, just as he was hostile to the practice of dubbing foreign films, but he wanted to impose a heavy tax on foreign films that were dubbed in order to subsidize French productions.

Ciné-Liberté was also a movie club that met at the rue Navarin and the mouthpiece of the Alliance du cinéma indépendant (Independent Cinema Alliance). Claude Gauteur has published a letter from Jean

[5]"Images," Le Canut, *Jean Renoir cinéaste* (Lyon, 1976), 57.
[6]Georges Sadoul, *Dictionnaire des films* (Paris, 1965).

dated September 26, 1973, according to which, at the club's weekly gatherings, Le Chanois acted as his representative; Jean "only showed up for big meetings."[7] With Le Chanois and others like him as intermediaries, Jean Renoir kept contact with the public that Pierre Braunberger had promised him, and he was already thinking vaguely about another film that could be made under the same conditions, without a producer. Henri Cartier-Bresson told me that the following winter he worked with him on melodrama plots, but he could not remember which ones.

◆

On May 3, the elections were won by a coalition of Radical Socialists, Socialists, and Communists. As a consequence of this victory of the Popular Front, sought for so long by the whole left, Léon Blum was to become prime minister. He was careful to respect the agreements that had been made with his Radical and Communist allies, and he did not want to breach the Republican code. So he awaited the expiration of the mandate of the previous Chamber of Deputies before forming his own government. He sought to respect the existing institutions and refused to throw over the structures of the capitalist regime. Few of his political adversaries gave him credit for it—in general, they were even unaware of his restraint. Léon Blum was very unpopular, and not just with antisemites. An intellectual who was artistic and cultivated, he had no resemblance to the jolly Socialist of caricatures." Instead he was a middle-class renegade like Jaurès, a man whom he admired.

The lame duck Sarraut cabinet had no desire to act, and during the month of May 1936, a sit-down strike movement spread over France and reached every branch of industry and trade. Only the state-run services continued functioning. This complete paralysis of the economy shocked the propertied and producer classes. There were also sit-down strikes that were an attack on the laws of property, and the way they spread seemed strange and suspicious. The strikers were not threatening; they were content to discover the force that comes with numbers and the power of the masses. The Socialists did not want to scare anyone; still less did the Communists. Their demands remained vague: just to be treated better, and after they won the elections, that was assured. The sit-down would have been warning enough. The new regime brought with it new laws and new salaries, that was certain. In the factories and workrooms, a festive atmo-

[7]Claude Gauteur, *Jean Renoir, la double méprise* (Paris, 1980), 44.

sphere prevailed. The October Group had the idea of adding to the fun by putting on *Le Tableau des merveilles (Tableau of Miracles)* by Jacques Prévert "in the religious articles department of the Magasins du Louvre." La Samaritaine and the other department stores followed suit.

Once the government was formed, work was to resume. The PC took a conciliatory stance. Thorez was still preaching compromise. "Everything is not possible," he said in a speech on June 11, in indirect response to an article in *Populaire,* the Socialist daily, which, on the day after the first round of the elections, ran the headline, "Everything is possible," implying that the revolution was at hand. There were no Communists in the government. Maurice Thorez, who had played a big role in the victory of the Popular Front, wanted to bring about unity in France, never an easy goal to reach. There were profound divisions that had existed for too long. Work was only slowly being resumed, even though management had agreed to raise salaries. Laws establishing work rules were also unopposed: workers were provided with fifteen paid holidays, and the work week was limited to forty hours. Those laws remained in force after the fall of the government, which seems never to have gotten itself firmly established.

There were some moments of great public joy. Bastille Day passed as usual, but four days later, the war started in Spain, with Franco's troops rising up against the Republican government. Léon Blum was a pacifist, and he easily aligned himself with the noninterventionist policy of the British government. Since Germany and Italy were aiding Franco's forces, many disapproved of his foreign policy and were not in agreement with his economic policy either. It soon became clear that the Popular Front was not going to last. The opposition, which had at first been caught off guard, rallied. The fascists were becoming more and more dangerous, and the Nazis were gaining strength. Tensions were growing, and the unity of the left was far from complete. What was going on in Spain was a rehearsal for what was going to happen in the rest of Europe. The government of the Popular Front intended to maintain the neutrality that Léon Blum had chosen, but many French volunteers went to the aid of the Spanish Republic with undercover support from those in power. Moscow's halfhearted support for the "Reds" was not brought to light until much later. On the other hand, the French right appeared ready to ally itself with Franco, desiring his victory because it was afraid of seeing Communism get a foothold in Spain.

It was a period of terrible confusion. Some rightist extremists were ready to undertake the basest political escapades, even going so far as to consider legitimate the crimes of the "cagoulards" [hoods], who disguised their assassination attempts so as to impute them to the PC. Terrorist provocateurs, they thought that was the way to arouse the army against the Republic. "We are dancing on a volcano," said Jean Renoir. As usual, though he was living in the midst of people favorable to the Popular Front, he understood very well what the other side was up to and why. And no one expressed it better than he did, in a masterpiece called *La Règle du jeu (Rules of the Game)*. The internal disarray of the middle class was something he knew well. Never would he recover the carefree and joyous elegance that his father loved so much and that he himself also knew how to enjoy. The good fun of large festive gatherings and meals in banquet halls did not displease him, but he also appreciated dinner served by a maître d'hôtel in white gloves.

Marguerite, his companion, had no regrets. Their life, which was very different from the one he led with Catherine, conformed to his habits. The "Little Lion," as she was nicknamed in the movie world, with a ribbon around her neck and her dresses "à la Renoir," looked like one of the painter's models, but she had an occupation and no one thought her a dilettante. She loved her work and Jean's films and was happy that he had made *The Crime of M. Lange* and *La Vie est à nous*. She also enjoyed talking politics with the group or in her family. There was no shortage of topics. Praising Léon Blum was not easy. There was reason to be pleased at the time of the Matignon accords, which raised salaries and increased the buying power of workers, but social reform was soon postponed. The Communists protested heatedly, and they were right, according to Marguerite.

Through her and her family, Jean Renoir met Maurice Thorez, "lay godfather" of Marguerite's niece. Jean Renoir let himself be impressed by the intelligence and charm of this politician. Thorez stayed at Les Collettes with Jean Renoir and Marguerite and the family of Jean's youngest brother, Claude. Thorez in turn asked Jean to be the "lay godfather" of one of his sons. But the friendship that arose spontaneously between the two never had a chance to flower. Their activities were too different. They appreciated one another, and they were always pleased to see each other on the rare occasions that they did so, when they discussed in a good-humored way the most varied subjects, each enjoying the other's breadth of knowledge. Although a Northerner, Thorez loved talking and having a good laugh. But their meetings did not lead Jean to become a card-carrying member of the party. And, though most of his friends did, he did not join one of those committees for antifascist and antiracist writers and artists that were springing up everywhere at the time.

◆

The summer that the Popular Front came to power, Jean was going to carry out a project dear to his heart. He had often discussed it with Pierre Braunberger, his producer-to-be. Both of them loved a short story by Maupassant called "Une partie de campagne" ("A Day in the Country"), and both dreamed about filming it with Sylvia Bataille. The young girl whom Jean had long ago told that she had to wait to be in the movies had become the wife of Georges Bataille. She cropped up in the October Group and was interested in poetry and painting. Her sister was the wife of the painter, André Masson, and much later Sylvia herself became the wife of Jacques Lacan. She was very seductive, and Jean had already filmed her in *The Crime of M. Lange*. Still sensitive to the sound of a voice, he said that he had made the screenplay from the story of Maupassant because of hers. "I found in it things to say that went well with her voice. It was completely improvised."[8] He also wanted to make her a movie with period costumes. The banks of the Seine, where the action is supposed to take place, were crowded with factories, but he found a perfect place to shoot the film near his house at Marlotte, on the banks of the Loing, at a home in the woods where a forest ranger lived. The way Renoir treats the riverine landscapes and the gentle countryside naturally makes one think of the impressionists. But he understood how to exhibit the charms of the countryside around the forest of Fontainebleau without just trying to screen a few Renoirs in black and white.

The history of this film resembles his own, since, not for the first time, what happens on screen and what happens in life strangely intermingle. As during the filming of *La Nuit du carrefour*, there was a lot of rain that summer, too. The team of technicians and actors were all living together in a hotel. Nearby was the ranger's home, adorned for the film's sake with a sign calling it an inn. Weeks passed, good weather did not arrive, and things were getting tense. Jean, who was soon supposed to start another film, would sometimes disappear for the whole day, and people understood that they had better hurry up and get done. Braunberger was in despair; there was not going to be enough money. There were also some lovers' quarrels that everyone

---

[8] Jean Renoir, *Entretiens et propos* (Paris, 1979), 156.

was talking about. As usual, Jean found them funny and did nothing to defuse them. People were living too close to one another to stop at pleasantries. It was a far cry from the brief idyll intended to teach Maupassant's heroine that happiness does indeed exist. There was no innocence in the amorous festivities that were unfolding between the clear days when they shot the film. The film, by the way, featured a rowboat, a swing, fishing rods, and a nightingale, in short, all the accompaniments of a day in the country at the end of the nineteenth century.

The film goes way beyond the anecdote of Maupassant. Sylvia Bataille's character is dramatically emotional, her voice and face expressing first joy and happiness, then the most profound distress. Her beauty and intelligence, and the rare excellence of the other actors, so well chosen and directed, keep the film from becoming sentimental, which would ruin everything. In other words, this short film has a kind of emotional distance that is a crucial part of its success.

That success was not a matter of chance. Whatever he might have said at other times, Jean Renoir, who always knew what he wanted to accomplish, adapted his story and dialogues to the inclement weather, and he knew exactly how to endow the female lead with a classic quality altogether lacking in the story. Henriette–Sylvia Bataille is another victim, another young woman swallowed up by domesticity after having known an afternoon of love that itself ends prematurely in a torrential summer rain. She is all women who botched their lives because they didn't have the means to do otherwise.

For this movie, which lasts only fifty minutes, there were numerous, excellent assistants: Jacques Becker, Yves Allégret, Jacques B. Brunius, Henri Cartier-Bresson, Claude Heymann, and Luchino Visconti, still just a trainee and a prop man. Some have claimed that they shot scenes in this film without Jean Renoir's supervision. Nothing is less certain than that, although we do know that the filming was rudely interrupted after a heated argument between Sylvia Bataille and Jean Renoir, who announced one fine morning that he had to leave to film *Les Bas-Fonds* (*The Lower Depths*). There were at least two scenes to finish that would have to be shot in a studio, and there was no more money. So, like the love of Sylvia Bataille and Georges Darnoux—in the film, mind you—the shooting of *A Day in the Country* came to a sudden end, due in part to the rain and in part to personal tensions that could no longer be contained.

Unlike his heroine, Jean Renoir was not about to give up. He would find a solution later on, when he had the time. Meanwhile, Marguerite could edit what there was. For his part, Pierre Braunberger was convinced that the film had to be made longer, and he asked Jacques Prévert to write the necessary additions to the screenplay. But Jean Renoir did not accept his text, which was too far from what he had in mind. Sylvia Bataille talked to me about it. She said Renoir was right, because Prévert added a character not in the short story who would have made the film unbalanced. In any case, Prévert's dialogues were published later on.[9] Pierre Braunberger was not easily discouraged, so he tried another tack: he asked Michèle Lahaye for a screenplay, and Jean Renoir accepted her work. When Braunberger told me this story, he explained that Jacques Prévert read them his screenplay in a café near the Salle Pleyel, while Michèle Lahaye showed them hers in one near the Flea Market. A whole panorama of life crowded with exciting activities came back to him with his memories of those unpretentious joy-filled bistros. But Braunberger also told me how he suddenly realized that time had passed, that the actors had changed, and that it was impossible to begin filming again.

Jean Renoir seems not to have had time to regret that the film did not make it to the theaters. Other setbacks had inured him. Two scenes were missing: the simplest thing to do was to stop thinking about it, since there was nothing to do anyhow! As always, he was busy, and he couldn't afford to pass up the opportunities he had.

Pierre Braunberger also told me that during the war, when he got out of Drancy, where he was imprisoned in the first wave of arrests of Jews that took place in Paris after the Nazi occupation, he escaped to Saint-Céré, in the Lot district. One day, he had an appointment to meet a woman near the village, at a spot where there was an island in the middle of the river. While he was waiting for the woman to arrive, the Reich division arrived. He dove into the water and hid on the island until no more green uniforms were to be seen. While he was there, all alone, the film of *A Day in the Country* passed before his eyes, as Marguerite had cut it. He remembered each scene, and he said to himself that the thing was just fine the way it was. Once the occupation was over, when he went back to Paris, he found out that the copy edited by Marguerite no longer existed but that the negatives were safe and sound. Jean Renoir agreed to replace the missing scenes with captions. At the time, he was in the United States, and there was no question of his returning. So Marguerite, with the help

[9]In *Art et essai*, May–June 1965.

of her sister, Marinette Cadix, and also Marcel Cravenne, edited the film again. Like Braunberger, she remembered it very well. The only addition, aside from the two captions that represent the missing scenes, is a song of Kosma hummed by Germaine Montero. The film finally had its premiere on May 8, 1946, at the César, and it was an immediate success. It still works today, since it is also a film for our time, as Jean Renoir dimly understood. Beyond his self-doubts, beyond the hunt for producers and the struggle to do what he wanted, he knew that some day his work would be appreciated. Along with the *Rules of the Game, A Day in the Country* is the last of his films in which he took a role. With Marguerite at his side as the servant, he plays an innkeeper, a role that amused him. In the beginning of the film, his son Alain also appears as a young fisherman.

Alain, almost fifteen years old now, was a problem for his father. Being the only son of divorced parents was not a common or comfortable situation in those days. Until 1934, the boy spent most of his time with his grandmother and Marie, his childhood nursemaid, but she had finally put an end to that security by getting married. Losing one's nanny is always a traumatic experience for a child who has already been rejected by his mother, so one can well imagine that Alain felt abandoned. The passing of time did not dull the bitterness of Catherine Hessling, and for her, Alain belonged to the other side. To compensate for all this, Jean spoiled the boy rotten. He adored him, but since he usually didn't have time to show his feelings, he made up for it with gifts. Alain kept on getting toys that he didn't want. His friend Dido was always nearby. They had a continuing and stable relationship that was precious to Alain but just as precious to Dido, who preferred to live in Paris rather than move in with her mother in England or Brazil, where she rarely returned. Frequent trips to carnivals with Alain taught her to shoot so well that she impressed her family one day in Brazil by bringing down a vulture with one shot after all the men of the family had missed it. She and Alain loved this story, but he was getting to the point where friends his own age were a necessity.

He did have Jean-Pierre Cézanne and Jeannot Slade, Gabrielle's son; but unfortunately, most of the time Jeannot was traveling with his parents or in school. After Marie left, it was decided to send Alain to school, and he still has a horrible memory of the high school at Fontainebleau where, as a "new boy," he had to submit to cruelties that he could not deal with. For the same reasons, his memory of the lycée in Versailles that they tried next was no better. Though he spent most of his life with adults, Alain had no notion of how mean their children could be. He missed his two teachers, the priest and the Communist. But Jean Renoir thought that the time had come for him to begin regular studies. Alain had been a student of real life for as long as Jean's own father had allowed him to be; in 1936, he took Alain with him and registered him in the Lycée Condorcet, next to the apartment he had moved into at 105, rue des Dames, on the corner of the rue de Rome. The windows of the apartment looked out on the huge network of aboveground train tracks behind the Gare St. Lazare. Jean Renoir used the view in *La Bête humaine* (*The Beast in Man*), the one from Victoire's apartment, which Séverine uses when she goes to Paris.

It's enough to make a kid dream of playing hooky, all those trains escaping from Paris. It was made clear to Alain that the Lycée Condorcet was the last of the schools he would attend. In that, too, Jean Renoir was thinking of his own childhood. All those schools at which he was equally unhappy didn't teach him much. He developed a taste for reading and learning by observing his father and his father's friends. If it hadn't been for Gabrielle, he would never have passed his baccalaureate. So he knew it was useless to lecture his son, but he did demand two things of him: the first was to eat everything, since doing so was good discipline, which led toward self-mastery and away from self-indulgence; the second was that Alain had to read three works of literature: *Memorable Deeds and Sayings* of Valerius Maximus, *The Good Soldier: Schweik*, by Jaroslav Hašek, and the poems of Georges Fourest. Coming from Jean Renoir, the eclecticism of the list is not surprising, but few boys Alain's age read such books. Alain's acceptance of the two demands, however, did not prevent him from acting like a rebellious child. He skipped classes and was expelled from the lycée in 1937. His father did not reproach him for it, but he did send him off to work at the Pathé factory in Joinville. He also offered him his first motorcycle, a still fondly remembered Royal Enfield.

So Alain's academic career seemed at an end, which did not displease the boy at all. To the exasperating question that people always ask children, he responded good-naturedly that he hadn't the least idea what he wanted to do later on. His father thought he noticed an interest in movies in him. Actually, the only world that he had known since his childhood was movies. Jean-Pierre Cézanne, who was also expelled from school, had one idea in his head: become a magician. His mother was totally opposed to the idea. Pierre Renoir suggested that he become an actor, thinking that it might be a solution to their conflict; the boy seemed talented to him. But Renée Cézanne was against that just as much, and Pierre was very disappointed.

Right before school started in 1936, the Cinémathèque française was founded, "thanks to the backing of (Paul-Auguste) Harlé, director of the industry's journal *La Cinématographie française*. His recommendation was enough to make possible something that had been only a pipe dream until then," as Henri Langlois put it.[10] Langlois signed the enabling documents with Harlé. When it was first founded, "the Cinémathèque française showed the films in its collection in a little theater on the Champs-Elysées that no longer exists, on the second floor of the Marignan building." The budget was limited, but Langlois, who was consumed with a love for film and a passion for collecting, had from the start "laid down the rule that the *complete* works of meritorious directors be preserved."[11] He lusted after the archives of production houses, collecting both silent films and talkies. With the help of his friend, Georges Franju, he gathered up all the pieces of film that he could find, saving copies that would have been destroyed were it not for the two of them. Langlois realized that "the art of film had, in twenty-five years, undergone an evolution parallel to the one that had taken centuries in the plastic arts, from Giotto to Picasso" (ibid., p. 64). From then on he never stopped saving movies. He was the one, in fact, who had saved the negatives of *A Day in the Country*. He was a pioneer and a model for several generations of movielovers and filmmakers. The first time he saw *La Fille de l'eau* and *Nana* was in 1936.

Jean Renoir had not yet met Henri Langlois. At the time of the founding of the Cinémathèque, he was absorbed in a film that could not be more different from *A Day in the Country*. Alexander Kamenka, producer of Films Albatros, whose *Le Brasier ardent* he had much admired long before, had offered him the opportunity to make a film version of Maxim Gorky's *The Lower Depths*. The play had first been performed by the Moscow Art Theater in 1902, and Eugene Zamiatin and Jacques Companeez had made a screenplay from it. Jean was evasive, since he was not sure that Kamenka would allow him to make a film the way he wanted to. Then, after doing some reconnoitering, he set down his conditions: he did not want to situate the play in the plastic Russia of Parisian nightclubs, with gilt and balalaikas, nor

---

[10] *Cahiers du cinéma*, 200–1, April–May 1968, 63.
[11] Richard Roud, *Henri Langlois* (Paris, 1985), 49.

could the actors pretend to be Russians. It would be enough if they kept their Russian names. Also, the action would take place in a non-descript locale. Jean was very excited about this project, since it was his first chance to make a film with Jean Gabin and Louis Jouvet. He had known Jouvet for a long time through his brother, Pierre, but Jouvet's only film was *La Kermesse héroique* (*Festival of Heroes*), directed by Jacques Feyder, in which he played a chaplain, a role that couldn't compare to the one that awaited him in *The Lower Depths*, alongside that movie workhorse, Jean Gabin.

In two weeks' time, with the help of Claude Spaak, Jean Renoir reworked the screenplay and sent it back to Gorky via Zamiatin. Gorky said he was satisfied despite "enormous differences" between his play and the screenplay. He was never able to judge the result, since he died a month later. The film was shot from the end of August to the end of October 1936, in the Eclair studio at Epinay-sur-Seine; the exteriors were shot between Epinay and Saint-Denis.

> To understand the characters in *The Lower Depths* and to be able to portray them in my film, I took long walks in the suburbs of Paris. You know the kind of place: unending gray space dotted with greasy bits of paper and tin cans, dull green geometrical canals with wretched dives along them, sad merry-go-rounds with dull-eyed painted horses turning slowly in the square, and factory chimneys belching smoke into the sky. . . . Strange, tottering shacks crawling with vermin, hopeless thousands of Belgians, both French speaking and Flemish, living off unemployment, since the depression has flushed them from their factories. They're the real lower depths. Among these outcasts, there's a Chinaman, a poetic appendage, sole survivor of the ghetto of his countrymen that had been very populous before bad times began. He's a worthy gentleman, well shaven, wearing an impeccable black jacket and a striped pair of pants. He plays records made in China, records that bring him back to his homeland. . . . do you know what's on his records? Songs like "They Play a Little Belote," a ditty all Shanghai was singing in 1925. . . . That's life. What do we have to do with all that, with our makeup artists and wigs? So instead of inventing the monsters, I went downtown to do my casting, in a murky place near Villeneuve-la-Garenne.

This is Jean's description from an interview he gave.[12] That's how he would work. Meeting someone like the Chinaman was not so unusual for him. He had a knack for finding people. The interest in people

---

[12] *Cinémonde*, October 1936, 417, cited in Claude Gauteur, *Jean Renoir*, 85–86.

that is exhibited in his films was tangible in him in person. Even if he gave the impression of talking nonstop, he knew how to listen and see what was happening around him, and people responded.

◆

The story he tells in *The Lower Depths* is pretty remote from the one in Gorky's play. The change of time and place has something to do with it, but more than anything else it's the personality of Jean Renoir that makes the difference, and with it his view of others. A play written in czarist Russia couldn't reflect the same attitude as a film made in France at the time the Popular Front came to power. The play is desperate and ends with a suicide. But at the end of Renoir's film, Gabin is about to start a new life with the woman he loves, and the very last shot is a wink at Charlie Chaplin. In the film, the character who commits suicide is played by Robert Le Vigan, a great actor who actually did commit suicide. Jean Renoir used him for what he calls "an extremely stylized character to whom I tried to give extremely lyrical words, words that are within an eyelash of being phony."[13] He has him recite some lines of poetry just before he hangs himself, "the lines from *Merchant of Venice* about cherubim and stars that begin with the word 'Jessica.'" And nothing does slip into phoniness or improbability. On the contrary, his real character is revealed. One can see here the passion Jean Renoir brought to his art form. Everything in the film that seems to happen by itself is the result of reflection and deliberate choice. Technique, which he says so little about, was actually of great importance. In this sphere, as in others, he had many fresh, original, and advanced ideas.

Le Vigan's suicide in Renoir's *The Lower Depths* is only a minor event. What is apparent in Renoir and does not even exist in Gorky is a feeling of kinship between the baron, played by Louis Jouvet, and the thief, Jean Gabin. One never lost his human dignity, and the other regains it, while in Gorky, it is a question of the downfall and decay of them both. To keep on comparing the two works would lead nowhere, but I should add that, as usual, when he redoes a work, even if on the surface things seem to diverge a lot, the essential ideas remain intact.

This film did not arouse public enthusiasm. Even so, it won Jean the Louis Delluc prize, founded in memory of the writer and movie director who died in 1924. Renoir was the first to receive the prize.

[13] Jean Renoir, *Entretiens et propos,* 142.

The Lower Depths came out in December 1936 on the Boulevards, in the Max Linder theater. Those who went expecting to see a film of the Gorky play were nonplussed.

A few days later, Jean Renoir gave an interview to *L'Avant-Garde*, a weekly published by the Young Communists Federation.[14] He speaks of his plan to make a film on the French Revolution, a project to be undertaken "with my friends from *Ciné-Liberté*, from the cultural center [the one directed by Aragon], and from the CGT."[15] It was an ambitious idea, and making it happen "will demand a terrific production; we'll need regiments, officers, and we'll show the troop movements; historians will supervise the reenactments. We will succeed!" Farther on, he complains about producers: "They're nothing but businessmen, and they reject anything new." Then, when asked about the CGT, he replies that a film demands a lot of collaborators, a lot of discipline, an idea, and some freedom: all of which, for films, can only be found and be done within the CGT. Today, the future of film lies in the hands of the CGT." To be sure, this last phrase appears in the headline.

At this point, the CGT was, in fact, permitting him to do what he wanted to. There has been much talk about his political involvement, but it was not a matter of a real commitment followed by a disengagement. Of all the interviews he gave, the most politically involved is the one in *L'Avant-Garde*. In it he says, "I admit that I am the victim of my surroundings. I belong to what happens to be around me."[16] Being integrated into his environment did not prevent him from retaining some clearheadedness. Like his father, Jean Renoir remained hostile to ideologies and politics. However, being aware of the dangers of Nazism and being surrounded by friends who were Communists or Communist sympathizers, he agreed to act and suddenly found himself praised to the skies by the party press, which was very eager to win over artists and writers. Henri Jeanson wrote of *The Lower Depths* in *L'Humanité* on December 23: "The Louis Delluc prize is intended to draw public attention to Renoir's whole career, to his whole life as an independent artist." The next day, Georges Sadoul picked up the theme: "The people of our country love Jean Renoir deeply, since they know that this great artist is their true friend, sin-

---

[14] Interview with Jacques Rivette, *Avant-Garde*, 2, 1937, cited in Claude Gauteur, *Jean Renoir*, 41–44.

[15] CGT is the labor union of the French Communist party [*Trans.*].

[16] Interview with Jacques Rivette.

cere and devoted." Sadoul echoes the theme that the party adopted for him, although Jean himself never spoke that way.

As regards the Delluc prize, Jean said, "It's always nice to have a prize." Jean had done without success for a long time, though he was never indifferent to it. This prize, however, was awarded by people whom he thought highly of and whose cause seemed to him just, so it was a special pleasure to receive. Having reached artistic maturity, he was surrounded by young people who believed in a better future, who considered themselves ready to take action, and who also believed in him.

When the Popular Front won the election, he saw all these happy and enthusiastic people elated not out of a desire for profit or from a charge to their egos but from the satisfaction of seeing the working class achieve a better quality of life. Their hope was what dictated the film's conclusion. He did not share that hope, but at the same time he was sympathetic to those who felt it. Later on, he wrote: "Because of these two films (*La Vie est à nous* and *La Marseillaise*) I witnessed the exaltation of the Popular Front. That was a time when French people really thought they were going to love one another. We felt borne on a wave of generosity."[17]

Despite a slight drawl, a self-conscious Paris working class tone of voice, and the right sort of slang, Jean Renoir couldn't pass himself off as a CGT militant. Nor did he want to. His father had taught him to respect manual labor, and he really did. Warm sympathy radiated from him and was felt by anyone who worked with him. André Zwobada tells how, in 1936, Jean Renoir became the hero of the workers in the Francoeur studio, who had his picture pinned up next to Maurice Thorez. Those who knew him then, like those who knew him later, remember a typical gesture of his that he always made on the set, just before beginning to shoot: he would doff his hat as a sign of respect for the work of the actors and the technicians. Everyone appreciated this polite gesture, but he was the only director who did it.

In the beginning of 1937, Jean Renoir was made a Knight of the Legion of Honor. On that occasion, he behaved in the same embarrassed way as his father had. He already had a Military Cross, which was the butt of jokes among his friends, especially Pierre Lestringuez, who got one about the same time as he did. But he was basically very pleased, and receiving this honor from the government of the Popular Front gave it more meaning in his eyes.

[17] Jean Renoir, *Ma vie et mes films,* 114.

Though things went bad quickly for the government, voters on the left held fast to their opinions. Jean Renoir had too many plans in mind to discuss politics. For a long time—for three years, he has said—he had been looking for someone to produce *La Grande Illusion* (*Grand Illusion*). According to Charles Spaak, who wrote the screenplay with him, the search actually began in 1935. It does not matter much. To Jean, it took a long time, and the project would probably have failed if it had not been for Jean Gabin, who usually went with him to woo potential producers. After trying and failing at the big French and foreign production companies, they started on the smaller ones. A picturesque character with a genius for negotiation named Albert Pinkevitch helped them out (ibid., pp. 126–30). He was their go-between with a producer who had been impressed by Gabin's "unshakable confidence." The negotiations were long and difficult, and they almost came undone because of a castle that Jean insisted on using and refused to compromise on. "Just when we thought the deal was struck, a problem about silverware almost queered it. I promised to be satisfied with silver plate" (ibid.). Jean Renoir had a reputation for being expensive when it came to sets and accessories. Details were very important to him.

Fortunately, Pinkevitch understood that. "He was a born negotiator, who knew how to give each of the parties the feeling that he had extracted important concessions from the other side. In fact, Albert was gilding the lily. The concessions extracted were insignificant; the really important ones were hidden in a lot of useless considerations" (ibid., p. 129). The idea of making a war movie dated from the time Jean was filming *Toni*. He went to the air base near Martigues one day to complain about the noise from passing aircraft, and there he found that his old war buddy, Adjutant Pinsard, was the general in charge. Their meeting reminded him of when he was an aviation officer and Pinsard an ace pilot. Seven times Pinsard's plane had been hit, but each time he had succeeded in making it back to allied lines; he had also saved Jean's life several times by protecting him during his photo reconnaissance missions, when his chicken coop of a plane made a nice target for enemy aircraft. During the shooting of *Toni*, these two old friends dined together often. Jean took notes, thinking that Pinsard's escape stories might make a good film.

Those notes stayed in his file boxes for some time. Then he called on Charles Spaak to help him build a screenplay around the escapes and the tales of life in prison camps, where men of different social backgrounds are forced to live side by side. The first version underwent big changes when the producer, Raymond Blondy, realized that Erich von Stroheim had just arrived in France and wanted to resume his acting career. Jean Renoir had always admired Stroheim as a director, and he immediately thought that the role of the commandant of the prison could be modified to suit such an extravagant character.

The story of their first meeting has often been told, and one can well imagine these two men together, so different one from the other: Jean Renoir, always relaxed, wearing a worn blue suit that had been bought ready-made, and Erich von Stroheim, as chic as can be, with diamonds on his fingers and a golden bracelet on his wrist, declaring in a burst of theatrical collegiality, "For you, sir, whatever you desire!" Jean Renoir, moved by this artist he considered a past master, offered him a cigarette and started fumbling through his pockets for his old tinder lighter, whereupon Stroheim immediately produced a gold one of the latest design. Stroheim adored uniforms, and he selected every detail of his. In order to make his character in the film even more imposing, he had the idea of putting on an orthopedic corset that featured a chin rest. Jean approved.

But storms were brewing.

> During the very first shots of *Grand Illusion,* Stroheim was unbearable. We had an argument about the scene in the beginning, the one in the German shack. He refused to understand why I hadn't put what he called Viennese-style whores in the scene. I was beside myself. My complete admiration for this great man put me in an impossible position. That I was making movies at all was due in part to my enthusiasm for his work as a filmmaker. For me, *Greed* is the pinnacle of my profession. My idol was standing in front of me, he was even an actor in my film, and instead of the oracle whose truth I hung upon, I discovered a creature knee-deep in silly conventions. I understood very well that in his hands such conventions became strokes of genius. Bad taste is often an inspiration to the greatest artists. Cézanne and Van Gogh, for instance, did not have good taste (ibid., p. 151).

Jean was so deeply disturbed by this violent quarrel that he began to cry, and when Stroheim also began welling up, they fell into each other's arms. Stroheim promised to be cooperative, and he kept his word, or at least he tried to.

There was another memorable encounter, this time with Koch:

> During the shooting of *Grand Illusion,* the team had moved into an inn near the castle in Alsace. The innkeeper was also a wine grower, and he quenched our thirsts with an especially nice little white wine, but it was

a treacherous one. Koch began criticizing Stroheim for the lavish dress of the actress who was playing his nurse in the film. Their quarrel turned nasty, with Stroheim defending the artist's right to transform reality, and Koch remarking that Stroheim hadn't fought in the war and so would do better to shut up. Stroheim was hurt, and responded by calling Koch a petit-bourgeois. It was a gratuitous insult, since in spirit Koch was a true aristocrat. He wanted to get up and have it out with Stroheim, who stopped him with a gesture inspired by the heroes of his films, then got up and made his way to the door. Koch, enraged, threw his glass at the head of his enemy. The glass arrived a few seconds too late and broke to bits on the door behind which Stroheim had just disappeared. Almost immediately the door opened again, to reveal Stroheim smiling broadly at his joke. He held another glass in his hand, which he offered to the dumbfounded Koch (ibid., pp. 149–50).

You had to know Koch. "Stroheim was his idol." But in the end, there were no lasting consequences to these conflicts, and Jean remained friends with Stroheim once the filming was over.

♦

Françoise Giroud remembers that the two of them spoke German during the shooting. Bazin tells us that Stroheim–Rauffenstein speaks English to his prisoner, Fresnay–Boeldieu. The two officers recognize each other immediately as belonging to the same class. For Jean Gabin, who plays the proletarian officer, Jean Renoir had dug up his old aviator's uniform, and he had this actor, whom he admired so much, wear his own tunic. He was sufficiently virile and also sensitive enough to allow himself these gestures of masculine friendship in which beauty and seduction play a part. Gabin was the kind of man he would have liked to be. There was no ambiguity in his feelings, nor any jealousy. On the contrary, he "adored" Gabin, whose success with women delighted Jean. Jean enjoyed admitting that he had been seduced, but at the same time, he never tried to discover if his own charm was effective. His father always used to tell him that he shouldn't waste time with women. For Jean, they were above all a subject of conversation with his peers. Most of the time, it was just a lot of talk. Gabin's conquests made him laugh, but basically he adapted himself very well to the situation. In his friend's shoes, he would have grown bored very quickly. In this sphere as well, he was a strange mixture. As with his father, his work was more important than anything else. Moreover, he had doubts about his ability to seduce anyone, he ate too much, drank too much, was gaining weight, dressed badly, and, to the delight of others, seemed unaware of his charm. Great talker that he was, he never confided about his private life, but it became clear that the break with Catherine Hessling had marked the end of his season of passion. On the other hand, the mother image represented by Gabrielle had made him exigent: because of her, he was a stranger to machismo, and he only liked intelligent women. He knew how to listen to them and recognize their good points. On the other hand, he really enjoyed talk that would make a sailor blush, though there was nothing vulgar about what he would say. Gabin's lower-class side pleased him a lot. He never got tired of hearing him sing "Quand on s'promène au bord de l'eau" ("When we walk on the seashore"), a song from a film by Julien Duvivier called *La Belle Equipe* ("The Good Team"). His friend's Parisian accent filled him with wonder, while he criticized Jacques Becker and Henri Cartier-Bresson for "talking teu-teu." Neither of them knew what that meant, and his imitation of their way of speaking didn't enlighten them either, though it did make them laugh.

The role of the aristocratic career officer, Captain de Boeldieu, went to Pierre Fresnay. Pierre-Richard Willm and Louis Jouvet had been sounded out for it. Fresnay is so perfect in the role that it is hard to imagine what others might have done. Jouvet was busy, and Pierre Richard-Willm wrote to Spaak that he found the role uninteresting. The character did not develop, he preferred the role of Maréchal (Gabin's), and better throw Boeldieu in the dungeon!![18] They had not planned on Dalio either, so his role had to be rewritten during the shooting, with the help of Albert Pinkevitch, whose advice Jean had specifically requested. Pinkevitch spoke amazing French, "a mixture of slang and grammatical purity."[19] On top of which he was nuts about cheap puns. He was Jean's inspiration for the poacher played by Julien Carette.

Jean Renoir kept on asking the same questions, and he tried answering them by observation and with the help of advice from many people. According to him, everyone on his team had a specialty, sometimes without even knowing what it was. His wish was to create human characters who were not stereotypes. For him, this particular film represents his experience of war. He had been thinking about it for a long time, since the way war was presented in the movies had nothing whatever to do with what he had known. Inspired by General Pinsard, he chose to tell stories of prisoners and escapes.

[18] This from a letter sent me by M. Michel Richard.
[19] Jean Renoir, *Ma vie et mes films*, 130.

As always, he wanted to portray individuals. Each of them carries a world around inside and so reacts in his or her own special way, and all of them are so plausible that the public became excited—the big public, the one that Jean had never really reached before. As François Truffaut wrote in his preface to an edition of the script: "If Jean Renoir's career wasn't always an easy one, that is because his work always highlighted the characters rather than their dramatic settings. In *Grand Illusion*, the action unfolds in two prison camps, so the powerful setting that the public always hankers for is built in; anything can happen in a prison camp, in which even the tiniest actions of daily life can take on the intensity of extraordinary disasters. For such reasons, the public accepted and appreciated in *Grand Illusion* many aspects of Renoir's style that it had rejected or snubbed in earlier films: the changes of tone, the taste for generalities in dialogue, the paradoxes, and above all a strong sense of the strange aspects of daily life, what Jean called 'reality's magic.'"[20]

The film came out in June 1937 at the Marivaux, on the Boulevards. It was also shown at the Venice Festival that same year, but the jury did not dare award it the Grand Prize. It "invented a consolation prize," as Truffaut notes: the prize for best artistic ensemble. The movie was banned in Belgium by Paul-Henri Spaak, Foreign Affairs Minister and the co-writer's brother, and also in Italy by Mussolini. In Germany, Goering appreciated it but Goebbels had all the scenes in which the Jewish character is attractive cut from the film, then banned it completely. He called it "public cinematographic enemy number one." On the day the Germans entered Vienna, *Grand Illusion* was playing in a theater. The show was immediately stopped and never resumed. On the other hand, that same year, 1938, in New York, Jean's work won the National Board of Review prize as the best foreign film. It showed as an exclusive for twenty-six weeks, and Roosevelt said of it, "Every democratic person should see this film."

The success of *Grand Illusion* should have brought an end to the long purgatory that Jean had been going through, but he didn't count on it. The future seemed more and more unpromising. As usual, you had to live a day at a time and profit from the picturesque and the pleasant that life sent your way. A spectator wrote Jean that he appreciated *Grand Illusion* but that Rauffenstein would never have shot Boeldieu with that kind of a revolver since it was impossible to kill someone at that distance with a firearm like that. Jean was interested and met the author of the letter, Antoine Corteggiani, an amateur ad-

[20] Jean Renoir, *Le Grand Illusion*, Bibliothèque des classiques du cinéma (Paris, 1974).

venturer who loved the desert and had crossed the Sahara on a Scott motorcycle with a three-cylinder, water-cooled, two-stroke engine. Jean loved such stories, and Corteggiani had many to tell. Alain, too, soon became fascinated: "I loved old firearms, I used to have an antique revolver," he told me. "Corteggiani was a devotee of historical and popular mechanics. For instance, he could describe, draw, take apart, and put together every firearm since Agincourt, every single one," recalls Jean.[21] When he met him, they were almost ready to start shooting *La Marseillaise*. Corteggiani was soon promoted to assistant director in charge of all troop movements in the film. "For example, the changing of the guard at Versailles happened exactly as in the film." The luck that brought him Tony Corteggiani delighted Jean even more than his public success, since he could actually use it for something worthwhile in his films.

[21] Jean Renoir, *Entretiens et propos,* 84.

DANCING

ON A VOLCANO

◆

Starting on March 4, 1937, Jean wrote a column every Wednesday in *Ce soir (Tonight)*, the Communist daily edited by Louis Aragon and Jean-Richard Bloch. They had offered him this pulpit from which he was free to express himself on any subject that caught his attention. The first column was called "A Plea for Laziness."[1] He wrote with amazing facility in a simple and lively style that gave inklings of a great and as yet undeveloped talent. The columns are interesting, since they reflect what was on his mind at the time, and they reveal his acute powers of observation. Several of them are called "Bourgeois Manias." They tell stories that reveal the penchant of well-heeled Frenchmen for saving little things, like matches and lumps of sugar. He also speaks of his affection for Germany, of the Germans who are his best friends, though he never misses a chance to condemn Nazism. "More than One Germany," is another of his titles. He had a strong sense of the ridiculous and a funny way of bringing out the grotesque side of dangerous puppets like Hitler and Mussolini. In another article, he compares the disaster of the zeppelin *Hindenburg* to "these other victims of Hitler, the people of Guernica."[2] He also deplores the silliness and vulgarity of music hall shows. There is an underlying good humor in his spirited columns, which are free of

[1] Jean Renoir, *Ecrits, 1926–1971*, ed. C. Gauteur (Paris, 1974), 96.
[2] Ibid., p. 112, article of May 20, 1937.

partisan exaggeration. Sometimes their author shows a cynical side, which saves him from the tedium of niceness. Incidentally, Jean Renoir wasn't the only nonparty member to whom the editors of *Ce soir* gave carte blanche. Jean Cocteau, the singer Yvette Guilbert, Jules Rivet, and writers like Lise Deharme and Luc Durtain also had weekly columns.[3]

When he began writing for the daily, Jean Renoir was already busy preparing for *La Marseillaise,* but the more work, the better. Out of friendship for Joris Ivens, the Dutch director, he agreed in 1937 to write and record by himself the commentary for *Terre d'Espagne* (*The Spanish Earth*), while Ernest Hemingway did the same in English. For Jean, documentaries were "the phoniest kind of movie." To him, the only way to get to the heart of a subject was to recreate it. Taking Erich von Stroheim's *Folies des femmes* (*Foolish Wives*) as his point of departure, he wrote: "Stroheim taught me a lot of things. Perhaps the most important is that reality only has value when it is transformed. In other words, an artist exists only when he succeeds in creating his own little world."[4] But Joris Ivens, one of the founders of cinéma-vérité, was a far cry from Stroheim. A disciple of Vertov, he wanted to bear witness to a country being torn apart by civil war. Renoir's commentary is much less politicized than Hemingway's, which had the director's approval, and the English version is the one generally used. In Renoir's case, his commentary was the profound reaction of a man sensitive to the rootedness of peasants in their land rather than to the political line, even though he, too, was strongly affected by the Spanish Civil War, the divisions that it caused in the French left, and the atrocities it brought about, which he saw as inevitable.

La Marseillaise, which was his main preoccupation at the time, was not supposed to be a film like his others, but "the first film made for and by the people (ibid.). The idea was to finance it by public subscription and have a C.G.T. cooperative produce the film. An announcement appeared in the July 31, 1937, issue of *L'Humanité:* "*La Marseillaise,* directed by Jean Renoir, whose sponsors are MM. Chautemps, Zay, Sarraut, Blum, Jouhaux, Frachon, Cachin, Paul-Boncour, Thorez, Bracke, Jacques Duclos, Basch, Aragon, etc., will be a landmark in the history of film. Support the production by subscribing at two francs each, exchangeable for the price of a ticket when the film is shown in theaters."[5] A big meeting organized at Huyghens Hall was

---

[3] Claude Gauteur, *Jean Renoir, la double méprise* (Paris, 1980), 18.
[4] *L'Humanité,* August 11, 1937, cited in Claude Gauteur, *Jean Renoir,* 32.
[5] Cited in Claude Gauteur, *Jean Renoir,* 32.

chaired by Jean Zay, with Vaillant-Couturier, Léon Jouhaux, Pierre Cot, Léo Lagrange, Jacques Duclos, Germaine Dulac, Henri Jeanson, Jean Renoir, and five thousand others, to raise the money.

Blum's government fell on June 21, less than a month after the opening of the International Exposition in Paris, from which the Popular Front had hoped to gain much in the way of propaganda. The Exposition had been delayed by a strike of construction workers during a spring marked by severe social disturbances, in particular the shootings at Clichy. There the government had refused to stop a demonstration by the party of Colonel de la Rocque—the local government was Communist, and its deputy, a Socialist. There was a counterdemonstration that resulted in five dead and five hundred injured. It was a far cry from the euphoria of the previous year. That had died down on February 13, 1937, when Léon Blum officially proclaimed the "pause" that he had given intimations of since the end of the year. The pause was in fact the abandonment of social reforms like retirement for older workers, a sliding salary scale, and national unemployment funds and a return to free-market economics that had nothing at all to do with socialism. The first *Marseillaise* project was a victim of this political reversal of the Blum government.

On February 2, 1937, Jean Renoir gave an interview to Georges Cravenne for the newspaper *Paris-Soir*,[6] and he still thought the film would receive "the complete, total, absolute support of the government." Besides the distribution of 1,500,000 subscriptions at two francs apiece that was already planned, the government was to provide the director with a reimbursable sum of fifty thousand francs to "get things started and to pay for advance publicity." The film was supposed to be ready for showing at the International Exposition, whose subtitle was "Arts and Techniques." The army was going to take part "in reconstructing the battle of Valmy, with technical assistance from qualified officers." It was also supposed to send trucks to transport extras and even to provide mobile kitchens to feed all the people involved. The government had also approved the use of the palace at Versailles and some objects from the national museums.

What a fairy tale! In the midst of all these promises, Georges Cravenne adds that Jean was counting on the participation of famous authors of the day, like Henri Jeanson, Marcel Achard, H.-R. Lenormand, J.-R. Bloch, and Marcel Pagnol; of composers like Roger Désormières, Arthur Honegger, Georges Auric, Darius Milhaud, Joseph Kosma, and Jacques Ibert. Then there were the actors: Jean

---

[6]Reprinted in *Image et son*, 268, February 1973, 24–26.

Gabin, Erich von Stroheim, Louis Jouvet. His brother Pierre would have played Brissot, a journalist who was a member of the Jacobins' club and a deputy in the Legislative Assembly. And Maurice Chevalier was going to sing the Marseillaise! It's hard to imagine what film Jean had in mind to make with such a hodgepodge. The reality was very different, and looked a lot like the way Jean usually made films.

He wrote the script with his friend Karl Koch, who "understood well the German side of Marie-Antoinette and everything about the German influence in the royal court."[7] Koch also taught him a mass of details about the daily life and manners at Versailles. Jean prized him greatly, and he realized that Koch, with his admirable logic and rigor, was having an effect on his own way of thinking. Koch had marshaled his friends to research information they needed. Tony Corteggiani was responsible for the weapons and troop movements, and Nina Martel-Dreyfus, a young American, for other historical research. Jean-Paul Dreyfus, who was her husband at the time, told me proudly that she spoke six languages and had studied ancient Greek. It was hard to say what inspired the woman more, her research or the company of Jean Renoir, who found her winsome. Marc Maurette, an assistant director of the film, remembers having spent many days at the Mazarine Library or the Bibliothèque nationale. "You, go to the BN and copy down all the speeches of the Legislative Assembly that you think are interesting," was Jean's charge to him on days when the industrious Nina was occupied with other things.

Pretty soon, Jean realized that the official help he would actually receive was less than what he had gotten from the Historical Film Society to shoot *Le Tournoi dans la cité*. It was out of the question to make the film at Versailles, so he had to make do with Fontainebleau. The shooting didn't begin until August of 1937, well after the inauguration of the International Exposition. The PC press did its best to support the undertaking, but despite articles, tracts, and posters, the money from subscriptions was quickly swallowed up, and the cooperative in the hands of the CGT turned into a regular production company.

◆

Well before it was finished, the film, whose title was supposed to be *La Révolution française,* aroused debate, even though at that point neither the right nor the left knew how Jean would treat his subject! There was talk of a great historical fresco. In the interview with Cravenne, the battle of Valmy comes up, and the issue of who would play

[7] Jean Renoir, *Entretiens et propos* (Paris, 1979), 84.

Brissot, but in an interview with Roger Régent that took place when the shooting had just begun, Jean had changed things around. So that the film would last less than a week, he decided to abandon the great figures as subjects and

> concentrate instead on the man in the street. . . . What I want to show . . . is the greatness of individuals in the midst of a collective act. We have kept the character of the king. He is even very important. But we idealize him in a certain way and have him express, as faithfully as possible, the ideas that all his partisans held in those days. The principles of the Revolution will take shape in this light.
>
> I would be lying if I said that, in this ideological struggle, I remain impartial. I'm shooting La Marseillaise with the firmest of convictions: what I want is to make a partisan film in good faith.[8]

In a way that was not customary for him, Jean worked on the basis of solid documentation that had been obtained for him through the devoted toil of his friends. His specific plan was to recreate, day by day, the major events but also the little ones, like the journey of a batallion of men from Marseille to Paris, where they arrived on the eve of the signing of the Brunswick Manifesto and then took part in the assault on the Tuileries on August 10, 1972. His goal was also to be well informed about the way people lived, not just the revolutionaries and their families and friends but also the court, the king and the queen, their immediate entourage, and also the aristocrats who had already chosen exile.

When Jean speaks of this period in interviews, he is like a contemporary historian. He knew tiny details of daily life in the various social classes, both in Paris and the provinces; also the fine points of etiquette and the taste in food of both king and people. Everything that gives depth to characters was within his grasp. He knew ten times as much as he let on, and it was useful knowledge. One can sense it working throughout the film, and it makes the images on the screen believable even for the viewer who is unfamiliar with the life of that time.

Despite its solid base, the film is often disconcerting. Many leftists felt irritated by it: the king is a nice guy, the exiles in Koblenz seem more pathetic than despicable. Only Marie-Antoinette was "a beautiful bitch," as François Truffaut describes her.[9] When the film came out on February 9, 1938, it was greeted in Ce soir with an article

---

[8] Pour vous, August 12, 1937, 456, cited in Claude Gauteur, Image et son, 268, February 1973, 22.

[9] Andre Bazin, Jean Renoir (Paris, 1971), 240.

(dated the following day) by Aragon at the top of his form. "Jean Renoir's great miracle—which by its mere existence shows up Hollywood-style "reconstructions" for academic fakery—is that despite the costumes and sets and the theme of La Marseillaise, he has made a film so current and powerful, so human, that you are taken, carried away, swept off for more than two hours, as though it were our own life that was at issue. And, in fact, it is." That's the way the first paragraph ends. Farther down, it continues: "Greatness and disarray, the pettiness of family life intermingled with tragic moments at the dawn of a new world, brief moments whose grandeur dwarfs the most famous psychological novels. In the avenue of the Tuileries, the dauphin can't keep from playing with dead leaves." Aragon had understood everything Jean intended and invented as a filmmaker. It must have pleased him to read his words. Truly, Aragon understood as well as anyone what Jean wanted to do, but their friendship did not last.

The right booed this film. Some writers admired it, like Alexandre Arnoux in Les Nouvelles littéraires,[10] while others, like Roger Leenhardt, criticized its faulty construction.[11] Two friends, Marcel Achard and Henri Jeanson, also criticized it. The first distinguishes between the director and the partisan.[12] The second violently berates the film for its pervasive pro-Communist stance. Both of these men had hoped to help write the screenplay.

The way Jean Renoir reveals himself in this film is interesting. There can be no doubt about his sincerity. But his characters are not black or white. He often wrote of what his stint in the cavalry had taught him: that no horse's coat is all white or all black. People aren't divided into the good guys and the bad. Each person has a redeeming quality, and he always discovered it. It's an important point about the man and the artist. Jean sometimes let himself get carried away by his loyalty to free revolutionary thought, and he went so far as to use the exaggerated vocabulary of his militant friends. Sometimes they would call people fascists who were really fascists, but at other times the term was used for people whose ideas were not in agreement with the party line.

In an interview, Marcel Carné said it wasn't enough for Jean to make up a spoonerism at the expense of his Quai des brumes (Port

[10] February 19, 1938, in Image et son, 268, February 1973, 61.

[11] Esprit, March 1, 1938; Image et son, 268, February 1973, 54–55.

[12] Marianne, February 16, 1938; Image et son, 268, February 1973, 64–65.

in Fog); he went so far as to accuse the film of being fascist. When Jacques Prévert warned him, "Say it again and I'll bust your face," Jean answered. "You know how I am, I only meant that the characters are fascist at the core."[13] It was a funny way to patch things up, but that is the way they left it. There were no fisticuffs between the partners of *The Crime of M. Lange*. It is also worth remembering that not long before this, there had been the anathemas of the surrealists. Going from one extreme to the next, less than two years later, people in the Vichy government accused *Quai des brumes*, the story of a sentimental deserter, of having cost the French the war.

In the screenplay of *Quai des brumes*, taken from a novel by Pierre MacOrlan, the dialogue is Prévertian, and, as a whole, the film's poetic realism is far too literary for Renoir. There was also the fact that Jacques Prévert and his gang at the Deux Magots were considered to be Trotskyites. Calling it *Cul des brèmes* (a vulgar pun on *Quai des Brumes*) was Jean's way of having fun with language; so was his use of the term fascist. It is the Jean Renoir who lets himself go with the current, like the cork that his father used to speak of. He repeated what he heard around him, and even added a bit to it, but he knew nothing about moderation or shutting up. He was not political "at the core."

◆

At certain points, Jean was ready to give up, according to Le Chanois. Even his articles in *Ce soir* were burdensome. But Marguerite, Jacques Becker, Lestringuez, and Thorez himself brought him back to his senses. Frotunately, in his work, he never let himself get caught up in the madness around him. Discussions with friends, statements to the press, even the quarrels, were all unimportant. The only things that mattered were the movies.

He expresses his love for the movies by way of his admiration for an individual in an article entitled "Homage to Elie Faure."[14] Jean was brought back to his own past by the death of an old man who knew how to keep alive the enthusiasm that young people feel for what is new in art or in thought. Elie Faure was a friend of his father's—he was one of the first to understand his late style of painting—and Jean had not forgotten the strong emotion he felt upon discovering that Faure had written about movies, in particular, about Charlie Chaplin. "It was the first time that such a "serious" writer, a universally re-

---

[13] *Les Cahiers de la cinémathèque*, 5, Winter 1972; *Image et son*, 268, February 1973, 73.
[14] *Europe*, 180, December 15, 1937, reprinted in Jean Renoir, *Ecrits*, 187–88.

spected philosopher, deigned to think about the profession that already had an unbeatable attraction for me. When I say "deigned," I mean what others would have said. Elie Faure never "deigned" to do anything. He went at things with all his heart and soul." Once freed from the noise of politics, Jean Renoir found his true voice.

At the time of the second World Youth Congress that took place at Vassar College in Poughkeepsie, New York, from August 15 to 24, 1938, Jean Renoir's name occurs in the minutes of the meetings of a committee in charge of compiling a list of anti-American activities.[15] The reason was that he wrote for the *Cahiers de la jeunesse*, a periodical published by Luc Durtain and Paul Nizan and edited by Georges Dudach. Jean had indeed responded to two inquiries in the journal: one about young people in movies,[16] the other on the question, "Does France have a mission?" which he answered from the point of view of film.[17] Aside from Jean, among other participants in *Cahiers de la jeunesse* who made the list were Romain Rolland, Jacques Madaule, Henry de Montherlant, André Malraux, Alexis Tolstoï, Raphaël Alberti, André Chamson, Jean Cassou, René Lalou, Julian Huxley, Jean Painlevé, and Marcel Carné. Not all of them are Communists, but they are all antifascists who were not afraid to associate with Communists. At the time, that was the position of most intellectuals of the left, at least in France. The truth about what was going on in Moscow at the time was not known, and the extent of Stalin's purges from 1936 to 1938 wasn't clear until the de-Stalinization period. Yet already in 1938, Americans were frightened of Communist infiltration. Fortunately for Jean Renoir, his name occurred on no other list of the commission.

With the spring of 1938 came the announcement of the end of the Popular Front after a short-lived second Blum government was formed at the time of the invasion of Austria by the Nazis. A month later, Hitler was threatening Czechoslovakia, and President Benes was having difficulty dealing with the trouble stirred up by the Nazis in the Sudetenland. Faced with these dangers, the far left gave a vote of confidence to the Daladier government, having decided to maintain a united front against fascism. But that wasn't going to work either, as became clear at the time of Munich.

◆

[15] "Hearings before a special committee on un-American activities," *Congressional Record*, 75th Congress, 3rd Session, August, 1938, 17.

[16] *Cahiers de la jeunesse*, 2, September, 1937.

[17] *Cahiers de la jeunesse*, 12, July 15, 1938.

La Marseillaise marks the end of Jean Renoir's honeymoon with the PC. There was no sudden rupture. He was recovering his autonomy little by little. Like his father, he was a complete individualist. Friends were there for distraction and for the teamwork that provides support and good times. But he could never accept a mentor, nor did he need one. While he was making *Grand Illusion* in 1936, he took Françoise Giroud, who was working on the movie, to hear Maurice Thorez. She found him "bewitching. . . . He was Jean Gabin and dialectic, too."[18] So he asked her, why not join the party? He himself had often been asked the same question and had always found a way to say no; which does not mean that he was not interested in what was going on.

In an unpublished article shown to me by Claude Gauteur, Jean reports a parallel drawn by his friend Karl Koch between Hitler and the "Schpountz," a Marcel Pagnol character in the film of the same name. The article was probably written in April 1938, when the film came out. Koch understood very well Hitler's story, and his "ideas," as Jean Renoir calls them, about the megalomania of the Schpountz seem to be a good explanation of the führer's; the hideous disaster that would soon result could already be foreseen.

The films that Jean Renoir wished to make had only a distant relationship to the political situation, except for the first one, whose plot summary he deposited with the Screenwriters Guild on January 8, 1938, entitled *Les Sauveteurs* (*The Saviors*, a "provisional title"). "We are on the verge of an international war," is the first phrase of his text.[19] First, in an expression of solidarity among peoples, war ships from opposing sides go to the aid of a ship in danger. Then war breaks out, with the helping and helped ships ready to fight one another. This idea of people with common interests having to fight against each other haunted Jean Renoir since his service in World War I. Another synopsis, *Les Millions d'Arlequin* (*Harlequin's Millions*), was filed three times, on March 24, April 9, and May 8 of 1938. It consisted of three different episodes in a story about an inheritance in the south of France. "Jean Renoir has invented the ménage à quatre," is François Truffaut's comment. The film's heroine is courted by three suitors at once. Jean hoped to make his film with Erich von Stroheim, Pierre Fresnay and his wife, Yvonne Printemps, along with the other stars from *La Marseillaise*, Louis Jouvet and Pierre Renoir. ("After that one, we decided to always stick together."[20]) He also had another, com-

---

[18] Françoise Giroud, *Si je mens* (Paris, 1972).
[19] Jean Renoir, *Oeuvres de cinéma inédites*, ed. C. Gauteur (Paris, 1981), 37.
[20] *Ce soir*, April 4, 1938, in Jean Renoir, *Ecrits*, 163.

pletely different film ready to go, *Histoires d'enfants* (*Children's Stories*), whose theme is still not out of date: it was about children who become delinquent as a result of miserable family situations and poverty.

None of these plans came to fruition, but because of *Les Millions d'Arlequin*, Jean for the first time took leave of his readers in *Ce soir*. He addressed them directly:

> When you see a show that makes you indignant or makes you laugh, you feel an irresistible urge to share your indignation or your laughter with friends. That is what I am able to do with you, my readers. It's a great thing. The only fly in the ointment is that I can't see you, and I don't know how you're reacting. I am not a writer, I am just a guy who doesn't know how to resist the temptation to tell a good story. But when I tell it to people I can see and touch, I swear it's a lot better. I can feel the effects, I see what works, I can lean on what I think is interesting or funny. It's a lot easier. And then I can "play" the story, like an actor, and punctuate it with hand gestures and winks and funny faces.[21]

This paragraph is typical of the tone and also of an important side of this man, who loved to laugh and be pleasing. He interrupted his column from April 14 to June 30, 1938, then stopped writing it permanently on October 7 of the same year.

◆

Amid all these uncertain plans, still thinking that *A Day in the Country* was unfinished and that there was no way to fix it, Jean got a surprising offer: Did he want to direct *La Bête humaine* with Jean Gabin in the role of Lantier? He had to decide quickly. Gabin, at the height of his career, wanted to live out a dream of his childhood; he wanted to drive a train. At first, they were looking at a screenplay called *Train d'enfer* (*Train from Hell*), but Jean Grémillon, the director, had given up on it. Since Gabin wanted a role as an engineer, Roger Hakim, his producer, thought of the Zola novel. A version by Roger Martin du Gard, who had just won the Nobel prize, was available, but it was too long, so Jean got inspired and wrote another one in twelve days.

Before he started the work, he had forgotten the book, but he did remember Zola visiting his father. He was so dark that he reminded Jean of an Arab. "He was a very kindly man, there was a smell of grease and leather about him. . . . he was really nice, and he brought me candy."[22] It's possible that Monet's painting, *La Gare Saint-Lazare*, inspired Jean. He must have thought of it often when he lived in the

[21] Jean Renoir, *Ecrits*, 162–63.
[22] Michel Ciment, "Entretiens avec Jean Renoir," *Positif*, 173, September, 1975, 16.

apartment on the rue de Rome whose windows looked out on the network of tracks behind the station. He had moved from there only recently, to a less spectacular spot, 7, avenue Frochot.

At the time that Zola wrote *La Bête humaine,* four years before Jean was born, the progress of science and engineering still had that sheen of novelty. "I think that any human creation is beautiful at first. Civilizations are magnificent in their early stages. Excuse me if I repeat myself, but I'm always citing the case of Greek civilization, of the little statuettes found at Mycenae, products of the oldest period of Greek civilization which are so grand, so marvellous" (ibid.), said Jean, who also thought that the appeal of the first films was due to the same phenomenon. He found in Zola "amazement at the technology of the time, appreciation of locomotives and the poetry of the train" (ibid., p. 17). And also of poetry itself.

> There's a certain phrase that attracted me and that is probably the reason why I made *La Bête humaine.* It really got to me. I found it in the chapter where Gabin, that is, Lantier, has a date with Séverine in the park. They meet there and he is so taken by the young woman's beauty that he can't say a word, he looks at her, and then she breaks the silence with the following words: "Don't look at me like that, you'll wear out your eyes." I find that so beautiful, and I said to myself that I had to make a movie in which you could put a phrase like that (ibid.).

François Truffaut also mentioned to me that reply of hers. I just saw the film again, without him; he was already suffering from the terrible disease that killed him a few months later, and I would sometimes stop by to give him my still fresh impressions of the films I had seen or the people I had spoken with. Bringing up memories of his friend transfigured him; his face lost for a moment the mark of death that was upon it. It was wonderful to see that he could still experience such joy.

Trains and poetry, which are not antithetical, dominate the film that Jean Renoir constructed as simply as a tragedy, "inspired by the novel of Emile Zola," as the credits put it. The writer-director set aside everything that was not directly related to the story of the love and death of Lantier and Séverine.

According to the notes of Emile Zola that he consulted, "Jacques Lantier is as interesting to us as Oedipus the King. This train engineer was under a cloud as dark as that of any member of the House of Atreus."[23] The producers, Robert Hakim and his brother, wanted

---

[23] *Cinémonde,* 529, December 7, 1938, in Jean Renoir, *Ecrits,* 264.

Gina Manès, the great tragic actress of the day, in the role of Séverine. But they allowed themselves to be convinced when Jean Renoir shared with them his desire to cast Simone Simon in the role.

> Séverine is not a "vamp." She's a cat, a real cat, with a silky coat that begs to be caressed, a short little snout, a big, slightly beseeching mouth and eyes full of promises. . . . There's another reason that made me ask Simone Simon if she wanted to act in my film: she has talent, and the kind of talent that most affects me. . . . It is discreet, and for that reason strong. She slides over effects, she's modest, she never tries too hard, and for that reason, she knew how to be my dear Séverine, that strange little character who is at once passive and destructive. They become a tiny center of the world, those women whose Louis XV heels are dogged by disaster.[24]

On August 8, 1938, Jean Renoir and Jean Gabin went to Le Havre to greet Simone Simon, who was returning on the liner *Normandie* in order to film *La Bête humaine*. "In America, without knowing what I had in mind, she herself thought about the role and dreamed of playing it," Jean tells us.[25]

Full of energy, Jean called in two articles to *Ce soir* (for August 9 and August 10, 1938) about waiting for and meeting Simone Simon, who was arriving from Hollywood. From the looks of it, he was bewitched by her, and Jean Gabin soon would be. Simone Simon is so extraordinary in the role that it is hard to imagine another Séverine. She asked to read her lines, so Jean gave her a text that, as usual, he would change a lot, usually to restore Zola's dialogue, since it seemed to him to suit the voice and bearing of the young woman. So as not to make a film with costumes and an antique locomotive, which would have diverted the viewer's attention, Jean transposed the film from the date of the novel, 1869, to 1938.

Before beginning to shoot, they had to get some familiarity with the world of the railroad. The administration of the SNCF [French National Railroad] and the Fédération des Cheminots [railroad union] provided "extraordinary facilities" to the production company. For several weeks, Gabin led the life of an express train engineer. He learned how to drive a train, and at the same time, Julien Charette became a true stoker, learning how to break coal and fill the firebox. Jean Renoir, Simone Simon, and Fernand Ledoux, who played the role of Roubaud, Séverine's husband, also lived at Le Havre, in order

---

[24] *Cinémonde*, 537, February 1, 1939, in Jean Renoir, *Ecrits*, 268–69.
[25] *Cinémonde*, 529, December 7, 1938, in Jean Renoir, *Ecrits*, 265.

to get better acquainted with the environment in which the film was to take place.

For the actual filming, the SNCF let them have an unused stretch of track. "We used two locomotives to get up to top speed more quickly. Behind them was a platform for the lighting and the generator, and behind it were two passenger cars that we used as dressing rooms for the artists and technicians. There was no trick photography for the speed."[26] Except for the final shot, in which Jean Gabin jumps from the tender to kill himself, which was shot in front of a fake backdrop, and with good reason, all the other shots were made on location. That caused some problems:

> My nephew Claude almost lost his life there. You remember, in the first sequence, there is a view of a tunnel. Suddenly you're in the dark, and you can just see a point of light in the distance, and it gets bigger as the train comes to the exit. The sequence was shot as if it was seen by Gabin, who looks out the side of the locomotive through the little window in front of him there. So we put Claude, my nephew and cameraman, outside the train, attached to the sides of the locomotive with his camera held in place by a little wooden jig that was made for the purpose. But it had been set a little bit too high, so that Claude realized at the last minute that the camera was going to be ripped away by a corner of the tunnel wall. He just had the time to duck, and the thing was smashed to bits before his eyes. We had built a true rolling studio on the train (ibid.).

Claude Renoir told me that it was his uncle who had attached him to the locomotive. He had his left arm free, and since he was wearing a leather jacket, he was too hot, but he didn't dare move even his hand for fear of catching himself on the tunnel wall.

This way of shooting a film recalls the good old days in the attic of the Théâtre du Vieux-Colombier with Jean Tedesco. Jean Renoir was having fun, and he hadn't changed, nor would he ever change. Which is to say that he would never stop inventing, and that his films are always experiments.

The idea of shooting this sequence in the tunnel of Bonnières as seen by Gabin was a new one, but no one has dwelt on such details because innovations like it are typical of Renoir's way of filming. In his day, there were no portable, hand-held cameras as there are nowadays. They worked with the 120 Parvo (ibid.). It wasn't always possible to record the sound directly. You had to put the microphones in places that the camera couldn't reach. In this film, the sounds and the

---

[26]Michel Ciment, "Entretiens avec Jean Renoir," *Positif*, 173, September 1975, 19–20.

music by Kosma are extremely well mixed. In general, it was especially demanding to make, and the team was, as usual, homogeneous: there are five Renoirs in the credits, including Jean, writer and director, Marguerite, editor, Claude (brother), assistant director, Claude (nephew), cameraman, and Alain, assistant cameraman-in-training. It was Alain's very first job. The other assistant cameraman, Guy Ferrier, was Jean Gabin's nephew. Kurt Courant, just arrived from Germany, was director of photography, and Suzanne de Troye was assistant director and editor of the railway sequences. Eugène Lourié designed the sets, and Sam Levin was the set photographer.

Jean Renoir was also among the actors in the film. He plays Cabuche, a free spirit, a marginal fellow who is unfairly condemned to death because justice demands that someone be responsible for the perfect crime committed by Roubaud. In Zola, Cabuche is a quarry worker, but in the film a poacher, because of Jean's predilection for poachers. Like Pappa Poulain in *A Day in the Country*, Cabuche resembles Jean too much. He is so unconvincing that one hardly takes offense at the judicial error. Jean Gabin is no longer around to ask if the realization of his childhood dream brought him the joy he'd hoped for, but the Louison, his locomotive, is one of the main characters in this exceptional film, the shooting of which ended around the time of Munich.

The Munich pact was signed on September 29, 1938. The week that preceded and the days that followed left a bitter taste in France. The nightmare was not dispelled, only postponed. The joy on the street when Daladier returned barely hid a tangible malaise. Yet the press was more or less unanimous in its invitation to rejoice. The Communists were the only ones to oppose the agreements, and Jean Renoir, in his last weekly column for *Ce soir*, without leaving off the "joking" tone he had adopted, did not mince words:

> Did you see them, those fat, smiling, self-satisfied faces, those pretty double chins, those greasy rolls of flesh at the napes of their necks, and those uniforms? The most handsome was Goering. If I had been Daladier or Chamberlain, the humble representatives of our self-proclaimed democracies in that sideshow, I'd have felt a little humiliated. When you've decided to go for a big laugh, you should really go all out, and not stop at silly principles about clothes or other nonsense that only inhibit the representatives of our old middle classes. To hell with Emily Post and her good manners!
>
> So the Germans are going into the towns of the Sudetenland. Will our papers publish the pictures as they did for Vienna, of the nice jokes that the Nazis are certainly going to play on the Jews in these regions? Will

we see again old men washing sidewalks with their knees in the mud? Or women forced to walk on the streets wearing ignominious signs around their necks? In short, will we again be indirect and distant witnesses to those jokes that the Nazis play so readily and with such finesse at the expense of those whom they have defeated?[27]

La Bête humaine came out just before Christmas in the Cinéma de la Madeleine, where it had an exclusive run for thirteen weeks. It was a great success in those troubled times, but Jean Renoir was too preoccupied to get any pleasure from it. On January 26, 1939, Barcelona fell into the hands of the fascists. A month later, the Daladier government recognized the Franco régime. And everywhere the Nazi menace was growing every day.

◆

After La Marseillaise, Jacques Becker had decided to work on his own, while remaining Jean's close friend. That is why you would search in vain for his name among the credits for La Bête humaine. The man who did not succeed in getting himself taken seriously by the producer of The Crime of M. Lange got the chance, at the beginning of 1939, to direct L'Or du Cristobal ("Cristobal's Gold") from a screenplay by Karl Koch based on the T'Serstevens novel. Dita Parlo, Georges Peclet, Paul Temps, and Léo Larive, actors in Jean Renoir's films, took part in this work, and Marguerite was supposed to have edited it. Claude Beylie wrote of it: "In the newspapers of the day, it says 'dialogue and technical supervision by Jean Renoir.' Indeed, Renoir did write a first draft with dialogue (the text has been preserved) [Beylie neglects to say where] but it seems to have been left by the roadside. Perhaps Becker used it for inspiration, but he directed the film on his own."[28] They ran out of money in the middle of filming and had to stop; later on, still during the war, they started up again, but with another producer, and Jean Stelli finished it and got credit for it. At the time, Jacques Becker had been drafted.

Claude Beylie mentions other projects that never saw the light of day: in 1938, Jean wrote, in collaboration with Erich von Stroheim, a screenplay called La Couronne de fer (The Steel Crown) based on La Toison d'or (The Golden Fleece) by Joseph Kessel. He and Jacques Becker are said to have written "an original, unpublished screenplay" from Erich von Stroheim's La Dame blanche (The White Lady). Le Baron de Crac is another one from 1939. Jean Renoir was to have directed this film

---

[27] Ce soir, October 7, 1938, in Jean Renoir, Ecrits, 178.
[28] L'Avant-Scène cinéma, "Spécial Renoir," 251–52, July 1–15, 1980.

with a screenplay by Hans Richter and dialogue by Jacques Prévert, Jacques B. Brunius, and Maurice Henry. Jean is also supposed to have done a version of *La Grande Menterie* (*The Big Lie*), a regional novel by André Suarnet, from Provins (just east of Paris), which describes the life of the claydiggers (ibid.). However, Claude Gauteur found no trace of these scripts in the archives of the Compagnie Jean Renoir, and Madame Anne de Saint-Phalle confirmed this to me. But Gauteur discovered two others from 1939: both of them take place in North Africa. One is called *Amphitryon* and the other is a *Romeo and Juliet* under various names: *Ida, Tibi, Artus,* and *Le Crime de la 'Gloire Dieu.'* At first it was situated in Paris and Burgundy, but it was restored to its original title, *Romeo and Juliet,* in May 1939, when Jean had finished shooting *Rules of the Game.* He did not know how his film would be received, so he wanted to go away and to revisit North Africa, which he had discovered 10 years earlier during the shooting of *Bled.*[29] We already know how easy it was for him to invent or reinvent film synopses. The Paris archives and those of Dido Renoir have an incredible number of film projects. But in the spring of 1939, he knew that this desire to leave was a fantasy. He still played around with the idea, revealing it in successive interviews with Maurice Bessy,[30] Jacques Berland,[31] and Pierre Barlatier.[32]

◆

During this same period, while the Western democracies were trying to convince themselves that the Munich agreements were safeguards of peace and when French society was coming unglued under the pressure of its internally divided parties, Jean Renoir felt the need to express his anxiety by imagining what he called "a happy drama." After the exceptional feelings of brotherhood during the Popular Front and films full of good humor and hope fulfilled, from *The Crime of M. Lange* and *La Vie est à nous* to *La Marseillaise,* Jean stopped and began asking himself questions. Which authors do we like? Those whose work has some relationship with what we are going through. As Proust put it, "You can only speak of yourself." That is all we know. Jean was about to do a strange, new thing with film, but without completely realizing that he was. He was not about to relate his life's story, but to express what he felt in that sad year and the way he

---

[29] Jean Renoir, *Ecrits,* 63–78.
[30] *Cinémonde,* April 5, 1939, cited in Claude Gauteur, *Jean Renoir,* 155.
[31] *Cinémonde,* May 17, 1939, cited in Claude Gauteur, *Jean Renoir,* 156.
[32] *Ce soir,* July 8, 1939, cited in Claude Gauteur, *Jean Renoir,* 156.

saw those around him. He reread the eighteenth-century classics, like Beaumarchais and Marivaux, his old friends.

Even before he finished making *La Bête humaine*, Jean started thinking about *Rules of the Game*. He tells us that it started with his listening to French baroque music. "I began a time of my life when my usual companions were Couperin, Rameau, and everyone from Lully to Grétry. Little by little, my idea took shape and the subject got simpler. I kept living on baroque rhythms, and after a few more days, the subject became more and more precise."[33] He saw contemporary characters "moving to the spirit of that music." Naturally, Simone Simon was among them. He saw her on the set every day, and he imagined her doing a very different dance from the memorable one of the railroad men in *La Bête humaine*. He wanted to make her into a lady of the manor. He was thinking of some of his friends, "for whom lovers' intrigues appeared to be their only interest in life" (ibid., p. 154), and he kept imagining, along with one of his "ménages à quatre," a transformation of Alfred de Musset's comedy, *Les Caprices de Marianne* (*Marianne's Caprices*).

Sologne, the place where he decided to make his new film, was dazzling: "Its fogs took me back to those great days of my childhood when I went with Gabrielle to the Montmartre theater to see *Jack Sheppard ou les chevaliers du brouillard* (*Jack Sheppard, or The Knights of the Mist*). Nothing is more mysterious than this countryside emerging from the mist" (ibid., p. 155). He took pleasure in the beauty of that landscape, and he remembered how his father regretted that he had been unable to paint it. In that time of crisis, he needed more than ever to escape from the humdrum and find something new.

In his eagerness to get back to work, he did not wait for the success of *La Bête humaine*, which might have led producers to him. He had not forgotten the endless trouble he went to in order to scrape up the cash to make *Grand Illusion*. Now, there was no time to lose. He was sure of it, and at the same time, he couldn't keep himself from devising long-term projects. With some friends, he decided to form a production company, the NEF (Nouvelle édition française, "New French Editions"), which moved into 18, rue la Grange-Batelière in rooms that were sublet from Marcel Pagnol's film production company. There were five associates: Jean's brother Claude, André Zwobada, Olivier Billiou, whom he had met at Hakim Bros., Camille François, a schoolmate of Jean's who wrote songs and lived at Renée Cézanne's, and Jean himself. They each put up 10,000 francs and

[33] Jean Renoir, *Ma vie et mes films* (Paris, 1974), 154.

formed a cooperative that was supposed to produce two films a year. Jean Renoir wanted to create a sort of French equivalent of United Artists, the associated artists of Hollywood. He contacted René Clair, Julien Duvivier, Jean Gabin, and Simone Simon, and all gave him their consent in principle. Starting on December 8, 1938, Georges Cravenne, who was press attaché for *Rules of the Game*, began reporting in *Paris-Soir* that Marcel Pagnol and Jean Renoir were about to sign an agreement and acquire exclusive rights to a large theater where they would only show "the films that they would direct from then on."[34]

◆

In January 1939, Jean Renoir went to London to speak to the London Film Institute Society. During the trip he met Robert Flaherty. He had seen *Moana* "maybe twenty times," and *Nanook* "was a great moment in my life, and an important one." The two men understood each other like brothers. The great American director had a huge studio in Chelsea at the time, and Jean would never forget the evening he spent in it. It was just behind a little chapel that had been destroyed by the bombardments. A group of Irish revolutionaries was there talking with Flaherty about Ireland's destiny and putting away large quantities of Irish whiskey. They had to go to the Café Royal to buy some chicken pies to feed this gang. When they came back with them, they had to turn around and go get some more, along with more whiskey, since more famished and thirsty Irishmen had arrived while they were away.[35] His meeting with Flaherty was the major event of his trip. In his speech, Jean talked about dubbing, which he heatedly disapproved of. He also brought up his plans for a production company and said, "If these cooperatives work, it'll be the end of all the schemes that you have to use in France to make a film.[36]

When he came back from London, it was time for him to shut himself up somewhere and write his script. In an interview that he gave Marguerite Busset, from *Pour vous*,[37] just when he was leaving, he said he didn't know whether he'd go to the Fontainebleau Forest or to Burgundy. He cultivated this kind of freedom because it was necessary for his work. Unforeseen changes and last-minute decisions were a part of his life at the time, and his companion, Marguerite,

---

[34] Claude Gauteur, *Jean Renoir,* 157.

[35] Text of an interview with Gilcher Bachman in 1951, shared with me by Alexander Sesonske.

[36] *La Cinématographie française,* 1060, February 24, 1939, cited in Claude Gauteur, *Jean Renoir,* 157.

[37] Cited in André Bazin, *Jean Renoir,* 182–85.

could hardly intervene. She had to figure out why and let him do it his way. In the past, Gabrielle indulged his whims, and since then he had not felt the need to get rid of them.

In the end he set himself up at his home in Marlotte, as usual, and he made up several versions of the screenplay. He wanted to tell the story of people dancing on a volcano. Simone Simon rejected the role of the lady of the manor, which had been written specifically for her, after asking for payment that was beyond the means of the NEF. Camille François suggested Michèle Alfa. Zwobada told me he went with Jean and Marguerite to the theater to watch this much-talked-about actress in her debut role. But that evening the only woman Jean was looking at was a young one sitting in a box. He had found his lady of the manor: she was a true princess who had fled Austria because her husband, Prince Starhemberg, had founded an anti-Nazi party with his peasants. They had just moved to Paris. Jean was delighted. She was younger than the role. Under the name Nora Gregor, she had done some theater, and she had had a part in *Michael*, a film that Dreyer shot in Germany in 1924. She hardly spoke French, but what did it matter! He would revise the script, that's all. She was the perfect person for the role. Zwobada tells how, in his enthusiasm for her, Jean Renoir went from a bar near the bal Tabarin, where he often went with his friends, to dinner at Maxim's. Marguerite, who took part in these expeditions along with the prince, bought herself a dress for the occasion. Jean Renoir himself made an effort to dress well, a rare event.

The more one looks, the stranger the birth of this film seems. There are ceaseless changes. The actors withdraw or slip away, always for some reason or other. Because of his theatrical duties, Pierre Renoir wouldn't even hear of shooting on location at La Motte-Beuvron for weeks on end. His role was supposed to be Octave. Jean thought of Michel Simon, but it was too late. Like Simone Simon, Jean Gabin refused the role he was offered, but Roland Toutain accepted it. Claude Dauphin wouldn't play the princess's husband; Marcel Dalio, who was Rosenthal in *Grand Illusion*, took the part, and Gaston Modot, who also had a role in *Grand Illusion*, played a role originally intended for Fernand Ledoux. Actors and roles were not the only things that changed; so did the names of the characters, sometimes in the same version of the script. If a character's first name did not change, the spelling of the last name would usually change instead!

After reading several versions of the screenplay, one can see how this clever man took cues from the look of his actors to recreate characters, to invent a past for them along with their tastes and occupations. Each one could identify with his or her role without appearing to act. We have already seen evidence of the importance he attached to the work of the actors and his technique of "breaking them in gently," as Gaston Modot put it; later on Modot wrote,

> Is it a question of genes? He works like a painter, in intimate contact with his theme. He lies in wait for it with his actors. Weeks before the shooting, depending on the role he has in mind for them, he sets them up in a printing factory or puts them on board a locomotive or sends them out in hunting parties in Sologne with poachers and wardens.
>
> The actor takes a real bath in it and undergoes a complete life change. Soon he knows how to handle a rotary press or conduct a train or lay nets and beat bushes. He speaks the lingo of his trade. His gestures are a specialist's gestures, not some pale imitation, and he's wearing his own costume, not someone else's.
>
> What results! One day, Carette, the poacher, and I, the warden, are chatting in the main square of a village in the Sologne; a man drives up in a car and asks us for directions, not doubting for a minute that we're local guys. So with his best Parisian accent, Carette answers, "Better ask a yokel from this dump, buddy, 'cause we ain't from around here!"[38]

Where does Octave come from? His name is a reminder of *Les Caprices de Marianne*. But Octave is also Mirbeau's first name, another strange character whom Renoir admired. After being deserted by Pierre, the director realized that he did not need to beg himself to take the role. "Ever since I finished my period of technical games and disregard for actors, one of my most stubborn dreams has been to be an actor," he wrote, without further explanation.[39] He changed the role, as he did all the others. But this autobiographical film betrays no confidences about its author. Jean Renoir disguised himself as a bear for the ball of his princess—a marquess in the film—and he really makes one think of a big, honey-loving bear. Tender, a little shy, he twists and turns and catches others in their secrets. To secure his place as the eternal guest, he offers joy and kindness, but he remains deeply melancholic—to please women, it seems—unhappy because he is a failure, a person used to compromise, which will in fact allow him to survive, in contrast to Jurieu the pure. Like Coelio in *Les Caprices de Marianne*, Jurieu will find death as the victim of his own distrust, rolled up in a ball like the rabbit shot dead in the famous hunting sequence.

---

[38] *Ciné Club*, 6, April 1948, provided by Claude Gauteur.
[39] Jean Renoir, *Ma vie et mes films*, 250.

Jean Renoir was not Octave. If he had not been a genius, though, he could have become him. Taking the easy way out is often the fate of the children of famous parents, who become convinced that they are incapable of doing as well as their mother or father. Jean knew all about Octave, just as he knew all about the other characters. He knew that the slaughter of rabbits and pheasants prefigures the death of men. War was inevitable, and he was thinking about it all the time now.

He left for La Motte-Beuvon on February 15, 1939, with his whole troop. Koch and Zwobada, who had helped write the script, were his assistants, as well as Henri Cartier-Bresson. Tony Corteggiani, indispensable as an adviser for the hunting scenes, was also an actor this time, and Alain Renoir, who had become one of the two assistant cameramen for Bachelet, asked him endless questions if he was not talking with Corteggiani about firearms and motorcycles. Dido Freire, his childhood companion, had been hired on as a script girl. Thinking of their stay at the Hotel Rat still makes Henri Cartier-Bresson laugh. Despite the bad weather—it rained as it had rained at Marlotte when they were making *A Day in the Country*—high spirits prevailed. The actors soaked up the spirit of the countryside, played cards, and chatted among themselves while Jean put the finishing touches on his screenplay. As usual, he filled in the spoken dialogue during the shooting. Madame Rat, the innkeeper, was shocked: Carette asked her to serve him a shot in the men's room, since his wife would not let him drink and he did not want to make a scene.

Georges Sadoul, who came to Sologne to observe the shooting,[40] remarked on the harmony between the stars and the technicians. On Sunday, the electricians invited Renoir and his actors to lunch. The following Sunday, they returned the favor.

They waited for days and days for the weather to clear up, but it never happened. If Jean lost patience, it was not because of the weather, though; it was because of his mistake in becoming infatuated with Nora Gregor. She could not play any character at all and was getting more and more depressed as she sensed the director's disappointment. There was no way to turn back the clock. The only cure was to give the husband's mistress and the chambermaid bigger roles.

> Cœurs sensibles, cœurs fidèles
> Qui blâmez l'amour léger

---

[40] *Regards,* May 11, 1939.

Cessez vos plaintes cruelles,
Est-ce un crime de changer?[41]

After the credits, a placard displays this citation from *The Marriage of Figaro*. They "flutter about," like love according to Beaumarchais, perhaps until they get dizzy. Actors easily forget the world around them, but in 1939, that was not possible. The partial mobilization of March 16 called them back to reality, as did the entry of German troops into Bohemia and the formation by the Slovaks of a satellite state of the Reich. The Munich accords were broken before the film was complete.

It was already clear that this film was not going to be cheap. Jean's partners were not surprised; they had foreseen that their estimates would be exceeded. While he was working at Marlotte, they found some money through friends and by getting advances on the foreign sales contracts. They thought that *Rules of the Game* would need a budget of 2,500,000 francs, which would make it the most expensive production in France for 1939.[42] There was no need to be frightened. Encouraged by the success of *Grand Illusion*, they could expect that everything would turn out all right. Even *La Marseillaise* had found its public in Moscow, where it was shown starting on May 13 in the twelve best theaters. It drew seven million viewers in the space of two weeks. Two hundred fifty prints were sent to the big cities and industrial centers.[43]

Jean Renoir had wanted to shoot his film in color. According to a letter from Dido Freire to Robert Flaherty dated February 14, 1939, the superb colors of Sologne in winter were especially tempting to him. He tried to arrange for Technicolor to pay for all costs beyond the usual price of black and white. But since the shooting started a week later, Jean was sure there was not enough time to get an answer from them. He was completely dependent on the unexpected funds raised by Camille François and Olivier Billiou. Yet it soon became clear that they would not be enough either. Their stay in Sologne lasted longer than expected; meanwhile, a double set was waiting for them at the Pathé studios in Joinville. The décor by Eugène Lourié and Max Douy was superb, with real parquet floors and real doors, authentic furniture and silverware. The wind-up toys that Marcel Dalio's character

[41] "Sensitive and faithful hearts, you who find fault with fickle love, cease your cruel complaints. Is it a crime to change?" [*Trans.*]

[42] According to Philippe Esnault in *L'Avant-Scène*, 52, October 1, 1965.

[43] Claude Gauteur, *Jean Renoir*, 19–20.

collects were expensive, as was the big hurdy-gurdy, which they also found in Germany. For the shots at the Château la Ferté-Sainte-Aubin, Jean Renoir had all the shutters removed because he felt that they ruined the facade. But he was satisfied with the sets designed by Lourié and Douy. He entrusted the shooting of the scenes of the massacre of the rabbits to Zwobada and Corteggiani. They had to sacrifice hundreds of animals and work for two months to obtain the result.

"Zwo," as he was called, also was in charge of another project: getting Jean Jay, a director at Gaumont who had managed the successful distribution of *La Bête humaine,* to provide an advance of two million francs on the rights that he would have to pay to include the *Rules of the Game* in his circuit. He allowed himself to be convinced, but he was not often to be found on the set or at the rushes. He did not like Jean Renoir's acting, and he wanted him to cut the character of Octave.

Jay was neither right nor wrong. It is not easy to disassociate Octave from Jean Renoir. He is no longer the amateur recognizable beneath a disguise like Cabuche in *La Bête humaine,* since Octave moves and speaks like Jean Renoir. He does not spoil the film; in fact the opposite happens. You accept him with curiosity and sympathy, and he has such presence, not necessarily as an actor but as a person, that you look on in fascination without knowing whether it is Octave or Jean Renoir commenting on this suicidal society and offering a kind of farewell to what he loved and hated at the same time.

In the end, the film cost more than five million francs, very expensive for those days. During the shooting, Jean Renoir was hoping the film would be shown at the International Exposition in New York that year. It was a dream that had to be abandoned. *Rules of the Game* had its premiere on July 11 at the Colisée and the Aubert-Palace. Viewers from the boulevards of Paris understood nothing and joked about such a senseless film. They were disappointed. The Champs-Elysées audiences could not stand the mirror being held up to them, a feeling that they expressed by whistling vehemently. Some worthy gentlemen went so far as to put matches to their newspapers and almost set the theater on fire. Jean Renoir was appalled. He had not foreseen such a setback. He tells us that after *La Bête humaine,* he wanted to get away from naturalism and to make a "classic and poetic" film. Henri Cartier-Bresson stressed that "Jean couldn't stand those messages," but formula films were not his style either. After so many different experiences and with his constant desire not to mine just one vein but to take new risks every time and to create, with each new subject, a new means of expressing it, he had invented a world of film. This film's unaccustomed form and the ethical stance of its director were both disturbing to the public. A new kind of movie, it was the work of a single auteur who thought up the story, the way to cut it, the dialogue, the shots, the soundtrack, and how the actors should play their roles. More than twenty years later, François Truffaut wrote, "It isn't an accident that *Rules of the Game* inspired a large number of young people who had first thought of expressing themselves as novelists to take up careers as filmmakers." There are an extraordinary number of critiques and commentaries on it. "It is the credo of movielovers, the film of films, the film most hated when it was made and most appreciated afterwards, to the extent that it ultimately became a true commercial success."[44]

To understand why the film was so violently rejected, one should return to the atmosphere of tension in that summer of 1939, when the French and the British were trying to make an alliance with Moscow and Poland was already being directly threatened. It was clear then that the pacifists were simply playing into the Nazis' hands. Still, no one wanted a new war. But despite the danger from without, right and left were as opposed as ever. For the public on the Champs-Elysées, Jean Renoir remained the man who made *La Marseillaise,* and his latest film seemed even more scandalous, since it was a representation of society in 1939. He became a scapegoat, like the politicians of the Popular Front, and he hadn't even thought about political rancor and was expecting a warm reception! Here he was again, on the verge of financial ruin, and his friends would never again see the money that they had invested in him. It was a real disaster. He asked Marguerite and Zwobada to go to the theaters and literally cut the scenes that were causing an uproar. Soon the film was only 85 minutes long. After Marguerite had edited it the first time, it was 113 minutes long. Jean Jay had her put it back to 100 minutes "to avoid a commercial disaster."[45]

The press was less wild than the public. Claude Gauteur has collected and categorized the major reviews. By his count, twelve were "unqualifiedly unfavorable," thirteen "favorable with reservations," and ten "favorable." After coming out of the Colisée, when René Clair, who was bringing him home to avenue Frochot, asked him

---

[44]François Truffaut, *Les Films de ma vie* (Paris, 1975), 60–61.
[45]According to Philippe Esnault, "Le jeu de la vérité," in *L'Avant-Scène cinéma,* 52, December 1, 1965.

what he wanted to do, Jean Renoir answered, "I don't care." It is an unconvincing answer; he was not a man who could forget a film in which he had invested so much, but he had forgotten that when you are completely sincere, people do not always understand. He wanted to run away. It was impossible for him to stay in Paris, to face his friends, and to keep on thinking of all the money lost, money from people who had confidence in him. He could not stand it; it was better to get a new job. His friends began worrying. Even Lestringuez, who was the man to call when Jean's morale was flagging, couldn't change his mood. Marguerite said nothing but seemed worried, too.

◆

On July 14, *Le Jour* and *Paris-Soir* announced that Renoir had agreed to film *Tosca* in Rome. His friends were upset and at first had a hard time believing it. How could it have happened? And why had he said nothing? He had gotten the offer during the filming of *Rules of the Game* by way of Jean Dewalde, who was his agent at the time. He kept it a secret because the offer had come from Scalera Films and the Italian government, which was held in contempt and for good reason. The Italians were offering Karl Koch to work with him on the script and promised that Luchino Visconti would be assistant director.

Jean had first left the offer on the table. He wanted to see Italy, but, like his friends, he felt it wasn't the right moment. Two years earlier, he had not thought it proper even to go to Venice to accept a prize awarded to *Grand Illusion*. Now, everything was different, and he left for just a few days. They invited him to come and take stock in person of the working conditions that were being offered him. He was thinking, according to the statements that are attributed to him,[46] that you could extract from *Tosca* "an extraordinary police film with chase scenes and everything that goes with it." His friends gave little thought to *Tosca* and a lot to the change in political orientation that his choice implied.

On August 12, 1939, in *Ce soir*, Aragon concluded an ecstatic review of Malraux's film, *Espoir* (*Men's Hope*), with the following lines: "I am writing these words for you, Jean Renoir, who left Paris without wanting to say good-bye to me . . . for all those who are weak and cowardly . . . for all who have despaired of France too soon and whom perhaps I will never again be able to look at calmly after this

---

[46] *Match*, August 17, 1939, cited in Claude Gauteur, *Jean Renoir*, 158.

film, and this war, and the great Passion of the Spanish people, my brothers."

It was the end of his friendship with Aragon, and with several others as well. But these accusers were mistaken. Jean had not left without daring to say good-bye to Aragon and some others. He had not changed. He hated Nazism as much as ever, and the absence of freedom, and racism, but he needed to forget the failure of *Rules of the Game,* he needed to get out of the country while he still could. After a lot of reflection during this period when he felt cut off from the rest of the world, he had come to the conclusion that his personal life should change direction. He had allowed misunderstandings to build up between himself and Marguerite, and their relationship had deteriorated. But Marguerite still thought they were going to live together. Despite what the others said, she had hoped to make the trip to Italy with him.

NEW WORLD EXILES

◆

The trip to Italy was supposed to be short. Jean Renoir left Paris on August 10, the day on which a Franco-British military mission reached Leningrad in the hope of negotiating an alliance that had been proposed by the Soviets three months before. He wanted to try to forget politics and profit from a summer that was already waning. He was also counting on making some discoveries. He did not go off by himself: Dido Freire and Karl Koch went with him. The three of them had known each other for years. She was still a youngster in boarding school at Dupanloup when Albert Cavalcanti had brought her to the Renoir home at Marlotte. In Jean's presence, she had always been extremely shy. Even when she was regularly taking Alain to the Paris Zoo, she still avoided him. She had huge black eyes that looked out in an extraordinary way at everything, both to ponder and to be amused. Little by little, she made friends with Catherine Hessling, since she loved dancing and the world of movies fascinated her. Dido admired Jean Renoir but did nothing to get close to him—quite the contrary.

Mr. Guillaume was the one who first got the idea of hiring the girl. His role was to offer sage advice in all aspects of life. Dido Freire didn't put up much resistance. Working for Jean Renoir would be exciting. So she became a secretary, then a script girl in *Rules of the Game*. She had a lively intelligence and that consuming look. When Jean Renoir finally began to look back at her, he realized that she had class, a quality that he loved just as much as beauty and intelligence. After the failure of his film crushed him so, she was the only one whose presence bucked him up. He was beginning to realize that he was smitten with the young girl who not long ago was taking his son to England and to the carnival at Neuilly.

During the filming, Dido had been so discreet—and secretive—that no one had realized what was going on. Once again, as in the script, there was a comical kind of amorous competition between the actors, but it reached the verge of drama. The "boss" seemed calm, as usual, just a bit excited about what was going on, and he was always ready to fan the flames of passion if some shots he was filming the next day might gain in intensity as a result. The gang had not gotten past his infatuation with Nora Gregor, which had subsided quickly once he realized the error he had made by casting her. Marguerite was not a bit worried. She knew that his emotional life and his work were linked. Dido also understood it very well. She knew that the most important thing for him was to keep on making films, and she was ready to do all she could so that the discouragement he felt about *Rules of the Game* would quickly fade.

◆

So the trip to Italy afforded a needed change. Even if it was unlikely to amount to anything because of the ever clearer prospect of a war, Jean had taken the job thinking of his father, whose footsteps he would have liked to retrace. But he and his companions never even had the time to go to Venice and Padua, the first stages of Auguste's journey. They met Barattolo and Ambrosio, emissaries from Scalera Films, at Montecatini Terme, and followed them to Florence, Pisa, and Lucca. Jean was rereading Marivaux, an author closely associated in his mind with Italian baroque; *La Double Inconstance* (*Double Inconstance*) inspired him with a yearning to see "angels on bridges wearing clothes with too many folds and wings with too many feathers."[1]

On August 14, they were welcomed to Rome by Luchino Visconti. While visiting the city, they were also picking out places where Jean might like to shoot. Visconti had had time to learn Renoir's tastes, and he was the best guide imaginable. Jean was won over. He had not dared to hope that things could turn out so well so soon. Moreover, Dido and he realized that they understood each other perfectly without trying to. She loved Rome as much as he and as much as they loved one another.

Unfortunately, they had to go home. On August 23, the German-Soviet pact was signed, in which the two powers shared Poland, thus freeing the Reich from preoccupation with an Eastern front. Jean was

---

[1] Jean Renoir, *Lettres d'Amérique*, ed. A. Sesonske (Paris, 1984), 13.

shocked. An alliance like that had seemed unthinkable. He kept on remembering about the hope that had animated the October Group during the shooting of *The Crime of M. Lang* and *La Vie est à nous*. He also kept on thinking about Aragon's article and of the angry reactions of his friends when they learned that he was going "to Mussolini's." He hadn't taken the trouble to tell them that Karl Koch was anti-Nazi and Visconti antifascist, nor that *Tosca* was not a glorification of the regime of Il Duce. That wasn't the first time he was apprised of the narrowness of militancy. But now what were they going to do? How could the French Communists adapt to this awful reversal? For the last several years, he had associated with them because of the vigor with which they combatted Nazism. It would be very painful to see them again. They would refuse his condolences, even if he sympathized with their disarray. Every day the situation grew worse, and the news was more and more alarming.

Before returning to Paris, Jean and Dido stopped at Les Collettes, now the home of his youngest brother, Claude. They stayed there until August 31, as we can tell from a postcard that survives, addressed to Luchino Visconti. On that day, Hitler was demanding Dantzig. The next day, he invaded Poland, and on September 3, England and then France declared war on Germany. Jean Renoir, still a lieutenant in the reserves, was drafted again, but this time into the army film service. His job was to write scripts for propaganda films and to shoot documentaries. Back in the saddle after his vacation, he began to write for himself and to think of new movies to make. With encouragement from the watchful Dido, he saw himself resuming his place within the community of directors. In an interview that appeared on October 18, 1939, he said: "For the moment, still under the spell of my stay in Italy, I'm reading St. Francis of Assisi, and I intend to make a movie though I'm certain that I won't. Sometimes you need to have big plans like that . . . you get attached to them because they get you going . . . but they don't come true because they're too grandiose."[2]

His break with Marguerite had been complete, as was that with his friends from the PC. The two things went together, as Jean realized when he got back from Italy. He wasn't surprised. He had spoken with Marguerite, but he had no chance to do so with his political friends. One day the PC was denouncing pacifism, the next it was announcing with pride that Stalin was "guaranteeing the peace." Eventually, the party was dissolved by the government, and *L'Hu-*

---

[2] *Pour vous*, 570, October 18, 1939, interview with A. Doringe, cited in Jean Renoir, *Oeuvres de cinéma inédites*, ed C. Gauteur (Paris, 1981), 80.

manité and *Ce soir* stopped publication. Maurice Thorez deserted France on October 4 in order to fight in the Soviet Union "against imperialism," because according to the new marching orders of the Komintern, it was an imperialist war. All of that seemed really pathetic, even awful, and Jean had to try not to think about it and to do what he had to do.

During this same month of October, Jean wrote to Robert Flaherty: "My dear, dear Bob, I'm going to make some movies that will really excite me, not with actors anymore, but with *people, real ones.*" This postcard was sent by the army from Wangenbourg in Alsace on October 24, 1939. Jean directed a short military instruction film, now lost, on daily life in an army camp.[3] As he wrote later: "I was filming soldiers who were yawning from boredom."[4] Alain, just eighteen years old, enlisted in the cavalry, as his father and grandfather had done. Worry began to eat at Jean, who luckily did not know yet how many years those worries would last. It was impossible to look ahead; now, more than ever, he had to live a day at a time.

In the past, Jean Renoir had been close to Jean Giraudoux. They would lunch together once in a while with Pierre Lestringuez and Louis Jouvet. After debuting the unforgettable title role in Giraudoux's *Siegfried*, Jean's brother Pierre had acted in most of Giraudoux's plays. Suddenly, Giraudoux resurfaced, named by Daladier to head the General Information Board. "Overwhelmed by attacks of favoritism and negligence, betrayed by incompetent or irresponsible helpers, Giraudoux had neither the time nor the opportunity to undertake any reform except of the language spoken on the radio for short addresses."[5] When he learned that Mussolini had invited Renoir to reconsider the *Tosca* project and to give a series of lectures at the Experimental Cinema Center in Rome on the role of the director, Giraudoux urged him to accept. Mussolini had so much admiration for *Grand Illusion* that he had his own print of it, he was told, although the film itself had been banned in Italy. Jean himself, in his articles and in an interview that had appeared in *Ce soir* two years before, had treated the man with irreverence.[6] Nothing suggests that Il Duce had also seen *Rules of the Game*. Yet he wanted Jean to give lectures at the Ex-

[3] See Claude Beylie, "Sur un film inconnu du lieutenant Renoir," *Ecran 79*, April 15, 1979.

[4] Jean Renoir, *Ma vie et mes films* (Paris, 1974), 158.

[5] Chris Marker, *Giraudoux par lui-même* (Paris, 1952), 157.

[6] Jean Renoir, *Ecrits*, 117–32, and Claude Gauteur, *Jean Renoir, la double méprise* (Paris, 1980), 58.

perimental Center he had created. Lieutenant Renoir was placed at the disposition of the Foreign Ministry and sent on a mission to Rome.

In the hope of keeping Mussolini out of the conflict, the French government was ready to do anything to curry favor with him. But since Jean Renoir's work was then and would long remain controversial, on August 28, 1939, *Rules of the Game* was blacklisted by the Ministry of Foreign Affairs. Suzanne Borel (later Madame Georges Bidault) was the head of the service that made up the list, and she explained its inclusion as follows: "In countries where we number many friends, but where we must also anticipate unofficial, tendentious German propaganda, we are especially anxious to avoid representations of our country, our traditions, and our race that alter its face, lie about it, and deform it through the prism of an artistic individual who is often original but not always sound."[7] It is not a pretty explanation, especially when one thinks of the period in which it was offered. As for military censorship, Gauteur, who studied the situation for the Renoir films, including *La Marseillaise, Grand Illusion, La Bête humaine,* and *Rules of the Game,* which were banned in some regions and freely shown in others, concluded that *Rules of the Game* "was banned because of the situation from September 1939 to February 1940, like a certain number of other French films, nothing more, and nothing less."[8]

In mid-January 1940, Jean Renoir and Dido Freire, who went along as his secretary, left for Italy in a Delahaye convertible without the top. They shivered on the way through the Alps. On arriving in Rome, they moved into a hotel that no longer exists, the Hotel di Russi. They were delighted to meet Karl Koch there, and together, they rented a large, sumptuous apartment near the church of San Stefano Rotondo. In honor of Dido, who was born in Belém, the two friends set to covering the walls and the ceilings with frescoes of Amazonia, including animals, jungles, and a river. The job kept their spirits high at a time when they had nothing else to do. The strangely stagnating war made them anxious. Dido, who was as worried as they were, tried distracting them. She remembers that they had a couple of well-trained servants who were anxious that their masters be "signorili [gentlemanly]" and were probably government spies. Cora was an excellent cook, and Vicenze served impeccably, so why not make the most of it? They entertained at home, and brother

---

[7] To Lucie Derain, *La Cinématographie française,* 1093–94, October 14–21, 1939, cited in Claude Gauteur, *Jean Renoir,* 140–41.

[8] Claude Gauteur, *Jean Renoir,* 142.

Claude, the singer Tino Rossi, and Harry Pilcer, a dancer who was all the rage, came to visit. Dido loved dancing and did a turn with him, to some popular tunes. They had 78 rpm records, which is all there was at the time. So they ignored the "passive defense" measures, the windows covered with black curtains and the lightless streets, and they asked themselves what spring would bring. The work was going slowly; Visconti was helping them with the screenplay.

◆

Jean got along well with this wealthy Italian aristocrat who was so taken with film. Before he became Jean's assistant, Visconti had gone to cavalry school; in 1940, he still owned racehorses. That delighted Jean, who made no secret of his own past in the cavalry. Visconti's respect for him was touching, and Renoir wanted to help him in his first efforts as a director. He brought him the French translation of James Cain's novel, *The Postman Always Rings Twice*. Visconti later made *Ossessione* (*Obsession*) from it, with his own brand of poetry and lyricism. It was considered the first Italian neorealist film, a direct descendant of *Toni*. Visconti's friends were already famous or would soon be so in Roman film circles: Vittorio de Sica, making his first movies at the time, Cesare Zavattini, later de Sica's screenwriter, Roberto Rosselini, and also Giuseppe De Santis, Visconti's assistant in *Obsession*.

The Experimental Center, which was founded in 1935, belonged to the Academy of Music in Rome, and it was the first great school of cinematography. Mussolini was very eager to develop the film industry in Italy, and he was hoping to profit from the war in order to broaden the market for his productions. In the center, teachers and students, most of whom were antifascist, like Visconti's friends, were not persecuted. They just had to evince a certain prudence; at least, that was how the situation appeared to an outsider. Jean Renoir was invited to take part in their discussions by Luigi Chiarini, the founder and director of the center. Chiarini was more of a theoretician than a filmmaker, but he had the knack of creating a lively meeting place that did not fail to stimulate his guest.

The trip went as well as possible, given the anxiety due to "that funny war" and infrequent news of Alain. Dido and Karl Koch spent their energy trying to keep Jean calm; he got absorbed in his work. At first, Jean told a Roman journalist that his version of Victor Sardou's play would turn out to be a French film with no relation at all to Italy.[9]

[9] *Film*, February 10, 1940, 3.

On the day that the interview in which he said this appeared, he was quoted as saying, in another magazine, that he had found "the subject matter for a great Italian film . . . the most typically Mediterranean land. . . . And we should create a Mediterranean cinema. . . . When I came here, I immediately sensed that it was the only place in which I could carry out my plan."[10]

Since his childhood, he was an adopted Mediterranean, and aside from the propaganda that he was supposed to provide and that had to include some compliments, it is not surprising that he was seduced by the Italian countryside and people. It is important to remember the ease with which he adapted himself everywhere. His enthusiastic and open-minded temperament was at home in Italy. In an article he wrote for *Tempo*,[11] he talks about having had the idea of filming *Tosca* in 1925 with Catherine Hessling. He had abandoned the project then because of problems with the rights to the story. But now he was getting ready to make a kind of detective novel that respected the tragic unities of time. He wanted to follow his heroes from hour to hour during a single day and night. A lot was to be shot on location outdoors, in order to "get the most out of the atmosphere of Rome." He continues: "My ambition is to make the viewer think that movies existed already in 1800, since the streets of Rome would appear to be part of a documentary made at the time." But to avoid the confusion that he especially feared in costume dramas, he wanted to dress those in the entourage of Mario Cavaradossi, Tosca's lover, in a style reminiscent of the Directoire, and the other group, those belonging to the court of the Queen of Naples at the Farnese Palace, to be dressed in the style of Louis XVI.

He had to change the casting of the film repeatedly. For the role of Cavaradossi, he had at first wanted Georges Flamant, who had played Dédé in *La Chienne,* but it turned out he had been drafted; Viviane Romance, whom he had wanted to play Tosca, was unable to get out of France because of the war. She was replaced by Imperio Argentina. Michel Simon, who was to play Scarpia, had no problem getting to Italy, since he was Swiss. And Visconti gave good advice about which Italian actors to choose. Ill-timed complications were disturbing to Jean Renoir. In a departure from his usual practice, he wanted to finish the cutting and the spoken dialogue before starting to shoot. This was because of the language barrier, but also because, without

[10] *Cinéma*, V, 1, 87, February 10, 1940, 90–91.
[11] *Tempo*, IV, 37, February 8, 1940.

knowing exactly why or how, he had a feeling that he would never be able to finish the film.

♦

In March, "heroic Finland," which had been invaded by the Red Army on November 26, 1939, and had fought with great vigor, signed a peace treaty with the USSR. The next month, Denmark and Norway were invaded by the forces of the Reich. The latter invasions took place in record time: four hours for Denmark, forty-eight for Norway. The Allies' response, long delayed, was centered around Narvik, where there was a siege that was about to last for weeks and weeks. Rome wasn't the best place to hear reports favorable to the Allies, but even a natural optimist would have to notice how superior the German forces were.

Dido responded furiously to the hostility that the French were sometimes treated to. At Easter, she had an experience with serious consequences for her private life; it also gives a feeling for her personality. Needing to confess and not being proficient enough to do it in Italian, Dido preferred to ask a French-speaking priest to take her confession. The man was a German and said to her: "The French will pay for their sins!" Indignant, she ran away without receiving absolution. He ran after her, but she refused to return to the confessional, unable to forgive the "man of God." From then on, she stopped practicing her religion and never wanted to reconcile herself to the Church even many years later.

Dido, too, was a mixture, of excitability and good sense. Her good sense on behalf of the one she loved caused her to write to Robert Flaherty on May 2, 1940. He was in Washington at the time, and she wrote him that she wanted to see Jean Renoir leave for America. She had already shared this wish of hers with him in Paris, where he was living during the filming of *Rules of the Game*. What was needed was a real contract, she added. So Jean got an offer from a major studio via a New York agent, Lois Jacoby. Dido provides these details: Jean was to receive "$500 per week during a three-month period of adjustment, then $1,500 per week while making the film." The offer interested him, but he wanted to get a round-trip ticket for himself and his secretary, who was to be hired by the company directly. He thought that the propaganda he could provide for his country in the United States would be a lot better than anything he could do anywhere else. In the same letter to Flaherty, Dido says that they were having a lot of problems with *Tosca* but that everything seemed to have been worked out, and that they were going to start shooting, probably next week. The inconveniences and the delays were mainly caused by distributors and studios.

In fact, Jean Renoir did shoot for two nights, on May 6 and May 9. The Piazza Farnese, where a curious crowd pressed against them, was lit up all night long until 7 A.M. Two horsemen emerged from the Farnese palace and went off at a gallop through the darkened streets, scaring off a few cats. The Castel Sant' Angelo was also lit up at night, and the horsemen advanced to the bridge at its entrance. A crane holding the camera was placed right next to Bernini's angel statue overlooking the bridge.[12] On May 10, after having shot five sequences in all, Jean Renoir stopped. That was the day of the German offensive; the führer's troops were in Belgium and Holland. There were many more exteriors to shoot, but he was ready to quit.

There were Germans all around the city— Michel Simon was the first to notice them. In Rome, Simon had two pastimes: taking pictures of the ceilings in palaces, and making conversation with the residents of whorehouses. During his almost daily visits, he would show off his pictures of ceiling frescoes. One evening, he found his usual seat taken by a German out of uniform. "When he asked the madam for his place back, she was terrified and refused to do anything. In disgust, Michel Simon went home to bed. The next day, he told me the story and, in his best Michel Simon voice, he concluded, "F— them and their ceilings!"[13]

There were other warnings: thugs paid by the Nazis were mugging people who bought copies of *Osservatore Romano*, the only newspaper that was sympathetic to France. That was how Jean Renoir got himself beaten up in a restaurant. As a result, the French ambassador advised him to leave Italy, which he did. Everything was falling apart. On May 13, panzer divisions established three bridgeheads along the Meuse. Two days later, the Dutch army surrendered. On May 27, it was Belgium's turn to do the same, on orders from King Leopold III. The next day, British and French troops boarded their ships at Dunkirk.

Dido spent several difficult days alone in Rome with Karl Koch, who hardly left the apartment. She stayed to get back a print of *Grand Illusion* and deposit some papers at the Brazilian embassy. She was

[12] According to *Cinéma*, 94, May 25, 1940, 355, in an article by Gianni Puecini, "Si gira di notte."

[13] Jean Renoir, *Ma vie et mes films*, 160.

there on June 10, the day Mussolini announced from the balcony of the Palazzo Veneto his intention of fighting at the side of Germany, barking out, "A chi il mondo?" and the crowd shrieked deliriously, "A noi, a noi!" On the other side of the Alps, it was a heart-wrenching day. Soldiers and civilians were wandering in the streets. France was suffering its most crushing defeat, and it brought with it a terrible wave of fear among the citizens, "un vent de folie [a wind of madness]," as Henri Amouroux called it. Dido Freire returned to Paris on the last train to cross the border. Jean was waiting for her there, anxious to go and find Alain, who had managed to let him know his whereabouts.

◆

Dido and Jean had no difficulty renting a Peugeot, and they went off to find the young NCO, a horseless cavalryman in charge of a big truck and fifty men. Their officers had disappeared. He didn't know what to do. His regiment's mission was "to stop the Germans at the gates of Paris, and only that!" (ibid., p. 164). A staff officer arrived and gave the order to regroup farther back in the lines. In the confusion that followed, Alain disappeared. Jean's account of this meeting evokes the tumult and disarray that people were feeling at the time. Jean and Dido did not know what to do either. After lunching from cans on a park bench, they decided to go find the Cézannes at Marlotte, since they had a car. They arrived just in time. The family had decided to leave their lovely home and hit the road with their most precious canvases. Only Aline, the daughter, refused to leave. She took it upon herself to take care of Madame Renoir's piano and Le Chasseur, a portrait of Jean at 14, dressed up as a hunter. They piled up the Cézannes, all wrapped and tied, in the back of the Peugeot. Renée and Paul got in the car with Jean, while Dido, Marjorie, the young, pregnant daughter-in-law, and Jean-Pierre Cézanne followed on bicycles. The highways, which were crowded with terrified people in flight, were a harrowing sight. Troops were retreating even more quickly than the flood of refugees was advancing. On June 12, the order to retreat was given by General Weygand, chief of staff; on that day he declared Paris an "open city." Two days later, the Germans entered a deserted city. On June 15, members of the government, who had been scattered everywhere, managed to meet at Bordeaux. The confusion was indescribable. The French were crushed by their disastrous defeat and flight. On the evening of June 16, Paul Reynaud, the Prime Minister, yielded his place to Pétain, and on June 22, the armistice was signed. After a meeting with the Italians in Turin, the armistice went into effect on June 25 at 12:30 A.M. Those who lived through that nightmare will never forget those dates, nor will they forget the appeal addressed to them on June 18 by General Charles de Gaulle from London via the BBC.

Meanwhile, the little group around Jean Renoir made its way without really knowing where it was headed. They felt they were at the mercy of chance. There were probably eight million Frenchmen and Frenchwomen on the roads. People came across relatives and old friends who were just as aimless and uncertain as they were. That's what happened to our friends. At La Motte-Beuvron, where Jean Renoir had shot some of the exteriors for *Rules of the Game*, they met Renée Cézanne's father, Georges Rivière, Auguste's old friend, and his son-in-law, Edmond Renoir, Jean's first cousin. They were heading for Limoges.

The group of friends spent the night in a barn outside of Sully-sur-Loire. They crossed the river just before the bridge over it was destroyed, and then, outside of Vierzon, they experienced their first air raid. It made them stop and think. Imagining that the Germans were probably going to occupy Bordeaux, they decided not to continue southward, but to find safety in a village off the main route. They had arrived near Guéret, and their choice fell on Chénérailles. They found lodging in a barn belonging to Antoine Dioton, a saddlemaker.

> We put the canvases up in the barn—it was terrific to see them hung in such an unusual way. Paul was delighted. The walls made of irregularly shaped stones, the crib with what was left of the donkey's dinner, and the farm implements themselves were a perfect backdrop for the paintings. The work of the master from Aix had never before been shown in so rich and authentic a setting. Paul Cézanne the younger, my dear friend, buffeted by the hazards of international politics, found himself able to give his father's works a showing that would have certainly pleased their creator. That night in the barn, we were lulled to sleep in the peace that radiates from masterpieces. Our oil lamps gave off the ideal light. Their flames dancing in the slightest breeze gave us the feeling that the people in the paintings were alive and actually about to utter words (ibid., pp. 165–66).

After that great storm, incredible peace, "a state close to complete happiness."

On July 23, Jean Renoir wrote to Gabrielle: "You must have seen Alain by now." The boy was his main concern. Then, as was his custom, he wrote of what was happening: "We eat a lot and well. We love our neighbors, and I think they have adopted us. Renée plays the gypsy queen," and he goes on to speak of the countryside, which is "amazing. Everywhere you look there are scenes from Dad's paintings, even more than in the south, and much more than outside Paris or at Essoyes."[14] He did not forget that they were in the Limousin, his father's native district, as he wrote to Robert Flaherty on July 8. In that letter he said: "The future is our main concern. We're wondering what will happen now to the film industry in Europe." On July 29, Flaherty responded in a telegram, now lost, to say that Hollywood would accept Jean, that he could work there. He was even sure that financial arrangements would be made to suit him and Dido and that advances would be sent to pay for their trip.

◆

But when Flaherty's telegram arrived, Jean Renoir had left the Limousin for Cagnes. He sent the following telegram from there on August 6, 1940: "Warm thanks impossible to leave France without special authorization affectionately." Two days later, he explained in a letter that he was still under contract to Scalera Films in Rome. He had to be ready to resume his work for them if they asked. At that time he had no way of foreseeing it, but during the occupation, Scalera actually did produce two films in the Victorine Studios at Nice, *La Vie de bohème* (*The Bohemian Life*) directed by Marcel L'Herbier in 1942, and, the following year, *La Boîte aux rêves* (*The Dream Box*), directed by Yves Allégret. As Gilcher has written, for a moment he might have wanted to go back and work in Rome for Scalera on *Tosca* or something else.[15] He also thought it was his duty to stand by his colleagues when everything was going so badly and when French filmmaking "is in such a state of confusion after our disaster." At the same time, he realized that there was nothing he could do. He still wanted to wait, thinking that the best solution was to work in France first, then, once the situation had stabilized, to join Flaherty and make a film in a faraway land, as he had dreamed of doing for so long. Robert Flaherty, who seems from his correspondance with Jean Renoir to be as devoted and warm in his friendship as he is in his films, had taken to heart the fate of Dido and Jean. He had the sense to realize that waiting was impossible and that it was time to act quickly. He telegraphed them on August 10, telling them to contact the American consulates

[14] Jean Renoir, *Lettres d'Amérique*, 15–16.
[15] William Henry Gilcher, *Jean Renoir in America* (Des Moines, 1979).

in Nice or Marseille. Jean ought to be able to leave. On the American side, all was arranged with the State Department.

In the meantime, it was better to live at Les Collettes. The Riviera was more accessible than the village in the Limousin, where the Cézannes spent the whole summer. Only Marjorie and Jean-Pierre left for the home of Albert André in Bagnols-sur-Cèze, near Nîmes. They stayed there until their baby was born the following January. Then they went back to Paris and moved into their parents' apartment on the rue de Douai.

Cagnes was in the so-called free zone. In divided France, at first people thought that in the south they were safe from Nazi interference. Jean soon had proof of the opposite. On several occasions, he had visits from "two Frenchmen working for Nazi cultural relations" who encouraged him as good friends to make films for "the New France," assuring him that he would have no restrictions. He could shoot whatever film he wanted, and considerable means would be placed at his disposal. These agents of the Reich had a Russian woman with them, "an adventuress of the mystery novel type" who worshiped Hitler "like the living god." Lestringuez, who was staying at Les Collettes, was present during these visits as well and made "commonsense, down-to-earth, aggressive remarks. 'Hitler,' he would say, 'peed in the soup.'"[16] But it was clear that they wouldn't always stand for jokes of this sort. Nor could Jean run the risk of exposing himself and his friends to less harmless visits. These were trying enough; they made Jean nervous, and he knew what was coming. He had no wish to embark on such a dangerous venture. The only solution was to leave before having to refuse to collaborate, which was what they were going to offer him next. If he stayed, things would end badly indeed.

Dido was right to take steps so that they could go to America. Since for the moment Italy was at war, Scalera Films was not asking Renoir to finish *Tosca*. He had even lost contact with Koch and Visconti, who had taken on the project with him. So the thing to do was to see how to get an exit visa from the French. Tixier-Vignancour was in charge of filmmaking in the Vichy government. Jean sent him a letter informing him of the American offers, and he received a favorable response, but a visa had to come from the Interior Ministry. On September 2, Jean left Dido at Les Collettes with Claude and his family and set off for Vichy to lay siege to the appropriate bureaucrats. There

[16]Jean Renoir, *Ma vie et mes films*, 166.

were some problems with his case because he was only forty-six. According to French law, he had two more years of eligibility for the draft. However, his war wounds meant that there was room to maneuver. But that took time, and Vichy had become an overpopulated town where you could meet a lot of old friends. They were not just people who came to court the regime. There were also many like him, who came to get papers that would enable them to leave the country, as well as those who came in order to find out what would happen next: all sorts of rumors were making the rounds.

Jean had already decided what to do. He met Sylvia Bataille, whom he had not seen since *A Day in the Country*. "He'd gotten the picture," she told me; "he said to me: 'Better get the hell out. You can't do anything here. It's going to be horrible. It's going to be the land of the raw deal: a hill of beans for a house.'" Once he got his visa, he went back to Cagnes on September 18 and worked on speeding up the final details.

◆

Even in their familiar old house, it was impossible to take up where they had left off. Everything was different now. They had to do without the car. That complicated things, even the shortest trips, since public transportation was overcrowded. Dido, who went to Nice to get the American visas, had to keep going back and forth. The bus would show up full, and before she'd finished waiting in one line and gotten to the next, the consular offices would close. As usual, Jean Renoir did his best to keep in touch with friends. Marc Allégret stopped by to visit, and also Jean Gabin, who was at Saint-Jean-Cap-Ferrat. In a letter to Denise Tual, Gabin speaks of "a very pretty idea [of Jean Renoir's] for a screenplay that would be very hard to produce at the moment, as anything would be, for that matter."[17] He's probably referring to the *Magnificat*, a synopsis of which Jean filed at the Screenwriters Guild on September 12, 1940.[18] Jean himself wrote to Denise Tual on August 24: "I've thought up two screenplays, one little one suited to the current scarcities, the other grandiose, which really thrills me and Jean Gabin, too" (ibid., p. 168).

Magnificat is a lovely, poignant story that he never filmed. It is based on a tale Dido told him: French monks leave for a remote region in Brazil to missionize some Indians who had until then refused contact with whites. To overcome the Indians' mistrust, the missionaries

---

[17] Denise Tual, *Le Temps dévoré* (Paris, 1980), letter dated August 25, 1940, 169.
[18] Jean Renoir, *Oeuvres inédites*, 79.

Auguste Renoir. *The Alphabet*
There are a number of double portraits of Gabrielle and Jean. The baby's long curly golden hair delighted Renoir.
Source: SPADEM

Gabrielle Renard just turned fourteen when her cousin, Mme. Renoir, asked her to leave their small Burgundy town and come to Paris to take care of the new baby, who came to depend on her completely. Gabrielle became the most famous of all Renoir's models and throughout her life remained Jean's best friend.

The golden locks are gone. Jean is nicely dressed but so fiercely independent that he resents looking like the other students at the elegant boarding school he attends.
Source: SPADEM

In 1913 Jean decided to join the cavalry. His aspiration was to be an officer.

Above, Jean Renoir was badly wounded in 1915. On crutches, in a mountain infantryman's uniform, he is photographed here with comrades and a nurse. His young brother Coco is wearing a black arm band in memory of their mother.

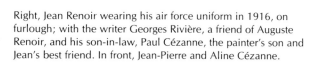

Right, Jean Renoir wearing his air force uniform in 1916, on furlough; with the writer Georges Rivière, a friend of Auguste Renoir, and his son-in-law, Paul Cézanne, the painter's son and Jean's best friend. In front, Jean-Pierre and Aline Cézanne.

Under the huge old olive trees, the studio that
Auguste Renoir built at Les Collettes, his estate
in Cagnes-sur-Mer, near Nice.

Jean Renoir in his twin-engined Caudron. Castor oil was used to lubricate the engines. Jean found
the smell of this "luxurious oil" intoxicating.

M. M. HAKIM présentent

JEAN GABIN · SIMONE SIMON

LA BÊTE HUMAINE

Un film de **JEAN RENOIR** · d'après l'œuvre d'**ÉMILE ZOLA**

Paris Film Location
78 Champs Elysées
Paris

A poster for the film directed by Jean Renoir in 1938. This adaptation of the Zola novel, starring Jean Gabin and Simone Simon, was a success. Here is the fatal couple with the well-known actors Carette and Fernand Ledoux.
Source: Cinémathèque française

Marcel Pagnol and Jean Renoir in 1934, when Jean was working on *Toni* and using Marcel Pagnol Studios in Marseilles.

Jean Renoir plays a leading role in his *The Rules of the Game,* 1939. On the left, Nora Gregor; on the right, Mila Parély.
Source: Cinémathèque française

Jean Renoir and his son Alain, who is making his debut as assistant cameraman in *The Rules of the Game*. Alain soon turned eighteen, and the year 1939 completely changed his life.

In 1963 Jean Renoir received an honorary degree from the University of California at Berkeley. To his right is Alain, professor of English at the university since 1955.

Jean Renoir and Dido in their house in Beverly Hills.

Jean Renoir, 1955, avenue Frochot,
where he kept an apartment for 35 years.
This private enclave in Montmartre, just a
stone's throw from the Place Pigalle, still
looks like a country road.

Jean Renoir with Ingrid Bergman filming *Elena and Her Men* in 1956, in Paris.
Source: David Seymour-Magnum

Dido and Jean Renoir visiting their friend, the painter Georges Braque, in his Paris studio, 1956.

In May 1966, Janine Bazin and André S. Labarthe produced a television series called "Jean Renoir, le patron," with Jean Renoir and some of his friends and actors. Here he is with Michel Simon, the memorable tramp in *Boudu sauvé des eaux.*
Source: Henri Cartier-Bresson-Magnum

Jeanne Moreau and Jean Renoir on the set of his last film, *Le petit théâtre de Jean Renoir,* in 1969.

Each year François Truffaut managed to spend some time in the Beverly Hills house of the Renoirs. Jean was his ideal and beloved mentor.

Dido was protective of Jean Renoir but with such grace that their friends always found him accessible.

Jean Renoir in 1978 in the Beverly Hills home Dido and he had built for their old age. It contained favorite furniture and objects that came from his parents' house: a bust of his mother, paintings by his father and, outside, the olive trees and the roses that reminded him of Les Collettes.
Source: Paris-Match-Sauer

never engage in retribution and never exhibit anger. They let themselves get slaughtered by the Indians without demanding vengeance, accepting martyrdom for their faith, and adding every day to a stock of gifts that the Indians refuse to touch. They clear some land and build a kind of monastery, with hedges and a garden, and do what they must to survive. The Indians remain invisible but spy upon them ceaselessly, day and night. Jean could well imagine these men, coming from various social stations, each with his past, his way of reacting, his way of living out his faith. He understood as well how they might be able to accept one another in a communal life that was pushed to extremes by other men, mysterious men who always left traces of their presence. There would also be the beauty of nature and the wild animals. For twelve years the mission endures; the forest animals become their friends before the Indians touch the gifts that have been laid out for them. Yet that day comes, and the mission is successful. "The slow conquest of spirits by humble and anonymous Frenchmen would delight audiences in all countries and reveal the most authentic and moving aspects of the spiritual force of France" (ibid., p. 83). So concludes the first version of this screenplay, which was filed a second time in 1959.

The choice of this subject at the beginning of the Nazi occupation and the way in which Jean Renoir elaborated it are both interesting. They show what his frame of mind was. First the patriotic feeling is explicit: the monks are Frenchmen, and Jean stresses "the spiritual force of France," something that is usually unspoken in his films. But after the defeat of France, he felt the need to anchor himself again in those old beliefs. More profound and still more important is the need to express his certainty that only love for our neighbors can save us. There wasn't much chance that he could shoot such a film in those days, however much people needed to hear what he was saying, which was totally the opposite of Nazi ideology. Later on, at the time of *Le Fleuve* (*The River*), people spoke of his 'conversion.' Jean Renoir had no need to convert. He was able to revise his ideas about one subject or another, but he was also one of those people who never lost his faith.

A combination of things—the dreaded war, the exodus, the uncomprehending reception of *Rules of the Game*—all set Jean on a long journey inside himself. There were also shocks to his private life: breaking up with Marguerite had brought to the surface misunderstandings that had been accumulating for many years, differences between them that he knew of, but that the rhythms of everyday life had kept hidden for too long. His horror of explanations led him not to announce his decisions until he had made them and even taken action as a consequence.

◆

Now he had to keep on being creative—there was that exuberant vigor in him—so he had to leave his sad, ravaged country. The first port of call was Marseille, to await Spanish transport visas. There were delays and complications. Dido and Jean left Cagnes on October 6, but on October 21 they were still at Marseille, where Dido sent Flaherty a telegram asking the U.S. ambassador in Madrid to intervene with the Spanish government on their behalf: that was the only way for them to get transit visas. Then it was Algiers, Rabat, Casablanca, and Tangier, where Dido had to wait behind while Jean was able to leave for Lisbon. Finally, she met him there on December 5 with her papers all in order.

Their stay in Lisbon gave rise to malicious comments whose traces can still be found. To understand why, one need only recall the atmosphere of this era, when everyone was suspicious of everyone else and people spread rumors that were often false and always unverifiable. Henri Jeanson, a journalist and screenwriter famous for his comic incisiveness, was film critic for *Le Canard enchaîné*. He had been bullying Jean Renoir since 1936, and he spread a rumor that Jean had been making antisemitic remarks in Portugal to curry favor with the Salazar regime. It is difficult to credit this accusation about the author of *Grand Illusion* and *Rules of the Game*. One should also take into account the way statements can be twisted by the newspapers of totalitarian countries, which are in the hire of their governments. Interpreters of the artistic work of Jean Renoir have attempted to shed light on this affair. Claude Beylie, after painstaking research to find the incriminating texts, published an apparently reliable summary of them.[19] He looked at the texts of two interviews. The first took place in November 1940, with a Portuguese newspaperman, Fernando Fregedo, and was only published several months later in *Hollywood em Lisboa*. The other was with the editor-in-chief of *Animatografo*, Antonio Lopes Ribero, on December 2, 1940. In the first one, Jean speaks about a Latin cinema that could compete artistically with Hollywood. Earlier that same year, he had been speaking in Rome of a Mediterranean cinema. It was an idea that he was developing and that he thought was not dangerous—it excluded Germans. The problem is,

---

[19] *Cinéma d'aujourd'hui*, 2, May–June 1975, "Jean Renoir, le spectacle, la vie," 30.

the Salazar regime put the stress on its "Latinity," and, worse still, the article contains an unfortunate buzzword: "The Latins are the great actors of the future. So we must create an intimate commercial and spiritual collaboration among all the peoples of our race." But who can guarantee that "collaboration" was a word used by Jean Renoir? One might rather think it was a word that a skillful and quick-witted fellow like him would avoid. He was speaking French to a Portuguese journalist, and he himself was in the United States when the interview was published. He certainly didn't ask to review the text before publication. He was not mistrustful, and he had no experience of the way dictatorships use everything to propagandize for themselves. In the second interview, he speaks of the character played by Dalio in *Grand Illusion*, Rosenthal, "to boast of his sentimental and emotional qualities," in the words of Beylie. From reading the analyses that he was providing of these articles in the Portuguese press, it becomes clear that the charge against Jean is false, despite the tendentious language in the first interview. That it is false is not surprising, since it does not fit the man's character and, on the other hand, it coincides all too well with the nasty rivalries and paranoia of the day.

At the time, Lisbon was a refugee city from which people hoped to escape to America. Often the wait for a boat or a plane was very long. Thanks to the American friends who had gotten their tickets for them, Dido Freire and Jean Renoir were lucky. They were able to embark on December 20 on the *Siboney*, headed for the New World. Another Frenchman was traveling with them. They were soon well-acquainted, because he shared Jean Renoir's stateroom—it was Antoine de Saint-Exupéry.

✦

Chance did well by them once again: the friendship among the three exiles was immediate. Saint-Exupéry was six months younger than Jean, and this writer/aviator had all kinds of qualities to please his older companion; intelligence, imagination, and an underlying loneliness. He was too different to be easily understood. The new friends shared spontaneity, passion, a talent for having fun, and a taste for laughter. They were also, all three of them, very well mannered. Jean's background in aviation made it easy for him to appreciate Saint-Exupéry's exploits. He had been a test pilot who set up the Patagonia line and had made a solo flight from Paris to Saigon. In 1931, he won the prix Fémina for his second book, *Vol de nuit* (*Night Flight*). He was already famous as a writer and reporter. In 1939, he had published

Terre des hommes (*Wind, Sand and Stars*), a book in which courage and grandeur exist without bombast, along with the love of others and of beauty. Jean Renoir had not read it yet. "We began a series of excited discussions about my old hobbyhorse, the power of the environment. Saint-Exupéry believed in it but did all he could to escape from it. He went so far as to refuse to learn English, saying that he'd already had enough problems learning French."[20] When they arrived in Jersey City at three in the afternoon on December 31, 1940, they parted with regret, promising to see each other again soon.

Robert Flaherty was waiting for Jean and Dido; their greetings did not lack warmth. They owed their being there to him. In the midst of their expressions of affection, Robert Flaherty, no less exuberant than the Frenchman, noticed his friend's short-brimmed felt hat and burst out laughing. He could not let him go out with a hat like that— he had to look like an American right away. So he put his own hat on Jean's head, a broad-brimmed Western one, and threw the other one in New York Harbor. Flaherty was not the least bit interested in fashion; it was just his way of expressing his joy and his desire to see his friends adapt to a new land that was so different from their old one. Dido and Jean did not have time to see much of anything in their short trip across Manhattan with him to the Hotel Royalton at 44 West 44th Street, across from the Algonquin. Louis de Rochemont, a friend of theirs and the director of *March of Time*, a newsreel that was updated each week and shown in every American movie theater, had gotten them rooms in this fifty-year-old hotel. Lilian Gish and other Hollywood actors were living in it, as well as Sherwood Anderson and the critic George Jean Nathan. Jean Renoir loved the slot in the bathroom wall for used razor blades.

It was New Year's Eve. They saw the lights of Broadway, and from their hotel they could hear the crowd in Times Square shouting at midnight in front of the *New York Times* building. The next morning, Bob Flaherty, generous and attentive, took them to brunch at the Hotel Lafayette. An eighteenth-century building, it was "ennobled by its age," in Jeans' words. Flaherty had an apartment in the Chelsea Hotel, another landmark for New Yorkers: Mark Twain and Thomas Wolfe had lived there, and later it became the watering place for another generation of filmmakers, from Shirley Clark to Andy Warhol. These hotels, which they visited in rapid succession, gave them the feeling that New Yorkers wanted to live in the past. They were indeed

[20] Jean Renoir, *Ma vie et mes films*, 167.

skyscrapers, but people seemed to flee the towering mirrors of steel and glass that the movies were full of. They seemed ashamed of what was brand new, and it reminded Jean of his father's notions about America and Americans: "He used to say that America was rich because Americans were the children of poor emigrants and that there were generations of illiterate ancestors behind them. 'Now that they have schools and that people work the virgin land, the result is surprising. But their grandchildren, after two generations of educated parents, will be as stupid as we are.'"[21] He began to wonder if his father wasn't right. It was too soon to pass judgment, and the people whom he was seeing, mainly Bob Flaherty and his friends, were not typical Americans. They had lived outside of the United States or were even born elsewhere. He was eager to see Hollywood, but he also did not want to leave the East Coast without going to Washington. His object was to go to the French embassy to see if he couldn't get authorization to bring Alain to the United States. Flaherty had spent the holidays in New York with Dido and Jean in order to welcome them, but he was working on a government-sponsored film in Washington called *The Land*. In fact, he was preparing to shoot in the offices of the Department of Agriculture. When he went back to Washington with Dido and Jean, he brought along several "close and not so close friends" and then invited all twenty of them to a big restaurant for a sumptuous banquet. When it came time to pay, Flaherty realized that he did not have enough money with him, but without hesitation he signed "the bill flamboyantly and exited to the bows of the maître d'. The trip gave us a good idea of Flaherty's style and a foretaste of American generosity."[22]

During their first stay in New York, an Irish taxi driver took Dido and Jean under his wing. On his day off, he took them on a tour of Manhattan on the elevated train, which no longer exists, and brought them home for a dinner of Irish stew cooked by his wife. All this was because they were French and also Catholic like him. It was a good example for them of the importance of ethnic groups in this huge country. But they had a lot to learn, and one surprise lead to the next.

Dido and Jean arrived in Hollywood on January 10, 1941, at one o'clock in the morning, after a long plane ride during which they tried to imagine what their life would be like in the Mecca of movies. Memories of films from the great days that inspired his youth kept coming

---

[21] *Renoir, par Jean Renoir*, 317 (= *Renoir, My Father*, 321–22).
[22] Jean Renoir, *Ma vie et mes films*, 169.

back to Jean. Besides Charlie Chaplin he thought of Mae Murray, "the actress who perhaps most influenced Catherine Hessling" (ibid., p. 171). The golden age of Hollywood had long since passed, and America is a place that doesn't spur one to look backwards, as he was soon to discover.

The life that was just beginning for them started in temporary quarters on the Strip, in a furnished apartment at Sunset Towers, 8358 Sunset Boulevard. Jean Renoir had two agents, Charles Feldman and Ralph Blum, whom he met on the day he arrived. They must have been hard workers, since he signed a contract on January 15 with Twentieth Century-Fox to make two films. Darryl Zanuck, who was vice president in charge of production at the time, was not yet forty and had already a long career in film behind him. Working with Zanuck was certainly the best Hollywood had to offer. Jean Renoir found the contract natural, but after all the setbacks he suffered with French producers, it seems unbelievable. But he told himself that in the land of movies, he was going to be able to make films his way. He had no idea what it was like to be a director in a big studio. To be sure, he knew that the way movies were made had nothing to do with his handcrafted art and do-it-yourself technique, but he believed that Zanuck was ready to let him have what he needed. The signing of the contract received a lot of publicity. Mention was made of the great Auguste Renoir, the most famous French painter in the United States. According to the press releases, exactly what films Jean Renoir was going to direct was still under discussion.

Jean was eager to write the screenplay for his first American film, but to work with Zanuck and the American production teams, he needed to speak English. Along with everyone else, he was well aware of that. Everyone was ready to help him with another job, one that was just as urgent for him, getting Alain to the United States. The help he got made Jean feel grateful to his producers—Twentieth Century–Fox provided an actor's contract for his son, and he got the necessary affidavit from his agent, Feldman, who also followed up on the steps taken in Washington with the French embassy.

The ambassador, Gaston Henry-Haye, was well known as a Pétain loyalist. Jean Renoir had to write to him several times. For several months, he worked very hard coordinating the differing procedures of the American administration and Vichy, and also to convince Alain, who does not seem to have been in much of a hurry to join them. The love that Jean felt for his son is touchingly evident in his letters. He addressed him with deep tenderness and much modesty. "I'm eager to see you come, since Dido and I are a little bored without you," he wrote on March 8, 1941.[23] The day before he wrote to Jean Gabin, "You can't imagine how happy I am at the prospect of seeing you here before too long. I think that you'll be happy here; I'd be completely happy if I had my kid here. I hope that the situation with him will get straightened out by Daven, who was willing to talk to Sidney Kent about it. I'm so depressed about it all that I don't go out and I'm not visiting my friends. The news of your arrival tonight was a ray of sunshine" (ibid., p. 23).

The number of letters in which he expresses his disappointment about Alain's absence is astonishing. His tone is always marked by that warmth of feeling that is so apparent in his films. Alain is his "kid," as he usually calls him, and he cannot stand being separated from him. But on May 6, he wrote to Saint-Exupéry:

> I have some good news to tell you. At least it's good for me, and since I like you, I know that it'll be good for you, too: finally, my boy has really decided to come here and be with me. I owe it to Moguy, who directed the last film that Alain worked in at the beginning of the war. Since Alain did such good work for him as a cameraman, he likes him and has confidence in him. It's the old story of Monsieur Perrichon. So Moguy sent Alain a telegram telling him that he was counting on him for the job, and now Alain's only interest in life is to get over here immediately (ibid., p. 37).

So his trial would soon be over. There was a false alarm from the ambassador, who wrote him in early June that a young man of Alain's age could not possibly be authorized to leave France. It provoked the following reaction: "I'm going to try to fall back on Brazil. And if things keep us apart for too long, I won't renew my contract and I'll return to France."[24]

As for mastering the English language, that, too, was a matter of time. It was not for lack of effort on Jean's part. Dido's lessons—her English was perfect—weren't sufficient. He immersed himself, as we would say nowadays, in the study of the language with the kind of specialized teacher that you can find in Hollywood, and for good reason. Her name was Mary Samelson and she was the mother of Paula Samelson, who, starting with the second of Jean's American films, was in charge of the dialogue. But his progress wasn't as rapid as he had hoped.

♦

[23] Jean Renoir, *Lettres d'Amérique*, 24.
[24] Letter to Claude Renoir, June 11, 1941, from Dido Renoir archive.

Jean was dying to get to work. Knowing what his next film was would free him from the anxiety he always felt when he had no work. Dido understood. She was the ideal companion, in good times as well as bad. During the dry spells, she was ingenious at distracting him, and her high spirits were unflagging.

Zanuck kept sending him screenplays, in English, to be sure, and after a while Jean could read them, but he kept on wanting a film whose script he himself had written. He had several projects. One of them, *Les Enfants de l'orage* (*Children of the Storm*) was inspired by a scene he had witnessed on the highways during the flight from Paris. Boys from a center for young delinquents were released because of the German onslaught.[25] Reading the scripts sent him by Zanuck had already taught him something: the synopsis he was writing with Dido's help, called *Flight South*, contains a well-written story logically developed with a certain amount of excitement and fine sentiments. It should have pleased an American producer. But Zanuck rejected it, since the subject didn't interest him. He wanted nothing of war or struggles rooted in social inequality. His own start was as a screenwriter, and he had good ones working on his team. He gave no serious thought to Renoir's ideas as the kernel of a film. What he wanted was a subject situated in France to which the director of *Grand Illusion* could bring his "foreign touch." There was no such thing available to him, but he did have a good screenplay by one of his favorite writers, Nunally Johnson. Called *Venezuela*, it was based on a novel by Stephen Wendt, and it featured an earthquake and a riot in a penitentiary. Jean found it uninspiring. He made a counteroffer: rather than his own script on the flight from Paris, he wanted to shoot a film based on *Terre des hommes* (*Wind, Sand and Stars*), the book by Saint-Exupéry that he really loved and whose English translation was a big success in America.

The idea of collaborating with Jean Renoir excited Saint-Exupéry. It was not easy as yet to talk by telephone between New York and California, so to start up their literary discussions again, Saint-Exupéry sent Jean recordings. In April, he went to Hollywood to meet his friend and see some agents and producers. But the trip did not help. Jean Renoir could not even get Zanuck to read the book.

In this waiting period, the burdens of exile began to weigh heavily. Jean was more and more anxious to get involved in directing a film so that he would be less preoccupied with Alain's absence, and so that

---

[25] Alexander Sesonske, "Jean Renoir in Georgia," *The Georgia Review*, 1982, 26, 11.

he would worry less about what was going on in France and in the world, where the war kept on spreading. Only the money question was resolved, and in a more than satisfactory way. In the year 1941, Jean received $54,000, a big sum in those days. "Dazzled by my salary, in my innocence I had no doubt that I'd be getting as much from then on, so I didn't hesitate to rent a very lovely home."[26] They moved in March to a large estate that had once belonged to George Eastman, founder of Eastman-Kodak Company in 1892, the man who had perfected the first rolled photographic film made of celluloid in 1898 and had industrialized its manufacture. In a letter to Alain, Jean wrote: "We're living in a very pretty house, with a fairly large yard, built on a hill that overlooks the town. It's in Hollywood, which is apparently not a very choice spot. Fancy people live in Beverly Hills, farther west, nearer the ocean. The most expensive villas are in Santa Monica. Dido and I are very happy in this house, which is a little old, a kind of Marlotte in America."

He tried to give Alain an idea of what this "big, funny country" was like, where he hoped he would soon see his son. "The streets are very long. For instance, we live at number 8150 Hollywood Boulevard, and before us, on our street, there are literally 8,148 homes. Hollywood Boulevard is the Boulevard des Capucines of Hollywood, but it's like that about two or three miles from us. The street then twists and turns in the hills and becomes a little street, and that's where we are. The place we're in is almost as rural as Les Collettes, except that there are more neighbors. At the foot of the hill, about the same distance as Le Béal is from Les Collettes, there's a bunch of shops and even restaurants, doctors, dentists, and markets."[27]

It soon became clear to Jean that social differences were a question of money. Your car, as much as your home and neighborhood, put you in one category or another. He wanted to buy a Chevrolet, like Harry, his manservant. But his agent assured him that he ought to have a Buick at least. So he bought a Buick convertible that he hated, while Dido drove around in an old Packard convertible "that was very cheap and much prettier than the Buick, I'm very jealous" (ibid., p. 25). Though he was a lover of fine cars, Jean kept the Buick until he went back to Europe many years later.

It was not hard for them to get a foothold in the movie capital. It did not matter that they lived on Hollywood Boulevard. They had just

[26] Jean Renoir, *Ma vie et mes films,* 174.
[27] Jean Renoir, *Lettres d'Amérique,* 25.

arrived and did not know the social geography, people said. His contract with Twentieth Century–Fox, even if we do not know the details, must have been a juicy one. So they were well off. What people thought didn't interest either of them, though. They made friends according to their taste and their choice. That would take time, as it would anywhere. Getting along with people on the street was simple, pleasant, and amusing. Jean Renoir enjoyed looking over the merchandise in the huge Schwab Drugstore at the intersection of Laurel Canyon and Sunset boulevards. You could find underwear, pots and pans, wine, and aspirin tablets all in the same store. He was delighted by the Farmer's Market, which seemed unreal after the food restrictions in the "new" Europe. In an open-air market, there were stands with all the farm produce you could imagine plus the best caviar, smoked salmon, and exotic fruits. They also explored the whole region, which was very varied and very beautiful. But soon after their arrival, Jean's war wound acted up, and he had to take it easy for a while.

◆

There were many French people there, either recent refugees or people who had moved there long ago, like Charles Boyer, who had come in 1930, or the directors Jacques Tourneur and Robert Florey. Even before World War I, foreigners had been working at Hollywood. Among the new arrivals, all branches of filmmaking were represented. Because of the unions, it was especially difficult for cameramen and set designers to find work. That was what happened to Eugène Lourié, who had worked for Jean in *The Lower Depths*. Others took whatever jobs they could find.

In general, Jean and Dido kept their distance from them. They were no more eager to spend their time with French people in a foreign land than they were to be with the Americans who welcomed them because their incomes were comparable. Both Jean and Dido were very courteous, but friendship was too important to them to develop relationships with people who did not interest them. That did not keep Jean from working to help his compatriots or any others, for that matter, if there was need. Generosity was his habit, and he did not hesitate to take steps to help others. That was how he learned from Haakon M. Chevalier, Malraux's translator, that the author of *Men's Hope* would be in danger if the Germans attacked the southern zone in France. Jean wrote immediately to Daryl Zanuck to ask for a contract for Malraux "even at a very low or even imaginary salary" so that he could get an entry visa for the United States.[28] He got a refusal from his producer without a clear explanation, but he understood what it was: Malraux was on file as a Communist.

There were two meeting places for the French in Hollywood: The Players, a bar on Sunset Boulevard that belonged to the director and screenwriter Preston Sturges, and, on La Cienega Boulevard, the home of Charles Boyer, who had become the soul of the French community. In his villa, Boyer had collected a large library of newspapers and documents that made it a real center for research on France. It soon became headquarters for French War Relief, which worked in partnership with British War Relief. Charles Boyer welcomed all political persuasions, since the French were, as always, never in agreement among themselves. Hanging side by side on his walls were a signed photograph of Pétain when he was still the hero of Verdun and a more recent one of General de Gaulle. Opposite both was a superb photo of Marshall Lyautey. "Charles Boyer's office was the oak of Saint Louis," as Jean-Pierre Aumont put it.[29] "I found there Kisling, Janine Crispin and her husband Georges Kessel, Louis Verneuil, Jean Renoir, René Clair, and two exotic, touching, poetic characters: Dalio, with his strange genius, his bitterness, his paradoxical nature, and André David, nearsighted, tenderhearted, giving off a kind of desperate joy, dreamy loneliness, and a continual fear of sin."[30] Kisling, Georges Kessel, Louis Verneuil, André Davis—so there were not just movie people in Hollywood. There was also a branch of France Forever, which was founded in 1940 to support Gaullism in the United States. Charles Boyer was a faithful member (according to William H. Gilcher) along with Julien Duvivier, Jean Gabin, Michèle Morgan, and Henri Diamant-Berger, who arrived much later.

Jean Renoir soon became aware of the tensions between various groups; he himself felt that he was leading a privileged life and found it unseemly to talk about the way French people who remained in France should lead their lives. He avoided these meetings in order not to get into fights with friends who took part in them. He would see them one by one for lunch or dinner now and then. Dido and Jean had a couple, Harry and Grace, who took care of household tasks for them. "He's pretty black, and she is a strange black-Irish mixture,

---

[28] Letter dated January 21, 1941, from Dido Renoir archive.

[29] Saint Louis (Louis IX, 1226–70), a king of legendary goodness, was supposed to have dispensed even-handed justice while sitting beneath the oak of Vincennes [Trans.].

[30] Jean-Pierre Aumont, Le soleil et les ombres (Paris, 1976), 95.

light brown with freckles, and very pretty. He was a bus driver in Pasadena. They're very nice and relaxed. His style is to say OK and give you a pat on the back when you ask him to do something for you."[31] Neither Jean nor Dido had any difficulty inspiring their devotion or adjusting to their different customs.

Jean's English was progressing, and, for fun, Harry and Grace got themselves a French conversation and grammar book so that they could learn some French. As time passed, Jean began writing and reading English, but he still didn't know when he would begin shooting a film. Zanuck was still thinking about *Venezuela,* but he was running into casting problems. Since several actors had refused the script, the subject of his film still hadn't been decided. Jean kept on suggesting things to adapt for the screen: making a film from Knut Hamsun's *Hunger,* or from Claude Tillier's novel, *Mon oncle Benjamin (My Uncle Benjamin)*—now there's a real French subject! Zanuck turned both down. Every once in a while a Twentieth Century–Fox press release would announce a future film by Jean Renoir. But that was just fluff to keep people's interest up. There was no reality to the releases. In addition to *Venezuela,* Zanuck had found another script, *I Wake up Screaming,* though he didn't want to let go of *Venezuela.* Jean had seen enough of Zanuck to realize that working with him wouldn't be easy.

Dido had the idea of sending for Bob Flaherty's younger brother, David, to give Jean a hand. "It would be great to feel as though we have a real friend with us. Afterwards, Jean will try to get them to give David a contract with Twentieth Century–Fox so he can make his first film with them. I already told his agent how happy Jean would be to work with someone whom he already knows and has confidence in. They don't seem to think it unreasonable, but with them you can never tell."[32]

◆

On May 14, 1941, since the shooting of *Venezuela* was still up in the air, Jean Renoir wrote to his agents, Feldman and Blum, that despite his sincere desire to please Fox, he was concerned about the risk he was running if the United States entered the war and his contract was broken; he asked what he would have to do. Since of the two subjects that had been proposed, he preferred *I Wake up Screaming* with Charles

---

[31] Jean Renoir, *Lettres d'Amérique,* 25.
[32] Letter of Dido Freire to Robert Flaherty, January 25, 1941, from Dido Renoir archive.

Laughton, Henry Fonda, and Alice Fay, to show his good faith, he suggested that this second script be the first film of his contract. Then he explained what he considered to be the most important point: "When I came to Hollywood, it was in the hope of offering the Americans what was best in me. Now, rightly or wrongly, I'm convinced that I can do something good with *Wind, Sand and Stars* by Saint-Exupéry. So I'd appreciate it if you could find a way for me to film it. . . . I'd also be very happy if you'd be so good as to draw the attention of any future producers to the fact that I am much more an author of films than a simple director of scenes, and that the little success I have had has especially been due to my scripts. To be sure, I do not expect to do in English what I have done in French, I mean making a screenplay from a story (which was usually a story that I myself had written, as in *Grand Illusion*), the editing, the dialogue, and everything except producing, in which I have no pretense of being competent. But the producer who would let me collaborate with him would profit from it, and the same is true of my work as a director, which will be much better if I share in creating the continuity."[33]

This letter lays out the problems that Jean Renoir met with in Hollywood. It shows his clearheadedness and also the way in which he went after projects that struck a chord in him. The letter was, however, never sent. Apparently its target was Darryl Zanuck, but, two days later, on May 16, Jean was editing a letter addressed "Dear Charlie" (Feldman) to say that he "wanted to talk over *Venezuela* in person," and he asserts: "I am incapable of making a film according to the big studio method whereby I am brought a script that I haven't made myself and I have to follow it like the Bible. . . . You have explained to me that I wouldn't be able to work in a spirit of free discussion here in Hollywood, and that, with Goldwyn, Selznick, Wanger, or Korda I would run into even greater difficulties than with a big studio. Should I conclude that I'd better leave Hollywood?

"Think it over and tell me frankly. I'm not ready to change countries, but if I think that I won't be able to do the kind of aesthetic work here that is my only goal in life, I'll go someplace else to do it" (ibid). Whether these letters were sent or not doesn't matter much. They give a notion of the anguish their author was feeling at age forty-seven, having already made more than twenty films, many of which, as he knew, were masterpieces. It had not taken him long to understand the problems that Hollywood presented him. Only he could re-

[33]Dido Renoir archive.

solve them and it was vitally important that he do so. They were worse than what he had known in France, where there was always some way to get around such obstacles. In America, it was simply impossible to use the methods of a craftsman. Once more, the son's life resembles that of the father. Each of them had a unique way of working that did not coincide with the expectations of other people.

In the end, they shot neither *Venezuela* nor *I Wake up Screaming*. Among the screenwriters that Zanuck liked very much was Dudley Nichols, the author of several scripts that were directed by John Ford, among them *Stagecoach*. Nichols had made a screenplay from a serial written by Vereen Bell for the *Saturday Evening Post*. Zanuck sent this script, entitled *Swamp Water*, to Jean Renoir, who read it on May 18 and was delighted. Finally, an American subject like the one he was looking for! It was a simple and violent story situated in the Okefenokee swamp at the border between Georgia and Florida. Zanuck had first thought of it for Fritz Lang, who was really hoping to shoot it, but if Jean Renoir wanted to try his luck, why not? Zanuck handed down his decision on May 23. Fritz Lang was not pleased, but that did not hinder him and Jean from becoming good friends later on.

◆

Zanuck expected some surprises from his new, much-admired director. He thought the major problem would be linguistic, and to get around it, he had required that the Frenchman have a "dialogue director" who would serve as an intermediary between himself and the actors, technicians, and set personnel. Jean Renoir, however, thought of this fellow, Irving Pichell, as a member of the studio who had been given the job of inspecting his work. The idea did not please him at all, even though he realized that his English was still tentative. It was also Jean's intention to refuse to make a film with stars. Directing actors is an exercise of power. Famous actors have their habits and tics, and they can be difficult to handle when one doesn't speak their language. Jean Renoir could not imagine that he would be able to persuade Hollywood stars to do what he wanted in his first film. That was what he explained to Zanuck, who had already announced that Linda Darnell, a beautiful brunette who was very popular at the time, and several others, would appear in the film. Jean chose Ann Baxter, Frank Lloyd Wright's granddaughter, for what was to be her first great film. Zanuck had a harder time letting himself be persuaded when Jean announced his intention to go to Georgia for location shots. What was the point of these huge studios in Beverly Hills if they were going to shoot on location? They were so big and so well-equipped that you could recreate anything you wanted in them. Jean Renoir was sure of it, but he stuck to his idea. It was all right with him for the houses to be built in the studios for interiors and exteriors, but the scenes that took place in the swamps themselves he wanted to shoot on location at the places described by the author, whom he was anxious to get to know. The night before his first studio meeting with Dudley Nichols, on May 27, Jean got authorization to go to Georgia.

Jean had no idea that the studio meeting would be what it was. Zanuck was not present, but everything revolved around him. Irving Pichell, associate producer, and a group of studio executives discussed in detail the way to adapt the screenplay. Their decisions would not be final until Zanuck had approved them. Jean Renoir did not take part in the discussion. He was too astonished. But from their first meeting, he had warm feelings for Dudley Nichols that quickly turned into friendship, despite the thousands of miles that separated them. Nichols was living in Milford, Connecticut, at the time.

On May 29, Jean Renoir set out for Waycross, Georgia, to discover a new land that pleased him very much. He still found it easy to relate to farmers. The notes that he took "on the Okefenokee swamp and its environs" are full of telling details:

> Lots of children, most of them blond. A little girl plays a drum consisting of a can strung around her neck. Another little girl plays on the roof of a hut. Lots of dogs, no cats. Sometimes a small tame animal, either a skunk or a fox. Cattle everywhere, along the roads, around the houses, the cows are small. . . . Some women do the ironing in the evening on the porches, which are all lit up. The roofs of the porches look like afterthoughts. In front of every house there's a huge, lovely tree often covered with Spanish moss. The earth is very light colored, almost white, which makes for a strong contrast with the dark, almost black earth around the swamp. Lots of dust on the dirt roads, which are very hard.
>
> Take many shots of trees loaded with moss and magnificent skies to use as backdrops for close-ups.
>
> Try to take shots for the film while there's work on the farms, as happens to be the case right now; that way, the countryside will be more than a lifeless backdrop.

And then he copied down snatches of conversations with the farmers. It was a mixture of the familiar and the exotic: alligators, beavers, rattlesnakes, water moccasins, turtles, wild black pigs, fields of cotton and sugar cane. But farmers are the same everywhere! "There's a place you'd like," he wrote to Gabrielle. "The people are the same as in Essoyes. I kept feeling I was with my cousins. Unfortunately, it's very far from here, and it takes two days by plane to get back."[34]

♦

Dido and Jean were back in Hollywood by June 4. Despite the discoveries of his trip, Jean was not relaxed the way he once was. On June 11 he wrote to Saint-Exupéry: "I'm not talking about current events. I think that you and I are both in the dumps. I can't for the life of me understand why boys the age of my son are on opposite sides of a barricade in Syria shooting machine guns at each other."[35] Alain's absence preyed on his mind and made him even more sensitive to the war.

In the studio, they continued preparing the script to suit Zanuck's wishes. On June 9, a new version was ready, and Zanuck announced that the film, which was originally supposed to be 11,000 feet long, couldn't exceed 8,000. On June 12, another meeting took place, in which Jean Renoir asserted himself and skilfully suggested to Zanuck the ideas that he hoped would win out. On June 25, he and Dido went back to Waycross to shoot, with Dana Andrews, Irving Pichell, Lucien Ballard (a cameraman who despite his name was not French but American Indian), and a small technical team. It rained for five days straight, but it was not a catastrophe. He could stay as long as he needed. They all returned on July 12, and shooting began in the studio on July 14.

On the set, his relations with the technicians and actors were excellent: "*Swamp Water* was my first encounter with American actors. It was the beginning of a romance that reminded me of my love affair with French actors. When we first started shooting, I got especially close to Ann Baxter. Her way of acting and her personality reminded me of Janie Marèze in *La Chienne*. The two films were completely different, but she had the same way of mastering a situation without appearing to. She made her way around problems instead of getting stuck in them."[36] Relations with the studio executives, however, took a turn for the worse. Jean found them comically grotesque, and he felt deprived of the advantages that come with independence. He was ashamed of his first Hollywood "sellout": he agreed to shoot a scene in several shots that he had originally shot in a single, moving shot,

[34] Letter dated June 20, 1941, provided by Jean Slade.
[35] Jean Renoir, *Lettres d'Amérique*, 54.
[36] Jean Renoir, *Ma vie et mes films*, 193.

"following my custom of combining into one shot all the elements of a given situation."

Orson Welles also used depth of field this way in *Citizen Kane* in 1941, and *The Magnificent Ambersons*, made in 1942, has a famous sequence shot of this type that lasts 167 seconds. Welles worshiped Jean Renoir and knew his work very well. It took film critics a long time to discover these innovative techniques, and Twentieth Century–Fox wasn't ready to accept them as yet. Without mention of the offending scene, shortly after Jean was obliged to retake the sequence at issue, he was informed that because of his slowness the rest of the film would be entrusted to another director. He was accused of going over budget. After saying his farewells to the technicians, the workers, and the actors, Jean went home "in despair." He tells us how he then got a phone call from Zanuck in the middle of the night: "The Clown King himself sprung me from the trap" (ibid., p. 184). The next day, when he went to the studio to resume shooting, there was an eerie silence when he first stepped onto the set; then everyone whom he had said goodbye to the day before burst into applause.

◆

Jean Renoir gave Zanuck credit for his talents, especially his savvy editing, which saved many films. But *Swamp Water* did not need saving, and Renoir was in the habit of taking part in the editing of his films. At Twentieth Century–Fox, he was lucky even to be present in the cutting room. Yielding to this system, which deprived Jean of an essential part of his job, cost him a lot. It did not take him long to decide that he wanted his freedom, and he did so even before his first film came out. Zanuck let him off his contract, which specified a second film. Jean Renoir remained dissatisfied, feeling he had somehow been cheated out of his status as an auteur.

When he wrote the following words, he had his own experiences in mind: "In film, what saves us is a little patience, even a little love. If you scratch off some makeup and push aside the lighting, you just might get a glimpse of that delightfully complicated creature, man. My dream is of a handcrafted cinema, where the auteur expresses himself as directly in film as a writer does in books or a painter in pictures. Now and then, that dream comes true. Some auteurs have really left a mark on their work" (ibid., p. 188). He himself was one of them, as he well knew. Hollywood was unable to destroy him. Despite the constraints he agreed to work under, *Swamp Water* has his mark upon it. On the surface, his relations with Zanuck were fine. He had not gotten what he wanted, and he understood that he could never change the work habits of Zanuck and his colleagues. The best thing was to withdraw. He still hoped that, with a smaller company, he could have more independence, despite the warnings of his agents.

Jean had not abandoned the idea of making a movie out of *Wind, Sand and Stars*. Before going off to reconnoiter for the exteriors, Renoir wrote to Zanuck and recommended that he read Saint-Exupéry's synopsis. He admitted that Zanuck might think it confusing. "Still, even in this shape, you may find exactly what won me over: the possibility of presenting to the public a human ideal that's the complete opposite of Nazism. That possibility is what gave me my enthusiasm."[37] Zanuck kept turning a deaf ear to these requests, but Jean did not let himself get discouraged. After breaking his contract, he became even more persistent. He and Saint-Exupéry had the same fiery passion for the project. The affection that had spontaneously arisen between them was especially precious in those days, when both of them were suffering from the war and from a lack of solidarity with their fellow refugees. Jean wanted to entertain his new friend in his big house: that was an old habit he had learned from his parents, whose doors were always open to friends. While he was shooting in Georgia, Robert Flaherty and his brother David stayed in the Renoir home in Hollywood, where they entertained many guests, including Orson Wells and Joris Ivens, whose wife was Flaherty's editor.

Saint-Exupéry did not like his life in New York and was really happy to move to Hollywood for several weeks. He arrived on August 20 with the manuscript of *Pilote de guerre* (*War Pilot*) far from completion. He had gotten into the habit of working at night and sleeping during the day, and so he did not see much of his hosts or his secretary, who held him in awe, in part because of the strange nature of their relationship: he would record on disks what she would type out the next day; his powerful voice resonated in the silent house, making it difficult to sleep. Dido is still amazed at the number of saucers, each one containing a drop of olive oil, that he put in the refrigerator. He used the congealed oil instead of butter for his breakfast, which he would eat when all the other members of the household were going to bed.

Saint-Exupéry stayed with Jean and Dido until the beginning of October. When he tore himself away from the writing process that was responsible for his bizarre schedule, he was the liveliest and most

[37] Letter dated May 22, 1941, Dido Renoir archive.

interesting guest imaginable, a great conversationalist with a repertoire of surprising card tricks. With his help, Jean Renoir got in touch
with Maximilien Becker, a literary agent in New York who had taken
care of the translation of *Terre des hommes*. He wrote to him on September 4 that he had read "what exists" of Saint-Exupéry's new book,
"a magnificent thing, even more beautiful than *Wind, Sand and Stars*. I
am sure that you will have a huge success with this book." He also
said that he himself wants to write a sequel to *Grand Illusion*. "I have a
few ideas about it. I'm hoping to turn out a pretty funny book that is
at the same time fairly dramatic, maybe too critical to make a good
movie."[38] The boredom that he said he felt during the shooting and
the absence of a contract with any other producer made him think
about writing. But writing for him was a second choice.

◆

Meanwhile, Jean was finishing *Swamp Water*. He went to the studio
until September 14. The end of his association with what he called
Fifteenth Century–Fox weighed heavily on him. He had learned a
good deal in the past few months. On July 29, 1941, he wrote to
Paulette Renoir, his brother Claude's wife:

> the work I'm doing isn't absolutely fantastic, but I think the problem is
> less with the film than with me. Once you have tasted the pleasures of
> individual creativity, it probably becomes very hard to knuckle under
> and accept the discipline of a screenplay. What's more, the least little de-
> tails of the production are decided by the studio, and the job of the direc-
> tor is very limited. Still, I spend whole days with terrific people who are
> loaded with talent. American actors are extraordinary, and the workers
> and technicians are first class. Working with them is a sheer delight.
> They're decent people, good-hearted and happy, and they're disci-
> plined, too. I'm sure that someone who knew the language well and the
> culture and had a little freedom could make extraordinary films here,
> working with such people.[39]

At that point, he was less optimistic about the future. His own
seemed insolubly blocked, and, given the prevailing working methods, he thought the American film industry was destined to become
the equivalent of the Odeon Theater in Paris in the old days: rhetori-
cal and out of touch. For a change of heart, he went to Arizona to visit
the Native American tribe from which his cameraman, Lucien Ballard, was descended. When he returned, Antoine de Saint-Exupéry

---

[38] Jean Renoir, *Lettres d'Amérique*, 77–78.
[39] Dido Renoir archive.

left to make room for the next wave of guests, Gabrielle and her family.

"Ga," Jean's lifelong friend since infancy, who married the American painter Conrad Slade in 1914, had come to the United States for the first time with her husband and her son, Jean. First they spent a few months in New England, Slade's birthplace. Slade was one of those supercivilized expatriates who have no difficulty feeling comfortable among European artists and intellectuals. He had been a student of George Santayana's at Harvard, who described him as follows: "The most Nordic of all my American friends was so Nordic that he seemed an American only by accident. When he went home, everything seemed to him unnecessary and inhuman; and he was content to live in Paris among poor artists and working people with none of the comforts or social pleasures among which he had been bred."[40]

From the time the Slades arrived, Dido and Jean really began to take root in California. Gabrielle's presence brought the past back to life. In Cagnes, after the flight from Paris, she was there with Jean and Dido, and they renewed the old ties of affection in the most natural way. Dido, the newcomer, was curious about their wealth of memories, had been accepted instantly, and asked questions even as she took in all of what they were saying. They got into the habit of explaining everything when she was around, and she laughed with them at their comic, freewheeling stories that were as colorful as the conversation once had been at the Renoir household. Time would pass quickly in that land where oranges, grapevines, and olive trees grew, just as in Cagnes.

Soon, *Swamp Water* was ready for release. It was first shown in public at the two theaters in the town of Waycross. The governor of Georgia declared that day, October 23, 1941, *Swamp Water* day. There was a parade in the streets and a ball to top off a banquet that was attended by the author of the novel, Vereen Bell. They even elected a Miss Okefenokee. All this was free publicity for Twentieth Century–Fox.

The New York premier took place on November 15 at the Globe Theater on Broadway. The film ran until Christmas Eve. During the first week it made $13,000, twice the average. By the fourth week, it was still making $7,500, and then the receipts went down normally. The reviews were generally favorable, and Southerners felt they were recognizable in the film, which is noteworthy since Jean Renoir's im-

[40] George Santayana, *Persons and Places, The Middle Span*, vol. II (New York, 1944–53), 144.

age of them was not the usual Hollywood stereotype: some of the film was shot on location instead of in the studio, and the film's acting is undeniably Renoirian. Jean Renoir was the first to be surprised at his success, but he still had no regrets about having cut his ties with Zanuck's powerful company. Thirty years later, Jean-Luc Godard said of the film: "*Swamp Water* works on the principle of *Toni* but with twenty years of experience behind it. It's not Renoir's taste for danger anymore, but confident daring. . . . He proves to us time and again that the only way not to arrive late is always to be ahead of time. He's already taking down the scaffolding when we're still admiring its boldness."[41]

It's important to realize that Jean Renoir knew what he was doing while he was doing it, and also to keep in mind the conflict between him and his producers, between him and other directors, to say nothing of the conflict that existed most of the time between him and the public. Nothing could keep him from striking out on his own, face front and eyes open.

But he had to find a way out one more time. Fortunately, hope was quickly reborn in him, because his driving need to create carried him past discouragement and disappointment. He ran into an old friend, Steve Pallos, who offered to help him "cook up a scheme that would allow us to make" the film about the children in occupied France. "I'm right where I was before starting *Grand Illusion*. I spend every day thinking about the screenplay, writing scenes of it, calling up its characters. I'll be terribly hurt if this film doesn't get made," he wrote Luise Rainer on November 18, 1941.[42]

Luise Rainer was a fine actress, Viennese by birth, who had been a member of Max Reinhardt's theater company. In 1933, she started working in New York theater, then she made several films in Hollywood, including Pearl Buck's *The Good Earth*, for which she won an Academy Award. She suggested to him another subject for a film adapted from a book. In the same letter, he told her he was overwhelmed with work. In fact, the film on the children did not pan out, but he had other ideas. David O. Selznick, producer of *Gone with the Wind*, wanted him to shoot a Jeanne d'Arc. It did not tempt Jean, who made a counteroffer: *Precious Bane*, with Ingrid Bergman. Although she was in favor of it, no producer wanted her to be disfigured by a harelip, like the heroine in Mary Webb's novel.[43] That, however, was

---

[41] André Bazin, *Jean Renoir* (Paris, 1971), 250.
[42] Jean Renoir, *Lettres d'Amérique*, 81.
[43] Jean Renoir, *Oeuvres inédites*, 134.

not the end of the story: he had other proposals to make, but he had to set them aside for a while to attend to his son's arrival in the United States.

In the beginning of November, Dido and Jean Renoir went to Washington and New York to iron out the details of Alain's trip. Questions about his French exit visa and his U.S. papers were answered in person in the capital. In New York, the ticket for the trip from Casablanca to New York on a Portuguese ship cost " a small fortune," but it did not matter. Jean wrote to some friends in the south of France: "I just got a cable from the fellow. He left Casablanca on November 19 on board the *Serpa Pinto*. At the moment, he should be between Bermuda and Havana. I believe they'll stop off in Mexico to leave off some people at Veracruz, and, with any luck, they should arrive in New York around Christmas. I reserved a room for him in the Hotel Lafayette, the oldest one in town; it's very small and very unmodern, and French people own it. The food there is very good. All that Alain will have to do is hop on the train, which takes a day and a night to reach Chicago, then three days to get from Chicago to Los Angeles via the Santa Fe Railway: then, after a year and two months separation, I'll have my kid back."[44]

During his stay in New York, Jean Renoir met Maximilien Becker, who suggested that he write a book about Auguste Renoir. But he had to make money to pay taxes, and a film would make a lot more money than a book. His spirits raised by the prospect of Alain's arrival, Jean revised his judgment on the experience he had making *Swamp Water*.

> Americans are good people and you can work here. I had some very tough times with Fox, but when you weigh the pros and cons, they were probably not tougher than what I went through with French producers. The competition is fierce, and the profession is lousy with parasites, as it is everywhere. I still think there is a place for people who really do good work. It's a much bigger change than people imagine. I see a lot of Gabrielle, who likes it here, but who claims that she'd feel less far from home if she were in China. I don't speak of Dido, because she's traveled so much that nothing surprises her anymore. As for me, I'll say it again—I'm beginning to understand and like this country."

This he wrote to his sister-in-law, Paulette Renoir, on the day of Pearl Harbor, while Alain was still at sea (ibid.). The boy arrived in New York the day after Christmas and made it to his Dad and Dido by year's end. Jean did everything he could to make it possible for him to

[44]Jean Renoir, *Lettres d'Amérique*, 83–86.

get used to the country quickly. He was surprised by a letter Alain had sent him from Bermuda. As he wrote to a friend: "It's a pretty scary letter. It's as though the boy has been liberated from a world where he had to weigh each word and can finally cry out what he feels and say what he wants."[45] He knew how to read between the lines, just as he knew how to listen and respond. Apparently, the letters Jean received from France did not really inform him about the way things were turning out there.

◆

When he arrived, Alain told them what he had seen, and he expressed his desire to join the Free French forces (FFL). There was no way his father could blame him for that. Since Germany and Italy had declared war on the United States on December 11, the attitude of the Vichy government grew harsher. The consul general of Los Angeles, who had been cordial until them, sent a letter on December 28 to Jean Renoir, René Clair, Julien Duvivier, Michèle Morgan, and Jean Gabin, as follows: "The French government has requested me, through our ambassador in Washington, to insist with you firmly that you return to France as soon as possible."[46] Not one of the people who received this missive obeyed it. Jean's reply was as follows: "For personal reasons, I would be very happy to make a film in France. So I am at your disposal to look over proposals that a truly French firm might offer me. At the moment, I am committed to two films, and, moreover, I am in the hire of Feldman-Blum Corporation. First I must make the two films in question. Then, or even during the filming, the French firm in question could discuss practical matters with Feldman-Blum Corporation." The letter ends with a postscript in which he asks for his passport to be renewed—it was about to expire a few days later (ibid., pp. 93–94). Actually, he did not have a contract and he was about to spend a few more months with nothing to do, but everyone knew then what it meant to go back to France and work there.

On Epiphany, Jean Renoir sent a cable to Saint-Exupéry to tell him that he and Dido were arriving in New York with Alain, who was en route to Africa to join the FFL. But the trip never took place. Jean proved to his son that the anti-American clichés, which he must have been treated to by his French friends during their long voyage across the Atlantic, had nothing to do with reality. He acquainted him with

[45] Letter to Estrella Boissevain, dated December 18, 1941, in Jean Renoir, *Lettres d'Amérique*, 89.
[46] Jean Renoir, *Lettres d'Amérique*, 93.

"a few high-quality Americans," as he put it, and then father and son together listened to Roosevelt on the radio, appealing to the country and announcing that foreigners could also be called to serve. Alain was so deeply impressed that he decided to enlist in the U.S. Army. "It's the least one can do," said his father; "the Americans offer us hospitality, it's natural that we should fight by their side." Alain Renoir told me that those were his father's words, and he hadn't forgotten them.

In a letter to the French ambassador who asked him for an explanation of Alain's attitude, Jean Renoir said that, by enlisting, his son

> was not acting in a rebellious way, but rather in response to the demands of a certain code of honor that can be defined in a few words: when you're twenty years old and you're French, either you stay in France and you share the suffering of your compatriots and you do what you can to help the government in the arduous task of putting the country back on its feet; or, if you leave the country, you enlist and you fight. Whichever it is, the idea of an easy life in Hollywood while his compatriots are unhappy seemed to him untenable (ibid., pp. 100–101).

Alain's enlistment entailed their separation once more, but this time it was a more acceptable separation. No one spoke of the risk that Alain was running. He was in an unavoidable situation that Jean had known himself when he was on the front lines. He was going to behave as his parents had, never saying a word about their worries. Alain signed up at the Army Recruiter's Office in their neighborhood and was sent on February 3, 1942, to Camp Roberts, 240 miles north of Los Angeles, and was instructed in artillery, even though he only liked the cavalry, like his father and grandfather before him. He was twenty years old and scarcely spoke English. His father also had been twenty in 1914, but their wars were not similar. The British were on the verge of being driven out of Singapore, which was a serious defeat for them. "This is going to be a long war," he predicted in a letter to Alain dated February 13, 1942, "and how can you tell whether destiny will make you more effective here, or instead, over there? The more I see, the more I believe that you can be helpful wherever you are, as long as you do your work conscientiously" (ibid., p. 97).

Alain had to spend two months in training camp before being sent somewhere on the Pacific front. Waiting for the mail became the event that established the rhythm of every day for Jean and Dido.

HOLLYWOOD ARTS

AND MANNERS

♦

n February of 1942, Dido and Jean found themselves a small house to buy at 1615 North Martel Avenue, between Hollywood and Sunset Boulevards. "It's about fifty years old; for Hollywood, that's a prehistoric relic." A bit decrepit, it had belonged to Agnes Ayres, who was in *The Sheik* with Rudolph Valentino. Hollywood legend has it that the two were passionately in love. Agnes built the house "in the old American style, part wood, part stucco," with a big, pretty yard. "The backyard was shaded by a huge mulberry tree whose branches fell from the trunk like a weeping willow's. At the opposite end of the yard, there was a giant avocado tree that bore no fruit, since all its sap was absorbed by the branches."[1] Dido quickly planted what Jean preferred and what reminded him of Cagnes: a grapevine and rosebushes. They moved there in April, leaving their large and luxurious mansion without regret; it had become a burden. At that moment, negotiations with Universal Pictures had concluded, and a contract was signed on March 30. Jean was guaranteed one film a year, at a high salary, and freedom the rest of the time.

What Universal offered him, via Feldman and Blum, was a kind of film that Jean Renoir had never tried before, musical comedy. The heroine was to be Deanna Durbin; at first its title was *Call Me Yours*, then *Forever Yours*, then finally *The Amazing Mrs. Holliday*. The script

[1] Jean Renoir, *Ma vie et mes films* (Paris, 1974), 214.

changed every time the title did. "It's chaos, fun, and tunes to go with them. My producer is Bruce Manning, a delightful fellow. He's from New Orleans, in other words, a Mediterranean, American style," as Jean wrote to Saint-Exupéry.[2] The film was a sequel to *Three Smart Girls*, which came out in 1936 and made the young Deanna Durbin famous. Shooting was supposed to start in June. The producer, Bruce Manning, was also the screenwriter. He improvised on the set during shooting, without preparing ahead of time. Jean Renoir was not hostile to improvisation as long as it was clear where things were heading. That was always the way he had done it, too. He wrote about this to Ralph Blum: "I believe in improvisation since I always improvised my own films. But the improvisation I did was always on top of scenes that were already totally written out in scripts that had been written and rewritten several times before the film began. I improvised depending on what I noticed on the set about the personality of the actors, to change a scene for the better. I would rewrite the dialogue to suit the feelings of the moment, to allow things to be more realistic and at times stronger."[3]

After a while, the confused, uninteresting, and silly script became unbearable, despite Manning's decency and the good fellowship with Deanna Durbin and the others. Moreover, his leg wound was hurting terribly, and standing up was not just painful, but impossible. Several times he suggested to Bruce Manning that he do the directing, which is finally what happened. On August 6, 1942, Jean withdrew for health reasons, and Manning took over the shooting, which lasted until December.

So his deal with Universal Pictures, which had seemed so promising because it was a smaller company than Fox and had a lighter-handed administration, was another setback. A few days before the end, he put down his impressions in a letter to his younger brother, Claude:

> Every once in a while I meet a big boss, and I think I'm going to get bawled out. On the contrary, I get consolation and pats on the back that would bowl over a bull. I can't figure it out. They have a strange combination of complete confidence and complete distrust in me. They get me involved in a feeble story that won't, at least in my opinion, make a good film, but they accept the most outrageous ideas I propose as long as they don't conflict with their established rules. If I want, I can have

[2] Jean Renoir, *Lettres d'Amérique*, ed. A. Sesonske (Paris, 1984), 262.
[3] Letter dated August 5, 1942, Dido Renoir archives.

Deanna Durbin make an entrance for her love scene doing a handstand, but if I want to make her laugh in a dramatic scene, for the sake of contrast, that'd be revolutionary. It will probably cost more than all my other films put together, but it doesn't matter.[4]

His morale was good, since he was regularly getting news from Alain—letters written in English arrived three times sooner because of the military censor. In addition, everyday life in the new little house was full of fun. In the garden "lettuce is growing, there are plenty of roses and there should be plenty of pears, persimmons, and avocados," he wrote in the same letter to his brother. That autumn, Gabrielle and her family moved into a furnished villa across the way, which they rented until they bought a house next door whose backyard adjoined theirs.

Jean had even more reasons to be in a good mood. In April 1942, after giving an interview to the French language weekly *Pour la victoire*, he worked on a screen adaptation of Steinbeck's *The Moon Is Down*, and he had just finished a script set in France, "maybe one of the first versions of *This Land Is Mine*."[5] He ascribes his problems with Fox and others to his shortcomings in English. But that was water over the dam, and in the same interview he expresses his intention to stay in America, where, as he says, he would have ended up sooner or later. A month later he wrote to Claude: "I've made my first request for papers. In three years I'll be an American citizen. That has nothing to do with what's going on at the moment, it's just because I feel more comfortable in this big country than in the confines of Europe. Alain is like me—he doesn't consider himself a refugee, he's an American."[6] In June, he got himself a divorce lawyer; he and Catherine Hessling had been legally separated since 1935.

A change of continents, a new nationality, a change of civil status—that's a lot of unusual changes for a man who was almost fifty years old. Jean Renoir did not even try to explain it later on when he returned to France to dispel the misunderstandings that they gave rise to. He did not feel that he had to justify himself. He lived life to the limit, just as his father had done, until the very end. Jean was impulsive, and he took sudden decisions, as we have seen, but he did so with a sure hand despite the way things sometimes appear. Those who judge him do so according to out-of-date criteria that have noth-

---

[4]Jean Renoir, *Lettres d'Amérique*, 114–15.
[5]William H. Gilcher, *Jean Renoir in America* (Des Moines, 1979), 375.
[6]Jean Renoir, *Lettres d'Amérique*, 102.

ing to do with his particular situation. They forget that he was, above all, a creative person nurturing his talent, even if he did so unconsciously; they are also unaware of the atmosphere that prevailed among French exiles in the United States between 1940 and 1945.

◆

After the Americans disembarked on the North African coast on November 8, 1942, relations between the United States and France were broken off completely. From that day, those living under the Nazi occupation neither received nor provided any news. It was difficult for one side to imagine what was happening on the other. Jean Renoir had learned long ago that there are no white and no black horses, and that men are not either good or bad—it comes out in his movies as well—but people who are actually subjected to exile, for instance, only rarely reveal their better side. Certainly there are human beings of exceptional greatness and also some genuinely innocent people who do not allow themselves to get caught up in petty factional rivalries, but most cannot keep themselves from speculating about the advantages that will accrue to them if they place their bets in one place or another. Gatherings are just occasions to look over the other guy and trade insults. In an atmosphere like a businessman's bar, people discuss each other behind well-protected blinds, and the only agreement among them lies in their mistrust of the generous country that welcomes them. "Since the last time I saw you, something very important has happened to me: I've come to hate the French in America," as Jean put it to Saint-Exupéry on June 2, 1942 (ibid.).

Saint-Exupéry himself published an "open letter" in the *New York Times* of November 15 that elicited broad protest among French emigrants: he suggested that his compatriots enlist and all fight under the same flag. "As for me, I hereby request to be attached to a combat squadron in North Africa."[7] Alain's decision to take part certainly led to his father's request for naturalization. Jean was disgusted to discover that most French people in the United States were even more mean spirited than the shirkers behind the lines in World War I. By his system of values, the main thing was to do what you had to. In fact, that was the subject of the film for which he and Dudley Nichols signed a contract with RKO.

His idea for a film about the children of the 1940 exodus changed into a script about the occupation, though he knew he could not imagine it without having actually lived through it. But he also knew

[7] Guy Fritsch-Estrangin, *New York entre de Gaulle et Pétain* (Paris, 1969), 82.

that the idea that people had of it in America was totally fake, and he was prepared to bear witness, one more time, that the world cannot be divided into two camps, the heroes and the traitors. His plan was to write the script with Dudley Nichols, who had become his friend since the making of *Swamp Water*.

Later, Jean wrote that as a child he had dreamed he met the noble knight Bayard "in a little grove on the banks of the Cagne, the riverlet that flows near Les Collettes; then one spring evening, in Hollywood, in an ordinary hotel room, my dream came true. Bayard was there. The bed with its quilted bedspread, the Mexican style dresser, and the countrified curtains faded into a haze. The copse along the Cagne came into focus, and he was there, ever so noble beneath the southern sky. It was Dudley Nichols, who smiled and stretched out his hand to me."[8] In Jean's eyes, Nichols was and always remained the irreproachable knight who knew no fear. He had been John Ford's main screen writer. After they worked together on *Swamp Water*, he became a great admirer of Jean, as we can see from the following excerpt from a letter to Theresa Helburn, assistant director of the Theater Guild of New York: "To my mind, he's the most amazing filmmaker around today, and he's not interested in money."[9] He often let out his anger at the managers of the big studios, whose spirit was far from chivalrous. The two friends first tried unsuccessfully to interest Walter Wanger in a film on Nazi Germany called *The Age of the Fish*.[10]

When Nichols and Renoir signed their contract with RKO, in mid-July of 1942, they took pains to specify what they really cared about. Jean Renoir was to be in charge of the story, the direction, and the editing. The script was then called "The Children," and it already had a teacher, a German colonel, and a train saboteur during the occupation. The plot really jelled after a conversation Jean had with Charles Laughton. Laughton and Renoir both recalled the story of Alphonse Daudet called "La Dernière Classe" ("The Last Class"), and on April 2, Jean filed a script in the Screenwriters' Guild entitled "Mr. Thomas." Mr. Thomas was the teacher's name in the screenplay, and who could play him better than Charles Laughton? Dudley Nichols was still at home in Connecticut. Once the break with Universal happened, Jean Renoir wired him and Dudley Nichols came to Hollywood on August 21, ready to begin work.

That was when Jean discovered that his good friend Bayard, the

[8]Jean Renoir, *Ecrits, 1926–1971*, ed. C. Gauteur (Paris, 1974), 201.
[9]Letter dated June 16, 1941, cited by William H. Gilcher, *Jean Renoir in America*, 378.
[10]According to Alexander Sesonske.

irreproachable and fearless, was afraid of daylight. To write, he had to have darkness and lamplight. When he would visit them in the morning, they closed the shutters, drew the curtains, and lit the lamps. Jean Renoir, who was curious about everyone's peculiarities, also respected them without expressing the least displeasure. He and Dudley Nichols worked without stopping. It was easy for them to work together. On September 13, Jean wrote to Alain: "I finished the script that I have been writing with Dudley Nichols for Charles Laughton. We're just delighted. It is very violent, and it shows, I hope clearly, that certain European leaders preferred to see the Nazis take over their countries rather than provide better conditions to workers. It's the history of the collaboration, conscious or not, honest or not, that we're about to try to explain."[11]

◆

Meanwhile, in the real but unimaginable Paris of the occupation that Jean Renoir did not try to recreate in his movie about resisters and collaborators, on September 30, 1942, at the Lord Byron Cinema (the fascists had forgotten to change its name) there appeared a dubbed version of *Tosca*, the movie that Jean had prepared with Karl Koch and Luchino Visconti. He only made five shots for it before hurrying back home amid the tumult of the French defeat. His sequence, which is the most masterful in the film, is a nocturnal gallop from the Palazzo Farnese to the Castel Sant' Angelo; it is an expression of his love for the baroque. Karl Koch, faithful friend, stuck to his cutting, and Michel Simon makes a superb Scarpia. Jean Renoir did not actually see this film himself until March of 1978. By then, it had become someone else's work. He found it strange that this story of a pure-hearted revolutionary, a victim of the corrupt and corrupting papal police, had been chosen with the concurrence of the fascist regime in Italy and shown under the occupation. At the time of its premier, Jean did not hear a thing about it, since that was when relations between Vichy and the U.S. government were beginning to disintegrate.

At that time, Jean's chief preoccupation was the casting of *This Land Is Mine*, which was not altogether to his liking. Opposite Charles Laughton, for whom he wrote the script, he wanted Erich von Stroheim for the German officer. He wrote him as follows:

> It isn't a lengthy role; there's more talk about the character than actual appearances. But the film's major scene takes place between him and the main character, who will be played by Charles Laughton.

[11] Excerpt from a letter provided by Alexander Sesonske.

This is no ordinary German officer. I got the idea for him from my recollections of a discussion I had in Lisbon with an important German agent. He claimed he was Swiss, but I learned later that he was German and that there was no big mystery about it. During our dinner together, he recited poems in French with only the slightest accent. He knew French culture extremely well, and he was a great admirer of it. His dream was a Europe in which the Germans were the organizers and the French the artists. It's likely that he meant it. I was impressed by this cultivated and refined person, since he seemed to me to be a lot more dangerous than some Nazi thug. He's more or less the point of departure for the character in the film (ibid.).

Stroheim answered that he regretted he could not accept the part since he was appearing on Broadway in *Arsenic and Old Lace,* and there was no way he could get free in time.

The final version of the script was ready on October 2, and the shooting started soon after that date. There were a few disagreements with Dudley Nichols. Since he wrote the dialogue, he wanted his text respected. Jean Renoir gave in and set aside his custom of modifying lines on the set when the personality of the actor affected the character in the text. That was where he improvised, and this time he gave it up, without complaining. The two men had aspirations of working together again, once the film was over.

An old partner of Jean's, whom he valued highly, turned up again: Eugène Lourié, set designer for all his films since *The Lower Depths,* had succeeded in getting to New York, where he was making a living as a commercial artist. It soon became clear that in Hollywood, where Jean kept trying to get him to come, he could not be authorized as head designer because of union rules. So he was thrust into the job of associate producer, which allowed him to oversee the design but kept him from making mock-ups and working on the set. Hunting around in the RKO Studios, he chanced upon the sets built in 1939 for the exteriors of a version of *Quasimodo.* It had medieval streets and everything that was needed! Secretly, Lourié fixed them up at night to avoid the watchful eyes of the union.

On January 3, 1943, Jean Renoir wrote Robert Flaherty that he had finished the rough cut of his film and that he was thinking of writing a book: "despite my happy experience with RKO, I keep thinking it's the only way I can express myself frankly" (ibid.). Before doing so, however, he had to have an operation. A few months before, it had been discovered that he had chronic appendicitis, but he had insisted on putting off the surgery until the film was over. He had about two months left to do the final cut, and that was something that for him required a lot of care. "Since the movie was a little propagandist, I thought I should be careful and should modify the cutting during previews until I had calibrated the effects on the public that I wanted to convince."[12]

The film was shown to the press on March 12. It came out at the same time as *The Moon Is Down*, which Fox finally produced, *The Hangman*, and other war movies, and was very well received. Jean was well pleased. He needed distractions, for that was when he was supposed to go into the hospital. But he postponed the operation until the end of June. Then they realized that it wasn't chronic appendicitis but a fistula. It was very painful, and Jean was slow to heal. Meantime, he had favorable responses to his film from all sides. He wanted it to be shown to different segments of the public, and from March to the end of May, when it was first shown publicly in New York City, the movie appeared in sixty-five theaters in the Midwest, Kentucky, and West Virginia. *This Land Is Mine* was also shown in military bases in Alabama, Florida, and Colorado, as well as in five big cities in New England.

Jean was especially moved by spontaneous responses from soldiers. He also was delighted by a telegram from Geneviève Tabouis and enthusiastic letters from Pierre Lazareff and Jean Benoît-Lévy. He wanted to make a propaganda film that was different from what he had done before. His technique was more conventional, with a large number of shots. Dudley Nichols had pointed him in this direction at the beginning of the shooting. He refused to allow him to open the film with an establishing shot from a mobile camera on a crane. His friend's firm position on this made Jean think twice; he did not want to confuse viewers who were accustomed to films in classic style, and he also knew that reviewers are not overjoyed by innovation. He did have the nice surprise of seeing *This Land Is Mine* receive the Academy Award for best sound recording of 1943. He had used sound in his own special way, without making concessions. It was the only prize he ever received for his American films. Renoir was unsure of the reception his compatriots would one day give this film, but a subtitled version of it was made in April of 1943 and shown in London that June, with great success and to a large audience. In August, it was shown in South America, which elicited the following telegram from Louis Jouvet: "Congratulate Laughton Friends very moved With love Vive la France." The following year, the film was shown in Portugal and North Africa.

[12]Jean Renoir, *Lettres d'Amérique*, 131.

In February 1943, Paulus and his army capitulated at Stalingrad, and in July, the Soviets started an offensive against the Reich; in May, the Allies entered Tunis. One month later, there was the landing in Sicily, soon followed by the unconditional surrender of Italy. Hitler no longer reigned supreme. The end of the war was still far off, but everything had changed. Americans under Nimitz and MacArthur had started reconquering the Pacific. The Japanese Air Force was no match for theirs. Jean and Dido followed these events with great excitement. Fortunately, they also had regular news from Alain, short letters that were "full of affection and confidence in his leaders and friends" (ibid., p. 147). He was in the Pacific theater, "in pretty unpleasant jungles." Jean Renoir says nothing about being concerned for his safety. Daily visits from Gabrielle kept his spirits from flagging during his long convalescence; what work he could do next was far from clear.

◆

Gabrielle spoke no English—in fact she never learned it—but she was so friendly that she managed to do everything without help from her husband or her son. Charming, funny, smart, and nice to boot, she made conquests everywhere. Jean and Dido's new friends soon became hers as well. Her favorite was Charles Laughton, whom she nicknamed "Gros Matou" ("Big Pussycat") and who purred with pleasure whenever he saw her. There were also Charlie Chaplin, who was about to marry Oona O'Neill, Ann Baxter, Lilian Gish, and Doris Kenyon. When they finally bought the house next door and the two backyards were joined together, Jean Renoir was a happy man: here was the family life that he had always sought in vain to recreate.

When he chose exile, he did not expect to find, on the other side of the world, the kind of everyday life that he had been searching for since his father's death. Gabrielle was the Gabrielle of his childhood, more available to him than his mother, as important as his father at the time that he discovered himself and others. Conrad Slade, Gabrielle's husband, resembled Auguste Renoir physically; he had known and loved the man. The memory of those days was alive to him; that was his youth. Then there was Dido, the newcomer, who, by education and origin, resembled the little Manet girls, Jeanne Baudot, Renoir's pupil and Jean's godmother, or the daughters of those collectors or friends whose portraits Renoir had drawn. She was also like Renée Cézanne, who had immediately adopted her and had had time to appreciate her during the exodus from Paris.

A diplomat's daughter, Dido had traveled a lot, which was still a rarity. She was quickly at home in California, where the climate really suited her. She helped Jean in his work, watched over his health, and wanted to get him to lose some weight. She shared his artistic and literary tastes, and, like him, she loved nature. Living with him only heightened the admiration she had of him as an adolescent. Once again, it was a confirmation of the theory of horizontal divisions: one of the reasons they understood each other so well was their equivalent social origin. Their frames of reference were the same, which tightened the bonds between them. For years, Dido had not dared go near him; but she soon became his inseparable companion, confident, reassuring, understanding him like the best of friends. She also got along superbly with Gabrielle, integrating herself with ease into the intimacy of the two Burgundian cousins. She shared their jokes, their curiosity about others, and their racy, often fictitious anecdotes. Both of them felt the same way about the French exiles in Hollywood, whom Jean called "the resisters from without." Their glib patriotism and their well-fed, well-sheltered criticisms were aggravating. Their American friends enjoyed dining on the simple fare at Dido and Jean's; the food and wine was excellent and the conversation also.

The two of them also became regulars at the gatherings of the "great salon," as those who took part called their Sunday night suppers at the home of Salka Viertel. A group mainly consisting of refugees ate black bread and lentil soup: they were Bertolt Brecht, Hans Eisler, Thomas Mann, Arnold Schoenberg, Christopher Isherwood, Leon Feuchtwanger and his wife Martha, Aldous Huxley and Maria, his first wife, Emil Ludwig, Franz Werfel, and Alma Mahler, as she was still called. They were artists, musicians, and writers. Some did not live in Hollywood but never missed a meeting when they were in town. What united them was their devotion to their art, their love of freedom, and their hatred for Nazism. Most had a past in Europe, and the few Americans who belonged to the group were cosmopolitan: Dudley Nichols, Albert Lewin, Robert Flaherty, and Clifford Odets were at home in an international gathering. Their intimacy with Jean and Dido increased as the years went by.

In a letter to Albert André, Jean described the life in Hollywood, "where people attach no importance to the question of 'material situation.' The only thing that's asked of you is not to be boring." But he added:

> I'm no fan of parties; I've stuck with the old-fashioned notion of a good dinner, your fanny ensconced in a comfortable chair at a table with

white tablecloths, with flunkeys to change your plates and fill your glass—it's a lot better than sitting on an ottoman and balancing your dish. We have a good friend whose profession is the same as mine, named Al Lewin. The only difference is that since he's been at it in this town for thirty years, he's amassed a pretty nice fortune. He shares my view of parties, and he gives absolutely impeccable dinners: French champagne, Russian caviar, real foie gras, to say nothing of an unrestrained passion for garlic, which is a real pleasure. His dinners remind me of what you used to get at Palazzoli. The same friends get together there, from the widest variety of professions: a German physician with a gift for anthropology, his wife, who is an American suffragette, an operetta musician who's ended up at MGM with his wife, a devoted anarchist, a very funny person, a couple of actors, Man Ray, and lots of people who aren't famous at all but are good drinkers and good company (ibid., p. 251).

Jean and Dido knew how to pick out friends and a way of life that suited them both.

Yet 1943 was not an easy year. Despite the success of *This Land Is Mine,* no other project succeeded with RKO. Ingrid Bergman and Dudley Nichols, resisting David Selznick's discouragement, were both enthusiastic about the idea of making a film from *Sarn* (*Precious Bane*). The two men tried to convince other producers but to no avail. The same was true of an attempt to make another version of *The Lower Depths,* this one set in Los Angeles. On June 29, Jean wrote to Jean Benoît-Lévy, "Since I finished *This Land Is Mine,* I've been working on projects that I don't believe in. The result: a big depression, doubts about the profession that you know only too well, and poor relations with the people in my trade" (ibid., p. 137). Once he got back his strength, his usual energy returned, and it kept him from being depressed for too long. He changed agents, leaving Feldman-Blum for Berg-Allenberg, who were apparently better equipped to defend his interests.

Pierre Lazareff, director of the French section of the Office of War Information in New York, wrote to Jean on November 22 about recordings that would be "distributed by American government radio throughout liberated France."[13] Jean recorded several of them, and at the same time, Robert Hakim, the producer of *La Bête humaine,* suggested that he make a movie from *Hold Autumn in Your Hand,* a novel by a Texan writer, George Sessions Perry, for him and David Loew, an

[13]Dido Renoir archives.

independent producer who had worked with Al Lewin in the production of *Portrait of Dorian Gray*. This idea did come to fruition, but it took time.

◆

In February 1944, Jean and Dido left for New York, where Jean was to work on a propaganda film for the Office of War Information. In those days, the train took three days to make the trip from Los Angeles to New York, including a change of train in Chicago. During the stopover there, they visited the Chicago Art Institute, which has a large collection of impressionist paintings, including the portrait of Jean sewing a dress for his camel. The trip was a kind of honeymoon for them; in fact, Jean's divorce from Catherine Hessling was made final on October 23, 1943, and on February 6, 1944, Dido Freire and Jean Renoir were married by a justice of the peace in Los Angeles. Jean, who had a reputation for being absentminded, arrived late, having somehow lost his way. Gabrielle, Dudley Nichols, and Charles Laughton, their witnesses, stayed and waited. Alain, still in combat on an island in the Pacific, wrote that the day he heard the news was the most beautiful of his life. He loved Dido, and she returned his affections; to her, Alain was always "my son." Their friends were also overjoyed, since it was plain they understood each other so well.

The honeymoon was not a long one: their stay in New York lasted several months, and the work was intensive. Jean had signed a contract as a consultant to the Office of War Information, which reimbursed his expenses but paid no stipend. The film he directed, *Salute to France*, was produced by the Bureau of Overseas Motion Pictures, headed by Robert Riskin. It was intended for American soldiers who would sooner or later take part in a troop landing in France. Ever since the Teheran Conference (November 28–December 2, 1943), it had been clear that the Allies would open a second front in Europe, bigger than the one in Italy. The film was going to be made in French as well, the idea being that the French would be well disposed to the Americans if they could see what a flattering image the Americans had of them. Burgess Meredith had just finished making *Welcome to Britain*, and he was happy to be returning from London to work on *Salute to France* with Jean Renoir.

When they arrived on February 14, Dido and Jean moved into the Algonquin Hotel, a famous meeting place for writers and artists that was right across the street from the Royalton, where Jean and Dido had spent their first night in America on New Year's Eve 1940. Jean immediately began writing the screenplay with Burgess Meredith, an excellent actor who knew nothing about France and the French, and also the actor Claude Dauphin, a lieutenant in the Free French Forces who was sent from North Africa to work on the film. Kurt Weill was composing the music for it, but its orchestration was entrusted to a soldier for financial reasons: the soldier didn't need to be paid or reimbursed for expenses. Shooting began in March. Garson Kanin, actor, writer, and director, was in charge of the English version, and Jean Renoir did the French one. Actually, the division of labor between them changed during the course of the next few weeks, and Jean Renoir actually directed both versions. From *La Vie est à nous* to *This Land Is Mine*, Jean had a lot of experience with propaganda films; this one, which was intended for two very different audiences, was especially tricky to carry off.

Fortunately, Jean Renoir got along very well with Burgess Meredith and Garson Kanin, both of whom became his friends. New York evenings with Jean and Dido were entertaining in large part because of them. Jean described Burgess Meredith as "astonishing," as was his current wife, the actress Paulette Goddard. "Before us was the kid from *Modern Times*. The only difference was that her rags had turned into the most elegant evening clothes. Despite interruptions that lasted several years, our friendship is intact. She's a pretty woman with a lot of spirit; you're never bored when she's around."[14] Garson Kanin and his wife, Ruth Gordon, of *Harold and Maude* fame, were "two extraordinary theater people" whom Jean and Dido loved to look at and listen to. They saw "the delightful Annabella" and also "Marlene Dietrich and Jean Gabin, who were living together. Marlene was singing patriotic French songs in nightclubs for the fun of it. She always ended with "The Marseillaise." Gabin thought it was idiotic. He and Dietrich fought ferociously. He called her "my Prussian girl." Her response to this was to tap him on the forehead and say, in her languorous voice, "What I love about you is that inside there it's totally empty. You've got nothing between your ears, nothing at all, I love it." This most subtle of actors did not respond at all to the insult.

"Marlene Dietrich was truly a superstar, not just on stage but in real life as well. At her home, she was the perfect hostess and a great cook: her stuffed cabbage was a triumph. On stage and in the kitchen, she was addicted to compliments, even though she was swimming in them." And Jean tells how "in a nightclub, she repeatedly asked Dido

---

[14] Jean Renoir, *Ma vie et mes films*, 207.

to go with her to the bathroom. Dido was surprised at the frequency of her need for relief, but finally she realized that Marlene just wanted people to admire her legs. Her pretext for bringing Dido was to protect her from the attack of women who would rush at her from behind. It was all just a ritual for her; one should add that the cult of her legs was indeed justified" (ibid., p. 209). In the end, when Jean Gabin had gone off to join the Free French Forces, in her loneliness she became something of a burden to the Renoirs.

During their stay, an important change took place in Jean's habits. He agreed to go to a good tailor. Until then, he had always bought his clothes cheap and ready made. But his friends had insisted with Dido that he get some suits made to order. Many letters have survived of a correspondence with a certain Steve Senyi, the New York tailor who for several years sent Jean the clothes he needed in California. Jean had always been the first person to make fun of the way he dressed. Even the fittings, which he went to with Dido, seemed to him a big waste of time.

All these varied distractions did not dull their desire to go back to California. From his astute comments and notes, it is clear that Jean did not really like New York, which "is like a giant pot ready to explode" (ibid., p. 207). Yet he agrees that in the city "ideas fly, currents change, and the life of the mind is intensified." Besides *Salut à la France* for the Office of War Information, Jean took part in some short training films, but he lost track of them (ibid.).

Finally, on April 17, 1944, Jean and Dido left New York for Hollywood. The film was done, if not edited, and the arrangement was for Garson Kanin to do that. But Jean could not keep them from disfiguring the film by exaggerated cuts that brought it down from ninety-five to thirty-seven minutes (according to Alexander Sesonske[15]). Many years later, Burgess Meredith was still complaining. "The copy of the film *Salute to France* that we received had nothing to do with the film that (Jean Renoir) and I made with Garson Kanin. There are maybe one or two scenes from the original, and that's it."[16] The French version, which is very good according to Philip Dunne, production head of the Bureau of Overseas Motion Pictures of the Office of War Information, was shown in Paris starting in October 1944, but it has completely disappeared.[17]

[15] Interview with A. Sesonske, April 19, 1984, at Santa Barbara.
[16] Letter to Margareta Akermark, July 21, 1978, cited in William H. Gilcher, *Jean Renoir in America*, 391.
[17] William H. Gilcher, *Jean Renoir in America*, 391.

Before Dido and Jean left New York, Jean had received several offers: an English producer was interested in *Precious Bane* and wanted to shoot the film in England along with, perhaps, a second film directed by Jean Renoir from a screenplay by him and Dudley Nichols. Louis Jouvet wrote to him from Mexico asking him to go there to shoot a film in French. In his delight at finding a group of people so interested in French culture that they were willing to finance a film, Jouvet immediately thought of his friend to direct it. Jean played with the notion, but Dido was at his side teaching him to be reasonable. "Since you've done it all your life, you know how insecure it is to be an independent director," Jean answered Jouvet.

> My absence from Hollywood these last few months has made my situation even more difficult. Even the film that I told you I had to do in September looks like it's falling apart. My agent, in whom I have complete confidence, claims that I can fix everything up when I return, either with the subject I was supposed to use or with another one that pleases me just as much. However, if I go to Mexico, it's possible that the work opportunities I now have will be lost forever, and that I'll have to give up on Hollywood. I should add that, from a financial standpoint, I'd be in danger of having to reimburse advances that my producers have given me, which would make it hard for me to meet my income tax payments and complicate my exit from the United States no less than my reentry thereafter.

There was also Alain, who was the main reason Jean couldn't leave the United States. "He's fighting in wretched jungles for months on end. A little while ago he received a 'Soldier's Medal' . . . in short, it wouldn't please him very much to see his Dad cut off from the country for which he's fighting. He's probably coming here on leave soon with his friends, all of them farm boys from the sticks who want to see California, and I'd rather not be held on the other side of the border when they arrive at the door of my home." [18] Rumor had it that the troops on the Pacific front were coming home on leave, and Jean was hoping very much to see Alain.

As he said in the letter to Jouvet, despite having signed a contract with Robert Hakim, Jean was not sure he was going to be able to shoot the film based on George Sessions Perry's *Hold Autumn in Your Hand*. Allenberg, his new agent, alerted him in New York that David Loew was losing interest. In order to get the project going again, Jean was going to have to be aggressive when he got back to California. On

---

[18] Jean Renoir, *Lettres d'Amérique*, letter to Louis Jouvet dated April 9, 1944.

the other hand, Dudley Nichols was pushing the idea of a film on the life of Sister Kenny, a faith healer with a clinic in Minneapolis. Jean Renoir liked the subject and wrote this to Nichols:

> In France, I was struck by a similar story: the wife of a fisherman in Berck-Plage along the English Channel, who, with the help of a doctor from Paris, was using a new method for curing osseous tuberculosis. That was eighty years ago. So you see you've touched on an old preoccupation of mine. As you say, it also answers to one of our joint aspirations: to show the life of a saintly person at a time when materialism seems (although perhaps it's only an illusion) to be gaining ground. In these times, it's a good idea to expose the purest forms of spirituality, devotion to a cause, and renunciation of this world's easy pleasures. I can also see that the story exalts the protection of one of God's greatest creations: I mean the human body.[19]

In another letter to Nichols, he says: "More and more I'm coming to believe that the only people who count in the history of a nation are its saints: but those saints, whether they are artists, peasants, men of state, or workers, will always be preoccupied by petty day-to-day concerns, ordinary things that look vulgar to theoretical minds."[20] There he expresses his deeper thoughts, the kind that give a special fullness to the characters in his films.

◆

In mid-June, shortly after D-day, Jean went to Minneapolis with Dudley Nichols to visit Sister Kenny. Those events and the news from Alain were disappointing and they preoccupied him, so that the visit did not have its expected results. The day after D-day, June 7, Jean wrote to an old British friend in Cagnes. "Alain's recent letters are upsetting me a little because he's announcing his return to the U.S. in about a year. That'll make it more than three years since we've laid eyes on him. He says they need experienced soldiers in the Pacific. He's in the middle of the combat zone. The last we heard, he got jungle rot and the doctor had to paint him blue from tip to toe."[21] He was more than "a little" upset. He was too worried about his son's fate to feel creative. He decided to urge Dudley Nichols to make the film about Sister Kenny on his own. He was not a "commercial" author, and he did not want to mess things up for his friend, who probably

[19] Letter to Dudley Nichols, April 2, 1944, Dido Renoir archive.
[20] Letter of April 9, 1944, Dido Renoir archive.
[21] Jean Renoir, Lettres d'Amérique, 152.

had a really popular film on his hands. Sister Kenny claimed she cured polio by wrapping affected limbs in hot, dry cloths. All of traditional medicine was against her. "Wearing a huge feather hat on her head that made you think of her Australian origins, she strode through life like a soldier going to war."[22] In the end, Dudley Nichols did as Jean suggested and directed the movie himself. Jean also received a request from Simon Schiffrin, director of the Free French Cinema, who was impressed by *Salute to France* and wanted Jean to make a film of Joseph Kessel's *L'Armée des ombres* (*Army of Shadows*). He answered him on June 30 that he was tied up with professional commitments in the United States and also because of Alain, that he wished "to be here when he returns."[23]

His first job was to redo the screenplay of the film for Robert Hakim and David Loew that he was afraid of losing. Loew accepted his ideas and his changes. "This man, David Loew, is the only person in Hollywood who is rich enough to be exempt from vulgar ambitions. He was born into the film world and he loves it. He doesn't intend to lose any money, but if he can make a good movie, it'd give him more pleasure than anything else in the world" (ibid.). Jean Renoir felt he would have more freedom than he had experienced with RKO. In the meantime, Paris was liberated on August 25, just before he began shooting the film. Jean was eager to hear about everyone, family and friends, whom he had left behind. Despite the last minute preparations for shooting, he found time to write. David Loew, whom he calls "a great guy," made things simpler for him by acceding to his wishes.

Loew allowed Eugène Lourié, whose status with respect to the unions had been straightened out, to design the sets. Since it was not possible to get the necessary authorizations to transport the material involved to Texas—most trucks had been requisitioned by the army—Lourié found the perfect location within California, on the banks of the San Joaquin River, near the small town of Madera near Fresno. It had the obligatory cotton fields and was as picturesque as you could ask for; the land belonged to a Russian colony, members of a sect that was persecuted by the czars and had settled there well before the Gold Rush. There were a few problems, since the most conservative members of the sect did not allow reproduction of the human face, but temporary purchase of the cotton field by the pro-

[22] Jean Renoir, *Ma vie et mes films*, 203.
[23] Jean Renoir, *Lettres d'Amérique*, 155.

duction company ironed out the issue. The shooting of the film was like a vacation for everyone involved, David Loew included. He was interested in learning the way the French worked. Technicians and actors camped out in tents provided by a company that specialized in such things; they also provided the food and everything else that was needed. It was very hot, but everyone got along well and had a good time. Norman Lloyd, one of the actors in the movie, told me that Hollywood directors were feudal lords, tough guys, "even Willy Wyler was like that. But Jean fooled everyone. He was as thick skinned as the others but you couldn't tell. He had a kind of poetic quality to him, and he was a human being of the highest sort." Lloyd also told me:

> He was the soul of France. When you worked with him, you were under his spell, you accepted him completely. He led you into his world and, as an actor, all you wanted to do was please him. He knew how to get the best out of us, and at the same time make us his creations. That's what happened with Zachary Scott, Betty Field, and Beulah Bondi, who was a great, classic actress. You're a great actor when you have the courage to be yourself. Jean gave you that courage. You accepted him because he accepted you.

For the lead roles, Joel McCrea and Frances Dee were the first choice, and they were overjoyed to work with Jean Renoir. When they read the script, however, they begged off, since they had no desire to play the part of miserable farmers, even if it did mean being directed by a French director with a famous name. Because of their rejection of the script, according to Jean, and for business reasons regarding the two companies, David Loew's and the one that included Robert Hakim, according to others,[24] United Artists Corporation was on the point of withdrawing from the project. By threatening to withdraw their right to distribute his other films, David Loew succeeded in convincing United Artists to hang in. However, they asked that the title be changed from *Hold Autumn in Your Hand* to *The Southerner*.

The script had several hands, including Nunnaly Johnson, perhaps John Huston, and assuredly William Faulkner. Zachary Scott said that Faulkner considered Renoir the best director of his time. For his part, Jean Renoir was an admirer of Faulkner. Knowing that he was in Hollywood, Jean made sure he asked his opinion on several questions. Faulkner did not just make observations that led Jean to redo several scenes; he also gave him valuable pointers on the dialogue.

[24] William H. Gilcher, *Jean Renoir in America*, 393–94.

Jean Renoir had had time to become familiar with America, and the diversity of his team amused but didn't surprise him. His assistant director was a gentleman from the East Coast driven by a passion for film, Robert Aldrich. Aldrich was the son of a Rhode Island banker whose family had roots going back to colonial America, and he was the cousin of Nelson Rockefeller; the production director, meanwhile, was an unpolished Irishman who was intemperate and had no manners at all. The cameraman was a Frenchman whose career went back to the glory days of French cinema, before World War I, when French films dominated the world market. The heroine of *Protea*, one of those silent movie serials that were appreciated everywhere, had a younger brother who was an assistant cameraman and who dreamed of going to America. His sister refused to leave her homeland, but the American businessmen who had hired the whole *Protea* team [one of its members, Gasnier, made *Les Mystères de New York* (*Mysterious New York*)], agreed to bring along Lucien Andriot. He took a little boat with him: seeing the Los Angeles River on the map, he imagined being able to paddle along it as though it were the Marne. Tales of his search for that invisible river were a highlight of the evenings encamped among the Russians.

The movie that was begun in September and finished by the end of January was handed over for distribution on January 31, 1945. The National Board of Review rated it third best film of the year 1945 and Jean Renoir best director. The next year, *The Southerner* won best film at the Venice Biennale. In France, it was not shown until 1949 at a horror film festival organized by André Bazin in Biarritz. Once again, Jean was full of hope. He was finally satisfied with a film he had made in Hollywood. The atmosphere he made it in as well as the reception it received from his fellow professionals combined to make him confident of his future there. There was not even a real interruption between *The Southerner* and his next project. And he had succeeded in making a movie that was so transparent to the American people that the Ku Klux Klan boycotted it in the South, which was great publicity. The film was first shown in Beverly Hills on April 30, 1945, and in New York, at the Globe Theater on Broadway, on August 25, 1945.

◆

Many things had happened between the beginning and the end of shooting. The war in Europe was over on May 8, 1945. The atomic bomb had been dropped on Hiroshima and Nagasaki, and Japan surrendered on August 15. Jean was still waiting for Alain to come home. Having become a second lieutenant, he had just been decorated again. At the end of the war, he and his men were occupying and administering a Japanese village. He left Japan on November 2 and was reunited with his father in early December. They had been apart for a total of four years.

It took some time for communications with France to be re-established. By the end of 1944, Jean had received a reassuring telegram: all of his loved ones had survived, but the first postcard did not reach him until February 15, 1945; it was dated December 24, 1944. It came from his brother Claude who at the moment of the liberation had been working in the underground for six months with his son. He also learned that Les Collettes was intact: a bomb that had fallen in the yard hadn't done much damage. Airmail letters did not begin arriving regularly until the end of September.

As soon as the mail was working again, Jean Renoir wrote on September 10, 1944, to "Dear Mr. Guillaume," his financial adviser, to ask for news about his world and to give some of his own. "If you see Catherine, you can tell her that she has something to be proud of in Alain. . . . He's been nominated for the Congressional Medal of Honor, which is the rarest of medals in America. Until now, during the whole war, only 56 have been given in the army and 50 in the navy. The president awards it in person, and the recipient receives a pension and an officer's salute. Unfortunately, Alain has only been *nominated*, and there's no guarantee that he'll get it. But the mere fact of being nominated is already a great honor.

"I wish to announce to you *alone* a piece of important news as far as I'm concerned. Dido and I have gotten *married* after I had my separation with Catherine changed to a divorce. As soon as things get going again, it would be prudent to go through the same formality in Paris. Otherwise, my marriage will probably be meaningless in France."[25] This important news never reached Mr. Guillaume, and it was a long time before divorce proceedings were initiated in France; a lawyer was not chosen until the end of August 1945.

Well before that date, Jean wired his brothers to tell them he had gotten married. Then, on January 15, 1945, he wrote to Claude: "We're living in a little house right next to Gabrielle. We hardly go out, and have few friends, but they're good ones. It's a little bit like the home of a retired gentleman in Chatou" (ibid., p. 171). A little later, he wrote this to the Cézannes: "Really, if I hadn't had Dido with me, I think I'd have done very badly as an exile. Thanks to her, the

[25] Jean Renoir, *Lettres d'Amérique*, 159.

end is near and I don't feel too washed out" (ibid., p. 195). As usual, he was concerned about those for whom he was responsible, Madame Heuschling, his former mother-in-law, whom Catherine's sister, Jeanne, was taking care of, his brothers, his friends. He sent them money, but "the news that I have about prices in France, and the fact that a dollar converted into francs has very little purchasing power, limit terribly my ability to help you financially. Perhaps there will soon be a Franco-American agreement to solve the exchange problem," he wrote to Mr. Guillaume (ibid., p. 177). The winter of 1944–45 was a harsh one in France, and he and Dido were worried, knowing how poorly heated housing was there. They sent packages with food and clothing. Dido became an expert packer, always filling boxes that she was sending one place or another and dealing with long lines in the postoffice. Worse still, they were never sure that their packages would actually arrive. But they knew that it was worth trying their luck, since wartime restrictions were far from over.

Impatient as they were for direct news, there was a special joy in greeting those who actually came to visit from France. Among the first of them was the actor Pierre Blanchar, on an official visit. He was president of the French Cinema Liberation Committee, which had been formed with the consent of the National Resistance Council; among its members were Louis Daquin, Jean Grémillon, and, from Jean's team, Jacques Becker, André Zwobada, and Pierre Renoir. There was also a dinner with Andrée Viollis and Jean-Paul Sartre. "I already knew Madame Viollis from *Ce soir*. What a pleasure to see her again! She's such a nice woman; of all the people I've seen, she made me feel the most homesick," he wrote to Pierre Renoir (ibid., pp. 180–81). He loved hearing people talk about what was going on in Paris. He wrote Mr. Guillaume on February 24, 1945: "As for me, I'm dying to go back to France, since at fifty you're too old to change your habits. What's more, perhaps our country will need all the energy it can get" (ibid., p. 177).

But he knew of two obstacles to his return. First, there was no way they would abandon Alain, whose discharge date was still unknown, and "my plans will very much depend on his. Secondly, I can't get rid of the idea that producers who made films during the occupation did so by somehow coming to terms with the Germans. I have nothing against them for it: you're free to save your skin and your money as you think best, as long as it doesn't mean selling your dear friends down the river. But I'm not eager to go and work for them. I can see their names in the newspapers; they get along with the Americans the same way they did with the Nazis. It all disgusts me a little, and I'd prefer to go and work in France once the film industry is in other people's hands" (ibid., p. 193).

◆

On July 2, 1945, when he wrote this letter to Mr. Guillaume, he was just about to begin shooting *The Diary of a Chambermaid*, a project that had been dear to his heart for a very long time. He and Burgess Meredith had become friends during the shooting of *Salute to France*, and in this venture they were partners. Meredith had been discharged from the service and was at liberty to do as he wished; like Jean, he thought that the role of Célestine was perfect for his wife, Paulette Goddard. He also saw himself as Captain Mauger, and Jean felt strongly that the film should be shot in a studio, far from anything real. They set to work, hoping that RKO would produce the film, but the script was considered too bold and they rejected it. So the three of them, Paulette Goddard, Burgess Meredith, and Jean Renoir formed a little company, Camden Corporation. Paulette's agents went to work raising money. They also had to find a studio and a distributor for the finished product.

They got in touch with Benedict Bogeaus, the owner of General Service Studios. You could rent space in his old studios. In fact, Jean had shot the studio sequences of *The Southerner* there. They had no sound equipment, but you could rent that somewhere else. Bogeaus, originally a real estate agent in Chicago, had bought these Hollywood buildings and started out working for the army. Then he produced a film, *The Bridge at San Luis Rey*, that was a success.[26] As the principal shareholder of Camden Corporation, he was guaranteed not to lose money, since it was renting his own studio. He came up with the $900,000 needed to produce *Diary of a Chambermaid* and its distribution was entrusted to United Artists. It was an arrangement that seemed to suit everyone.

For a time, there was discussion as to whether or not Anita Loos ought to get the script. She wrote *Gentlemen Prefer Blondes*, and Jean says he admired her very much. "Although still something to look at, she was a Hollywood veteran. She had written screenplays for the first films of Douglas Fairbanks, Sr., and the young Mary Pickford."[27] In the end, though, Jean and Burgess Meredith were credited as sole authors of the screenplay and dialogue, and the film was shot from

---

[26] William H. Gilcher, *Jean Renoir in America*, 407.
[27] Jean Renoir, *Lettres d'Amérique*, 190.

mid-July to the beginning of September 1945. That spring, Jean had received from Paul Soskine, "one of the Arthur Rank producers" (ibid., p. 187), an invitation to make *Vanity Fair* in London. It was an idea that did not displease Jean, but he couldn't think of leaving the United States because of Alain. There was nothing to do about it, and anyhow, *Diary of a Chambermaid* was a new experience, with new partners who were as adventurous as he was. Paulette Goddard is indeed an astounding Célestine, and Burgess Meredith's Captain Mauger is extraordinary. The script took a lot of liberties with the novel as well as the play that had been extracted from it by André Heuse, André de Lorde, and Thielly Nores. But this burlesque drama—Jean called it a "cine-novel"—is faithful to the spirit of Mirbeau and shows how fascinated Jean was by the position of domestic servants and the egoism of their middle-class masters, which knows no bounds.

American reviewers did not understand the film. They were hoping for plenty of erotic scenes, at least insofar as that was possible. One should remember that the Hayes Code was still in effect. It had been promulgated in 1934 as a response to the demands of the National League of Decency, which wanted "good" films. The original code had even been strengthened by Joseph I. Breen, a Roman Catholic journalist who headed the Production Code Administration in Hollywood. Films that were not approved by the administration prior to release were subject to a fine of $25,000, and, worse still, they were shut out of the big distribution circuits if they contained love scenes that appealed to "baser instincts" or even obscene gestures and language. Nudity was forbidden. Producers and distributors were both careful not to infringe on the code. When *Diary of a Chambermaid* (*Le Journal d'une femme de chambre*) was first shown in Paris on June 9, 1948, two years after it opened in New York, the French press was as mystified as their American counterparts had been.

◆

The film came out in the United States on February 15, 1946, with the premier in Chicago. Public response was lukewarm. Even so, the film was listed among the year's ten best films, and it made money, as Meredith told William Gilcher much later (April 12, 1978) in a telephone interview. He had great memories of working with Jean Renoir. "Enthusiasm . . . was his characteristic quality. No other man taught me as much: I mean, we were carried away by his enthusiasm. . . . His ideas were always good and way ahead of other people's."[28]

[28] William H. Gilcher, *Jean Renoir in America*, 409.

Paulette Goddard loved her part, the film, and the director. You can see it in the way she acts. "Jean adored Paulette Goddard," Dido explains, "and we all had a lot of fun during the shooting of the film." Jean himself said little about this movie, perhaps because he was disappointed by its reception, which made him wonder if he had failed, although he really had succeeded.

In presenting the film for French television in August 1961, Jean said that "*Diary of a Chambermaid* belongs to one of my antirealist crises."[29] André Bazin, who didn't like the film the first time he saw it, realized that he'd made a mistake and wrote of it: "There isn't a single film in all of Renoir's film output that has more freedom of invention and style."[30] People have written and will continue to write a lot about *Diary of a Chambermaid*. Jean Renoir, who thought he had reached Americans with *The Southerner*, disconcerted them and the French with this film. Neither of them got anything out of it. The American public expecting to see a French film instead found one that reminded it of westerns, since it was filmed in a studio and because of the actors it had and the period in which it took place. On the other hand, French audiences could not stand Célestine and a Mauger who hops around and speaks English.

The film is a rare mixture of the burlesque and the tragic, and Jean had hardly finished making it when he received a tempting offer. Joan Bennett, who was supposed to star in a film for RKO called *The Desirable Woman*, requested that Jean Renoir be the director. Since *This Land Is Mine*, he had kept on good terms with RKO, and Charles Koerner, vice president in charge of the studios, was a good friend of his. Jean signed a contract for two productions.

The screenplay was based on a thriller entitled *None So Blind* by Mitchell Wilson. Jean rapidly wrote the script with Frank Davis, about whom he wrote to Robert Flaherty, "Our partnership is really important for me, since I think he's the perfect collaborator, and he seems to think that I, too, am good to work with. Here in Hollywood, it's very hard to fight by yourself for the film you want to make. Two souls with the same taste and ideas are worth more than their weight when it's a question of defending what you want."[31] The way they conceived of the script left lots of room for improvisation and working with actors on the set, which, once again, gave Jean Renoir the

---

[29] Jean Renoir, *Entretiens et propos* (Paris, 1979), 136.
[30] André Bazin, *Jean Renoir* (Paris, 1971), 90.
[31] Letter dated December 21, 1946, in William H. Gilcher, *Jean Renoir in America*, 412.

impression of having greater artistic freedom. The shooting looked like another one of Jean's extended holidays. The story of the film, which featured sexual attraction without sentimentality, was a new experience.

Jean Renoir was much interested in Joan Bennett. Born into a family of actors, she had a cosmopolitan upbringing and spoke French very well. Seeing her live on the set, in the spotlights and between scenes, made Jean laugh. He wrote to Paul Cézanne:

> Joan Bennett, who plays the desirable woman, is amazing for her complete lack of vanity. She talks about her false eyelashes, about the gadgets she puts in her mouth to make her teeth look more regular and shiny, about her wig, even about her age with bemused irony and a complete lack of shame. She spends the whole day knitting, and I find it really funny to think that this homey person is considered by the American moral groups to be the most dangerous sexpot on the screen today.[32]

However, just as the shooting began, Charles Koerner's companion died of galloping leukemia. Without his support, the whole project turned sour. The film was finished on April 4 and shown to the executives at RKO on April 25. They decided to try it out in Santa Barbara on an audience consisting mainly of high school students. Dido was against it and warned that no importance should be attached to the reactions of viewers who were so far in age from the characters in the film itself. But her view was not heeded, and these youngsters were unable to understand such a stark, stripped-down film featuring characters they could not identify with. Jean Renoir and the RKO executives were disturbed by their response. In fact, Jean was so unhappy that he allowed his film to be dismantled, remade, and disfigured. Scenes were added, and another screenwriter was called in. By the end of November, half of the film was reshot with his agreement and participation. The title became *The Woman on the Beach*. Physically, Jean was exhausted; he got bronchitis, and to go to the studio everyday they pumped him full of antibiotics and other medications. He needed a rest.

For the past year, things had really been happening in his life. The most important was Alain's long-awaited homecoming in December of 1945. On his arrival, the young officer—he was just 24—came down "with a violent attack of malaria, or at least of something that looks a lot like it. The doctor said it might simply be the result of

[32]Jean Renoir, *Lettres d'Amérique*, 211–12.

suddenly stopping the quinine treatments he had been having regularly for three years. It is a marvellous drug—in fact, they say that because of it they won the war in the East—but its side effects are powerful" (ibid., p. 205). As a veteran, Alain had the right to a university scholarship, but he arrived too late to register that year. Courses had already started. Until he could begin school at the beginning of the next academic year in the fall of 1946, he decided to make a living by using his hands. His first thought was to resume work as a cameraman, beginning with the filming of a short subject on Big Sur. But he soon gave up the idea because of insurmountable problems with the union. One after the other he worked as a photographer, a bricklayer's apprentice, a garage mechanic, and a stableboy for an Indian friend who raised horses on a little ranch near San Francisco. It was a great joy for him to be with Dido, his father, Gabrielle, and her family, and everyday life in Agnes Ayres's old house was calm, happy, and enriching.

At the beginning of 1946, however, Jean and Dido saw that a little hillside was for sale near Lilian Gish's house along Benedict Canyon, and they quickly decided to buy it, wisely, Dido thought. The land on which their Hollywood home was situated was about to drop in value, since they were building a synagogue, shops, and parking lots near it. The increase in traffic would lower the property values. So it was time to sell and move, and, with their old age in mind, they wanted to build themselves a house without steps to climb. More and more, they were planning on staying in the United States. For her part, Gabrielle felt the same way. The gypsy life was over for the Slades. As Jean and Dido's neighbors, they were putting down roots in an area that looked nothing like New England or Burgundy, their respective birthplaces. They had made friends and were closely involved in the life of Jean and Dido. Gabrielle's absence is still felt every day by Dido, who has not yet forgotten those days, happy ones despite Jean's disappointment with his latest film.

◆

Before Alain arrived, letters came from France announcing that *Rules of the Game*, which came out again on September 26, 1945, in its eighty-minute version, had been banned again. "Fights broke out at the exits. Now there's a film that doesn't leave its viewers unmoved!" wrote Claude Renoir to his brother on October 22, 1945; a week earlier, Jean had this from Pierre Lestringuez: "Your ears must be ringing . . . since at this very moment, you have taken on the role of high priest of film here; in all sectors of the business, from the crooks on top to those at the bottom, they're saying with a sigh: 'Ah, if only we had Jean Renoir!'" (ibid., pp. 199–200).

"The opinion people have of me in Paris makes me delightfully conceited, and I'm not hiding it from my friends!" Jean replied (ibid., p. 200). People were showing his films again all over France. Every town had a movie club then, and young people were enthusiastic about the originality of Jean Renoir's films. It inspired many to make a career in movies, as François Truffaut wrote later on. Renoir made people aware that a film could express a person's dreams and complex thoughts as well as the reality of an era, a place, or a region. It was all the more exciting since for four years everything that people loved to see they couldn't.

Aside from the truncated version of *Rules of the Game*, they began to show his older films. *Grand Illusion* had to win the censor's approval before it could be shown. Jean Dewalde, Jean Renoir's representative in Paris, and Charles Spaak, the co-writer, had to agree to "two little sacrifices," as Spaak put it in a letter dated April 10, 1946. "They had to cut parts of the scenes where Maréchal and Boeldieu are invited to join the French prisoners' party (to see people eating and drinking on a movie screen in France was a provocation!). And also, there was Maréchal's answer to Elsa: 'When the war is over, I'll come back and get you.' (As everyone knows, lots of French prisoners came back from Germany with wife, children, and mother-in-law: the censor was the only person in France who didn't know about it)" (ibid., p. 222).

A Day in the Country was shown for the very first time on May 8, 1946. The original version of the film had been destroyed, but Marguerite Renoir supervised a new edit on the negative in the Cinémathèque. Jean Renoir lost confidence in this film, which he never had time to finish, but Pierre Braunberger had the idea of replacing the missing scenes, two indoor scenes that they lacked the time and the means to shoot, with narrative titles. *A Day in the Country* was the chief competitor to *La Bataille du rail* (*The Battle of the Trains*) by René Clément at the Cannes festival that year. It is one of the most powerful and perfect films Renoir made. The critics praised it to the skies, and *Rules of the Game*, shown one more time, finally succeeded. "People suddenly understood what wasn't explained," wrote Lestringuez in May 1946 (ibid., p. 209).

Amid all the praise, and after the lukewarm reception given *Diary of a Chambermaid*, came an old-fashioned attack on *Vivre libre*,

231

the dubbed version of *This Land Is Mine*, first presented in France on July 10, 1946. Jean Renoir heard of it via "a Hollywood newspaper" and he wrote as follows to his brother Claude on July 26:

> I won't refrain from telling you how upset I was to hear of it. It wasn't convenient for me to take on a subject like this one at a time when, in America, anything French was thought of as the enemy. It seemed to me that my first duty was to show the Americans by means of a film, which was the only means I had, that there really was anti-Nazi feeling in occupied Europe. I think I succeeded in doing that, and my proof is the numerous letters I received from soldiers. I can sum them up in a word: "Until now, I thought all those Frenchmen were bastards, but your film made me think again, and I believe my opinion was perhaps exaggerated."
>
> In addition, underground fighters from various countries, including a delegation of Russian cameramen sent on leave to the U.S. for their heroism during the war, saw the film and told me it represented very nearly the state of mind in an occupied town and the ways in which the Germans acted to ingratiate themselves in certain places.
>
> Anyhow, I think RKO was wrong to show a film that was news back in 1942. But whatever they did, if what I read was correct, I can't forget the deep hurt I feel at my countrymen's lack of compassion (ibid., p. 238).

◆

After all his years of exile, Renoir was even more sensitive to the inability of the French to understand him than he was at the time of *Rules of the Game*. He felt he was the victim of pent-up anger from four years of occupation. It had nothing to do with his film. There was no point in seeing the film to judge it, people thought. Renoir had not lived under the Nazis, so he could not express what was happening then. Yet his reluctant hero is no cardboard figure. He has the same depth of character as others have in his films. The German in command of the place gives an intelligent explanation of collaboration. As always in his films, everything is scaled to human proportions, reflecting the weaknesses and strengths in each of us. I saw the film again with a friend who had been a deportee, and it moved us both, despite the clumsiness of the dubbing; at no point were we disappointed or annoyed.

Despite *Vivre libre*, Jacques Mortier, Jean's childhood friend who had given him the subject of *Toni*, wrote to Jean in November 1946: "A long article the other day put you at the top of the list of directors who are the pillars of French cinema, and it deplored your absence!" (ibid., p. 209). Later on, the *Cahiers du cinéma* group appreciated the film, but Jean Renoir needed encouragement right then and there. He already knew that *Woman on the Beach* was a bomb, and for the first time, he totally lost confidence in what he was doing. He was at a standstill, and it led him to refuse a *Madame Bovary* suggested by Robert Hakim, which tempted him very much. There were also some difficulties in his personal life that kept him from returning to France. He had to get a divorce so that his marriage to Dido in Los Angeles would not make him bigamous under French law. Catherine Hessling contested the divorce in her desire to complicate things for him.

On August 21, 1946, Jean Renoir wrote to Mr. Guillaume, who was Jean's go-between to his divorce lawyer, Jacques Masse: "We're really in a funny spot. At one point, Dido and I thought of getting divorced in order to make us legal in France and in order to allow me to ask for an uncontested divorce from Catherine. The trouble is, we have no grounds for divorce in the California courts, so that way out wouldn't work for us. The only reason could be Dido claiming that she had been deceived in marrying a man who wasn't really free. But California law wouldn't recognize that reason since it is, in fact, this law that made me free to marry" (ibid., p. 242). He made no reference to this "funny spot" in his letters to his friends or his family. Jean was too well mannered to complain even though one year later, on July 27, 1947, Mr. Guillaume wrote him: "Everyone is interested in this case, the judge, the lawyer for the accused, and the lawyer for the defense. For them it is a strange case without precedent, and everyone is doing research on the subject. Since the first hearing, the president of the court has not made a secret of just how interested he is in the case under his jurisdiction." It was going to last a long time. "This ridiculous reason," as Jean called it, kept him from returning to France, where he could have been arrested for bigamy.

He wanted to see his friends again. He also wanted to accept some tempting job offers. Sam Siritzky, who was in exile in New York and whose father had premiered *La Chienne* in a theater he owned in Biarritz, wrote to Jean in February of 1946. "Your fame in France has never been as great as it is now," and he hoped that the first film his father and his family would produce on their return to Paris would be a film by Jean Renoir (ibid., p. 281). André Bernheim, in June of 1947, asked him to make a film with Jean Gabin, Pierre Fresnay, and Gérard Philippe. Jean realized that the time had come when he could do whatever he wanted. In the United States, things were hardly the same. No one was making him any offers at all, and RKO was offering him compensation not to make the second movie on his contract. Even though the film was to be *Madame Bovary*, he accepted the offer.

Nevertheless he had not given up on Hollywood. He still dreamed of making his great American movie. He tended to think of *The Southerner* and *Diary of a Chambermaid* as just exercises. Moreover, he wanted to free himself from the big studios, and he revived the idea of a production cooperative. In an article, he stated his intention of forming an independent production company. "My 'first new film' will be from a play by Clifford Odets, *Night Music*, with Dana Andrews and Joan Bennett."[33] That film was never made, but the company did get created.

Without speaking of his legal mess, which had become the main obstacle to his return to France, Jean wrote to Renée Cézanne that he was staying in the United States mainly for the sake of Alain. He had no doubt that Alain would adjust better to American life than he would to life in France. The young fellow was still far from reasonable. "I'm certain that I was like him when I was his age," writes Jean, "and even that I stayed that way until I found Dido, who changed everything with that energy of hers, as you know. (One of the reasons that I like the United States so much is that this is where we were married and where I found a kind of peace that had eluded me before)."[34] Their union was a rare success. Once a shy adolescent, the marriage brought out her lighthearted good sense; Jean needed joy and laughter but also the security that she provided, the lighthearted security that he had from Gabrielle in his childhood. What's more, he saw that Alain had great confidence in Dido and "displayed great affection for her."

♦

At the University of California in Santa Barbara, where he finally was accepted, Alain was not slow to get excited about his studies. His father was a little "amazed," but on the other hand, "your exploits, or rather those of your buddies, of the 'happy-students-at-Heidelberg' variety, give me the heebie-jeebies. Don't go and get yourself kicked out. That would really be a shame, after all the trouble you've taken to learn. On another front, a little scandal in my family wouldn't help my own business. Hollywood movie people are even more conservative than the suburban middle class in Paris. The latest thing is that Hans Eisler is being insulted in the papers because he's a foreigner and, it seems, a Communist. The same thing could happen to me, even though I stay away from politics, not out of fear, but from

[33] *Cinévie-Cinévogue*, nos. 3 and 4, June 1 and 8, 1946, cited in Jean Renoir, *Ecrits*, 54–55.
[34] Jean Renoir, *Ecrits*, 289.

boredom. There's nothing more boring than an American Communist."[35] As he had during the war, Jean still kept away from political involvement with French refugees, but that did not prevent him being preoccupied with what was happening in the world and worrying about another conflict arising. The tension between the USSR and the USA was growing worse every day. Also on his mind was the inevitable war in Indochina and the divisions it would, once again, create in France. In September 1946, Jean wrote this to Renée Cézanne: "Even here the times are troubled. Yesterday the cooks in Los Angeles went on strike, and not a single restaurant is open. Furthermore, the cattle and sheep got annoyed that the government wants to regulate their price and have dropped from sight. You can't find the least piece of meat in the butchers' stalls. A great wind of madness is blowing on the world" (ibid., p. 245).

Still, aside from the labor problems, day-to-day life was easy and pleasant. Jean wanted to perfect it by surrounding himself with familiar objects from his past that could find a resting place in their new home in Beverly Hills. He began working on the plans for it. First he wanted to bring over the large portrait of himself at age fourteen called *The Hunter*. Apparently Goering had lusted after it, but Aline Cézanne kept it hidden during the whole occupation. Jean awaited its arrival "anxiously," as he wrote to Mr. Guillaume, who undertook to send it to him (ibid., p. 242). The painting's journey is the subject of many letters and required a lot of activity on both sides. When it arrived, the customs officer whose function was to open the crate exclaimed that it looked just like the *Blue Boy*, the Gainsborough portrait that hangs in Los Angeles.

Jean and Dido had a good laugh over that remark. Jean had stumbled across some American relatives of his. Grandpa Charigot, the one who fled Essoyes and his wife's mad passion for housecleaning and scrubbed floors, had at least two wives in America. After living in Canada, he settled on the banks of the Red River in North Dakota. "Except for himself and a Jesuit priest, the only inhabitants in those parts were Indians."[36] This grandfather's daughter, Victoria, a retired postmistress, spoke French with the local accent of Essoyes, just as her father had, and she lived with one of her daughters, Dora, who was "married to a dentist and, strange to say, living in Santa Monica, on the seashore, five or six houses down from one of my good friends, Al Lewin, where I've visited many times since I arrived

[35] *Cinévie-Cinévogue*, nos. 3 and 4, June 1 and 8, 1946, cited in Jean Renoir, *Ecrits*, 269.
[36] *Renoir par Jean Renoir* (Paris, 1958), 308 (= *Renoir, My Father*, 309).

here."[37] "She also told me that some members of the family married Indians, so that I probably have some cousins with feathers on their heads, if they still wear such things" (ibid., p. 215).

This picturesque American side to his family, the presence of Gabrielle who enjoyed it as much as Dido and Jean, and, still more importantly, Alain, the well-loved only son—all these combined to make Jean put down roots. He had no illusions, but he also judged clearly what was going on, what he saw. On April 10, 1946, he wrote to Marie Lestringuez, the sister of his friend Pierre:

> Life here is so similar to the way things were after the armistice in France in 1918 that it's hard to tell them apart. The country is bigger, so the reactions are perhaps a little more sluggish. But I often have a feeling of déjà vu; there are ideas abroad that are all too familiar. The leftist movements that are called "Socialist" and "Communist" in France are here represented by certain labor unions. Rightist movements, like the ones we had twenty-five years ago, try to involve war veterans and set them at odds with working people. L'Action française is replaced by groups that are more or less spinoffs of the Ku Klux Klan, and instead of wanting to massacre Jews, the same kind of jokers have a strange desire to set fire to black people. Fortunately, as I was saying, the country is big, and its size gives it a kind of wisdom that may really only be sluggishness: at least, it seems to stop people who are on the brink of dangerous excess. Whatever size a movement may have in the United States, there is some part of the country a few thousand miles away that is not taken in by it, and that allows an opposed movement to grow in reaction to the first one and create some kind of balance. So to sum up my view on the postwar period here, I think the horrible development of mechanization is less dangerous here than in a smaller country, because there is some breathing room around the monster" (ibid., p. 217).

As people would realize forty years later, he wasn't mistaken.

For all that, movies were his main preoccupation, and he was always on the lookout for a subject he would like to film. As always, he wasn't looking for something easy. In October 1946, he noticed in the *New Yorker* a short critique of a novel written by an Englishwoman born in India, Rumer Godden. There were two reasons for his attention to the praise it was given: *The River* was a minor work, and not many people would read it.[38] He bought the book and found it terrific; it had no elephants and no tiger hunts or maharajahs, so he got an option on it.

---

[37] Jean Renoir, *Lettres d'Amérique*, 220.
[38] William H. Gilcher, *Jean Renoir in America*, 420.

THE RIVER OF LIFE

◆

The death of a friend is that much sadder when you live half a world away. On October 6, 1947, Paul Cézanne, Jean Renoir's lifelong friend, died in Paris. The two had not seen each other for seven years. In several letters, Jean had suggested that Renée and Paul come to visit them. Renée called Jean her brother; as for Paul, "my father and mother thought of him as their son. His disappearance leaves me feeling lost. In my affections and memories, he lies somewhere between my father and my brothers. I also happen to have admired him. He didn't really express what he had inside himself; instead of being a writer or a painter, he gave his gifts to his friends. If it's possible to think of friendship as an art, Paul's place in that art is as important as his father's in the art of painting." Jean wrote these words to Mr. Guillaume, who was equally grief stricken.[1]

In the same letter, he sums up his feelings: the worst thing is not to have seen him again.

> But you know my situation, you can't always do what you want; these days it seems it takes me more time than ever to accomplish the least little thing. Obstructive officials, visits to consuls and travel agents, these things now scare me. And, frankly, I'm not sure I'm ready to start up again with the country where I was born. Exile hasn't exactly been a walk for me, as it has for many others. It's been heavy, and it's changed me deeply. Paul's disappearance has brought home to me all the doubts I've had. I spend my waking hours regretting that I wasn't at his side when he was sick, and I wonder why I didn't go. But you're right. It doesn't matter how he's gone. He is gone, and that's the terrible part.

[1] Jean Renoir, *Lettres d'Amérique*, ed. A. Sesonske (Paris, 1984), 294.

Jean often had doubts about being in exile, but he didn't admit it easily. More often than not, he claimed he was happy in the United States and gave all sorts of good reasons for loving the life he led there. He worried about being criticized for taking the easy way out, for running away from danger, and the more time passed, the more he feared this reproach, though he always kept it in the back of his mind. He was too multifaceted and too fascinated by what was going on around him to let himself be inhibited by fear of criticism.

He was also disappointed in his work, and his setbacks inspired disillusionment. He wrote this to Pierre Lestringuez about *Monsieur Verdoux:*

> People here are indignant about Chaplin's latest. Dido and I loved it. But in the eyes of modern man, Chaplin has committed the sin of expressing his personality. That's something no one wants anymore. Down with the individual! Long live the salad made with store-bought mayonnaise! You can't tell its ingredients apart! On either side of the barrier that'll soon separate East and West, the big deal is "leveling." If you want to stay alive, you've got to stay on the same level as everyone else, you've got to dance the communal boogie-woogie, you've got to put your feet in the footsteps of whoever's beside you and whoever's in front of you (ibid., p. 278).

He became a close friend of Chaplin's, and their friendship lasted because they admired each other. That was a rarity for Chaplin, who was often cruel to his colleagues. Jean devoted a long article to *Monsieur Verdoux,* which made him laugh until he cried. Here is its last paragraph:

> Some day *Monsieur Verdoux* will assume its rightful place in the history of artistic creations that deserve the respect of our whole civilization. It will stand beside the pottery of Urbino and the paintings of the French Impressionists, between a story by Mark Twain and a minuet by Lully. On the other hand, the films that are full of money, gimmicks, and advertisements, that thrill their fans, they'll take their place beside God knows what, in the land of oblivion, alongside the rows of fancy mahogany chairs, all alike, spewn from chrome-plated factories.[2]

Jean Renoir makes no secret of what he prefers. Nor does he hesitate to stand up for what he loves. Hollywood, it seemed to him, took the wrong route in trying to please a wide audience that was getting

---

[2] *L'Ecran français,* July 15, 1947, 107, in Jean Renoir, *Ecrits, 1926–1971,* ed. C. Gauteur (Paris, 1974), 196.

smaller due to the fear of war and the political situation. An antitrust law was passed that prevented the big studios from controlling the distribution of films. It both threatened their funds and weakened their power. Henceforth, they could not afford to take risks. They wanted to be assured of the viability of what they produced from the start. The blight that fell on the film industry as a result was impressive to Jean. Still, during the course of 1947 he kept up hope that he would make a feature film entitled *Woman of a Hundred Faces,* the story of a model in Paris between the wars. Nothing came of the project, as nothing did of so many others. For a long time, he had been wanting to make a film from the novels of Knut Hamsun. But he abandoned the idea when he found out that the author of *Hunger* had been a collaborator. At one point, there was the possibility of making an opera like the *Threepenny Opera* from *The Crime of M. Lange.* Hans Eisler was to be his partner in this adventure, and he thought they had "a good chance of getting their work accepted by a Broadway theater." Their partnership would have been a lot of fun. He also had another project in mind, one that he was very hopeful of succeeding with, even though he knew very well the inherent difficulties it faced. The idea was to create a small production company that would bear his name, Jean Renoir Productions. The company would not make more than four films a year. They would be distributed by Allied Artists, "the deluxe wing" of a larger company, Monogram, that made only cowboy movies and gangster movies. "These are the only people who seem disposed to let me do whatever I want," as he wrote to Flaherty.[3] During 1947, he and Forrest Judd, a screenwriter for Monogram, put the company together. It was not possible for him to shoot a film that year, but the plan was for the first one to come out in 1948. It was going to be called *Children of Vienna* (ibid., p. 266).

◆

As usual, life saw to it that these plans changed. First of all, in January 1948, the name of the company changed to the Film Group. Other partners joined Forrest Judd: "A young businessman, a young actor, a very old lawyer, and my friend Lourié." Jean forgot *Children of Vienna* in favor of a version of *Romeo and Juliet* by Anouilh, but it, too, was soon abandoned because of a dispute about author's rights. Then he began thinking about the Clifford Odets play, *Night Music.*

Fascinated by what was happening in the theater in a land that

---

[3] Jean Renoir, *Ecrits,* 308.

was still new to him, Jean found it tempting to make plays into films. With his usual powers of persuasion, he had no trouble convincing his partners that the Film Group should in fact specialize in producing movie versions of both classical and modern plays. But his old friend Simenon turned up in the spring of 1948. He had moved to Tucson, Arizona, and was spending a few days in Los Angeles. With him, Simenon brought several of his latest novels, including *La Fuite de M. Monde* (*Monsieur Monde Vanishes*), which really excited Jean Renoir. Simenon was ready to give him the rights to it, and the Film Group was supposed to inaugurate its productions with *M. Monde.* Jean worked on the script during the summer of 1948. His hope was to begin shooting in August in Chicago and New York. His confidence had returned. Once again he would be able to make films his own way, and he had proven that you had to keep away from the big studios. Nor was he the only one to have this opinion. A telegram sent to Robert Flaherty after the debut of *Louisiana Story* proves it: "Have just seen your marvellous film. Keep it up and you'll be immortal and get excommunicated by Hollywood, if you're lucky. Congratulations." The telegram was signed by Oona and Charlie Chaplin, Esta and Dudley Nichols, and Dido and Jean Renoir.[4]

Soon Jean had to abandon his fine optimism. Once again, his outlook grew dark. He had his contract with the distributor, his company was formed, but banks refused to lend them money. The bank that had agreed to finance their first two films reversed its decision because Congress had ordered the Federal Reserve to limit loans to small businesses. "Still, this story about the Federal Reserve isn't what really stopped me," Jean wrote to a painter friend on October 4, 1948. "I'm convinced there's another worm in the apple, which is my complete incompetence in business matters" (ibid., p. 331).

Fortunately, he had some other offers. Claude Heymann, who was his assistant from 1926 to 1936, asked him on behalf of Films Universalis to shoot Anouilh's *Eurydice* in Italy; and B. P. Schulberg proposed that he make a film about Goya, also in Rome, with his friend Paulette Goddard. He did not take up Heymann's offer because he found out that Marcel Carné was interested in it, and he did not want to get into difficulties with him. "Even as things are they don't speak well of me in France. I don't really care, but in order not to care, I have to be sure that I haven't got anything on my conscience" (ibid., p. 327). Before it, too, was abandoned, the Goya project was post-

[4]Claude Mauriac, *l'Amour du cinéma* (Paris, 1954).

poned several times, because Paulette Goddard wasn't available. He refused another Italian film with Louis Jouvet, and another with Paul Muni in England on the life of Van Gogh. It was suggested that he direct *The Reckless Moment* (*Les Désemparés*), which was made the following year by Max Ophuls, with James Mason. Robert Hakim asked him to return to Paris and make *Casque d'or* (*Golden Helmet*). Jean withdrew on the advice of his lawyer, Mr. Masse. As he told Mr. Guillaume, who was in constant contact with the man, "Tell him clearly that I won't set foot in Paris until he gets me out of this mess once and for all" (ibid.).

♦

It was frustrating not to be able to go where he wished; and then distance, memory, and imagination deformed what actually happened. In Paris in 1946 the producers of *Grand Illusion* put the film back into circulation. The negative was destroyed during the first Allied bom bardment of Paris in 1942, so the version that was shown had censor's cuts. Georges Altman went after it: "We don't have the moral right, two years after the Wehrmacht, the SS, and the crematoria to ask the arts to remind us of Franco-German friendship. The blood is still fresh. It's neither hatred nor chauvinism that makes us voice our amazement and indignation; it's just memories."[5] Perhaps it was too soon to avoid this kind of misunderstanding. Even though Altman seems to be the only one who didn't understand it, *Grand Illusion* wasn't as successful as had been hoped. Jean's American films were shown in France during 1948, all except *The Southerner*, which did not appear there until 1950. People did not have it in for him, despite what he thought. His old friends did not like the American movies simply because they wanted to see him there making films together with them, as before. They thought that if he came back, and the group was assembled again, they would rediscover their youth. Sadly, none of that could happen. The past does not come back to life, as Jean Renoir knew very well, and misunderstandings are unavoidable. Even if they did not yet have it in for him, when they saw him working the way he wanted to, they would! Each new subject set its own form that was distinctive and that had not even been imagined before.

On the other hand, more and more young people admired him. Magazines and cinema-club newsletters spoke of him frequently.

[5] *Franc-Tireur*, August 29, 1946.

François Truffaut wrote his first article for one of the latter, the *Ciné-club du quartier Latin*. He did it "for Bazin, who was in the sanatorium and was already working on his book on Renoir," as he noted on the photocopy of the article that he provided me. It consists of a column on *Rules of the Game*, which was circulating among the ciné-clubs in an eighty minute version that was also shown at the Cinémathèque. The negative of this version was made from a safe, new copy kept hidden during the war. François Truffaut thought it was a complete version.[6] The journal *Ciné-club*, which was the mouthpiece of all the French movie clubs, had grown rapidly in importance and size. Its sixth number (April 1948) is completely devoted to Jean Renoir and contains, among other things, an interview with Gaston Modot. Modot, who played an extraordinary Schumacher in *Rules of the Game*, had this to say about its director: "He was insatiably curious in the service of his art, and so he learned all he could about everything. It was amazing to hear him talking enthusiastically about the capacity of automobile engines, the physiognomy of Lavater, the varieties of clock movements, the sense of direction in migrating animals, the notions of revolution among the Jacobins, and other, even less expectable subjects."[7]

His Californian friends would not disavow this description of Jean, despite the changes he perceived in himself since being there. Jean Renoir's personality was so strong that it left a mark on his surroundings instead of the other way round. As in his films, he was not interested in recreating a part of Paris in Beverly Hills; he knew how Hollywood differed from Les Collettes, or the Mediterranean from the Tropics, and that Californians have nothing to do with the peasants in Provence or Burgundy. Life in California had another rhythm to it. You had to take pleasure in nature's luxuriance, appreciate a certain kind of *joie de vivre*, play at an exaggerated sort of friendliness in your relationships with anyone and everyone, and accept a lack of refinement in people's reactions.

Everyday life was a consolation. The new house, which visitors thought had a Provençal flavor to it, was being built. It was just what he and Dido wanted it to be, not too big or too small, all on one level, full of light and with a superb view of the ocean, reflecting their needs and their taste. They presided over the construction site with affection, taking great pains to get the details right. After a long bu-

---

[6] *Ciné-club du quartier latin*, 5, 3, 1.
[7] Information provided by Claude Gauteur.

reaucratic struggle, Dido succeeded in bringing over her governess, one Bessie Smith, from England. She moved in with them in December 1947 and was a great help to Dido, who had always remained close to her. Bessie, for her part, adapted very well to life in California and to daily interaction with Gabrielle and her family. There was a marvellous understanding among them all, and no pettiness. Dido was continually sending all kinds of packages to friends across the Atlantic. It was a job that consumed more energy and time than she would have wished, but certain commodities that were still rare in Europe were indeed useful to those who received them: things like coffee, sugar, and powdered milk.

On February 12, 1948, Alain married Jane Wagner, a young dietician he met in Santa Barbara. Their marriage took place in Ohio, her birthplace. Alain wanted to undertake graduate study. A writer, or a newspaperman, or a university professor—he was not sure yet what he wanted to become, but it was clear that the old incorrigible had become a brilliant student. His lifestyle was typical of an academic's, modest and orderly; it was a far cry from what his father would have anticipated when he first came to America.

In June of 1948, Alain received his diploma from the University of California and entered Harvard in September of that year to study for his doctorate in English and Comparative Literature. Having obtained it, he taught in Athens, Ohio, before returning to the University of California at Berkeley, where he has remained for the rest of his career. He became a great specialist in medieval English literature. His youthfulness has not deserted him; his voice is strong, and he has the heartiest of laughs. Alain resembles his father more than just physically. Like him, after first detesting school, he achieved excellence in the specialty of his choosing.

As of 1948, Jean knew he would not have to worry about his son any longer. In a letter to Marie Lestringuez, his friend's sister, he describes in minute detail their first dinner at Alain and Jane's, "in their little apartment over a garage in the backyard of a house in a pretty seedy neighborhood (of Santa Barbara). The dinner was magnificently serenaded by gospel songs from a black church housed in a decrepit warehouse on the other side of the street."[8]

In September, Jean and Dido went to Arizona to visit with Georges Simenon. Jean still thought it would be possible to shoot *M. Monde*—not long afterwards, though, he gave it up. The Simenon

[8]Jean Renoir, *Lettres d'Amérique*, 317.

household amazed Dido. His surprising Canadian companion/secretary was pregnant; Jean agreed to be the child's godfather if it was a boy, and Dido its godmother if it was a girl. They spent a day on the far side of the Mexican border, hanging around in strange, awful places. Simenon insisted he and Jean visit the local whorehouse, while Dido and Denise drank beer from dirty glasses in a depressing bar. Jean had fun imagining Simenon "transformed into a cowboy"; his own fantasies made him double over with laughter. Jean was as available as ever to his friends, and he was always passionately interested in what befell them and what they were up to. His wit was effervescent; he spoke with ease, joy, and vigor, always punctuated by peals of laughter. Here was a man who could bring a smile to the lips of the grouchiest person, but he was as reserved as can be about his personal life. He always had been, too. It was yet another trait that his parents had as well. For a long time they kept their relationship secret, and they were always shy in public with one another, as shy as they were with other people.

Once more, a tragic event occurred in which film and reality intermingled, like the accidents in which Janie Marèze and Pierre Champagne had died. This time, it was Marguerite who was the protagonist of a drama like those in Jean's films. In legitimate self-defense, she used a pistol to kill the man whom she married, without enthusiasm, after her breakup with Jean. The news caused an uproar among film people in Paris. But after she spent a month in preventive detention at La Petite Roquette, the case against her was dismissed. Free again, "she regained her composure and did an excellent job of hiding the terrible shock she had received," as Pierre Lestringuez wrote.[9] She also resumed her work as a film editor, working with Jacques Becker, who had always given her support. Jean Renoir was "very disturbed" when he heard what happened, but he could do nothing about it, as he told Pierre Lestringuez: "One fine day two parallel roads diverged and ended up in totally different places. If you see her again, tell her I hope she puts all that behind her and that her life gets back together very soon."[10] He was honest, and also too clear about himself to pretend to sentiments that were not really his. His past with Marguerite was completely erased. As he said to Renée Cézanne, in the last few years with Dido, he had found a kind of peace that he had not known before. Before, always on edge, he felt a

---

[9] Letter dated December 18, 1948, Dido Renoir archive.
[10] Jean Renoir, *Lettres d'Amérique*, 348.

need to please other people that no longer overwhelmed him in the same way. He still loved being loved, but he felt somehow freer. It was the calm that comes from shared love and from faith.

◆

His next film was destined to express that faith, always in the background in his other work, more clearly than ever before. The option he had gotten on the Rumer Godden novel had already lapsed when one of the partners of the Film Group, Forest Judd, introduced him to a Beverly Hills florist named Kenneth McEldowney, who wanted to go to India to shoot *The River.*

McEldowney was pretty far from the standard Hollywood producer. He knew the film world because his wife, Melvina Pumphrey, worked at MGM in the publicity department. She was a publicist for Esther Williams, "champion swimmer and film star," then at the height of popularity for her aquatic ballets. McEldowney had discovered India during the war. He had served there in the American Air Force and had stayed in touch with "important people in India" who were ready to finance an American film on India that would be shot in India. That would allow him to make a foreign investment all the while respecting the law against the export of capital. McEldowney, who was very skillful, succeeded in convincing the British National Film Finance Company to lend him some money on his assurance that the film would be produced by the British Commonwealth since Indian princes were his principal backers—even though, at the time in question, representatives of the Indian government insisted, for their part, that India no longer had any ties to the British Crown.[11] The way McEldowney finagled things was of no interest to Jean; what he wanted and had been wanting for some time was to shoot the film. Nor did Jean attach much importance to what his rather unusual producer was telling him. Had McEldowney met Rumer Godden by way of Santha Rama Rau, an Indian woman who had spent a lot of time abroad and written a book called *Home to India,* or had he met her through Nehru's sister? Whichever it was, she assured him it was better to show India through the eyes of an Englishwoman who had lived there for a long time than for Westerners to make a film with Indian characters and an Indian storyline. McEldowney was smart enough to see that she was right.

McEldowney was very good at adapting to other people, at lis-

[11] William H. Gilcher, *Jean Renoir in America* (Des Moines, 1979), 422.

tening to them, and at knowing what language to use with them. Although he could lie himself, Jean Renoir took a little time to notice his producer's lies. His own were gratuitous embellishments of the truth, he was conscious of that and admitted it willingly. As for McEldowney, his lies were of a different sort. More elaborate, they were also more useful. Jean Renoir at first thought he was a nice guy, and he hoped he had come across the ideal partner. Still, he made clear that he wanted to be in charge of the direction and editing, and that he also wanted to write the script in collaboration with Rumer Godden. Their agreements were all properly written up and signed. The film was to be shot in India with actors who were not stars.

McEldowney claims he had to force Jean Renoir to go to India, but Jean himself said this: "There's one condition to our partnership, and that is that you pay for a trip to India to let me see if it's really possible to shoot a film there. Because if not, and if we have to shoot *The River* in a Hollywood studio with fake sets, I'd rather quit now."[12]

Dido and Jean left for India on January 29, 1949, and did not return to Los Angeles until April 6. Their first stay in the East made a great impression on Jean, who wrote as follows to Clifford Odets on February 15:

> We've been in India for two weeks, including two days in Pakistan. I won't tell you everything there is to say, since we still don't know anything. The only thing that is clear is that in our whole lives, we have never been in a country in which people live so differently from the way we do. We like the Hindus very much, and the few contacts that we have had about making a film here have been very encouraging. I've shot a few test shots with an Indian cameraman and technical team; I edited them with an Indian editor. They're very competent, and they have a respect for our craft that I wouldn't mind finding in white technicians. We have met young people, students, and they were fascinating. The strange part is that even in the so-called scientific domains, they do not try to pass themselves off as Europeans. Hollywood people would take a Hindu director or writer for a beggar and would have a hard time believing that he has any education at all. On the other hand, Hindu intellectuals are probably more broadminded and don't find our clothes too silly looking.
>
> Calcutta is a good imitation of a London suburb, including the fog and the smoke. Huge, old-style factories spread a kind of cloud of black soot over the city. Sometimes, a whiff of air from the ocean dispels the haze: a little temple appears that might have been painted by Matisse, or the

[12] Jean Renoir, *Entretiens et propos* (Paris, 1979), 149.

crumbling facade of a house, crowded with complicated, lacy shutters in the style of Dufy, or a little bit of a garden where you wouldn't be surprised to come across Scheherazade resting in the shade of a mango tree. A sheer delight.[13]

The day before, he wrote this to Gabrielle:

We're in our hotel room. The ceilings are very high, as they are everywhere in India. Since I'm very precise (gaga, you'd say), I brought a thing to measure with, and I measured a little over thirteen feet high. There are big fans hanging from the ceiling that turn horizontally and at their leisure. (You've seen the same ones in little towns in the desert or near Fresno.) Dido is trying to make a phone call. Someone has pinned a calendar on the wall with a picture of almond-eyed ladies in the nude on it. She underlines today's date, and that arouses the "monzamis" who serve us. When we eat in our room they stay here with us, two or three or four of them, with magnificent turbans. They comment on every gesture we make and giggle, and if we read a letter, they read it at the same time as we do, over our shoulders, without understanding a word.

There are cockroaches here as big as dates and the same color as them, too. We're still delighted with our trip, despite the inconvenience of a country in which you can't drink the water without boiling it first or else you'll get cholera. But it is magnificent, and the people are amazing. Hugs and kisses to you all.[14]

Several times, he repeats that he is hooked. He adds: "It's an extraordinary country, with extraordinary people, and, I'll tell you right away, it's one of the least mysterious places there is."[15]

He hated tourism, that's clear. What he wanted to do was "learn India." Practicing his craft there was a good way to do just that. With his passion for observing others, he soon noted that "Hindus are thirsty for human contact: they need to feel the warmth of life."[16] Later he said:

It's perfectly possible that Eastern philosophy can help Westerners once again. In India, the people who really lead the philosophical life (really, it's not philosophy, it's just a point of view about life) reach the following result: if they are very poor, they set up housekeeping on the window ledge of a large building, for instance, a bank. In such a spot they store the covering in which they sleep (because sometimes it gets chilly at

[13] Dido Renoir archive.
[14] Letter provided by Jean Slade.
[15] Jean Renoir, *Entretiens et propos*, 149.
[16] Jean Renoir, *Ma vie et mes films* (Paris, 1974), 233.

night, and it also rains during the monsoon), and also whatever utensil they have to cook food, if they find any. There are trams that make a lot of noise, there's a lot of shouting in the street, but they succeed in isolating themselves completely, in thinking about their little concerns with as much intensity as if they were in a country home that was completely isolated and surrounded with greenery. Well, it's a pretty amazing thing! It's a system that's worth learning, and that could be very useful for us (ibid., p. 65).

Then he sums things up: "A few weeks in India have taught me this essential truth: that people do not exist in a vacuum, that what surrounds them *exists*."[17]

It was a safe bet that he would understand and adore India. He found out what he had to very quickly, but their stay lasted much longer than had been foreseen. Initially the plan was to stay in Calcutta for two weeks and then go to Bombay and then, on the way home, stop off in Rome, where he had made contact again with Salvo d'Angelo from Films Universalis to discuss shooting Anouilh's *Eurydice,* and from there to London. But he and Dido went to Pakistan to visit the home in which Rumer Godden had grown up. Picking actors and the members of a technical team takes time. They stayed in the Great Eastern Hotel in Calcutta and set about looking for a home in which to shoot the film. "The house I have found is a little bit run down," as he wrote to Lourié, his old friend who was doing the set design. "I just wanted to add that we're going to set up the house so that we can also live in it. It'll be a little rustic, but the beauty of the garden, with its monkeys and mongeese, will be a substitute for luxury."[18] They also went to Delhi, with McEldowney, whom they accompanied in several of his attempts to get import licenses and other necessary authorizations. McEldowney showed off his skill in dealing with the administration and his Indian friends. This film was the greatest adventure of his life, and he wanted to get the most publicity he could for himself out of it.

Jean and Dido became good friends with Indians like Hari Das Gupta, whom Jean had met during a visit to USC. Gupta had been a student there in 1946–47, and he was to become his assistant. Gupta introduced them to his family. "This group was the model of the enlightened Hindu middle class. It included professors, lawyers, doctors, civil servants, other professionals. Many young women graduated from Shantinikitan University, a school founded by Tagore that

[17] *Cahiers du cinéma,* 8, January 1952, in Jean Renoir, *Ecrits,* 270.
[18] Jean Renoir, *Lettres d'Amérique,* 353.

succeeded in preserving Indian ways at the same time as it taught the essence of Western culture. That was a success all right."[19] Jean also tells the story of his first meeting with the dancer, Radha, in the palace in Benares, the holy city, where her future husband, Raymond Burnier, lived. "Radha taught me the 'katakali' dances and, in general, the music of Madras province, where she lived" (ibid., p. 237). He made her, a Eurasian woman, into a key figure in the film, in which everyone else is Western.

◆

Meantime, the film took shape in his head. The country was beautiful, and so were its creatures: the women draped in saris who walked like queens; all the pure colors, which he wanted to show. "I saw the colors in India as marvellous motifs with which to test my theories about color films. I'd been wanting to make a film in color for a long time, even though I believe that black and white are powerful factors in making a film into a spectacle. Black and white profits from the advantage that lies in the impossibility of its being realistic: whether you want it or not, the world outside is in colors" (ibid., p.233). He did shoot *The River* in Technicolor, but for all that, it was not a realistic film. He went to London to become familiar with the color process, which was new to him. He took along "an aged gentleman to work the clapper that coordinates sound and picture" during the trials in Calcutta. "He had a distinctive look to him, so I asked the others about him and finally learned that he was a very famous cinematographer who was just curious to see how I worked. So I asked him if he wanted to be the cinematographer in my film, and he said yes, so he came to London to study Technicolor. He was in charge of framing the film."[20] Jean's nephew, Claude, was the actual camera operator. He told me that he had gone through a long training period in London—six months of classes on Technicolor film.

When Dido and Jean finally left India, McEldowney went with them. That was on March 15, 1949, and they did not make the stop that had been planned for Rome. "Dido and I met Rumer Godden in surroundings that could not be more remote from India: an inn on the Thames called 'The Perfect Angler.' From that day, the three of us were faithful friends."[21] The novelist promised to meet them in California to write the screenplay with Jean. During their stay in London,

[19] Jean Renoir, *Ma vie et mes films*, 236.
[20] Jean Renoir, *Entretiens et propos*, 14.
[21] Jean Renoir, *Ma vie et mes films*, 233.

Jean worked with the people in British Technicolor, auditioning actors with the help of Rumer Godden. On April 6, 1949, he and Dido returned to the United States.

Their return was a festive one, because while they were away, Bessie Smith had moved them into the new Beverly Hills house on Leona Drive. It was just as they had hoped it would be: all on one level, simple and suited to their needs, with a garden that would soon become very beautiful, thanks to Dido, and a superb view that the smog was not yet ruining. They soon had another reason for rejoicing: a letter from Mr. Guillaume dated June 15: "I hasten to inform you that the court of appeals has transformed the separation agreement into a divorce and ordered their decision to be transcribed into the civil acts." So Catherine Hessling had finally lost the case that she tried so hard to drag out. She did in fact appeal to the Court of Appeals, but its decision prevented her from taking any further action against Jean Renoir. He was finally free to return to France. How good it felt! For all these years, he had refrained from complaining, which was all the more admirable since he was paying for Catherine's lawyer—she was still dependent on him—as well as his own.

To be unable to return to your birthplace is very hard to bear; unfortunately, many of our contemporaries know just how hard. Although he never said anything about it, Jean suffered from it. But he did not want the peace and calm that he was enjoying with Dido to be tarnished by Catherine, who kept trying to set him up for public vengeance. He was going to be busy for several months with the film, so at that moment he was unable to take advantage of his newfound freedom.

◆

Just before the good news, Rumer Godden arrived. An Englishwoman who was raised in India, she lived in the countryside, in Buckinghamshire, with her husband and her children and her writing. Two films had already been made from her novels, and she had not intended a third. It was easy for her to adapt to the life of Jean and Dido, and she and Jean worked well together. The screenplay they were constructing did not stick to the text of the novel. She had no problem accepting the principle that Jean close her book and put it on a shelf. There were to be new characters and other anecdotes, and she yielded to his views. She was not surprised at what her new friend had found in India. The essence of her book is a hymn to life incarnated in the ever-present river, and she knew that would remain intact. Unlike many authors, she had no frail vanity or pettiness. Dido and Jean had understood that from the first time they met. Once the day's work was done, she joined readily in their amusements. She got along well with their friends, who were glad to welcome her and sad to see her leave.

When she left California on July 31, the screenplay was far from complete, and some roles were yet to be cast. The actors whom Jean had thought of, James Mason, Robert Ryan, and Mel Ferrer, couldn't make themselves available, so finally they were obliged to settle for a young, unknown male lead. This meant modifying the role and also reviewing the choice of female actors in order to keep things balanced. He wrote Rumer Godden of these developments as they occurred, and the way in which she responded reveals the deep agreement they had achieved on the concept of the movie. Yet his choice of a young, inexperienced actor for the role of Captain John troubled her, and the subject comes up in several of their letters. Jean stuck to his decision, but in any case, he had no other choice. Films had not been her domain before, but Rumer Godden was excited and voluble. In India, she helped train the young people they chose who had no prior experience. A former dance instructor, she really made them work at it. "She made them dance and recite poems. The results were excellent: our young actors don't look the least bit ill at ease" (ibid., p. 239).

She wrote:

> The world of film was new to me. I found it terribly interesting and terribly exhausting. I was overwhelmed by that world and my work. We were living in the polyglot atmosphere of the Great Eastern Hotel in Calcutta, a place far removed from peaceful nostalgia. The air was thick with all sorts of machinations, discussions, consultations, quarrels, tensions, and conflicts, the kind of thing that surrounds an emotional event like the shooting of a film, especially in such a difficult setting. We were working too hard to be able to dream, but I was carried away again by all those familiar things: the colors of the past, the noises, the smells, the tastes, the thoughts; I wasn't searching them out; they took charge of me, in spite of myself.[22]

Because of no-shows and changes, auditioning took longer than expected. In their part of southern California, where the barometer gets stuck at beautiful, fall succeeded summer without Jean even realizing it. He was so busy that he didn't hear the jeers and whistles that greeted *The Southerner* at the first festival of banned films organized by André Bazin in Biarritz in July 1949; that was its first showing to a

---

[22] Rumer Godden, "The Author and the Film of *The River*," manuscript provided by Alexander Sesonske.

French public. But at least it was in good company. Also shown were the complete version of *L'Atalante* by Jean Vigo, as well as his *Zéro de conduite* (*Zero for Conduct*), *The Lady from Shanghai* by Orson Welles, Grémillon's *Lumière d'été* (*Summer Light*), *Les Dames du bois de Boulogne* (*Ladies of the Bois de Boulogne*) by Robert Bresson, *La Bataille du rail* by René Clément, John Ford's *The Long Voyage Home*, *Jour de fête* by Jacques Tati, and Jean Rouch's first film. Orson Welles and Raymond Queneau were members of the jury, which was headed by Jean Cocteau. Godard, Truffaut, and Rivette, all under twenty at the time, were there as well. André Bazin, wonderfully honest, notes "the shock and disappointment, but they were tempered by the certainty that it was the man and not his film that was to blame."[23] Dido remarked, with typical naturalness, "Jean was used to being treated badly. After his disappointment over *Rules of the Game*, nothing could get to him."[24] A little while later, he would actually meet Bazin. That was the beginning of a friendship that death alone interrupted.

Before leaving for India, he had to rewrite the script with Rumer Godden and find a few actors in England. He and Dido stopped at Boston on the way to London in order to visit with "the children." Alain was working on his doctorate in English and Comparative Literature at Harvard. They arrived on the East Coast on October 31 and left on November 3. From London, it was not hard to stop off in Paris to greet the family, Mr. Guillaume, and a few friends. Though there was nothing to fear legally speaking, Jean and Dido preferred to keep their arrival on November 21 a secret. They only wanted to spend forty-eight hours in France because of the press of work. The short visit seems not to have made much of an impression, except for the meeting with André Bazin, which took place at the Invalides air terminal.

Janine Bazin remembers that her husband could not find a parking space. Since "he wasn't the kind of guy who'd leave his car just any place, he told me, 'Go see Renoir while I look for a spot.' I was sure I'd recognize him, so I was the first member of the Bazin family to meet Renoir; but I found him very intimidating," she told me. Jean suggested that they join him on the trip from the station to Le Bourget, where he was taking a place for London. That's how André Bazin had his first interview, which he published with a photograph of Jean and Dido. The headline read, "The Author of *Grand Illusion* Has Not

[23]Dudley Andrew, *André Bazin* (New York, 1978), 150.
[24]Interview with the author.

Lost Confidence in Creative Freedom."[25] The periodical called *L'Ecran français*, which had come up from underground and was supported by the PC, was a weekly that Bazin contributed to on a regular basis, though he was not part of its editorial staff. Usually he refused to do interviews, but Jean Renoir was his favorite director, and he knew that the man would not disappoint him. The Bazins and Renoirs had much in common: a simple, direct way of relating, and a love of movies. They understood each other from the start.

In London, Claude Renoir realized that it would not be easy to send the equipment they needed—an electric generator and projectors—to India. "It happened that the ship that had loaded these things received an order to put them back on the dock and replace them with arms destined for Indochina. The French war in Indochina was in full swing, and the arms trade between London and Calcutta was flourishing."[26] MacEldowney took "two whole months" to find another ship. Meanwhile, Dido and Jean returned to India. With Rumer Godden, her young sister Nancy, Claude Renoir, and Eugène Lourié, they got acquainted with the locations where the film was to be shot.

Lourié quickly decided it would be easier and less troublesome to build a street resembling the ones they were walking down instead of deploying their cumbersome equipment in a place that was already overcrowded; arc lamps so close to the straw roofs constituted a fire hazard; "huge masses of greenery" hanging over one-story buildings posed insoluble lighting problems as well as significant human problems: they would have to close the street while shooting was going on, which would necessitate reimbursing the shopkeepers for many days' worth of business, and then, where would the villagers do their marketing while the filming was going on? With figures to back up his claims, Lourié succeeded in convincing the production team. A film street like all the other streets in the village became a reality.

◆

Jean Renoir warned his nephew: "You'll see, it's a beautiful country, the light is really extraordinary. . . . The area around Calcutta is like the banks of the Loire. If the technical procedures are up to what we want, things could be very interesting."[27] In fact, Claude was as

[25] *L'Ecran français*, 230, 6–14, November 28, 1949.
[26] Jean Renoir, *Ma vie et mes films*, 235.
[27] Interview with Claude Renoir, *Cinématographe*, 46, April 1979, 38.

amazed as he was by the beauty of the place and the people. Neither of the two failed to be struck by the human misery—how could they not be?—and later on, during the shooting, they were outraged by the bloody clashes between Hindus and Moslems. Why should we be surprised to find nothing in their film on that subject? The characters belonged to an earlier period, before those troubles. Jean's assistant, Hari Das Gupta, has recorded some of his memories.[28] He speaks of Communist riots, and he insists that, despite what was said at the time, no sound engineer was killed during the fighting. He says that "Jean was deeply attached to the river . . . and totally taken by the country. Masses of refugees kept arriving, and his heart went out to them; he wept when he saw them, softhearted as he was. When we went out on location, he asked me all the questions that were boiling inside him. We would ride along, and he had so many questions to ask." Sometimes, Gupta would bring along a friend of his, Satyajit Ray, who was the artistic director of an advertising agency. "He could talk endlessly—and beautifully—about Bengal and its people, and Renoir listened." Ray and Das Gupta, for their part, learned by listening to Renoir. Sometimes they were surprised by Jean's interest in things that were so familiar to them, and they got charged up with enthusiasm and affectionate attention," as Gupta recalls. "We started seeing through his eyes."[29]

"For a man of his age and dimensions, Renoir's enthusiasm and energy are phenomenal. He would trudge across miles of impossible territory to find the right viewpoint for the right locale. At times, the absorption in his work was so complete that his wife would have to administer some gentle admonishment like: 'You shouldn't be out in the sun so long, Jean,' or, 'Jean, you haven't forgotten that appointment at six o'clock, have you?'"[30] One day, Jean said to Ray, "'Look at those flowers,' . . . pointing to a *palas* tree (a tree with red flowers that is very common in Bengal) in full bloom. It was the first of several occasions on which I was fortunate enough to accompany him on his trips in search of locations. 'Those flowers,' said Renoir, 'are very beautiful. But you get flowers in America, too. Poinsettias, for instance, they grow wild in California. But look at the clump of banana trees, and that green pond at its foot. You don't get that in California. That is Bengal.' One could see that while searching for locations, Re-

[28] On magnetic tape, provided by Alexander Sesonske.
[29] Erik Barnouw and S. Krishnaswamy, *Indian Film,* 2nd ed. (New York, 1980), 190–91.
[30] Satyajit Ray, *Our Films, Their Films* (Bombay, 1976), 115.

noir was also searching for *la couleur locale,* for those quintessential elements in the landscape which would be pictorially effective as well as being truly evocative of the atmosphere of the country. As he put it: 'You don't have to show many things in a film, but you have to be very careful to show only the right things.'" (ibid., p. 137).

Ray also tells another typical anecdote:

> Renoir had met a family of refugees who had come all the way from Pakistan by boat. "And they had all sorts of fantastic adventures," he said. "I am sure their story would make a very good film." I said India was full of such stories which simply cried out for filming. "And no doubt they are going to be made," said Renoir with naïve conviction. I said, "No, because the Indian director seems to find more inspiration in the slick artificiality of a Hollywood film rather than in the reality around him." "Ah, the American film . . . ," Renoir shook his head sadly, "I know it's a bad influence" (ibid., p. 112).

But five years later, Satyajit Ray made *Pather Panchali.*

With all sorts of reasons for delay piling up, and also because of the astrological chart and the position of the stars—in India, you always have to take them into account—shooting did not begin until December 29, 1949. They knew from the outset that nothing would be easy. Jean Renoir had chosen to perform his first experiment with color film on a continent in which the film, with its three separate bands, could not be developed. So it was impossible for them to judge the results immediately. They had to send the rolls to the lab in London, and the rushes did not arrive for three weeks. In the meantime, they had to make do with telegraphed conversations with Technicolor. Claude Renoir tells it this way: "We could trust no one but ourselves. For *The River,* Jean Renoir and I did a lot of work together with Renoir, the painter, my grandfather, in the background. All our research on the colors, their rendering, the contrasts between them, were dictated by that. One day, there was a blue vase inside that was not very beautiful (what's more, blue was still a risky color in those days), and I remember Jean telling me, "Listen, Claude, your grandpa would never put a color like that in one of his paintings. . . . Take it away!"[31] This is Jean's way of telling it: "Lourié and I, we sure used a lot of paint on the greenery, on the trees of Bengal! We walked around with big buckets of the stuff and changed things around completely."[32]

◆

[31] *Cinématographe,* 46, April 1979, 38.
[32] Jean Renoir, *Entretiens et propos,* 50.

Also in this film he used a process that no one had used before for a feature length film: recording the soundtrack on magnetic tape. Until then, the Hollywood studios thought it was too chancy, but Jean Renoir, never afraid to take risks, gave it a whirl. Recording the sound this way allowed him to find out immediately if it was good or not and to redo it immediately if not; otherwise, he would have had to send the sound to London as well and to fix things by dubbing, which Jean hated. The music for the film was "Indian music, Hindu chants, and, sometimes, a piano melody issuing from the house where the British family lived" (ibid.).

Perhaps there were even more accidents than usual during the shooting, because "the Indian electricians weren't used to these heavy machines. When they moved them, they forgot to tighten the screws that kept them in place. Some members of the team, one of whom was a Brahman, suggested that perhaps these unfortunate incidents were due to the way in which we had treated the goddess Kali. Kali plays a very important role in Hindu life, especially in Calcutta. It was she who founded the city. . . . The people on the team advised us to perform a little *puja*, a religious ceremony to honor the goddess. They performed the *puja*, which I filmed, in the big living room of the villa.

> A puja consists in bringing to a designated place a clay statue of the goddess, which will actually become the goddess for a few seconds. There are chants accompanied by dances and the burning of incense. At the end of the night, the statue of Kali is thrown into the river: clay returns to clay. The goddess was probably satisfied with the homage we paid her, since no more hands got caught in projectors.[33]

Jean Renoir was satisfied, too. An event like that delighted him greatly, and he enjoyed every moment of it, the way he savored Indian food. "How can you be unhappy with a curry on your plate? The British in my team were unhappy, they would have preferred their eggs and bacon. Not I. I was very happy, and I said to myself, "There aren't two curries in the world that are the same, you can be very happy with curries."[34]

◆

While shooting this film in a land that immediately endeared itself to him, he felt he was expressing himself more completely than ever be-

[33]Jean Renoir, *Ma vie et mes films*, 239–40.
[34]Maurice Bessy and Claude Beylie, *Jean Renoir. Le spectacle, la vie* (Paris, 1989), 38.

fore in his life. The subject of the film, what lay before his eyes, the people around him, the crowd that he could not keep himself from mixing with, everything tended to give a new dimension to his work. Despite the complications that were imposed by the distance between Calcutta and London and Los Angeles, where *The River* was finally edited, he was certain he had not gone astray. As Jacques Rivette wrote much later, "The ultimate subject of this film, the richest of metaphors, is simply metaphor itself, or absolute knowledge."[35]

In theory, they were to finish shooting the film around the middle of April 1950, but on May 7, Jean Renoir wrote this to Prince Fateh Singji of Limbdi: "I hope to finish filming next Wednesday, then I will record the music here and also some sounds that I will never find in Europe."[36] The Renoirs were unable to decide to leave India immediately thereafter, and they accepted Radha's invitation to visit Madras.

> We went to visit her at the Theosophic Institute, of which her father was president, at Adyar, where we lived the life of Brahmans. It did us much good to refrain from meat, alcohol, and cigarettes (except that Dido cheated terribly and would disappear into the bathroom to smoke). From Adyar, we brought back images of religious serenity.[37]

They also witnessed some traditional spectacles in Madras, concerts and dances that they especially enjoyed. The day finally came for them to leave; the farewells were difficult, since they knew that they would never return to that land. But they also knew that they would never lose their Indian friends, that they were certain to see them again in the United States or in Europe. Yet that did not make the separation any easier.

On the way home, Jean had decided to stop in Athens, "to rediscover Western culture." "It's a pilgrimage my father had always wanted to make, and now I understand why. It's Grimaud in an even more transparent light."[38] His love of Provence was returning, along with nostalgia for the past; it had been a very long time since he had seen Grimaud, Cagnes, the hillside at Les Collettes . . .

In Athens, the actress Katina Paxinou was waiting for them with her husband, Alexis Minotis, a producer of Athenian dramas in the ancient theaters in Greece. She had worked in Hollywood in *For*

---

[35] André Bazin, *Jean Renoir* (Paris, 1971), 259.

[36] Dido Renoir archive.

[37] Jean Renoir, *Ma vie et mes films*, 240.

[38] Letter by Jean Renoir cited by Alexander Sesonske in a letter to me dated January 21, 1984.

Whom the Bell Tolls, which was how they had met and become friends. As promised, Jean and Dido let her know they were coming, but they did not expect the result. She took care of them during their whole stay. She met them with "her whole tribe" and decided on the spot that they had better change hotels. She took charge of bargaining with the management and moved them into an old hotel where they had the best room, with a balcony looking out on the Parthenon. She and Minotis showed them the sights and fed them well. Their few days there went by very quickly. The memory of his father followed Jean everywhere. The hospitality of Katina and her husband turned every meal into a banquet and filled every site they visited with unexpected excitement; as he looked at the monuments, the statues, and the other objects, he could not keep from thinking about what his father would have said of them.

On June 8, the Renoirs were back in New York. At that point, they were eager to get home. "Paris dazzled us, but we really regretted not seeing your father," as Jean wrote to Claude Renoir on June 17. "London was magnificent and Koch very funny. But the brightest memory of our trip was all Athens." He decided that less time would be wasted if he did the editing in Los Angeles instead of London, as had been discussed at first. "Here, I think I can get it done in two months" (instead of five).

In the same letter, after his long absence, he says he is

> struck by the paralysis that has come over Hollywood. I feel full of indulgence for Kenny (McEldowney), who, without knowing it, allowed us to make a film we could never have made in the framework of a regular production.
>
> Television is what's killing movies here, and what's strange is that the killer isn't rich enough to pay for films that are executed correctly. All the studios are full of producers who can make terrible films in a couple of days to suit this new master. The public loves television, since it lets you stay at home in your bathrobe, have a drink, and turn it off when what you see is boring; it also keeps children busy and makes you popular with your neighbors; finally, it's cheaper than taking your whole family out to the movies.[39]

Relations with McEldowney were not always simple, nor would they be so in the future, but when it was necessary, Jean Renoir knew how to be reasonable. The time spent in India made a difference for him. He was able to direct his film in complete freedom; and for the

[39]Dido Renoir archive.

first time since his stay in Rome at the beginning of the war, he was closely associated with young filmmakers who thought of him as their ideal. He was not indifferent to recognition like that after those long years when he had such difficulty being accepted and when his most promising projects often ended badly.

◆

Daily life took its course. Dido and Jean could hardly believe they had stayed away from home for so long, but the olive trees had grown a lot, and the garden they found upon their return was superb, thanks to "la Bessie," as Dido called her in a letter to Conrad Slade. "We miss you very much, all three of you, and la Bessie, and the Toutous."[40] The Toutous are two dachshunds, Nénette and Tambeau, who were also Gabrielle's four-footed friends. Old habits were quickly revived, and the rhythm of visits between the two households resumed, despite the hours Jean was spending at the HalRoach Studios, where the editing was being done. Unfortunately, in September, three days before Jean's birthday, Conrad Slade died. While he was sick and until his last moments, Dido did her best to comfort and sustain him. The grief they all felt strengthened still more the ties of affection between Gabrielle, Dido, and the two Jeans.

During the editing, which Jean Renoir was doing with Georges Gale, a competent and friendly Hungarian, McEldowney, back in Hollywood, had calmed down, as Jean wrote to Prince Fateh Singj of Limbodi.[41] The laboratory that was to develop the color film was in London, which was not helpful. They could not shoot even the shortest linking scene, and there were also problems editing the soundtrack. They had to invent solutions to suit the new technique. Even so, the first cut was done pretty quickly and they even gave it a provisional sound mix.

Jean had decided to show this print to professionals and friends, to get some impressions. In a letter the prince dated September 18, 1950, he wrote: "A film is like a watch; the hands have to keep on running without stopping, so you have to be pitiless and cut whatever it is, good or bad, that can stop them."[42] He cut the beginning and decided to introduce a commentary by an off-stage narrator to make things even clearer; it seemed to him that viewers might have a hard

[40] Letter from Calcutta dated February 15, 1949, provided by Jean Slade.
[41] Letter dated December 3, 1950, Dido Renoir archive.
[42] Dido Renoir archive.

time following the story, since there were so many characters. He re-stored a few poetic images that he had cut because they had nothing to do with the unfolding action; but anything that touched life in In-dia and the riverine landscape would hold the viewer's attention. Jean sent long, detailed letters to Rumer Godden, and he took into account the changes she suggested in the text of the narrative that he had written with the help of a Hollywood screenwriter who was also a friend of Jean's, Salka Viertel. She saw that the film would be a success.

The final cut was finished in May of 1951 by Georges Gale, who went to London to verify the colors—he and Jean had only been working with samples. To promote the film, McEldowney deployed his genius for publicity: he signed a contract with United Artists that put him in charge of distribution. He also arranged for the Theater Guild to be a patron of the film, and he orchestrated a massive press campaign for it.

When the film came out in New York, McEldowney's wife, Mal-vina, wrote a long article in the *Saturday Evening Post:* "We Have Made a Movie—without Hollywood." *The River* was shown exclusively at the Paris Cinema for thirty-four weeks, starting on September 10, 1951. Two months later, when it appeared in other cities of the United States, an article appeared about it in *Life* magazine along with many photographs. The movie was a great success with the public, if not always with the critics.[43] It was put on in Paris in time for the Christ-mas season at the Cinéma Madeleine and at the Biarritz, starting on December 19, 1951. But before then, in September, it won the first international prize in the Venice film festival.

Jean Renoir didn't sit in Beverly Hills waiting for his well-deserved laurels. As he wrote to Jean Dewalde: "Claude [his nephew] is right. I like to stay at home and try my hand at being a writer, but I'm really a filmmaker first and foremost."[44] As soon as he had fin-ished his part of the editing, he left for Europe with Dido.

◆

Before arriving in New York, the couple stopped in Connecticut for Johnny Simenon's baptism. "It was funny to see him so serious, lead-ing his fat godfather by the hand down the path to the church and climbing the steps with him. The ceremony was simple. The air al-

[43]William H. Gilcher, *Jean Renoir in America,* 434–35.
[44]Letter dated July 2, 1950, Dido Renoir archive.

ready had the color and the taste of springtime. There were just a few of us around the baptismal font, and Johnny didn't flinch when they poured the holy water on his bushy hair or when they put a few grains of salt on his tongue. Jean Renoir was the one who was moved," as Georges Simenon tells it.[45] Jean could have extended this short visit that had been so long in coming, because he was leaving for Europe without a specific project in mind. But he seemed to have more choices than he needed, and he was eager to find out more about them.

While still in India, he was offered *The Madwoman of Chaillot* in English and French versions, with Louis Jouvet and Martita Hunt starring in both. Gérard Philipe had also written to ask him to direct *The Stranger*. There had been some discussion of Jean shooting *The Plague*, with Charles Boyer, but he learned on coming back from India that the producers couldn't wait for him and were obliged to start shooting before *The River* was finished. In fact, the whole project foundered. As for *The Stranger*, Jean Renoir soon learned that he could not count on it. "The publisher is asking $30,000 for the film rights. That would be expensive for a film intended for the American market, but for the French market, it's completely crazy."[46] Gérard Philipe was very eager to make a film with Jean Renoir. He suggested *Till Eulenspiegel*, a subject that was dear to him but did not excite Jean Renoir. Finally, a few years later, Philipe made his own film of it, with the help of Joris Ivens.

Offers were arriving from all directions: Canon Maillet, director of the famous choir school of the Petits Chanteurs à la croix de bois [Little Singers of the Wooden Cross], after meeting Jean Renoir in Hollywood, suggested that he make a film on *The Children's Crusade*. Jean's response was, "If I were a producer, with the means to make films, I would do it as soon as I could, since the world needs a film like that. Give me the time to ponder your suggestion a little. I would like to speak to you about it again after I have weighed the artistic possibilities and, if I can, the commercial ones."[47] To Georges Simenon, who asked him to film *La Neige était sale* (*The Snow was Black*), he replied on December 30, 1950: "I'm more and more excited about *La Neige*. I can see an extraordinary film coming out of it, but I'm also very anxious to find a way to do it in English in the context of an

[45] Georges Simenon, *Mémoires intimes* (Paris, 1981), 351.
[46] Letter to Claude Renoir, dated October 21, 1950, Dido Renoir archive.
[47] Letter dated December 15, 1950, Dido Renoir archive.

American town. I've written to my agent, Dewalde, about it."[48] In his
letter to Dewalde dated the same day, he wrote:

> [I'm] convinced I could make a very beautiful film from it. I even think
> it's a better subject than *The Stranger*. . . . I think Gérard Philipe might
> like the story. The lead role looks tailor-made for him. . . . Since the
> Americans, luckily for them, have never been invaded, a story about a
> foreign occupation taking place here would bowl them over and have
> unprecedented success. . . . Usually, I'm against double versions of the
> same film, but for once, I think it might be justified (ibid.).

He also wanted to make a movie with Gérard Philipe. He kept looking
for a story that would suit them both, and he was tempted to do a
remake of Clarence Brown's film, *Flesh and the Devil*, one of Greta
Garbo's first hits, with John Bilbert as the co-star.

On May 8, Jean and Dido arrived at Le Havre. Aside from his
other projects, Jean had a few pages of a script in his luggage entitled
Christine, a drama taking place in France with mainly American characters, except for the heroine, whose mother was from Réunion; Jean
had Lena Horne in mind for the part.[49] He wanted to spend the rest of
the spring in Paris, where his friends welcomed his arrival. But some
Italian producers offered him a film with Anna Magnani. He was
never one to refuse a fight with a wildcat. What a windfall! He was
ready to go there immediately to check things out.

His first thought was that he would come back to France, that the
film, *Le Carrosse du Saint-Sacrement (The Holy Sacrament Coach)*, based
on the play by Mérimée, would be shot in Paris. It was a Franco-
Italian coproduction, but the work had to be done in Rome. That
didn't displease him either—both he and Dido loved Rome, a city
they had discovered together when they first fell in love.

◆

Their quick passage through Paris was not, however, useless: Jean
saw André Bazin again, and he met Ginette Doynel, who would become a close collaborator of his and a family friend. André Bazin
wrote an interview for *Radio-Cinéma-Télévision* that, as François
Truffaut noticed, marked the beginning of their friendship.

> If you doubted that Jean Renoir was a great man, either from not know-
> ing or from not loving his work, spending a little time with him would
> convince you.

[48] Dido Renoir archive.
[49] Jean Renoir, *Oeuvres de cinéma inédites*, ed. C. Gauteur (Paris, 1981), 137–59.

A great man, first of all physically: he's tall and fat; when he comes upon you, all smiles, with his slight limp, he looks like a clown in a teddy bear suit, or an elephant with a sprained ankle. Teddy bear is a role he has actually played, in *Rules of the Game*, as well as clown; maybe he fell in love with an elephant on his recent trip to India. But let's leave aside the zoo, including rabbits shot from blinds in Sologne and monkeys who play the tambourine on a hurdy-gurdy. The only reason why he looks like one of Benjamin Rabier's animals is to charm us even more.[50]

The Bazin family was indeed "charmed," and it included, aside from Janine and their son Florent, just two years old at the time, François Truffaut, whose adoptive father Bazin had become in 1949. The affectionate friendship between Truffaut and Renoir dates to this time. Ginette Doynel also fell under his spell. Since he had no secretary, Jean asked her to come "to help out for a day." She came back the next day because she was unable to say no to him, and at the end of that second day, he called out to her, "See you next week in Rome!" She did not reply, but she was part of the film world, and she knew it was impossible for financial reasons. Moreover, she had some commitments. But Jean Renoir telephoned one of his producers from Rome, "Unless you send me Ginette Doynel, you won't have the script on time." Within the week, she arrived in Rome, and he asked her to collaborate with him on the script.

The whole thing had to be redone. The producers first thought Luchino Visconti would make a film for them in English that would take place in Rome and Venice and would also include scenes among the Indians, without going as far afield as Peru, however. As soon as Renoir met Anna Magnani, however, he saw how to change the film. This actress had a reputation of being a tigress, Jean was delighted to know, but he had to begin working immediately and postpone all his other projects; otherwise he would lose the opportunity. He was a little sorry about *The Stranger*, because Gérard Philipe thought he had found a producer. Too bad!

Jean set his conditions: Magnani was not to be Mérimée's La périchole, she would be the actress, Camilla, in a commedia dell' arte troupe, and the name of the film would be *Le Carrosse d'or* (*The Golden Coach*). The story would resemble the one in the play. To Jean it was clear that a film shot in Italy had to be Italian. Italians should take part in it, not just actors but technicians and also a filmmaker/screenwriter named Giulio Macchi, as well, who quickly became and remained a

---

[50] André Bazin, *Jean Renoir*, 94–95.

friend. Along with Ginette Doynel, he collaborated on the script and brought Jean Italian actors. "I assembled the whole team of commedia dell' arte actors," he told me. "I introduced him to Eduardo De Filippo, who gave us advice about actors from Naples, his specialty. Jean Renoir accepted our ideas and the actors I kept bringing him. For the role of the viceroy, they had found an American living in Rome. Jean had in mind a weak man, but he was so weak he couldn't handle the role. He was immediately replaced by Duncan Lamont, an Englishman, who did very well." Giulio Macchi does not say that he was the one who initiated Jean Renoir into the music of Vivaldi. Jean tells it this way: "My chief collaborator for this film was the late Antonio Vivaldi. I wrote the script to the sound of this master's music. His dramatic sense and his spirit taught me the best aspects of Italian theatrical art."[51]

It took a long time to get ready to shoot this film, but no one dreamed of complaining. The Renoirs loved Rome more and more. They were overwhelmed, as they had been twelve years before, by the varied and familiar beauty of it, the charm of its distinct neighborhoods, and its human scale. They had found a tiny penthouse apartment that pleased them very much on a little terrace, via Jacopo Peri, in the house of Princess Rufo of Calabria, the mother of Princess Paola. There were constant comings and goings of young people. The women were elegant and pretty, the men handsome: it was a mixture of Italian aristocrats and the Roman film community. "In those days, Italian cinema had some sinew," as Giulio Macchi recalls. "That was when Italian neorealism was at its height. All the great producers and creators were there."

Rome itself was bubbling with life. They worked hard, but they also had fun, just the way Jean Renoir liked it. He wrote the script in French even though the film was going to be made in English. He also wrote the dialogue in French. "He changed those dialogues of his dozens and dozens of times." Macchi said he has tons of pages of rewritten dialogue. They spent long evenings out of town, dining with friends in the country. Old pals would turn up, like Robert Capa, the photographer, who was doing an article for *Holiday*. Jean Renoir had not seen him since a memorable dinner in Paris in 1939, after the fall of Barcelona. Now that nightmare was well behind them. Jean, finally rid of his American car, bought himself a Jaguar. There was a festive atmosphere all the time, and Dido felt at ease and happy.

◆

[51] Jean Renoir, *Ma vie et mes films*, 248.

In September, they went to Venice to be present when the prize was awarded to *The River*. They had decided to take advantage of the situation to scout the possibility of shooting some scenes there. But Jean realized immediately that it would be impossible for him to work there. All those staircases to go up and down would be too much for him. Nevertheless, their visit was a success. "There was a reception at Torcello to celebrate *The River*," according to Giulio Macchi. "The producer had rented boats to transport his guests, and everybody had fun. Jean was singing the tune from *Threepenny Opera* about Macchi instead of Mackie, and he was in no hurry to go back to Venice. But the last boat broke down, so we spent the whole night outside under the stars. We saw the sunrise from the tower." Jean was in ecstasy, since he had long since passed the age of all-nighters. In the morning they took the first vaporetto for the Fondamenta nuove.

Back in Rome, everyone went back to work with the same spirit and good humor as before, but toward the end of September, while shooting on location, Jean Renoir jumped off a jeep, and his bad leg began hurting. First he tried hiding it, but he could hardly climb the narrow staircase of his apartment, and Dido soon discovered that his wounded leg had become infected. Jean refused to get treatment. He was terrified he would have to have it amputated, so he would not go to the clinic. Finally he had no choice. On October 29, 1951, he wrote this to Clifford Odets:

> Ever since a surgeon opened up my leg and cleaned the infection, I feel a little better every day. But it's awfully slow. The wound is very big, and when I take a good look at it, a complete cure seems pretty far off. I don't know if I'll be able to finish my Italian film. My only hope is that the import permits for the cameras, the equipment, and the Technicolor films from London require more than a month's worth of formalities and paper chasing.
>
> I'm really lucky to have Dido at my side. She spends almost all her time in the clinic, which is a frigid and uncomfortable place. These Italians have a strange affinity for discomfort. They have no idea about a decent heating system or a lamp that allows you to read in bed. But that's not important. I'm completely fed up after being in pain and in bed for the past six weeks. Now it only hurts when they redo my bandage once a day, a very disagreeable ritual. Though the comfort around here isn't what it should be, I think the surgeon is good, and the nurses and aids— they're all women—are funny and sweet.[52]

On November 19, Jean and Dido left Rome for an appointment with Professor Merle d'Aubigné in Paris. It had been arranged by

[52] Dido Renoir archive.

Ginette Doynel. He, too, wanted to hospitalize the patient, who was still healing, for a week. But the Renoirs chose to stay in the Royal Monceau. A severe vitamin deficiency was keeping the wound from closing up quickly. Jean Renoir began the therapy to counteract it in Rome, where he returned on December 2. He took it easy over the holidays. The way the Romans observed them aroused his curiosity. Eager to start directing, he kept working on the screenplay and the dialogue.

◆

In the beginning of January, still gift-giving season, he received the biggest encouragement of his life: a special issue of *Cahiers du cinéma* was devoted to his work. It was a review that had started in 1951, taking up where *La Revue du cinéma* left off—*Cahiers* had actually adopted its trademark yellow cover. Starting in 1946, Jean-Georges Auriol along with Denise Tual had resumed publishing (for Gallimard) a review that he had originally started up in 1927. The review led to the formation of a ciné-club, Objectif 49, which only showed new movies. It was "a very exclusive club, influential and chic, that was frequented by editors and readers of the big Parisian intellectual journals."[53] Cocteau, Bresson, Rossellini, and Welles were invited to it. Bazin dreamed of getting Jean Renoir to come, but that was while he couldn't enter France. *La Revue du cinéma* stopped appearing regularly in December 1948. One double issue was published in September 1949, after the Biarritz festival, but when Auriol died in a car crash in 1950, the review ceased publication. Then his assistant, Jacques Doniol-Valcroze, and André Bazin founded *Cahiers du cinéma*. In effect, it trained a whole new generation in French film, the critics-soon-to-be-directors whom Françoise Giroud called "the new wave." It was these young people who saw Jean Renoir as their ideal and gave him the position he deserved to have.

The January 15 issue was a real pleasure to him. He got recognition from people who spoke his language and loved what he did. In one of the texts included, he says:

> Something very important happened to me and millions of others like me, namely, the Second World War, which was the reason I left for America. I met many people who were important to me there, and I felt as though I was reborn. . . . Today, new creature that I am, I realize it's no time for sarcasm, and that the only thing I can offer this illogical, irresponsible, and cruel universe is my 'love.' Clearly, this attitude involves

[53]Dudley Andrew, *André Bazin* (New York, 1978), 144.

an egotistical desire to be repaid for it. I'm as bad as everyone else, and I need an indulgent smile as much as they do.[54]

Recognition had been every bit as long in coming for him as for his father. When it finally did, it, too, came from those who practiced the same art as he. Jean Renoir had not forgotten:

> His [Auguste's] nudes and his roses declared to the people of this century, already deep in their task of destruction, that the eternal equilibrium of our universe was something solid. Certain people were so grateful for this reassurance that they made a pilgrimage to Les Collettes to tell him so. Sometimes they came from far away and, being poor, made the journey under difficult conditions. When Zaza, our big sheepdog, began barking, we knew we were in for an unusual visitor. Bistolfi, the young Italian chauffeur, would open the door, and find a blond, bearded Scandinavian wearing crumpled clothes standing before him, or a meticulously dressed Japanese. My mother would ask them into the dining room where Big Louise would serve them food and wine.[55]

Wasn't what Jean also was hoping to see finally happening to him, providing a confirmation of himself that he did not dare hope for? Always true to himself, he put his art in question each time he exercised it, and by so doing he succeeded in expressing the truth that was his, just as his father had done. Each film had to be different, or at least he had to think of it differently.

The Golden Coach was a new experiment with Technicolor. Claude Renoir managed to free himself to be the cameraman. Later on, in presenting a retrospective of his films on French television, Jean Renoir said: "*The Golden Coach* is a film I was able to take to the limit, thanks to the patience and kindness of its producers, down to the last detail. Claude and I were able to study the color contrasts for it with a lot of care. For instance, it once happened that we didn't shoot a scene because the costumes were not exactly matched to the background color. We had the sets completely repainted, we changed people's wigs and makeup base. The result, I think, may interest some of you."[56] When Visconti withdrew from the production, the costumes had already been drawn and some sets were already selected; but, as Giulio Macchi told me, "Jean Renoir saw the costumes completely differently. He wanted them to be more tailored, and more French."

♦

[54] *Cahiers du cinéma*, January 1952, 8, 31.
[55] *Renoir par Jean Renoir* (Paris, 1958), 445 (= *Renoir, My Father*, 447).
[56] Jean Renoir, *Entretiens et propos*, 150.

On February 4, 1952, Jean was about to begin shooting this extensively prepared film, in which he wished to express his affection for the theater and his sense of wonder at the way real life and the theater could fold into each other and become one. By one of those strange and yet frequent coincidences, Pierre Renoir, the oldest brother, died in Paris one month after the shooting began. In Jean's eyes, Pierre was the quintessential theatrical actor. His whole life was dedicated to his art. When he was twelve years old, he used to recite poems to the little girls of their family circle. Even in everyday life, he seemed to be on stage, while in the theater, he forgot his name, his face, his arm paralyzed by a war wound, and he became the character that the public believed him to be. Jean respected his talent. Pierre's death, which grieved Claude (Jean's nephew) deeply, brought back to his son and his brother their share of distant memories. It also brought Jean back to those thoughts about the theater that had been haunting him for several years. Because of them, he had been willing to shoot film adaptations of plays when he was still hoping to become an independent producer in Los Angeles. These obscure feelings he always had about the mystery of theater were more prevalent now than ever before, and Anna Magnani incarnated them to perfection.

Working with that famous artist promised to be difficult at best. In the beginning, the hard part was getting her to show up on time. Every day, she was two hours late.

> Working with Magnani was particularly exciting, especially when she was tired. When she was tired, she arrived in the morning in a terrible state. She had probably spent the whole night out in cheap cafés, and naturally she looked pretty tired when she arrived. She would look in the mirror and then call to Claude and say: "Hey, Claude, what do you think? Look at my face, my eyes are so sunken they're on the same level as my mouth! You can't film me when I'm like that." So I would say, "Listen, Anna, we won't film you, but at least we can rehearse." So we began rehearsing with the other actors, and the first rehearsal was pathetic, but the second one was a little better, then, by the third one, the words started coming out of her mouth a little more sonorously, and then she began to soak them up and make them her own, and her face actually started changing. By the time we got to the fourth or fifth rehearsal, Anna looked exactly like a young girl. I like telling this story because it's typical of the great actor or actress. In them, art goes beyond the physical, the spiritual takes over (ibid.).

When Ginette Doynel, who had gone from screenwriter to script girl, asked Magnani about her unexpected docility, she said she had never worked with people who knew their trade as well as Renoir and his team. "Real pros," she said, and she liked that. She was learning English in order to play her role in English. For the Italian version, she dubbed herself in Italian. There were some tiffs with Jean because she wanted to change everything to Italian, to speak another text without taking into account the constraints implicit in the image that was already fixed. But Renoir had the knack of calming her down; whenever he saw that she was depressed and unhappy, he took her by the arm and took her off for a walk for ten minutes. When they came back, both of them were laughing.

Most of the time good humor prevailed on set 5 in Cincecittà, where the whole film was shot. On the next set, Léonide Moguy was directing *Domani è un altro giorno* (*Tomorrow's Another Day*) with Marina Vlady. She would come over with a few other young women to visit Renoir between shots. There were also various friends passing through or staying in Rome. There even was a visit by the "American cousins": Aunt Victoria, Grandfather Charigot's daughter, and her children. Also Dora and her husband the dentist arrived from Santa Monica. They followed Dido and Jean to Santa Marinella, to the home of Roberto Rossellini and Ingrid Bergman, where they all spent a weekend together. They had a great time. The Americans were very natural and completely relaxed. Dido and Jean loved going to the beach house, where Bergman and Rossellini were always happy to welcome them.

On May 4, 1952, Jean Renoir wrote this to Clifford Odets:

> As always, Rome is beautiful. Dido and I are spending our first quiet Sunday at home in weeks, nursing colds. In three weeks, we hope to take a little trip to France to visit my father's house near Nice and to make a brief stop at the village in Burgundy where my father, mother, and brother are at rest in the little local cemetery. We'll drink a little glass of the village wine, and then we'll come back to the cutting room in the studios here in Rome. It's just the type of trip we'd love to take with you.[57]

◆

They edited the film in Rome. Despite their affection for the town, Jean and Dido ran off on short trips to Paris (once for the premier of *Limelight*, to meet the Chaplins who had just arrived in Europe), or to England to visit Dido's mother and youngest sister. As usual, Jean took part in the job of editing.

[57] Dido Renoir archive.

The mistake I made was not to insist on having a good American editor. My Italian producers were terrified of the expense involved. Finally we hired a young Englishman whose main virtue was that he lived in Rome and didn't demand a much higher salary than an average Italian. But he had no experience and I had to do almost everything myself, with the help of my French assistant who, fortunately, spoke English, and of an Italian editor who spoke none. . . . That's why I'm afraid that *The Golden Coach* isn't so much an Anglo-American film as a translation into English of a French film in the Italian style.

This is from another letter to Clifford Odets dated October 5, 1952 (ibid.). Ginette Doynel says he knew how to keep the film's line intact. "With him, it didn't change. He was the only director of them all who knew how to cut a film in the editing. He did so without an author's regrets."[58]

Once the film was over, Dido and Jean went home to spend Christmas with Alain, Gabrielle, and their families. They were delighted to be at home again, and to find that their garden had once more been very well tended by Bessie. When they left, they did not think they were going to be gone for so long.

The Golden Coach was not premiered until February 1953. It didn't have the commercial success of *The River*. Some of the critics were reticent about it, but in others it aroused passionate admiration. François Truffaut wrote this about it: "In any case, it's the noblest and most refined film ever made. It contains the spontaneity and inventiveness of the pre-war Renoir alongside the rigor of the American Renoir. In it, everything is breeding and manners, grace and freshness. . . . *The Golden Coach*, which is closed, is a finished work that you must look at but not touch, a film that has achieved its final form, a perfect object."[59] The first day the film was shown in Paris, Jacques Rivette watched every showing of it from 2 P.M. to midnight. He could not tear himself away.

Such enthusiasm notwithstanding, Jean could not find money to make another film for two years thereafter. In *The Golden Coach*, he has the director of the commedia dell' arte troupe say to Camilla/Magnani: "You weren't cut out for what they call real life. Your place is with us, the actors, acrobats, mimes, clowns, and tumblers. You'll only find happiness on the stage every night for the two short hours when you do what an actress does, that is, when you forget yourself.

[58] Interview with the author.
[59] François Truffaut, *Les films de ma vie* (Paris, 1975), 62–63.

Through the characters that you will embody, perhaps someday you'll discover the real Camilla." For Renoir's father, real happiness was canvas and brush; for Pierre, as for Camilla, it was the stage; and for Jean, it was the movie set.

As he was finishing this film, he began thinking of new subjects, as usual. He wrote several outlines that he filed with the Screen-writers Guild: *Premier Amour* (*First Love*), after Turgenev, *Les Horreurs de la guerre* (*The Horrors of War*), and *Le Masque* (*The Mask*). In all three, "once again with Renoir, there were the contrasts between the regulars and the irregulars, the conformists and the nonconformists, the middle class and the anarchists," as Claude Gauteur stresses.[60] And like so many others before, these projects were never completed.

[60] Jean Renoir, *Oeuvres inédites*, 163.

THE MONTMARTRE LAMENT

♦

For Dido and Jean, home was now on Leona Drive. There the present intermingled with mementos from the Renoir past: paintings, sculptures, drawings, furniture, and other objects from France. They had a wonderful time in Rome, in Paris, and in England as well, where they were wined and dined; but their life was on that hillside, its terraces flourishing with fast-growing olive trees and a welter of tropical flora. There were also other flowers more familiar to Jean, which had been planted to bring back the past. "Dido works very hard in the garden and gets amazing results. The roses are magnificent. We're surrounded by geraniums and all kinds of other plants. It makes me think of *La Faute de l'abbé Mouret* (*The Abbé Mouret's Sin*)."[1] Alain was teaching in a college in Athens, Ohio, while Jane had quit her career as a dietician because they had a son, John, on December 27, 1951. Gabrielle and Jean Slade were thinking of moving to Beverly Hills, too, which would be more practical for their daily visits with the Renoirs.

Coming back after an absence of more than eighteen months, they really felt the void left by the departure of the Chaplins. "We read in the newspapers that Chaplin wants to sell his house. For me, it's like a symbol." Jean remembered when he discovered Chaplin films in the winter of 1915. And, a few months later, "some people like Elie Faure began to write about Charlie Chaplin in books that also

[1]Letter to Clifford Odets dated May 19, 1953, Dido Renoir archive. (Emil Zola's novel, published in 1875, is a quasi-mythological tale about a young churchman who loses his memory and is reborn into an Eden-like garden, where he lives on fruit and plants until he has his first sexual experience with the garden's other denizen, the lovely Alberine. [Trans.]).

contained essays on Cézanne and Debussy. Partly because of that, movies went from store fronts to palaces, and the public put up with paying a dollar instead of a nickel. Even so, nowadays, not a single film tycoon has gotten the idea of wiring to beg him to come back here."[2]

Chaplin was not the only one who left. Ever since Senator Joseph McCarthy had started his witch-hunt in February of 1950, and ever since the House Un-American Activities Committee had started investigating the so-called Hollywood Ten—screenwriters who were suspected of having opinions favorable to the Soviets—the climate had changed a lot. Everyone suspected everyone else, and informing against your associates was encouraged. Jean and Dido had largely escaped this wretched phase. They were in India when McCarthy began his campaign; then the editing of the movie and the sickness and ultimate death of Conrad Slade had been their main preoccupations, all of which set them apart from "all Hollywood" even more than usual. Jean's free time had been eaten up by Kenny McEldowney, who had extremely idiosyncratic ideas about distributing *The River*. Jean's colleagues didn't want the film, whose production looked crazy to them. Accordingly, no one even dreamed of adding Jean's name to those of suspected Communists. People had also long since forgotten how he had been mentioned in 1938 in a report to the sadly famous Committee on Anti-American Activities. At the time of his entry into the United States, Renoir was persona grata because of the recommendation of Robert Flaherty and of American producers impressed by the success of *Grand Illusion*, a favorite of Roosevelt's, and *La Bête humaine*.

In California, Jean Renoir was careful to stay away from political activity of any kind. He wasn't even tempted to indulge during the war—we've seen what he thought of the French in Hollywood. He had adjusted with ease to the American state of mind, and he thought it proper that his son fight on the American side. He himself had shot a movie for the Office of War Information called *Salute to France*, after having offered his services to the Army Signal Corps in vain.[3] But his real friends, like Bertolt Brecht and Hans Eisler, left in 1948—they were accused retroactively of having been Communists, or they were worried, like Clifford Odets and Dudley Nichols. Jean was closer to them or to Robert Flaherty, who died in 1951, than to those who gave up their individual freedom while pretending to defend it. "My father

[2] Letter to Clifford Odets dated February 17, 1953, Dido Renoir archive.
[3] Jean Renoir, *Lettres d'Amérique*, ed A. Sesonske (Paris, 1984), 141.

never passed judgment on other people," says Alain Renoir. His brothers, his nephew, and many of his close friends had joined the resistance, but some others had fallen into the trap of collaboration. They hadn't done so in their own interest but were driven by a personal ideology to which Jean did not subscribe; yet it suited their character. How could he condemn them? He had been well fed and in safety while Europe was living in starvation at the time of Hitler. He had not been surprised to learn what happened to both sides. He understood their strong points and their weaknesses.

◆

When he did return to France, Renoir could not help noticing that anti-Americanism was widespread. The cold war, the Korean War, and McCarthyism had done nothing to diminish it. His friends still had an idyllic image of the Soviet Union. Everyone who had given testimony at the time of the Kravchenko affair denied in court that the regime in the Soviet Union was arbitrary and brutal. After publishing a book entitled *J'ai choisi la liberté* (*I Chose Freedom*), which denounced the Soviet system, Kravchenko won his suit against the Communist weekly, *Les Lettres françaises;* but this did not persuade them to change their views. In the United States, people knew better about the trials in Moscow and Stalinism. Arthur Koestler had published *Darkness at Noon* in 1941. On his return from a reception in Los Angeles at which a Russian had spoken of the way the mentally ill were treated under Stalin, Jean Renoir, who had never said a word against the Soviets, revealed his indignation to his son, who was so amazed by it that he still recalls it. But in those days of McCarthyism, it was better to keep your indignation to yourself so as not to seem to share "bad" attitudes that were officially accepted. Jean was not pleased by this climate of silence. Dido kept encouraging him to take it easy, but she, too, had a hard time restraining herself. On radio and television, the bombastic McCarthy was ubiquitous and hard to avoid. It was a harsh test for Jean's acquired and Dido's innate wisdom. What was happening in his profession worried Jean more than everything else:

> If we stop to examine our lives in detail, we seem to be in charge of things. Yet we have the feeling that there's something going on that isn't right. Maybe it has to do with the appearance of the latest silly trend, 3-D. The few brief contacts I have had with movie people here have been scary: they really think they can solve their problems with a technical trick. So it's certainly a fine time to go back to the old stories and to throw away everything that is a little strange or different. I haven't tried

it, and I don't want to. I have the feeling that it is more impossible than ever to make a good film in Hollywood.[4]

The first movie in Cinerama was shot in 1952, and the next year witnessed the first examples of Cinemascope. By these processes and with 3-D the producers hoped to bring back the old days. But Jean Renoir was correct this time, too. It was not the right answer to the twofold crisis in Hollywood: the first problem was competition with television, the second, the absence of the good screenwriters, great actors, and great directors whom the anti-Communist witch-hunt had scattered over the landscape.

For a long time, Dido had been eager for Jean to write a book about his father. It was now or never, a good way to escape from those pathetic times. It was time for others to benefit from the stories that he and Gabrielle told so well, and it was time that both of them record their marvellous recollections. Dido volunteered to do the typing, and on May 19, 1953, Jean wrote to Clifford Odets: "A few weeks ago I started something I should've done a long time ago. I got together some notes for a book about my father. I'm doing it now with Gabrielle. At summer's end I'll go to France to visit the various places where I lived with my father."[5] Dido was greatly interested in this project, which was close to her heart. Whereas for his screenplays Jean was in the habit of working with a secretary, he was going to dictate this book to her. It would take a long time for the manuscript to see the light of day, however; it was not published until 1962.

The world of the theater was still Jean Renoir's world, and as yet he had no reason to renounce it. In this particular year, 1953, he wrote "a kind of experimental play called *Calla Lilies*. I did it in order to acquire a kind of discipline that is really a necessity for the stage: one set, five characters. I'm doing without the twenty-four-hour time limit."[6] In this same letter to his friend Odets, Jean Renoir speaks of *La Dame de la mer* (*The Lady from the Sea*) by Ibsen, which he was going to shoot in Norway. It was another experiment with theater, but it never got beyond being a dream. He was ready to find any excuse to get away.

◆

On October 21, Dido and Jean embarked on the *Liberty*. "A fantastic trip," as Dido remembers it, great food, a luxurious suite, and all the

---

[4]Letter to Clifford Odets dated February 17, 1953, Dido Renoir archive.
[5]Dido Renoir archive.
[6]Letter to Clifford Odets dated August 9, 1953, Dido Renoir archive.

tensions of the McCarthy era melting away as they left the port of New York in their wake. They arrived at Le Havre on October 27, and moved into an apartment on the avenue Frochot where Jean had lived from 1937 until the beginning of the war. He had lent it to his nephew, Claude, during and after the occupation.

The avenue Frochot, just a few steps from the place Pigalle, is one of those marvellous places that has somehow escaped the ravages of time. Legend has it that Alexandre Dumas, Sr., one of Jean's child-hood heroes, had lived at number 7, in the house where Jean had an apartment on the third floor. As he was to describe it in a 1954 script entitled *Paris province,* it was "a funny place, a kind of village marked off in all directions by nightclubs and exotic bars. At night, the neigh-borhood was invaded by drug dealers, vagrant Arabs, whores, tourist buses, and all the hardworking people who live off other people's pleasure. A single, sturdy fence defends [avenue Frochot] from inva-sions. It has resisted neon signs and the hustle and bustle without. It has remained an island of greenery and calm. Cars do not venture within. Children, dogs, and cats rule there."[7]

Even today, grass still grows between the paving stones of this street lined with sycamores, but beneath the windows of Jean Re-noir's apartment was a linden tree. The houses, which had been built around 1830, were seriously in need of the restoration that Malraux ordered for them at the end of the fifties. The inside of the apartment houses must have been pretty dilapidated, which wouldn't have dis-pleased Jean: old as it was, his apartment must have had more than its share of charm. To be sure, the furniture and other things shipped to Beverly Hills were now missing. Pierre Renoir had been Jean's neighbor there as well, on the second floor, and Jean Gabin's nephew, Guy Ferrier, was still living on the fourth floor, while the actress, Francine Bergé, lived in the next house down. Across the boulevard Rochechouart, Jean rediscovered what remained of the Montmartre of his childhood. Except for an occasional shopping expedition with Dido (which they always enjoyed), he hardly ever had time for a stroll in the neighborhood where he and Gabrielle used to wander. Friends old and new called them, invited them out, or came to see them.

André Bazin and François Truffaut held a special place among the many newer friends. Bazin had dedicated his life to film. At the time of the liberation, he belonged to the little group that created the IDHEC (Institute for Advanced Studies in Cinematography). He set up ciné-clubs in the schools and factories of Paris and its suburbs. He

[7]Jean Renoir, *Oeuvres de cinéma inédites,* ed. C. Gauteur (Paris, 1981), 215.

was director of a "center for initiation in film" for Travail et culture, a Communist organization in which his leftist Catholicism was acceptable until the day he published an article in *Esprit* called "The Myth of Stalin in Soviet Cinema," which was a sin in that shrine of strict Stalinist obedience. Starting in 1949, he was the head of Objectif 49, the ciné-club originally founded by Jean-Georges Auriol. He and Jacques Doniol-Valcroze wrote regularly as a team for *L'Observateur*, which started in April of 1950. That year, he entered a sanatorium at the end of January, but he never stopped working and writing. He wrote for the new journal *Radio-Cinéma-Télévision* that was founded to compete with the Communists' *L'Ecran français*. Since he was bedridden and couldn't go to the movies, he started a column for them on television. The weekly soon changed its name to *Télérama*.

When he first became friends with Jean Renoir, André Bazin was already very ill. At his death in 1958—he was only forty years old — Jean Renoir wrote this: "André Bazin, by formulating the basis of French cinema, contributed to the creation of a national art. He was our conscience. Personally, it has befallen me to modify certain plans of mine in anticipation of Bazin's judgment of the result.

"When I think of his work, my first impulse is not to categorize it as criticism. The label that comes to mind instead is inspiration. He got that good not by tossing out vaguely generous phrases, but by means of precise analytical procedures. Bazin worked religiously at his craft. . . . We became very good friends, and we met over a meal more than once. The man was as captivating as his work, and generous as well. The marvellous luncheons assembled by Madame Bazin were a sheer delight for me. The food was always delicious, and André loved to eat and to eat well. As for Madame Bazin, she was as skilled at the detailed classification of documents as at the creation of a culinary masterpiece. Both of them strove hard to make their friends forget that their host's days were numbered. He knew that the illness consuming him had no cure; she had reached the limits of anxiety and exhaustion. And both of them kept smiling, happy to see that their friends were happy; never that mask of a smile that always seems to repeat, 'Look how brave I am.' On the contrary, their joy was real joy."[8] Jean Renoir understood his virtues as a person and a writer on film.

François Truffaut, whose tutor was Bazin, became very close to Jean, as one can see from this letter: "I am a lucky man. My parents

[8] *France-Observateur*, 446, November 20, 1958, in Jean Renoir, *Ecrits*, 1926–1971, ed. C. Gauteur (Paris, 1974), 202.

were wonderful people, and nature gave me a sound constitution. Now that I'm reaching the end of my journey, here you come! There's something magical about it all."[9] François wasn't as fortunate as Jean, and he didn't outlive him by much. He died on October 21, 1984, at the age of 52. The affection between him and Jean Renoir was one of his most prized possessions. He was a mine of information for me concerning his friend. With unfailing generosity and intelligence, he provided recollections, letters, documents, and film cassettes.

◆

There were other friends, and there would be more over the months and years that Dido and Jean divided their time between their home on Leona Drive and their apartment in the shadow of Alexandre Dumas. In France after the war, the world of film was divided, like everything else. Jean quickly saw the overall picture. The Blum-Byrnes agreements that were signed in 1946 between the provisional government and the U.S. government were partly to blame for the bad state of production in France, which was poorly protected by import quotas on foreign films. A demonstration that was orchestrated by the Communists, actors, directors, and technical workers protested the situation they were in. Maurice Thorez, secretary general of the party, declared on April 18, 1948:

> These American films that have invaded our screens thanks to Léon Blum not only deprive our artists, workers, and studio technicians of their livelihood; they are also, literally, poisoning the minds of our children, of our young men and women, whom they want to make into slaves of American millionaires rather than Frenchmen and Frenchwomen steeped in the moral and intellectual values that created our grandeur and the glory of our fatherland.[10]

It was not designed to make Americans popular among movie people. As for the public, it sought out foreign films because attractive French ones were few and far between. The year that Thorez made his speech, Cocteau's *Les Parents terribles* (*The Fearsome Parents*), G. H. Clouzot's *Manon*, and, in 1951, *Le Journal d'un curé de campagne* (*Diary of a Country Priest*) by Robert Bresson were the only French films that made the lists of the year's twenty best films. Later, when the government understood the importance of what some people still considered an idle distraction for the masses, it offered subsidies as a reward for quality and in order to encourage production.

[9] Letter to François Truffaut dated March 16, 1978, provided by François Truffaut.
[10] François Courtade, *Les Malédictions du cinéma français*, 247.

When Jean Renoir came back to Paris, there were no such subsidies as yet. His old gang expected that he, with a reputation that
had been broadly reaffirmed since war's end, would find the money
to make films the way he had twenty years before. They were also
disappointed that he had not remained a fellow traveler with the
Communists. Because of the strong participation of Communists in
the resistance and of the battle that the Soviet people had fought with
the armies of the Reich, many artists, writers, and intellectuals had
become party members either clandestinely or after the liberation.
The PC was known as "the party of the slain," because its members
had died fighting heroically for their country and freedom. The crimes
of Stalin's regime were ignored by some and denied by the rest.

That ignorance stemmed from a certain honest idealism, and Jean
Renoir was not of a mind to combat it; nor was he ready to adopt it
either. He stuck to the trenchant neutrality preached by his father.
Now that Nazism had been defeated, he only felt concerned for individuals. The generalities purveyed by politicians and partisans seemed
unreal to him. Not long before he had had the same impression. The
French have been tearing each other apart for centuries in useless and
unavoidable strife, as his father used to say, but now was the time to
act, to try to save people and their freedom. His old friends were still
repeating their old slogans. There was no way they could agree with
him, and they even felt betrayed by him. The Jean that they rediscovered wasn't the same fellow: they claimed that America had changed
him. They hated his recent American films, and, now, instead of
going back to what they had done together when they were young,
Jean had projects in which they could not take part. Soon their resent-
ment grew. Few people are generous enough to try to discover other
people's motivations. Jean knew it only too well and wasn't surprised.

His friends from *Cahiers du cinéma*, on the other hand, required
no explanation of his political evolution since the days of the Popular
Front. In the Cinémathèque or ciné-clubs, they saw his films again
and again, all of them, and most of them uncut, and they were not
disconcerted by his work since *Rules of the Game*.

♦

Jean Renoir was always fond of reaching his public through the press.
Now, thanks to these young people who had not yet found the means
to make their own films but were writing about movies all over the
place, he indulged himself more than ever. Interviews with him appeared not only in print but also on radio and television. His surprising presence and the ease and clarity with which he expressed

himself made him an ideal subject, and he went at it with gusto. Newspaper reporters, movie critics, everyone was ready to stick a microphone in front of him, point their camera at him, or start their tape recorder. He had no illusions about it all. As he confided to Truffaut: "I would have made the same mistakes in Paris that I did in Hollywood. . . . I have certainly had my plans aborted, . . . but when I have an idea, it's general enough so that I can use it over in a different shape."[11] He wrote a synopsis called *Les Braconniers* [*The Poachers*], characters for whom he had a special feeling since his boyhood and who appear and reappear throughout his work.

No producer showed interest in that idea, but he used it in the play *Orvet* in 1955. He also says he was tempted to make a film about the life of Van Gogh. The idea came to him while he was watching television. "I had always refused biographies, but now I think it's possible to conceive of them as a sort of narrated documentary that here and there crystallizes into sequences that are acted out with a kind of dramatic intensity that is therefore even more searing," as he explained it to André Bazin.[12] Renoir filed the "complete screenplay" with the Screenwriters Guild on December 11, 1953.[13] But the subject had been taken: Vincente Minelli made *Lust for Life* based on Irving Stone's novel in 1956. Alain Resnais had also done a beautiful short on it in 1948, but Jean Renoir did not know of it.

What was he going to do now? *The Golden Coach* was not a commercial success, so producers were not well disposed to him. They never missed an opportunity to tell him that the nature of his talent was no guarantee of success. It was an old refrain in his family, alas! Moreover, 1954 was a terrible year in France. On May 7, the battle at Dien Bien Phu was lost, and in June, Pierre Mendès France, the prime minister, signed the Geneva accords that ended the Indochina War. Then, on November 1, the insurrection began in Algeria. Even so, in the spring of that year, Jean Renoir was tendered two offers: the producer Deutschmeister proposed that he shoot a film called *French Cancan*, and he was offered the job of directing Shakespeare's *Julius Caesar* for a single performance on July 10, 1954, in the arena at Arles, to honor the two thousandth anniversary of the founding of the city by Julius Caesar.

According to Claude Beylie, "the production of *French Cancan* must have deeply offended Yves Allégret." Jean Renoir was willing to

---

[11] *Radio-Cinéma-Télévision*, May 2, 1954, in Jean Renoir, *Oeuvres inédites*, 133.

[12] *Radio-Cinéma-Télévision*, November 29, 1953.

[13] According to Claude Gauteur in Jean Renoir, *Oeuvres inédites*, 173, n. 1.

take on "a film almost in progress" on condition that, as always, he had the right to adapt the script his own way. The basis of the story was the life of Ziedler, founder of the Moulin Rouge. André Cerf, who by his own admission was "a movie drudge," told me that Walter Neubach had hired him to make a film called *French Cancan*, but "the thing dragged on and on, it took a trip on the Orient Express that I didn't like. Neubach was in trouble, so he sold the title, the story, and me" to Deutschmeister. John Huston's film, *Moulin Rouge*, made in 1952, was the kind of success that made producers drool, which explains Deutschmeister's reaction. So, after so many years, André Cerf met Jean Renoir once again: they had not worked together since *Le Bled*. The big fellow who was always ready to laugh and chatter, was full of ideas, and had a charm that won over everyone, seemed to him no different from the "amateur of the old days."

The screenplay, which had to be rebuilt, tempted Jean because "*French Cancan* fulfilled an old dream of mine, to make a movie in a very French spirit, one that would be a simple and convenient bridge between me and the French public."[14] Indeed it was an important event: it was the first film he made in France since 1939. Getting ready to shoot it turned out to be very complicated.

Not having lived in Paris for a long time, he was offered all kinds of opportunities. Roberto Rossellini arrived. He had become a close friend. Jean greeted him in an article as follows: "I'm waiting impatiently for him to tell the story of our city as he did for Naples, which was Italy's holy city according to Rossellini."[15] Then there was a very well-received lecture at the IDHEC entitled "Here's How I Make a Movie"; it was reprinted in part in *Arts*.[16] Meanwhile, Deutschmeister had chosen Pierre Kast, André Cerf, and Jeanne Witta-Montrobert to work with Jean on the script of *French Cancan*, and he wanted to get going on it. But another commitment hindered him even more than these.

◆

His first job as a theater director! How many years had he been dreaming of such a chance! The film that he was supposed to be readying at the same time returned him to the problem of the show, as in the *Golden Coach*, where he was able to express all his notions about the magic of the stage. For his first play, as usual, he did not

[14] Jean Renoir, *Entretiens et propos* (Paris, 1979), 65.

[15] *Arts*, 468, June 16, 1954, in Jean Renoir, *Ecrits*, 198.

[16] *Arts*, 470, June 30, 1954, in Jean Renoir, *Ecrits*, 198.

take the easy way. Dreading as he did the declamatory style of tragic actors, he chose movie actors to play *Julius Caesar;* after all, it was being put on in an arena whose proportions were a far cry from those of an indoor theater. He had to fight to get the town authorities to accept a cast so alien to the legitimate stage: Françoise Christophe, Paul Meurisse, Jean-Pierre Aumont, Henri Vidal, and Yves Robert. After winning this first battle, he negotiated an "agreement with Philips whereby they would install fifty microphones all around the arena. No matter where an actor had to go to deliver lines, there was a microphone to pick up the faintest sigh." [17] "I had drafted some inhabitants of the town to play the Roman mob. In the south of France, people know their politics. I first explained the situation in depth to these amateur players. They really loved it, and they played the part of the mob as though they were attending a contemporary campaign meeting" (ibid.). However, the rehearsals took place way ahead of time in Paris, inside the main hall of the Théâtre de Paris. Loleh Bellon told me she was very intimidated by Jean Renoir despite the consideration that he lavished on the actors. She asked him, "Mr. Renoir, can I take my time here?" The least gesture, the slightest intonation meant something. He worked with the actors as he was used to doing in film.

Once they got to Arles, things got complicated. Jean Serge, the originator of the project and the play's stage manager, suddenly was put on notice that everything had to be taken down because the town had organized a bullfight. The electricians and machinists would hardly have time to put everything back in place for the performance. "On the evening of the show, the actors and I gathered in the lobby of our hotel. Outside, crowds of spectators were on their way to the arena. We were terrified. We didn't even have time for a dress rehearsal. Some actors warned me that they had completely forgotten their lines. Parédès, who was playing Casca, complained that his toga was too long and made him trip. Panic spread through the cast. One person said he envied the serenity of Orientals. Another asked me if I had had to confront crowds in India. The question started me explaining the essence of Hindu religion to them. I spoke of Brahma, the master of the gods, Shiva, destroyer and creator, and his female counterpart Kali, and of Krishna, the preserver, and his beloved Radha, protector of cows. They all listened to me, and they forgot their fear. When the moment arrived, the troupe was good and relaxed."

Typically, Jean says nothing about what he was feeling at the

[17] Jean Renoir, *Ma vie et mes films* (Paris, 1974), 253.

time. It was second nature to him to master the situation and calm the team down, as he describes it. But on July 10, 1954, in Arles, the series of misfortunes continued: "The sound system went out. We were to have begun the show with Beethoven's Fifth Symphony, the symphony of destiny, which went well with the fate of Brutus. Minus Beethoven, the only accompaniment was the whistling of the frustrated spectators. Finally the sound system was fixed and the Fifth Symphony resumed a losing battle with the anger of the populace. Just when the actors were about to walk on stage, I told Parédès-Casca to trip on his toga as he had in the hotel. The procession made its winding way into the hostile arena. It reminded me of a spectacle in which not the performers but the spectators were the lions. Parédès, as agreed, stepped on the hem of his toga and just missed falling flat on his face. First the crowd was silent for a moment, and then, almost immediately, there was an enormous laugh. They were with us" (ibid., p. 254).

"He had us make our entrances through the bull's gate," as Loleh Bellon tells it. "Caesar's court was spread out over the floor of the arena beneath the spotlights. It looked very, very beautiful to me." She also said that he had her put on an extraordinary wig. A black, leonine wig. " 'She's a woman who dies by swallowing pieces of charcoal,' Jean explained to me." Jean-Pierre Aumont, who had often gone to visit Dido, Gabrielle, and Jean from 1944 to 1950, thinks he remembers having confided to them his secret wish to play Mark Antony. He wrote that this show had "an unforgettable grandeur to it,"[18] and he talked to me about it as one of the most beautiful memories of his career. The actors were astounded by the inventiveness of the direction. It was a night of magic, of unbelievable beauty, so they all say.

As Jeanne Witta-Montrobert remembers it, "Young movie technicians made the trip from Paris in tiny, overloaded cars just to witness this one performance. All of them, including my son Jacques who came to meet me there, were extras in the Roman mob that first yells,

"Long live Brutus!" and then later "Vengeance!" . . . It was a one-night show that left no traces except in the memory of those who had the privilege of being there. But what traces it left! Jean Renoir knew how to take advantage of his natural surroundings with his extraordinary adaptiveness, with the suppleness of his mind—some have criticized him for it, mistaking it for spinelessness—that was the dominant trait of his character and the surest sign of his genius.[19]

[18] Jean-Pierre Aumont, *Le Soleil et les ombres* (Paris, 1977), 209.
[19] Jeanne Witta-Montrobert, *La Lanterne magique* (Paris, 1980), 199–200.

Among the young movie people was François Truffaut, who introduced Jean-Claude Brialy to Jean Renoir, and both of them were hired to play walk-ons. André Bazin was there, too. He wrote several pages on it that are as penetrating as ever, and he concludes: "Once again we witnessed the miracle of theater, but the miracle that made 10,000 people from the south of France into Elizabethan spectators was only half the story: the other being that there was actually a show to put on. It wouldn't have happened without the improvisational skills and the reassuring humanity of Jean Renoir. So we weren't surprised to see him appear in answer to the crowd's appeals and to greet them with the unforgettable lopsided walk of Octave stuck in his bear suit during the party at the chateau in *Rules of the Game*. The tears in his voice as he thanked the audience reminded me of the emotions of La Chesnaye showing off his hurdy-gurdy. The distance between an ironical, heartrending masked ball in a salon and this *Julius Caesar* played under the stars before the population of a whole town bespeaks Renoir's loyalty to his own goals as well as the spiritual and artistic breadth of our greatest filmmaker."[20]

After such a triumph, all the more noteworthy since his staging never took the easy way out, the only thing to do was go back to Paris. All the people who were working with him on his next film had come to Arles, so they all went back to work together at the Avenue Frochot.

♦

Meanwhile, life went on in Beverly Hills. Gabrielle and her son, whom the Renoirs still called by his nickname Jeannot, had finally succeeded in buying a piece of land on Leona Drive next to Dido and Jean's. They immediately began building on it and moved in with Bessie Smith so they could supervise the construction. The possibility of again being able to visit each other several times a day delighted all concerned. The Renoirs sorely missed the presence of Gabrielle, Jeannot, and Bessie, but Gabrielle, who had made two trips to Europe, in 1949 and 1951, wasn't eager to return: too many of her relatives and friends had disappeared. They were all becoming rooted in that corner of California. Jean and Dido still didn't know when they would be able to go home. There was a lot of work to do before the filming of *French Cancan* could begin in the fall. On August 30, Jean wrote David Loew, the producer of *The Southerner* who had become his friend: "An-

---

[20] André Bazin, *Jean Renoir* (Paris, 1971), 117.

other thing makes me happy, which is that you're not the only young fellow like me who's taken up a new career (painting and tree surgery, in your case); the possibilities that have come up as a result of my staging a play have given me more joy and excitement than I felt even while preparing my first film thirty years ago. Life is marvellous!"[21]

Just before the beginning of autumn that year, Jean reached the age of sixty. François Truffaut asked him for an article to be published in the weekly *Arts*, and he dictated it immediately: "Writing was as easy for him as speaking, and it came out in beautiful long phrases," Truffaut told me. "I'm sixty years old and I've made thirty-five films," Jean began. "I'm often asked if I prefer to work in one country or the other. It's one more thing that doesn't matter much. I prefer to work in France because of the friendships, because the "family" feeling of film teams is stronger in France, but I think each movie is a country of its own, a little world whose frontiers are not like the ones that separate nation states. That's the way it is in all of show business."[22]

For *French Cancan*, Jean's plan was to use Technicolor for the third time, and to shoot the whole film in the studio. Max Douy's sets were to recreate the atmosphere of the lost Montmartre he still dreamed about, its streets, its terraces lined with cafés, the studios, and the caf'conc' shows that Uncle Henri and Aunt Blanche used to take him to, and where at a tender age he learned—and never forgot—all that "delightfully filthy repertoire." He says he was tempted because there was going to be music in the film: "Since 1924 I've been haunted by the idea of making a movie opera. But in 1924, it was impossible, since there wasn't any sound."[23] For *French Cancan*, he wrote "Montmartre Lament" and, with the help of Georges Van Parys, who wrote the music for the film, he put together a medley of songs from 1900. It was all a lot of fun, reviving his oldest memories and inspiring him to use, self-consciously but deftly, his knowledge of the painting of that era.

◆

Choosing from among so many actors was a problem for Jean after such a long absence. He made the rounds of the Paris cabarets to find young actors: Jacques Jouanneau, who became his "postwar Carette," as François Truffaut rightly put it, Pierre Olaf, Michel Piccoli, and Jean

---

[21] Dido Renoir archive.
[22] *Arts*, 482, September 22, 1954, in Jean Renoir, *Ecrits*, 63.
[23] Jean Renoir, *Entretiens et propos*, 65.

Caussimon. He did not know Françoise Arnoul, who was going to play the lead role, Nini. One day she came to his house

> dressed à la Renoir. It was summer; reddish blond hair, pink cotton dress, pink ballerinas. Jean sat me down in a huge wing chair. He began walking up and down and talking. It was utterly fascinating; he went from one subject to the next, his talk was very colorful. Then he began talking about Nini. He talked for a very long time, and then he stopped. He burst out laughing, a big, loud laugh, with his hands on his hips. And then he said to me: "Well, all right, you can be Nini. I was talking to you and I saw that you knew how to listen, so you can act. An actor who knows how to listen to others knows how to act."[24]

Jean also reenlisted some actors who had been in his films before the war, people like Valentine Tessier, Gaston Modot, Dalban, and Léon Larive. Above all, there was Jean Gabin, whom he had not seen since New York. *La Bête humaine* was the last film that they had made together. The engineer Jacques Lantier was pretty different from the character whom Gabin was going to play, Ziedler, with three mistresses pining after him. But Gabin had a fourth conquest as well, his director, who was as dazzled as ever by this "huge actor" who "could express the most violent emotions with just the slightest shudder over his impassive face."[25]

"Le Jean," as Gabrielle called him, said in an interview during the filming: "I'm very happy to be working with Renoir again, though I was a little scared at first. People change in fifteen years; . . . It might well have happened that we couldn't stand each other. But my fears were unfounded; in person, he was the same Renoir as ever. 'They' didn't change him a bit. Right now, I think he's doing a fine job."[26]

Jean Renoir wrote this about him:

> I sense that his tastes in life are about the same as mine. Without saying anything ahead of time, we end up in the same restaurants. When we work together, we don't need long discussions to analyze a situation. And we hardly need the script to find out where we are. Gabin is a born actor, as I'm a born author/director. But our strategies aren't the same: Gabin is imposing and he gets his way without trying. I'm the opposite: I offer elaborate excuses and then I try hard to convince.[27]

And in the same vein:

[24] Interview with the author.
[25] Jean Renoir, *Ma vie et mes films*, 118.
[26] *Cinéma 55*, 2, December 2, 1954, in André G. Brunelin, "Jean Renoir au travail."
[27] Jean Renoir, *Ma vie et mes films*, 250.

During the shooting of *French Cancan*, when he had nothing to do but wait, he kept busy by giving Dido recipes. "Do you know how to make rabbit in mustard sauce? You take a tablespoon of Dijon mustard . . ." He would stop to play his scene, magnificently, then go back and continue the recipe right where he had left off, switching from his role back to the rabbit without any problem (ibid., p. 251).

They had started shooting on October 4, first in the Francoeur Studio, then at Saint-Maurice. As Françoise Arnoul tells it:

Every night, Jean looked at the rushes and edited the film with the editors. Every morning, he went to makeup. He would walk round in circles there. He always called me Nini, never Françoise. He'd take little pieces of paper with notes on them out of his pocket and put them on the makeup table and say, "If you like this, maybe it can help you." He had written a song about Nini. How Nini carries her laundry basket, how she bows to say hello, how she puts up her hair. . . . Jean worked with his actors in such a way that it was very hard for them to remain in their own world. The truth is that he had the fantastic intelligence to use exactly what people had to give.[28]

Filming ended on December 20, after "three months of extreme happiness, three months of holidays," says Françoise Arnoul. "At the time, people shot on Saturdays. Jean would say: 'Nuts! Tomorrow's Sunday. Have to wait till Monday to see you all again.' The end of a film is like the end of a love affair, you go back to real life after it's over." That particular love affair had been especially successful, and the actors felt lonely without the man whom, in general, and deferentially, they called "Monsieur Renoir."

To introduce his film on television, Jean Renoir spoke about Nini:

The great impresario . . . will teach her more than how to make money and to be radiant, he will teach her the beauty of her trade. That's something extremely important. I believe in having your trade. It seems to me that that's what we should base our lives on, and I think that *French Cancan* is above all else an homage to a trade. And in this case, what a trade! Dancing! Anyway, if I had tried not believing in the idea of having a trade while I was shooting *French Cancan*, I would have been reconverted to my belief in it by the women who were working with me. It was absolutely fantastic. We lived in an incredible atmosphere! You should have seen the courage, the good will, and the kindness of those dancers.[29]

---

[28]Interview with the author.
[29]Jean Renoir, *Entretiens et propos*, 137.

The film came out on April 29, 1955, and was an immediate success. Beneath its frivolous atmosphere, the beauty of its colors, and the frank and generous sensuality that pervades it, the public probably did not get an inkling of the real depth of the film, but it was still dazzled. Bazin got the point: "*French Cancan* is a return to origins, a beautiful homage to the memory of Auguste Renoir."[30]

Françoise Arnoul, who lived through the experience, came to this conclusion:

> Before the film was released, my ex-husband, Georges Cravenne, who was the publicist for *French Cancan*, organized a dinner for Dido, Jean, Jean Gabin, his wife, and the two of us. I was all excited about seeing them again, since I thought the excitement of those three months would return spontaneously. Not at all! At the time, Jean was rehearsing *Orvet*, with Leslie Caron. During the whole dinner, he talked only about Leslie and *Orvet*.

"He's a creative artist," she added, sensibly. But she also told me that she detested Leslie Caron that evening, even though they had never met. She admitted it to Leslie later, and Leslie said, "I'll tell you the sequel. After *Orvet*, Jean told me he was going to make a film with Ingrid Bergman, and he only talked about her and his film." They both had a good laugh over that one.

Jean had sent fifteen thousand spectators into rapture in the arena at Arles, and he had received unanimous praise from the press for his staging of *Julius Caesar*. As a result, the director of the Renaissance Theater, Jean Darcante, agreed to produce *Orvet*, a play that Jean Renoir had written for Leslie Caron. Jean Renoir wrote about his first encounters with this actress, and Leslie Caron spoke to me informally of them as well. They both remember, but the ways they do are different and typically so.

For Jean Renoir, Leslie was a little girl sitting with a lady on the platform of Victoria Station in London. "Dido immediately thought this unknown actress would be perfect for the role of Harriet in *The River*, which I was in the midst of working up," but she didn't have time to go and speak to them. The next day, at the Gare du Nord in Paris, "it was a mob scene and all I could do was watch her long tresses disappear amid the flood of travelers." The "little girl" reminded him of the daughter of the poachers who had rescued him when he was hurt in the car crash that had killed Pierre Champagne.

According to Leslie, she was seventeen years old at the time and

[30] André Bazin, *Jean Renoir*, 130.

288

had just had a big success in a ballet presented at the Théâtre des Champs-Elysées, *Oedipe et le Sphinx*, with Jean Babilée. She had gone to London at Arthur Rank's invitation. On the way back, since there was a thick fog, everyone had rushed to get on the Golden Arrow. She had noticed Jean and Dido at the airport and the train station. She knew who he was, and

> his wife looked like an Indian sculpted in stone. One year later, I had already made *An American in Paris,* and we met at the home of Pierre Sicard, a New York painter. I remember the atmosphere there, which was very "Georges Simenon," with Jean hailing a taxi in the rain after the party. Then, in Hollywood, I began to go and visit them in the afternoon. You could show up after five o'clock; there was some salami, some olives, and some red or white wine. There were two big armchairs and a clock that Jean had designed, which had two chimes, one to incite you to pray, the other three minutes later.

At the time, she had made three or four films, and she was wondering whether she should keep on dancing or become an actress. "Jean said: 'I think you are an actress.' Less than a year later, he offered me the play. He taught me everything, down to the littlest details. For instance, he said you ought to put a big block of butter on the table. In my house, there's always a big block of butter on the table."

Jean also remembers a second meeting they had at Pierre Sicard's, but he says it was at Los Angeles.

> The Sicards had invited us to their home with all the female dancers of the Ballet Roland Petit. A few years had passed, and the little girl in Victoria Station had become a young woman. The way she was seated and hiding behind her hair, there was no way I could fail to recognize her. . . . We approached each other like old friends. I noticed at the time that she looked like a cat. Later, Dido and I met her on the sidewalk in Times Square in New York, waiting for something in a driving rain: that time, she looked like a drowned cat. This kind of meeting is typical of all my meetings with Leslie: she always seemed to be looking for something.[31]

◆

The premiere of *Orvet* took place on March 12, 1955, before *French Cancan* came out. The critics were reticent. Jean wanted his play to be as accessible as his films, but only those who appreciated his cinematic work could understand the poetry of the little savage and listen to the meditation on art that is the play's real concern. In it, Jean

---

[31] Jean Renoir, *Ma vie et mes films*, 255.

expresses his fascination with the women whom his father loved to paint and his obsession with poachers. The play is, once again, a return to his childhood. In connection with *Orvet*, Jean wrote an homage to Hans Christian Andersen, whose fairy tales Gabrielle used to read aloud to him to keep him quiet while he was posing for his father. Their favorite story was "Soup on a Spit," which takes place in the kingdom of the mice. Jean tells how a visitor once asked his father if it was not dangerous to let children believe that mice can talk. "Renoir looked at the man with amazement and said, 'But they do talk!'" [32] The anecdote explains not just *Orvet* but a good portion of Jean Renoir's adult behavior.

Waiting for Godot had been put on only two years before, and Adamov, Ionesco, Vauthier, and Tardieu had only appeared in the tiny theaters that critics do not take the trouble to attend. So it was not surprising that in a large, old theater that was far from having a reputation for being avant-garde, Jean Renoir's work was considered disconcerting. The public reaction was better. Leslie Caron performed *Orvet* four hundred times, until she had to leave for Hollywood.

The Renoirs had no thought of doing the same. The success of *French Cancan* had led Deutschmeister, its producer, to suggest to Jean that he make a new film for him in two versions, one English, the other French. Jean proposed several subjects, but none was suitable. Then the idea came to him to make a film about General Boulanger. "Everyone says: 'Ah! That's terrific! It really could be very funny.'" Maybe so, but not the general's suicide at the end. At the same time, Jean was dying to make some kind of a jolly film with Ingrid Bergman. Deutschmeister was not against finding a place for the fair Ingrid in the screenplay. Then the general's family got wind of the project and threatened a lawsuit if a film was made on the life of their great man that actually used his name. Jean Renoir regretfully acceded to Deutschmeister's desire not to run that risk. Then why not construct a film around Ingrid, create an imaginary person who would only be distantly related to "the brave general"? Finally, Ingrid became Eléna, the Polish countess, which was actually just another name for Venus. "Venus doesn't know how to say hello without giving you the impression that she's offering herself to you completely, and in fact she is offering herself to you completely. She is the opposite of those decadent femmes fatales who only evoke despair, whom the devil has sought to make fashionable" (ibid., 281).

The eccentric Eléna resembles Misia Sert, but Jean had such a

[32] Jean Renoir, *Ecrits*, 200.

dread of psychology that he rejected the parallelism. The film was to be a fantasy in which unreal characters would evolve in a world that was just as unreal. It took him about six months to write the screenplay. His first thought was to call the movie *L'Oeillet rouge* (*The Red Carnation*), but then he changed it to *Eléna et les hommes* (*Elena and Her Men*). He kept on revising the script, and finally he asked Jean Serge to help him with it. Since his house at Marlotte had been sold during the war and he had to stay near Paris, he and Dido moved into the Pavillon Henri IV in Saint-Germain, where they could live in peace. The filming began on December 1, 1955, and ended on March 17, 1956. It took place in the Saint-Maurice studios, with exteriors filmed at Ermenonville and in the park at Saint-Cloud. Jean had his nephew Claude as chief cameraman again, and "we had fun, incredible fun using full red lighting" for a sunset effect. Using color (this time it was Eastmancolor) gave him the chance to monkey around with technique the way he always loved to.

Ingrid Bergman, whose relationship with Rossellini and the son that they had together scandalized Americans, had lived in Rome for four years and acted in several Italian movies, but she had never before made a film in France. She was that much more embarrassed about her French, since at home Rossellini spoke to her in Italian. One of her "men" in the film, Mel Ferrer, also had problems with French. Jean Renoir had first offered his role to Gérard Philipe, who found it "weak politically speaking" and had rejected it. So they had to correct and help Ingrid Bergman and Mel Ferrer, but there was worse: in an interview with François Truffaut and Jacques Rivette, Jean Renoir admits with a frankness that is hardly common among directors that he was "held in check for practical reasons." He had not realized how complicated it would be with two versions and actors who spoke no English.

The filming "was extremely difficult, extremely tiring, for the actors, the technicians, and for me. Circumstances were such that, bit by bit, I threw some cargo overboard, and I didn't develop all the situations the way I could have. It got to the point where I actually scaled them down so that I could present them in oversimplified language." He adds: "I was always having to devise shortcuts. . . . *Eléna* owes its unity to a certain spirit that I kept to throughout the film by clinging to its main character. That's the glue that holds it all together."[33]

He mastered these problems, as he mastered his interlocutors, by

---

[33] *Cahiers du cinéma*, 78, Christmas 1957, 48–49.

the lucidity and intelligence of his answers. He found some solutions by using the means at hand, but he did not try to hide the fact that there may have been better ones. Even so, he succeeded in transforming the lovely Swedish actress into an irresistible Polish noblewoman. Beyond Eléna's high spirits and those of Renoir himself—he assures us that he had a great time even so—and beyond the very successful opera buffa style, the film has a melancholic, not to say hopeless, undertone. It's a supersophisticated film of daring beauty, but it did not please the public when it came out in Paris on September 12, 1956. Shown with it was a short entitled *L'Album de famille de Jean Renoir* (*The Jean Renoir Family Album*), made for television by Pierre Desgraupes; it features Jean, born storyteller, bringing back to life some of his childhood memories and recalling some of his films.

◆

During the twenty months that Jean and Dido spent in Paris, they visited England twice in 1955 and twice in 1956, always to see Dido's mother and sister. Jean got along with them extremely well. His theory about the horizontal levels of society, about the affinities among people on the same social level being more important than the distinctions among nationalities, was proven true once more. He felt close to these women who were born on the other side of the earth but had received the same education as he and possessed the same culture. For her part, Dido was curious to meet his childhood friends, some of whom had dropped from sight. In particular, there were "the little Manet girls," who had become old women and whom no one called that anymore! She telephoned them and they went to tea with Julie Rouart, the daughter of Berthe Morisot, and her cousins, Madame Paul Valéry and her sister, Paule Gobillard. That mansion on the rue de Villejust (since become the rue Paul-Valéry) had been so familiar to Jean during his childhood, and his father had gone there so often to visit Berthe Morisot! "The little Manet girls" were full of memories and delighted to listen to Jean who, as usual, talked and talked.

Paul Cézanne's absence was painful, but it had been a great joy for them to see Renée, his wife, once more. Dido and Jean had the feeling that they had never left Pierre Lestringuez and Mr. Guillaume, their great friends. Henri Cartier-Bresson had been to see them in California a few years after the war, when he came to do a story with an American writer. They noted with satisfaction that Henri had kept his mischievous boyishness, his strangled outbursts of laughter, and his loyalty as a friend. Jacques Becker was the other young man whose accent Jean had laughingly imitated, calling it "teu-teu." In 1948, Becker wrote: "I was fifteen years old when I met him and thirty-three when we were separated. In the intervening years, I was his assistant for about ten years. There's no man whom I love more. I love him because he gave me the trade that I wanted, and I also love him because he gave us some movies without which French cinema wouldn't be what it is." [34]

Aside from these two friends and Braunberger, Jean's movie friends from before the war were lost. Each of them was working in one place or another, and the idea that Renoir had become an American, as I said before, displeased most of them very much. In Rome, Jean saw Marc Maurette again, who had been his assistant for *La Marseillaise* and *The Golden Coach*. Marc Maurette remembered how Jean Renoir had stood up for him in Rome with the producer who had taken sides with the wardrobe mistress in a violent argument. "The wardrobe mistress was very talented, but she was pretty old, and she forgot to bring the costumes once they were all ready. I got angry and the producer said I had to quit. Jean Renoir took my side very firmly, and I stayed on." The painter Jean Castanier had reappeared and played a small role in *French Cancan*, as had Claire Gérard in *Eléna*. Jean Renoir was very hospitable to actors and filmmakers. He kept on saying, "I'm bored to death with people who aren't in film." [35] Roland Stragliati, who had started as property man in *Madame Bovary*, told me he lunched with Jean in Rome and found him as passionate and warm as ever. Jean remembered details about people that revealed how much other people really interested him. In Paris, Dido and Jean met Georges Braque and his wife, and a lively friendship developed between them. They visited each other in the Braques' house near the Parc Montsouris or at Varengeville in Normandy, where they had a country home. The world of the painter was not alien to Jean, and Dido, like him, loved the work of their new friend.

Jean tried to put his business affairs in order. Mr. Guillaume stayed on the job until his death in 1956, when Ginette Doynel (who was also called Anne de Saint-Phalle) took over from him with the same attentive devotion. A passionate person, she threw herself into whatever she took on; she was much more demanding of herself than she was of others. One evening, she fought to get back the lavender print of *Grand Illusion* that had been shown by mistake at the Ciné-

---

[34] *Ciné Club*, April 1948, cited by Pierre Leprohon in *Jean Renoir*, 161.
[35] Jean Renoir, *Ecrits*, 63.

mathèque. She had gone there with Jean, who wanted to use a clip from it (the gloves scene with Fresnay and Gabin) in a television program called *Les Joies de la vie* [*The Joys of Life*].

♦

Dido and Jean did not wait for *Eléna et les hommes* to come out in France. They had to go back to the United States and do the post-synchronization of the English version. They got on the *Queen Mary* at Cherbourg on July 13, 1956, bound for New York. They stayed there for three months, working hard. At first they lived in the Waldorf-Astoria, where they once met and talked with John Kennedy, then a young senator from Massachusetts. Jean thought he was a very nice fellow. Then they went back to the Royalton, their first New York hotel, and their old habits. Their dear friend Al Lewin, the producer who had also directed films like *The Portrait of Dorian Gray* and *Pandora*, with Ava Gardner, was living in New York, so they saw each other often. Dudley Nichols was still living in Connecticut, which wasn't far. In the meantime, Jean had written another play, *Carola ou les cabotins* (*Carola or the Hams*) which he intended for Danielle Darrieux and Paul Meurisse, the Brutus in Jean's *Caesar*. He also wanted to find a producer for another project, a black-and-white version of Simenon's *Trois Chambres à Manhattan* (*Three Beds in Manhattan*), to be shot on the streets of New York with Leslie Caron. He had also translated and adapted Clifford Odets' play, *The Big Knife*, from which Robert Aldrich, Renoir's assistant in *The Southerner*, had scripted and produced a film the year before with Jack Palance, Rod Steiger, and Ida Lupino. On August 12, 1956, he wrote to Clifford Odets: "I have some good news from Paris about *Le Grand Couteau* [his translation of *The Big Knife*]. We can count on Michel Simon and Daniel Gélin. Maybe we can get Danielle Darrieux to play Marion. It would be a terrific cast. The only thing that bothers me is that I can't do the directing. After having been away for so long, I have to spend some time in California. Can I add that Dido and I are eager to see our children and friends again?"[36] One week later, he wrote to Gabrielle:

> Dear Ga, Finally we know when we'll see you and Jeannot again. Dido has bought the train tickets, on the advice of Maurice [their cousin, Maurice Renoir], for September 15. Try to be healthy so we can have some fun! . . . According to the TV, it's more than 100 degrees in Los Angeles. You must be nice and warm. Poor Bessie must be pretty tired of

[36] Dido Renoir archive.

watering the garden. She's a wonderful girl, and being away from her proved to me just how much I feel for her.[37]

As they had expected, the joy in coming home was great. There were their friends: Gabrielle and Jean Slade had moved into their new home adjacent to the Renoirs' in February of 1955, and since May 31, 1954, there was a new grandson, Peter, in the home of Alain Renoir. Alain and Jane had moved to Berkeley in June 1955, after Alain spent two years teaching in Williamstown, Massachusetts. In Hollywood, movies were going nowhere. The House Un-American Activities Committee had created a serious crisis of conscience, and to compete with television, which was becoming more and more important, they were still resorting to technical novelties like Cinemascope, 70 millimeter film. Jean Renoir's technical daring took him in a very different direction. Only a few directors of his generation were still working in Hollywood: John Ford, George Cukor, King Vidor, Raoul Walsh, Henry Hathaway, and Fritz Lang, who had done a frigid, mechanical remake of *La Bête humaine* the year before called *Human Desire*. He had done the same thing in 1945 with *Scarlet Street*, a remake of *La Chienne*. Fritz Lang and Jean Renoir were friends and thought highly of each other, but Fritz Lang had adapted himself much better to the demands of the American film industry. He was within a system that, once again, Jean could not succeed in getting into.

However, film attendance was dropping, the big studios were in trouble, and most of them shifted from production to distribution, which meant that independent producers were multiplying. The plan for *Trois Chambres à Manhattan* should have been more attractive to them than a low-budget film. But Renoir was disappointed to find that no one wanted to take the risk. Moreover, the American version of *Eléna*, which he had a very hard time postsynchronizing, caused him great discouragement. It had been "massacred."

They went out and edited it again, and they even shot a new beginning and a new ending with Mel Ferrer. I have no idea what's in them. I didn't want to see the film. This kind of stuff makes me sick! It really hurts! I guess it comes from some fear that the public won't understand. I gather that there are explanatory beginnings and endings. The film appeared in the U.S. just when Ingrid Bergman received the Academy Award for *Anastasia*. According to the publicity agents, the public expects her to make sentimental love stories. Since *Eléna* isn't sentimental, they have tried to change it or make excuses for it. As for me, I'm not interested in

---

[37] Letter provided by Jean Slade.

sentimental tales."[38] This disfigured version of the film they entitled *Paris Does Strange Things*. Jean was so "distressed that I couldn't go into a movie theater and look at a screen for six months. It really made me sick" (ibid.).

◆

In May 1957, the death of Erich von Stroheim reminded him that the professional world in which he chose to live was cruel and that some irreversible situations can break the spirit of the greatest geniuses. For Jean, *Greed* was "the absolute masterpiece." In his eyes, Erich von Stroheim remained "a great actor" and "an even greater creative force."[39] Jean did not forget Irving Thalberg's dismissal of Stroheim in 1922. Thalberg, whose righthand man was Jean's friend Albert Lewin, was then head of production at Universal. He hired someone else to finish shooting Stroheim's *Merry-Go-Round*. Then, after Stroheim made three other films, including *Greed* (someone had decided it was too long, cut it blindly, and destroyed the negative), Joseph Kennedy (father of John Kennedy), a Hollywood producer at the time, repeated Thalberg's gesture and stopped the shooting of *Queen Kelly*, which effectively ended the great Austrian director's career.

Jean could not got to France for his friend's funeral, which took place in the village of Maurepas, where Stroheim lived in exile, not far from Paris. The following year he wrote this of him:

> Stroheim taught me many things. Probably the most important of his teachings was that reality has no value except when it is transformed. In other words, an artist only exists if he succeeds in inventing his own little world. The characters devised by Stroheim, Chaplin, and Griffith do not live out their stories in Paris, Vienna, Monte Carlo, or Atlanta, but in the lands of Stroheim, Chaplin, and Griffith.[40]

During this period, Renoir's theater seems to have been more successful than his films. His version of *Big Knife, Le Grand Couteau,* went into rehearsal as planned at the Théâtre des Bouffe-Parisiens with a cast consisting of Daniel Gélin, Paul Bernard, and Claude Génia. Jean Serge directed the rehearsals, and the preview took place on October 4, 1957. Jean did not want to stay in Paris for long, and Dido did not want to go with him, so he arrived there alone in September. It was the first time he and Dido had been separated after

[38] *Cahiers du cinéma*, 78, Christmas 1957, 22.
[39] Jean Renoir, *Ecrits*, 189.
[40] Jean Renoir, *Ecrits*, 189–90.

living together for twenty years. He wrote to her every day, and because of the numerous letters, which she guards jealously, Dido speaks of this trip as she does of those they took together. He kept her informed of everything that happened to him. During the rehearsals of *Le Grand Couteau*, he shot a 16-millimeter film that lasted not more than fifteen seconds. It was "a miniature film noir," according to Claude Beylie, in which Daniel Gélin played the part of a Hollywood actor doing a dramatic scene. No copy of this film, entitled *Un tigre sur la ville* (*A Tiger on the Town*), has survived, though it occurs in every serious filmography. It was made to be shown on stage during the play. François Truffaut asked Jean Renoir later on if *Le Grand Couteau* was really a violently anti-American play, as people said it was. "I consider Clifford Odets one of the three or four best American playwrights. His success stems from the time of the Great Depression of 1929. The play is indeed very violent, and probably critical, but it is an acceptable critique since it was made against America by an American who loved America: Molière adored the society whose faults he denounced."[41]

Jean and Dido had the kind of brotherly affection for Clifford Odets that was an essential part of their lives.

> Clifford is the most civilized of men. His knowledge of music is huge; his understanding of the plastic arts amazing. He knows how to recognize a good wine or a fine fabric. For all that, he has preserved in himself the innocence of a primitive creature. He recognizes evil not by analyzing it but with his nose, as the angel Gabriel can sniff out the devil. What is good attracts him. He goes at life fearlessly. Language is his sword: his is working class, funny, and biting.[42]

On October 10, Jean wrote to his friend Clifford:

> The audience [at the preview] was a mixture of actors, authors, producers, and also, to be sure, members of the press. They applauded vigorously several times during the play, and also for ten minutes at the end. That doesn't mean that we'll get good reviews. I'm even pretty sure they'll be mixed. It's fashionable to be unpleasant or to try to present anything new with ironical jokes; and this Jean Renoir, who just arrives from California to open a successful show in the most Parisian of theaters, he's a good target. But even if there are some discouraging articles, I won't be depressed, because I know we've won over the public.[43]

[41] *Arts*, September 18–24, 1957.
[42] From the program at the Théâtre des Bouffe-Parisiens, provided by Claude Gauteur.
[43] Dido Renoir archive.

While he was in Paris, Jean signed the papers for a company he organized specifically around *Grand Illusion*. In Rome in 1951 he had learned that in 1945, in Munich, the photographic services of the army had seized a double negative of the film as war booty. After long drawn out negotiations with its producers, Jean repurchased the rights to the film and, at the end of 1957, he created a company with Charles Spaak, the co-author of the screenplay, called FRS (Films Renoir Spaak) whose managing director was Ginette Doynel (Anne de Saint-Phalle). When Spaak decided to withdraw in 1959, the FRS became the Compagnie Jean Renoir. After consulting with Jean, Renée Lichtig reedited the film into a complete version by assembling the various corrected ones.

◆

Renoir's films were everywhere becoming the subject of study and discussion. Some spoke of their spirituality, others saw Jean as the father of neorealism. At the French Institute in London in 1957, Jacques Brunius claimed that *La Chienne* was the inspiration for *Ossessione*, the film that Visconti made after having read *The Postman Always Rings Twice* at Jean's suggestion. Brunius had been following Jean Renoir's career since the filming of *On purge bébé*. Along with Luchino Visconti and several others, he had been Renoir's assistant in *A Day in the Country*, in which he also had an important acting role. Jean said of him that "he had a kind of magical quality. Like a character on the silver screen, he was a fairy tale sort of person. But he was also a creative man, and an excellent novelist. In a word, he was what people in the eighteenth century called "an honest man," that is, someone who knows a little about everything, but not superficially, and who is also capable of an overall view of the world."[44] Before devoting himself to movies, Brunius had studied aeronautics. Jean Renoir also says that "he epitomized Prévert's friends, a group of terrific people in whose discussions Brunius took part, not as an avid debater, but more like someone who was half asleep." Always in a daydream, smart and droll, he actually did seem nonchalant and alert at the same time; like the boatman he played in *A Day in the Country*, he stayed tall and thin.

In July 1957, Sacha Guitry died. In 1915, he had made a short film called *Ceux de chez nous* [*Our Gang*], which contains a sequence shot in Auguste Renoir's studio. His films, which were derived from his plays, went way beyond the boulevard theater on film that they could

[44]Jean Renoir, *Ecrits*, 209.

have been. Guitry had a kind of inventiveness and an inborn under-standing of the theater that made it possible for him to go beyond re-alism. There are masks everywhere in his work, and even his dia-logue is a form of disguise. But despite his own fascination with the magical world of the theater, Jean Renoir was never interested in Sacha Guitry's characters. At the time Jean didn't think his friends at *Cahiers du cinéma* were going to "discover" him, but later on they in fact did so. Jean was even busier than usual, since he felt obligated to accept requests that he participate in conventions or interviews.

For Christmas 1957, *Cahiers du cinéma* devoted fifty pages to him, reprinting a talk he had given "at the request of the Cinémathèque française at the International Congress on Research on Film History" on October 31, 1957, entitled "Ce bougre de Nouveau Monde ("This Confounded New World"), and a long interview with Jacques Rivette and François Truffaut that goes over all his films, beginning with the silent ones; Jean also lists his current projects and plans. On Novem-ber 22, he filed a ten-page synopsis with the Screenwriters Guild that went back to the themes of *Paris province*, an older project whose point of departure was the daily life in a "villa," a group of protected houses like the ones of the avenue Frochot. *Cahiers du cinéma* had pub-lished *Paris province* in May 1954.[45]

Before returning home to Dido, Jean went to England. On De-cember 4 he met with Leslie Caron in London to discuss a film project, and from there he went to Liverpool to see Madame Freire, his mother-in-law. On December 10 he boarded the *Sylvania* for New York, where he arrived on the 17th. He got home in time to spend a quiet Christmas with Dido in the brick and glass home they had built, along with Bessie and also Gabrielle and Jeannot, once again their neighbors. Alain, Jane, and their children were there, too. Jean took them to see the huge lit-up Christmas tree in Harold Lloyd's backyard on the other side of Benedict Canyon. Like his father before him, Jean thought Christmas trees were a fire hazard, so he told his grand-children that Harold Lloyd's tree was their tree, but it was so big they had to put it somewhere else. It was also too beautiful to touch, and it had to stay far away, like a dream.

In 1958, two avid young admirers of Jean's work, Jean Gaborit and Jacques Maréchal, started the Société des grands films classiques. Their goal was to restore and distribute *Rules of the Game*. They con-tacted Camille François who, after the NEF, the film's original produc-

---

[45] Jean Renoir, *Oeuvres inédites*, 213.

tion company, was dissolved, tried to "wipe out the deficit." So he ceded world rights to the film to them. He "handed over to them the negative of the copy that was rediscovered in 1946 and all the documents on file. From then on they spent their time repatriating all the old copies that remained the world over," amounting to two hundred boxes "of positives, negatives, various clips, and sound mixes" that were recovered after the bombardment in 1942. "With the assistance of Jacques Durand, an editor," they succeeded in restoring "the original 113-minute edit, thanks to Jean Renoir's advice. They even got up a 118-minute screening." [46] This meticulous labor of love took more than a year, and the restored film was shown at the Venice Festival in 1959. Its first public showing was not until April 1965, in Paris; finally, it was a triumph.

In business matters, Dido was a good adviser. She was more realistic than Jean, and he had complete confidence in her discretion. Their friends all say that without her he would have ended up living on the street. He was always ready to give and spend on others and with others. They had exchanged continents, but not life-styles. They had a stock of friends whom they stayed close to even when an ocean apart.

[46] *L'Avant-Scène cinéma*, 52, October 1, 1965, 9.

BETWEEN TWO WORLDS

◆

J ean still loved Paris but no longer felt completely at home there. Things were not the way they were before. First of all himself: he had lived through the war elsewhere and spent time in India, and he was also transformed by his deep relationship with Dido. Too much time had passed. The city was changing, and he returned to find it had changed, like a person one no longer lives with. The town was losing its face, and it was a face that he loved very much without ever realizing it. The shops in his neighborhood, like the people, were becoming nondescript. Since his last visit, the political atmosphere was also different. Shortly before he left, in June 1956, *Le Monde* published the Krushchev report denouncing Stalin's crimes, and then, at the end of October, the Hungarian revolt was brutally repressed by the Soviets. No one could deny these facts. For many people, it meant a break with the party, a painful break because Communism represented their hope for a more just society that would give everyone a chance and in which people would really have equal rights. The consequent disillusionment lowered morale. On the other side, the beginning of the year had seen the victory of Poujade, who brought together the middle-class malcontents, all those who were frightened by the country's modernization and by an economic development that was squeezing out small businesses. The war in Algeria, which heated up after the arrest of Ben Bella, was also dividing the French. Misunderstandings that should have been cleared up remained. There was no way to go backwards, and, as before, the two camps were not talking to each other. But now some were looking without malevolence toward the United States.

A new way of thinking was also coming into being, and Jean recognized the signs of it. He had witnessed the same developments in California. Already the distances were less great than they had been at the end of the war, and now, from one continent to the next, everyday life began to look the same. The consumer society was gaining ground in the West, and it was depressing to register its acceptance even on the streets of Paris.

The year 1958 was a year without a film, but Dido and Jean still had to leave Beverly Hills for Europe on April 14. They found out that *Grand Illusion* was chosen by an international jury as one of the "ten best films in the world." This was under the auspices of the Brussels World Fair. But as he said later on: "I'm not so interested in my old films. The joy was in making them. I remember filming some of them, and also my happiness when *Grand Illusion* was chosen for the New York World's Fair in 1939."[1] This time, he was going to do what was expected of him, in the hope that the future would bring other reasons for happiness.

◆

Jean and Dido landed in Paris on April 15, the day the centrist government of Félix Gaillard fell. The eventual consequence of this was the proclamation of the Fifth Republic by General de Gaulle a month later. As soon as he arrived, Jean made a preview for his film, which was scheduled to be shown that fall. He had not forgotten that he was a familiar face on French television, where his cocky voice and nonchalance worked wonders. He loved speaking as a director to his film's viewers, and it was something that he used to his advantage on several occasions. In the preview he introduces himself, relates some memories of the film, and shows some pictures of old airplanes: the Voisin, in which he learned to fly in 1915, and the one "in which Gabin and Fresnay get themselves shot down in the film," a Caudron. He provides some information on these different types of planes that must have pleased his male audience. He also says: "*Grand Illusion* is the story of people like you and me who get lost in that harrowing adventure known as war."[2] The film was shown in Paris in October, and its popularity hasn't abated since.

At the end of April, Jean and Dido went to Munich, again for the sake of *Grand Illusion*, which was going to end up moving them

[1] *Cahiers du cinéma*, 191, June 1967, 10.
[2] Jean Renoir, *Ecrits, 1926–1971*, ed. C. Gauteur (Paris, 1974), 244–45.

around more than they might have wished. On June 5, they were in Brussels, to which they returned on October 18. On November 1, they left for England, where they stayed until December 5. Jean introduced the film himself on British TV. During their stay in England, on November 11, while the public was expressing righteous indignation over Louis Malle's film, *Les Amants* (*The Lovers*), André Bazin died at the age of 40.

"He watched *The Crime of M. Lange* on television and devoted his last essay to it."[3] Thirty-six hours later he was dead. When Truffaut arrived, exhausted by his first day of shooting *The 400 Blows*, Bazin was already in his final agony. The young director was devastated, as were the other close friends who had gotten there a few hours before. His adopted father was never to hear all Truffaut had to say about an experience that so delighted Bazin and of which they had spoken so much. Jean and Dido were unable to attend the funeral, which included the family of young author/directors whom Bazin had trained and who, during that same year, had made their first feature films: Claude Chabrol, *Le Beau Serge* (*Handsome Serge*), Jacques Rivette, *Paris nous appartient* (*Paris Is Ours*), and François Truffaut, *The 400 Blows*. With Jean-Luc Godard, Pierre Kast, and a few others, they were to form the New Wave. It probably would never have existed without Bazin.

Jean Renoir wrote two articles about his dead friend, one for *France-Observateur*, the other for the issue of *Cahiers du cinéma* in his honor.[4] The extent of his sadness is plain from the neutral seriousness of his tone, which is so unlike his usual style. Bazin's simplicity and humaneness had made a deep impression on him.

As this year ended, Jean Renoir was preparing to shoot two films. One screenplay became, after many transformations, *Le Testament du Dr Cordelier* (*The Testament of Dr. Cordelier*), and the other, very different, *Le Déjeuner sur l'herbe* (*Picnic on the Grass*). In both he employed television techniques.

He had been thinking about them for a long time. Television was no longer a novelty in the United States, where it had produced the expected result. France had gone from 60,000 sets in 1954 to 680,000 in 1958. It was time to use them. Inspired by his theatrical experience, Jean wanted to use four or five cameras (he even went up to eight!), not for shots, but for whole scenes acted from beginning to end with-

---

[3] Dudley Andrew, *André Bazin* (New York, 1978), 212.
[4] Jean Renoir, *Ecrits*, 202–4.

out interruption, as in the theater, with microphones scattered all over the set. This meant working methods that were completely different from those he had used before. Even more than in a regular movie, this kind of filming requires teamwork and professional technicians who have mastered their art.

No television/movie coproduction had ever before been attempted in France. Jean Renoir's idea was to release the film simultaneously on television and in movie theaters. But he had a struggle on his hands. The National Federation of French Cinemas was against it. In a letter dated January 22, 1959, its president wrote to him as follows:

> You certainly are already aware of the unanimously negative opinion handed down by the Committee of the National Center of Cinematography, to whom the project was submitted yesterday.
> I do not wish to delay any further before informing you that such a project could in no case receive a favorable vote from the federation that I represent. In order that there be no shadow of a doubt, I even wish to explain that our unions would consider it their duty, in such a case, to inform their members very clearly of the conditions under which this film was made so that conclusions might be drawn which would necessitate preventing the film from appearing on theater screens.

What hostility! Fortunately, Jean Renoir did not allow himself to get discouraged. It was not the first time people had tried to rain on his parade. With his usual powers of persuasion, he succeeded in convincing the director of French TV that he should undertake this unprecedented experiment. Pathé, which was supposed to distribute the film, advanced the necessary funds.

Le Testament du Dr Cordelier was a modern version of Stevenson's *Dr. Jekyll and Mr. Hyde.* "Jean-Louis Barrault acted this double role as a dancer would have," Jean wrote. "To make the change from Jekyll to Hyde, he used no makeup whatever. As for props, he was satisfied with a set of false teeth and a hairy wig."[5] The way he created the two roles is amazing. I was very eager to meet him. Since he himself had done some remarkable directing in the theater, I wanted to know what he thought of working with Jean Renoir, who could not have imagined a better Opale or another Cordelier. I could not get the two characters out of my head.

Jean-Louis Barrault met me in a small and strangely empty office in the Théâtre du Rond-Point, which was so open and so well suited to the needs of his company and of today's public. He immediately

---

[5] Jean Renoir, *Ma vie et mes films* (Paris, 1974), 257.

began talking about the experiences he had twenty-five years ago as though they had just taken place.

> Technically speaking, making the film was very exciting. Jean had thought of a way to do it that I've never seen anyone try since. We rehearsed for two or three weeks, the way you rehearse in the theater, with the actors' places marked on the ground. We rehearsed a scene at a time, each one lasting about twelve or fourteen minutes. By the end of it, we knew exactly where the cameras were going to be, and that gave room for a little spontaneity. No more questions to ask. It didn't matter any more which camera was shooting you. Working with him was a joy. He knew how to make actors purr. He had a genius for putting you at ease, and I loved his conception of the double character: the doctor was the one who was repressed and anxious, while the monster, on the contrary, was relaxed and like a happy child. *Cordelier* is one of my happiest memories, even though I never got paid for it. When the film was finally distributed, the production company had disappeared. I had signed another contract with French TV, a very modest one, which was honored, and that was it. But the experience was worth it. I have no regrets.

When François Truffaut was shooting *Fahrenheit 451* in London, he saw *Le Testament du Dr Cordelier* at the British Film Institute, which was doing a Renoir cycle.

> In *Le Testament du Dr Cordelier*, Jean-Louis Barrault plays Opale, a fabulous character, original down to his incredible saunter, which was borrowed from Michel Simon in *Boudu* and Burgess Meredith in *Diary of a Chambermaid*. To animate a human being one has invented, make him slide instead of walk, endow him with a set of characteristic gestures, have him randomly thrash passers-by in the streets, there's an artist's, not to say a filmmaker's, dream. *Le Testament du Dr Cordelier* is that dream come true, just as *Picnic on the Grass*, I'm willing to bet, arose from this simple visual idea: "Hey, wouldn't it be fun to show a windstorm in the country raising women's skirts?"[6]

This strange work expresses the anguish that Jean always felt when confronted with the phony moral rigor of the middle class. Although Jean sometimes praises hypocrisy with a twinkle in his eye, he does so ironically, and it allows him to play games with every type of equivocator, even to hold the opinion of his disconcerted adversary in a dispute; that has nothing to do with the behavior of Dr. Cordelier. The fantasy mined in this film is a difficult and dark one.

◆

[6] *Cahiers du cinéma*, 178, May 1966.

When he was shooting over a ten-day period in January of 1959, Jean had no idea that a time of sadness in his life was just beginning. He knew that Gabrielle was sick, but he tried not to think about what was going to happen. He was hoping to see her again, to hug her and make her laugh. At the end of *Cordelier*, before editing was over, Jean had to rehearse a ballet called *Le Feu aux poudres* (*Light the Powder Keg*); he had written its plot. Jean Serge had asked him to help since he had just been given the artistic direction of the Ludmilla Tcherina company. The show comprised a ballet by Raymond Rouleau, *Les Amants de Teruel* (*Teruel's Lovers*), with music by Mikis Theodorakis, another ballet, this one by Roger Pierre and Jean-Marc Thibault, and then Jean's, also to music of Theodorakis. The idea was "very Renoir," as Jean Serge put it: on a stage divided in two, there were revolutionaries on one side and totalitarians on the other. The rehearsals went well. They took place right next door to Jean, in the Théâtre Pigalle, which was soon to be demolished. Jean had high admiration for the amount of work that dancing required, Jean Serge told me. His old friend Jean Castanier was in charge of the sets. Despite the annoying presence of Ludmilla Tcherina, whom he couldn't stand, Jean was ready to continue, but he had to enter the hospital for a hernia operation that he had already postponed for a year despite the advice of his cousin, Maurice Renoir. Without telling him ahead of time, Tcherina changed the choreography and had a new set made. Castanier started legal proceedings against her, and Jean Renoir demanded that his name be taken off the program. On February 20, 1959, he wrote this to Gabrielle:

> The dumb girls of the corps de ballet were very nice, and so were the boys. The girls have brains as big as chick peas, and the boys are all gay, except the principal dancer of my ballet, a Serb from the mountains, who's as naive as a sheep, as lazy as a lizard, and as badly brushed and combed as a boar from his own country—but he's still a very beautiful dancer with a lot of nobility in his stance and poses. I haven't worked very hard at this ballet because I was shooting a little film at the same time. I'll tell you about it another time. And then, with Tcherina around, it's hard to do anything at all, except get mad, a prospect that horrifies me more and more. So I've decided to leave well enough alone. I'll learn something from it that will be useful in my next movie, which will have dancing in it.[7]

Gabrielle never read this letter, for she died on February 26, 1959. On February 27, Jean wrote:

[7] Letter provided by Jean Slade.

Dear Jeannot, We were expecting your telegram, but the certainty is harder to bear than the fear. What could I tell you that you don't already know?

I'll indulge myself in a practical supposition, which is that in the midst of the emptiness you feel you may want the company of people who also feel it but don't think it necessary to make a big deal about it. In this case, perhaps you could come to see us. You'd find something to keep you busy in the context of the film that I hope to make when the weather gets better.

And if you want to stay in our house on Leona Drive, you know that our house is your house.

A tender hug from us both.

The letter is also signed by Dido (ibid.). Gabrielle's death deeply distressed them. Dido says that even a quarter of a century later, she still misses her. Gabrielle and Jean merited one another. Every day for them was a rich and always different adventure.

She's the one who influenced me most of all. I owe to her the Punch and Judy and the Montmartre theater. I owe to her my understanding that the unreality of the show helps the study of real life. She taught me to see faces through masks, to track down the cowardice behind the excess. She gave me my horror of the cliché.

My farewell to the world of my childhood can be expressed in the words: "Wait for me, Gabrielle."[8]

That paragraph closes his book of memoires. Gabrielle was life, and life did not allow him to see her dead. This woman, who had linked her fate to that of the Renoirs, whose beauty was revealed by Auguste, and whose miraculous and sensitive intelligence was revealed by Jean, died on the Pacific coast in a house that she had built beside Jean's. She was buried in the frozen New England ground, where it is colder than the worst winters in Essoyes. She lies beside her husband, Conrad Slade, in the Mount Auburn Cemetery in Cambridge, with Henry James, his sister Alice, his brother William, the philosopher, and all the Boston Brahmins: the Cabots who speak only to the Lowells, and the Lowells who speak only to God. Gabrielle spoke to everyone, and everyone understood her, even though she refused to learn English.

◆

In another letter to Jean Slade dated March 6, Jean wrote: "Until her final sigh, Gabrielle had a genius for peaceful reality." He also said: "I

[8]Jean Renoir, *Ma vie et mes films*, 262.

start to get up, to take a couple of steps, and I sit down in a chair." According to Anne de Saint-Phalle, his being sick protected him somehow from the despair that his passionate nature would have brought him to.

As soon as he felt better, he had to take care of his film, which was causing problems. Renée Lichtig had finished editing it while Jean was attending the rehearsals of *Feu aux poudres,* but the film could not be distributed as had been planned. The theater owners refused to show it because it was a television coproduction, and they considered television their worst enemy. Pathé got scared. One more time, Ginette Doynel took on the fight. *Le Testament du Dr Cordelier* was screened at the Venice Festival in September of 1959, but the disputes went on for three years. Finally, there was an agreement between the Compagnie Jean Renoir and Sofirad to guarantee the film's distribution. Sofirad was allowed to collect the profits, and in fact it was the only television film that made money. It first appeared in the provinces, and then, on November 18, 1961, the evening when showings finally began in the theaters of Paris, it was also broadcast on television there. *Cordelier* was not as successful as *Grand Illusion* or *Rules of the Game* four years later, but that was no great surprise. In fact, Jean was used to it.

At first, he was disappointed that he had to wait to have this new film shown. But since there was nothing he could do, it was better to concentrate on the next one. Television and movies were still on his mind.

◆

Le Déjeuner sur l'herbe (*Picnic on the Grass*), like *Cordelier,* was conceived for both media. The Compagnie Jean Renoir was its sole producer, so the conflict he experienced with his first experiment of this kind could not arise. This film swallowed up all the money that the reruns of *Grand Illusion* had made him. He rewrote the screenplay several times. Most of the actors in the production had already worked with Jean, but he gave Catherine Rouvel her first chance. He had met her at the Cinémathèque on the rue d'Ulm one evening when they were showing *Louisiana Story.* She remembers the dark green coat and the white fur hat she was wearing. What struck Jean was her accent. She had recently arrived in Paris from the south of France with her husband, who was taking a job as a teacher in the experimental high school of Mongeron. Because of the contrast between her fur hat and her accent, which for him suggested warm weather and sunshine, he found her "a little 1900-ish." "Take some pictures of this young lady," he asked the photographers who were there because of him. She never saw Flaherty's film, but she got the role of her dreams.[9]

Jean left with Dido to scout locations around Cagnes, mainly at Les Collettes, the Renoir property where Claude and his family were still living. He was glad to go back to the countryside that he loved so well and that held so many memories for him of his father and Gabrielle. He spent a month lovingly picking out the most beautiful places to film. Then they took a lightning-fast trip to Berlin on June 29 and 30 to pick up a gold medal for his work as a whole at the West Berlin Festival. On returning, Jean rehearsed *Picnic on the Grass* for several weeks in Paris, at the Francoeur Studios. Then they all left for Nice. The actors were not at all disoriented in the yard at Les Collettes. Jean had reconnoitered the landscape so well that he had left nothing out. His marks were in the exact spot he said they were. Shooting lasted for twenty-one days over July and August. It was done scene by scene, with five cameras. Despite the use of such television methods, the film cost almost as much as one made in the regular way. Jean made it clear that he was not using television filming techniques for financial reasons but to create "a kind of poem on film." Giving in to "economic factors" had never been his style. Once again, he allowed himself to say what he wanted to say.

Before the film was released on October 17, it was the subject of one of Pierre Cardinal's programs called *Gros plan* (*Close-up*). "I believe that our function is, above all, to look at the world, to look at it and then to tell of it. Looking at the world the way it is, and trying especially hard to see it without putting colored lenses in front of our eyes. Because we are surrounded by colored lenses, the world is full of colored lenses. They go by different names: education, prejudices, all that people have told us, all the tall tales that our life is made up of. So! You have to get rid of all that stuff and see the world with naked eyes, with the purest vision. And then you tell about it, you tell the viewers, who are sometimes surprised, because they're not used to it. So they say, 'It ain't so!' And this function of ours, it has a name that was discovered by young people, by the young auteurs of our time, and I like it very much, it's a word which says exactly what it means. They call that 'demystification.'"[10]

Picnic on the Grass came out in Paris on November 11, 1959, and

[9]Jean Renoir, *Entretiens et propos* (Paris, 1979), 115.
[10]Cited by Pierre Leprohon, *Jean Renoir* (Paris, 1967), 121.

was a complete flop. The critics, and the public as well, were not ready for this defense of ecology—no one was using the word yet—and stories about artificial insemination didn't excite them either, and as for what Jean Renoir thought of Europe, they made fun of it. They were disconcerted as well by the technique, which seemed to muddle things. Years later, the film was rediscovered, but Jean by then had long ago stopped thinking about it. When it came out, he wasn't interested in it any more.

Jean was constantly writing synopses that he faithfully filed at the Screenwriters Guild. On August 19, 1959, he registered *Que deviendra cet enfant? (What Will Become of This Child?)*; on November 13, it was *Magnificat,* which he had already registered before on September 12, 1940. According to Claude Gauteur and Claude Beylie, there were also "historical" subjects: *Henri IV, le Vert galant (Henri IV, the Noble and Chivalrous King),* and *La Chanson de Roland.* He also wrote up and registered the outline of a little film fifteen minutes long that was made by Claude Labarre, *Le Voyage de Monsieur Quiou,* a film never shown commercially. It is the story of a postcard-style trip across France, in which "he retraces the invention of the magic lantern," as Claude Beylie puts it in his filmography.[11]

On December 30, 1959, Dido and Jean left Cherbourg for New York. Before going back to see Jeannot Slade, they stayed in New York for a few days after their arrival on January 4 to discuss the publication of *Renoir, My Father,* with McGraw-Hill. The French manuscript was far from complete at that point. When they finally got back home, to try to feel less deprived of Gabrielle, they concentrated on the book project. With Jeannot at her side, Dido listened to the conversations that Gabrielle and Jean had taped. They both noticed that Jean did more than his share of the talking. Jeannot worked with them just as his mother had. He knew lots of anecdotes from the time before he was born, since Gabrielle talked about it endlessly. So Dido typed the text that Jean dictated to her. It was the first time they had worked together, and the first time that he had written a book.

They were not about to leave Beverly Hills, where the sun shone every day. Being back in their own garden was a joy. Bessie Smith had taken care of it while they were away, and the dogs and the house had not suffered in their absence, thanks to her efforts. Their friends welcomed them. Meanwhile, Jean began thinking again about making a film of Knut Hamsun's *Hunger.*[12] He wanted Oskar Werner in the lead

[11] *L'Avant-Scène cinéma,* "Spécial Renoir," 251–52, July 1–15, 1980, 164.

[12] Jean Renoir, *Oeuvres de cinéma inédites,* ed. C. Gauteur (Paris, 1981), 259–89.

role, and Pierre Braunberger, who was interested in the idea, tried to put together a joint French-Scandinavian production. But it did not work.

On February 21, 1960, Jacques Becker died in Paris. For Jean, it was another big loss that brought back a whole era of his life.

Jacques knew very well that I was his accomplice as much as he was mine. He knew that his cinematographic puns would get a rise out of me, the warm kind of laugh that you get from in-jokes. For my part, I counted on his civilized laugh to punctuate my pomposities. In a little while I'm going to do a screening for some American students of *La Nuit du carrefour*, which sticks in my mind as the clearest witness of Jacques's complicity with me. What memories! I can see us racing at night in ungodly old cars at insane speeds. We had to find a roll of film for [Marcel] Lucien; he, too, has just died. Or maybe we were missing an indispensable accessory for Jean Gehret's rôle; him, too. . . . My brother Pierre had migrated from Jouvet country and was one of us. . . . My brother is gone as well. Time marches on.[13]

That's his precise and sensitive way of summing things up, all right. Life continued for him, on one continent or the other. Jacques Becker, with whom he exchanged letters that were tokens of tender and masculine affection, touching for their complete lucidity on both sides: Jacques Becker was no more. They knew each other so well that their misunderstandings left no scars. Jacques was the young man who listened to jazz with Catherine Hessling, and his pal from the days of Marguerite, whose good friend he had remained without losing his friendship with Jean; in 1945 he wrote to him: "According to the people who've gotten to know you in America, Dido has made you very happy, which makes me love her without ever having met her."[14] Marguerite Renoir, in his words "my closest collaborator," (ibid.), edited all of Jacques's films, including the last one, *Le Trou* (*The Hole*), which dates from 1959.

◆

A return to Catholicism and the discovery of Buddhism helped Jean Renoir accept the inevitable. But he still missed the conversations forever broken off, like his daily one with Gabrielle. That year, Dudley Nichols, his American Chevalier Bayard, was also going to disappear. They only saw each other rarely, but they meant a lot to each other even so. In his memoirs, Jean tells of another death that touched them

[13] *Cahiers du cinéma*, 106, April 1960, in Jean Renoir, *Ecrits*, 205.
[14] Letter dated May 8, 1945, Dido Renoir archive.

deeply, that of Clifford Odets; they followed him through all its stages, but the end did not take place until four years later.[15]

In November of 1960, John F. Kennedy, the young senator from Massachusetts whom Jean had met at the Waldorf, was elected president of the United States. After the disastrous landing of anti-Castro forces at the Bay of Pigs in the beginning of 1961 came the break between Cuba and the United States. That spring, Jean Renoir was invited to the University of California at Berkeley. He was the first occupant of a chair founded by the Council of Regents, having been selected for it by the English and Drama departments.

Jean was interested in being in contact with students. People were fascinated by the wealth of his experiences, his vast culture, and his easy manner with people. They were clearly ready to profit from all the information he could provide. Renoir aroused their curiosity and made them ask questions. There was still too much wonder in him for him not to be as enthusiastic about the experience as his students were. Pauline Kael, a Berkeley alumna who has since become one of the most respected film critics in the United States, at the time was tending a little movie hall where she and her husband, also a former Berkeley student, were showing old films, "a real flea pit," according to Alain Renoir, "patronized by the campus movie freaks, whose numbers increased after my father's appearance."

Jean Renoir gave a few seminars and, more importantly, he directed the play he had written in Paris in 1957 for Danielle Darrieux and Paul Meurisse, *Carole et les cabotins*. It was put on in English by the students. When he had just finished writing it, Jean said this to Jacques Rivette:

> It's as honest a look as possible at the conflicting feelings that people have when there's an occupier and an occupied. I can't exactly call it a sequel to *Grand Illusion*, but it's part of the same set of preoccupations, though after twenty years' time and space. I put Germans in it, I put Frenchmen, there are collaborators and resisters, and there are the people who don't have a clue. . . . The hardest part is to find a small framework; stories on a grand scale happen all the time, but a story that really holds together, that means something, and that's self-contained, that's not so easy! Well, I've done it, I've got my self-contained story. It lasts three hours, just enough time to put it on a stage, including intermissions, from 9 P.M. to midnight, in an actress's dressing room, in a theater. That's why I'm so happy.[16]

[15]Jean Renoir, *Ma vie et mes films*, 242–45.
[16]*Cahiers du cinéma*, 78, Christmas 1957, 54.

As he says elsewhere, the play's subject is also the "magic of theater and the magic of life." The distinction between reality and illusion becomes a pressing one. More than ten years after the end of the occupation, a period that Jean often tried to imagine, he takes some distance from it and sets forth what he sees beyond the behavior of the different groups of people. Once again, his father is not far away. Carola is an actress whose world is bounded by the theater. It is a world he knew well, as well as he knew its people, and the German general who falls in love with Carola resembles both his subordinates and the French whom they are oppressing. You've got to look more deeply, his father taught him, and get beyond the ideologies. In 1973, *Carola* was shown once in English on American TV with Leslie Caron and Mel Ferrer, directed by Norman Lloyd, one of Jean and Dido's best friends. Eventually, the text of the play was published in French but never produced in Paris, which is where they returned on May 16.[17]

◆

Alternating visits to Paris and California had become their habit, but it was always understood that their real home was in Beverly Hills. At avenue Frochot, they were camping out, and they never took a lot of trouble to fill in the gaps left by what they took away to give a past to the house that they built together. There was something of the nomad in each of them. Until disease made him a virtual invalid, Auguste Renoir loved to move in to one home or another and stay there for a certain amount of time in order to paint. Dido, a diplomat's daughter, was also used to change. This time, in France, where things were always pretty depressing because of the war in Algeria, Jean had two plans: he had been offered the possibility of filming a screen adaptation of Jacques Perret's novel, *Le Caporal épinglé* (*The Elusive Corporal*), and he also was thinking about a film with Leslie Caron, with the subject coming from his friend Rumer Godden's *Kingfishers Catch Fire.* In July he spent a week in Aberdeen discussing the possibility of a screenplay with her.

Le Caporal épinglé didn't tempt him because of the circumstances in which it was offered. The director Guy Lefranc, still a young man, had submitted his adaptation of the book to Madame de Carbuccia, a producer. She accepted it, but Pathé, which was supplying the guaranteed minimum and distributing the film, did not want it and asked Jean Renoir if he would be willing to make a film from the novel. It was a situation not much different from the one that arose between

[17] In *L'Avant-Scène théâtre*, 597, November 1, 1976, 7–44.

him and Jacques Becker around *The Crime of M. Lange*. Since Jean had no offers after *Picnic on the Grass*, and there was nothing happening with *Cordelier*, which had still not come out, he read the book. That really got him interested. As for Guy Lefranc, he knew him slightly because of *Knock*, with Louis Jouvet, made ten years earlier, and also *Une histoire d'amour* (*A History of Love*), Jouvet's latest. He ran into him in Rome, while making *The Golden Coach*. When the chips were down, Lefranc did not react the way Becker had. He agreed to be his partner and did not dream of questioning the revisions Jean wanted to make to the screenplay.

Perret's novel is an account of the attempted escape of three friends who had turned up in the same prison camp in June of 1940. Jean Renoir had no intention of doing a World War II version of *Grand Illusion*, and the film he had in mind was as distant from the story of Fresnay, Stroheim, and Gabin as it was from the work of Perret. For example, he suppressed the part of the novel that takes place in Berlin in 1943, when, in the same city, you could find prisoners of war, STO workers, and life under Hitler, which went on as well as it could. That Berlin was too far from what Jean had known, and he wanted nothing to do with it. From the beginning of the film, he condemned the triumph of the New Order by inserting newsreels that confirmed his own images and are a context for the series of vignettes that constitute the film. He had imagined the vignettes in black and white. François Truffaut told me that *Le Caporal épinglé* was a film that he loved more and more; it was a film that could not have been made by a person who had not made silent films. Each vignette is perfectly articulated; you are reminded of Mack Sennett as the film progresses.

When he was writing the screen version of *Le Caporal épinglé*, Jean was interviewed on film by Jacques Rivette. It was a long interview that took place in a little room in a café of the Buttes-Chaumont for a program jointly sponsored by the film service of the ORTF (French National Radio and Television) and the government research service. Janine Bazin was the associate producer,[18] and Jean Renoir says in it that he does not know if "the multiple camera technique" could be used. But he already knew that in this film he wanted "to try to get, at least in some scenes, a continuity that develops from the actor's expression, from his inner movement, instead of the continuity that is usually constructed artificially in the editing room."

On October 3, 1961, Jean and Dido left for Vienna with the film team. But after being there for ten days, Dido had to return to Los

---

[18]"Jean Renoir vous parle," in Jean Renoir, *Entretiens et propos*, 93.

Angeles. Bessie Smith was sick and wanted to go back to England. After her departure, Dido had to stay there to take care of the dogs and the garden. For part of the winter, Jean was alone in Vienna, where the film was shot both outdoors and in the studio. The cold tired him, but as always, the work bucked him up. He loved being in Vienna, a city that was too big and as sad as ever. But the spirit and warmth of the group working together balanced out the cold, the sad, and the gray.

While making this film, he set aside the techniques of the two previous ones and went back to the way he had directed actors before *Cordelier.* Later, he said the following of the way he had gone about making it and *Picnic on the Grass* (from another interview with Jacques Rivette):

> It (the filming procedure) is practical. It lets you shoot with a certain security, it keeps you from spending too much money, from going over budget, from not shooting the number of shots you'd planned for a day; but, in my opinion, it destroys something that's really important: the actor's surprise in response to his setting, and I think that surprise is very interesting and that the actor should assimilate himself to his surroundings without the intermediacy of a director who has made little chalk marks all over the ground.[19]

Jean pushed his experiments to their limits, but he never was stubborn. He inherited a judicious openmindedness about such things, a rare quality that great artists seem to have.

One of his dreams was to make a series of short films, one with Simone Signoret, another with Paul Meurisse, which would make up a whole called *C'est la révolution* (*It's the Revolution*). He finished the manuscript of the book on his father. *Renoir par Jean Renoir* was published in Paris at the end of 1962. He entrusted its translation to a couple of British friends whom he had known in the old days at Cagnes. In April 1962, he spent two weeks in London with Anne de Saint-Phalle (Ginette Doynel) polishing up the result. Collins, the British publisher, was pressuring him, so they worked fifteen hours a day with help from A. J. Cronin's son. From London, he left for the United States and Dido without waiting for his film to come out on May 23.

It was an immediate success with the public and the critics as well. But without asking his permission, they had cut parts of the newsreels he had inserted, which were intended to set the political

[19] "Jean Renoir le patron," May–June 1966, in Jean Renoir, *Entretiens et propos*, 115.

context of the story of the escapees. Jean Renoir registered his protest in *France-Soir* on May 28.[20] By this time, Jean felt no discontinuity between his life in Beverly Hills and the one he led in Paris. *The Elusive Corporal* was chosen for the Berlin Film Festival of 1962 and was presented at the inaugural session of the London Film Festival on October 16.

◆

Despite his film's success and the ease in going back and forth between two continents, the years that followed were among the darkest of Jean Renoir's life. At his age, his professional life was more important than anything else. He was nearing seventy. In fine shape, he felt capable of making plenty of movies that were as innovative for their time as the ones he had made until then. Which is where the problem lay: producers are afraid of newness. He knew it well, he had often said so himself in the past. But he never accepted it. He could not stop creating, and more than before, he felt that time was pressing.

He would abandon one project for another if it seemed to him more likely to succeed. Sometimes he went in reverse and recouped an abandoned idea if it seemed too good to leave behind. In 1962, he wrote another screen version of *Hunger*, this one called *Vladjali*. In 1967, he also went back to a screenplay based on the life of Van Gogh. "I'll concentrate on his beginnings, on the drama at Arles and his meeting with Gauguin."[21] He was more oriented toward French producers, but he had not given up hope of finding a way of financing a film in America, too.

Welcome encouragement came from some new friends who were to play an important role in his life in California. In 1961, he met a young man, Brother Basil, a novice in a Benedictine monastery who was a student at Loyola University in Los Angeles. He wanted to put on some of Jean's films there the following year. Brother Basil was Greek by birth and a movie fanatic who only knew "the American Renoir." He found the director "very accessible" and went to see him at Leona Drive. He decided to show *Rules of the Game* and *Grand Illusion* at his university's film festival, where "they were a huge success." Jean Renoir, who was present, expressed his wish to go to St. An-

[20] André Bazin, *Jean Renoir* (Paris, 1971), 278.
[21] "Lettres françaises," November 8, 1967, cited by Claude Beylie in "Spécial Renoir," 168.

drew's Benedictine Monastery at Vallermo, to which Brother Basil belonged. Most of the monks came from Bruges, and their monastery had been in China, from which they were expelled by the Maoist revolution. So they withdrew to this village in the Mojave Desert, where they founded a little monastery that resembled the one they had been forced to leave.

Dido and Jean went up to the monastery in the fall of 1962. The foliage of the cottonwood trees was bright yellow. They spent the whole day with the monks, and immediately became good friends. In 1965, Brother Basil felt the need to resume secular life. He became Nicholas Frangakis, but he remained friendly with the monks and also with Jean and Dido. Jean Renoir's recommendation got him into UCLA, where he learned directing and began to make movies. Starting in 1963, the monks, who sponsored a festival of sculpture and the other plastic arts, asked Jean to be the head of the selection committee. The works to select were mainly by artists from Los Angeles and southern California, and they were exhibited at the home of Bernard Hilton, who had a house on the beach at Santa Monica; two years later, they were exhibited at the home of Marguerite Staudi, a Hollywood sculptress.

In those days, Jean Renoir met often with Peter Bogdanovitch, Robert Aldrich (who had been his assistant for *The Southerner*), Colin Young, who was head of the film department at UCLA and who became director of the British Film Institute, Philip Chamberlain, the film curator of the Los Angeles County Museum of Art who later organized a big Jean Renoir retrospective, as well as John Houseman and Fritz Lang. He was a popular man. But he had to keep going back and forth between Hollywood and Paris in the search for a backer who would give him the chance to express himself once more. He could not get used to the silence that writing meant for him. He was too used to working with actors, a whole team of people, he needed conversation, he needed to impose his view of the world on other people, he needed to see an actor transform himself right before his eyes and become the person he imagined him to be. The film director works with the human material as much as with the camera and the film. As for a painter, the activity has a physical side to it, whereas the world of words is something completely different. Jean Renoir knew it, since he was clearly gifted in that domain as well.

When *Renoir par Jean Renoir* appeared in Paris at the end of 1962, it was well received, but it did not gain the attention it deserved. It is a powerful book and a marvellous one. You do not forget it, and you come to know both the father and the son. Perhaps it, too, was ahead of its time in terms of its richness and simplicity, as were the other works of father and son. Autobiography involved less research then than it does now. Jean Renoir was not worried about it, and he was hardly amazed for the opposite reason when the English translation became a best-seller in the United States. His old trade was still his major, not to say his only, preoccupation. According to Claude Gauteur, "At the request of the producer of *The Elusive Corporal*, Renoir had also outlined a film version of Vladimir Pozner's *Le Lever du rideau* [*The Curtain Rises*]; he had Leslie Caron and Vittorio Gassman in mind to star in it." [22] He also had two projects in mind for Jeanne Moreau, whose bearing, face, and voice appealed to him. Nor had he forgotten the short called *La Duchesse* that he wanted to make with Simone Signoret. Unlike producers, actresses had confidence in him. They knew that Jean Renoir could elicit the best they had to offer: people in the profession had realized that long ago. When Simone Signoret went to Hollywood to film *The Ship of Fools*, directed by Stanley Kramer, she dropped in at Leona Drive every evening, "when the grind was over," to drink her scotch. She could be the grouchiest person, but she also could transform herself into the warmest and funniest of friends, just waiting to tell stories. Like Jean, she enjoyed discussing anything and everything, being outraged or charmed just for the fun of talking about it.

◆

In the United States no less than in France, Jean's reputation kept on growing among young people. On April 4, 1963, he received an honorary doctorate from the University of California at Berkeley. In 1965, he was invited to give a Spencer lecture at Harvard University. People in Cambridge at the time still remember it as an emotional experience. He spoke with such passion and sincerity that it brought tears to the eyes of even the most sophisticated.

When Dido and Jean stopped in Boston for that lecture, they were on their way to Paris, where Jean was taking to Gaston Gallimard, the producer of *Madame Bovary* whose father had been a friend of Auguste Renoir, the manuscript of his first novel, *Les Cahiers du capitaine Georges* (*The Notebooks of Captain Georges*). It is a strange book, written in a very restrained style, that tells of the wild love of a young middle-class man for a little prostitute. The theme of the fatal love affair recurs in several novels and in some of the screenplays that

---

[22] Jean Renoir, *Oeuvres inédites*, 25.

were never filmed as well. *Orvet* has it as well, but there it comes directly from "The Little Mermaid." A young, lower-class girl is exploited by a rich man. He loves her in his way, and she loves him, but she pays with her life for his capriciousness, which he understands too late. "A new episode in an old story," as he says himself, "that I will never finish and all of whose secrets I'll never succeed in revealing. Because for me this story remains mysterious, and that's exactly what makes it interesting."[23]

Probably because of all his father's talk about "frogs," and also because of the models, who seemed so free and happy, as a young man of the world Jean only had to do with women not of his own class. Without wanting to and even without realizing it, he treated them harshly although he thought they were as strong, not to say as indestructible, as he was. Jean never spoke directly about the amorous exploits of his youth. He always was totally reserved about that, but his stories all have an autobiographical element to them and all go back to the same "sin" committed by an inability to imagine the real needs of another. Until his relationship with Dido, there seem to have always been misunderstandings between Jean and women. The ecstasy and happiness never lasted. Their differences were so great that the unspoken became the unbearable.

His discovery of Dido dates from the time of *Rules of the Game*, the film which, according to François Truffaut, was "the great watershed in the love life and the career of Jean Renoir." In 1965, the film was revived in its original, complete version, the one that had been presented at the Venice Festival in 1959. Its public premier and commercial distribution began in April, and, finally, the film was a hit. When it came out in the movie theaters of Paris, Jean and Dido had already gone back to Los Angeles, having left on March 31 after three days in London visiting with Rumer Godden. Also in 1965, Jean registered a film project called *La Mort satisfaite* (*Death's Due*).[24] In addition, Pierre Braunberger was poised to produce the film composed of five sketches that Jean called *C'est la révolution*.

◆

The year 1966 did not spare them grief and disappointment. Dido's mother died in England on January 29, while they were in Beverly

[23] *Français de notre temps, Hommes d'aujourd'hui*, No. 52, 33 rpm recording (serial no. b51 FT 66), cited in his preface by Claude Gauteur, ed., *Julienne et son amour* (Paris, 1979); 16.

[24] Jean Renoir, *Oeuvres inédites*, 291–327.

Hills. In the spring, Jean went to Paris alone to attend the opening of the Jean Renoir Cinema, an art film house at 43, boulevard de Clichy, his old stomping grounds. Seven of his films were shown to open the theater: *Boudu, Toni, The Crime of M. Lange, French Cancan, Eléna et les hommes, Le Testament du Dr Cordelier*, and *Picnic on the Grass*. *Les Cahiers du capitaine Georges* came out at the end of April. In May and June, he did three programs for French television, each one an hour long. They were combined and shown as "Renoir le patron" ("Renoir, the Boss") in a series called *Cinéastes de notre temps* (*Filmmakers of Our Day*) by Janine Bazin and André S. Labarthe. Jacques Rivette was the director and interviewer. They shot these pieces in several spots around Paris, at Essoyes, and in Sologne. Janine Bazin told me that as she listened to Jacques Rivette and Jean Renoir singing together after dinner at the inn in La Motte-Beuvron, where they had gone to film a section about *Rules of the Game*, she suddenly got a sense of the happy atmosphere in which Jean and his friends used to work.

Jean was working on two new outlines: one was a very free version of Edgar Allen Poe's novella, "The System of Doctor Goudron and Professor Plume," which was supposed to be part of the film *Histoires Extraordinaires* (*Spirits of the Dead*) made in 1967 by Roger Vadim, Louis Malle, and Federico Fellini (ibid., pp. 329–30); the other was *Apollon et Alexandra* (*Apollo and Alexandra*), in which he wanted to "make much use of current events" (ibid., pp. 337–40). Ultimately, these pages stayed in their drawers. He was getting ready to go to London to check the translation of *Cahiers du capitaine Georges* when he learned that the Committee on Advances on Receipts of the National Cinematography Center had refused Braunberger's request of an advance of one million francs [$300,000], the estimated budget of the whole film being three million.[25] The newspapers cried foul. Henri Chapier, in *Combat,* launched a polemic: "While the greatest French film director was busy thinking about shooting his newest film, the Committee on Advances on Receipts abruptly informed him, without any explanation, of its refusal. In other words, the only official French entity that today ensures the survival of French films has made a decision against a project that concerns a French director whom the whole world envies. Given the stupidity of this attitude, Renoir should decide to leave France permanently for the U.S., from where we have, however, begged him to return after the triumph of his revivals, especially *Rules of the Game*."[26] A few days later, Chapier

[25] According to Claude Gauteur, in Jean Renoir, *Oeuvres inédites*, 341.
[26] *Combat*, August 1, 1966.

has this headline: "The Renoir Affair: Scandal or Sinister Machinations?" followed by citations of insults addressed to him.[27] Finally came the "official" response from the director of the committee: "Just because I love and admire Renoir, do I have to consider him infallible?"[28] and it goes on to state that the script did not please the committee. It could not be the point of departure of a good film, so they did not fund it. Pierre Braunberger disapproved of that, but he could not consider financing the project without the help of the Committee on Advances on Receipts.

Jean Renoir left on August 3 for Los Angeles, not for the reasons given by Chapier, but still a disappointed man. As always, though, he bounced back and explained dispassionately why he should be the one to run up against that kind of incomprehension. "I can only reveal the true meaning of a subject in the excitement engendered by working with actors and technicians. I can only give shape to what I produce after discovering the quality of the material I'm working on. I'd be wrong to have it in for people who prefer having to do with filmmakers who are less interested in last-minute discoveries. . . . I think competition with TV is inciting producers to support projects that are more and more de luxe. In America, successful films cost millions of dollars to make; that means that the greatest prudence holds sway over their fabrication, and that they must rest on fixed and precise screenplays, which I am incapable of doing. It will probably be marginal production of amateur films that will keep moviemaking in the experimental stage that it needs to have in order to exist."[29]

♦

People everywhere were telling him he was the greatest, but they wouldn't let him work. And the years were going by more quickly than before. He was seventy-two years old, and there was a lot left for him to do. The impossibility of getting money paralyzed him. Seeing the situation as it was didn't make it any less painful.

He went to Paris that spring to supervise a new editing of *La Marseillaise;* he had bought back the rights to it in 1960. But the prints at their disposal were unusable. Since

> Jean Renoir really wanted to recut the film in its entirety, we set out to find prints whose quality was good for certain shots in order to consti-

[27] *Combat,* August 6/7, 1966.
[28] *Combat,* August 9, 1966.
[29] *L'Ecran lorrain,* 232, October 1966, cited by Claude Gauteur in Jean Renoir, *Julienne et son amour,* 15.

tute a complete negative. The positive that was made from it wasn't adequate because some shots were scratched and their sound feeble. At that point I realized there was a good chance that the USSR had a negative. So I wrote to the Ministry of Culture to explain that the Compagnie Jean Renoir, which had purchased the rights to the film and wanted to reissue it, asked if they would be willing to lend them their versions, which they did. In fact, what they sent us enabled us to make a negative from which current prints are made.[30]

That was also the film that Jean revised himself and that was shown in theaters on October 27, 1967.

He showed it before that date in Montreal, where he attended the World's Fair from August 7 to 13. While Charles de Gaulle was going around saying, "Vive le Québec libre!" Jean Renoir was head of the film jury at the fair. From his home in Beverly Hills, he gave an interview to *Cahiers du cinéma* in which he tackled the problems of low-budget films and of television. "Movies should be imperfect, should contain surprises, and should stimulate others to new discoveries. Several of the greatest works of art were created by unknowns, but today anonymity is no virtue, since mass culture is threatening to strangle the individual." He also said: "A few years ago, I believed that television had more to do with contemporary life than film. Now I believe it less. I don't know, television has remained and probably always will remain a means of transmitting information and nothing else."[31] That year, *Boudu Saved from Drowning* was shown commercially for the first time in the United States.

At the beginning of 1968, Jean Renoir was in Paris again. From January 17 to 31, at the communal theater of Aubervilliers, the following films were shown: *La Bête humaine, Grand Illusion, A Day in the Country, Tire au flanc, Le Testament du Dr Cordelier, The Golden Coach,* and *Rules of the Game.* François Truffaut wrote a kind of introduction to them: "It all looks as though Jean Renoir spent most of his time avoiding what a masterpiece could offer in terms of fixity and definitiveness in favor of half-improvised work that is deliciously incomplete and 'open,' so that each viewer can complete it as he or she wishes, pulling it one way or another."[32]

Jean Renoir took advantage of his stay this time to make a short film with Gisèle Braunberger, the young wife of his friend Pierre,

[30] Letter of Anne de Saint-Phalle to the author, September 26, 1984.
[31] *Cahiers du cinéma,* 191, June 1867, 9–10.
[32] *Le Monde,* January 18, 1968.

called *La Direction d'acteur par Jean Renoir* [*How Jean Renoir Directs Actors*]. It took him four and a half hours to make this twenty-minute movie in which a student acts out a scene from a novel by Rumer Godden called *Breakfast with the Nicolaides*. The film shows how he got the most out of actors by getting them to value themselves, which he did with irresistible grace and charm. He also wrote some blurbs and prefaces for exhibitions of his father's artwork. In 1968, there were two of them: first "Intimate Renoir," at the Durand-Ruel gallery. What memories! Paul Durand-Ruel was a friend of the Renoir family, and one of his sons, Georges, was Jean's godfather. The other show was simply called "Renoir and his Friends." [33] Jean started writing a second novel and did a series of television sketches.

◆

On February 9, the Langlois scandal broke. With the help of Georges Franju, a set designer who had become a director of short films, Henri Langlois had founded the Cinémathèque française in October 1936. He had remained its artistic director. A film historian and, above all, a fanatic collector, he had with the smallest of means managed to gather up and preserve prints of films from all countries that would have been lost forever without him. He saved them from the Nazis and from the neglect of both film studios and film professionals. This man, with his gray face and rumpled clothes, always gave the impression of being both extraordinarily smart and completely paranoid. He plainly had an immense knowledge of movies. For film professionals and fans, Henri Langlois was the soul of the Cinémathèque, a special and very strange place where, thanks to him, you could make amazing and often unexpected discoveries, because most of the time, the programs that had been announced were not followed!

Such an exceptional person could only arouse jealousy among the bureaucrats who could not even come close to him in abilities and intellect. He had a tendency to believe that he was the object of plots and persecution. People did not pay much attention to his tales, which were pretty unclear anyhow. But suddenly, although Malraux, then Minister of Cultural Affairs, was his natural protector, Langlois was fired and replaced. It was scandalous. The next day, forty filmmakers (among them, Renoir, Bresson, Gance, Truffaut, Resnais, Godard, Franju, Marker, Astruc, Chabrol, and so on) boycotted the Cinémathèque under its new director and forbade it to show their

---

[33] Jean Renoir, *Ecrits*, 29–31.

films. The press was also on Langlois's side. Messages of support came from abroad, and the offices of *Cahiers du cinéma* became headquarters for a petition that called for "all the friends of film to join in solidarity with any event that might thwart the arbitrary decision that has victimized Henri Langlois." Feeling was unanimous among young and old, left and right, directors, technicians, actors, artists, writers, and intellectuals in France and abroad. Everyone signed petitions, and demonstrations started. There were encounters with police that foreshadowed what would happen later that year in the month of May.

Jean Renoir remembered that in 1955, in the film museum on the avenue de Messine, there was an "Homage to Jean Renoir" organized by Henri Langlois. He accepted the honorary presidency of the Committee for the Defense of the Cinémathèque française, of which Alain Resnais was president. He took part in a press conference on February 16, one week after the story broke. In his words, "The Cinémathèque would not exist without Langlois" and "if it weren't for the Cinémathèque, there would be no focus for the struggle against the horrors of commercial filmmaking. The farther things go, the more we have two kinds of cinema: we have the one that makes a lot of money and that, shall we say, stupefies the public with the most ordinary pap. Then there are the people who try to do something that's a little better. For the people trying to do a little better, the Cinémathèque was a focal point, a rallying symbol. That's all I have to say."[34] The statement is in character, for he took advantage of the situation to utter a profession of faith. He was not just with young disciples who shared his views, but also with friends like Michel Simon or Simone Signoret and Yves Montand. "The Langlois affair is just another episode in the long, open conflict between democracy and administrative technocracy," in the words of Pierre Mendès-France.[35] In view of the administrative embarrassment, it soon became clear that Langlois would be reinstated.

While all this was going on, Jean Renoir was hoping to make a movie with Jeanne Moreau called *Julienne et son amour*. "I'd like to do *Julienne et son amour* in the style of Bonnard or Debussy," he told a newspaper reporter.[36] He had given up on his first project with Jeanne Moreau, the story of a female tramp called *En avant, Rosalie!*

[34] *Cahiers du cinéma*, 199, March 1968, 34.

[35] Statement made in Grenoble, March 21, 1968, *Cahiers du cinéma*, 200–201, May–June 1968, 62.

[36] *Le Figaro*, January 13, 1968, cited in Jean Renoir, *Julienne et son amour* (Paris, 1979), 12.

There are just a few pages left of this fantasy. No one knows why he gave it up for the other one. Dido herself could not remember. There were so many derailments over the years! Perhaps it would have been "a kind of spoken opera interspersed with a few songs, in a romantic-realist style," he wrote.[37]

♦

The events of May 1968 and the disturbances that followed put a halt to activity in the film studios—as they did to all other activities in France—and postponed shooting indefinitely. Jean Renoir left for California, a discouraged man. From now on, there was no point in stopping in New York on the way home: their dear friend, Al Lewin, had also died. That added to Jean's already low morale. Talking with this man, who was so cultivated and who loved what he loved, had often been a consolation for Jean. "At the moment, I don't know if I'll ever make another movie, which I regret, since I still have things to say," he said to Alexander Sesonske, who interviewed him that summer in Beverly Hills.[38] Nothing could satisfy him except making films, which was his life. The time for honors had come, but they meant nothing to him. He got respect and admiration everywhere. Dartmouth College in New Hampshire put on a Renoir film series; in August, he and Dido left for Venice, where, under the auspices of the festival, seventeen of the films he made between 1924 and 1939 were to be shown in a retrospective.

However, in that year of student revolts, contradictory rumors were rife, and no one knew until the last moment whether or not the festival would actually take place. In the end, everything went well. Jean got a medal and, most importantly, was reunited with his Italian friends, such as Giulio and Adèle Macchi, in that country he loved so well. He also got to see Pasolini's *Theorema*, which he was curious about.

He complained that he could not find himself a producer, and so Giulio Macchi arranged for RAI (Italian National Radio and Television) and French Television to coproduce some sketches Jean had written. He made a selection from them that in theory were to be filmed in Rome. Jean clung to this hope, which was the only one he had, as he was well aware. Before leaving for Venice, in the interview with Sesonske he was still pretending to believe that he would shoot

[37] Jean Renoir, *Julienne et son amour*, 147.
[38] *Cinema* (U.S.), 6, 1, 17–20.

Julienne et son amour that October. He spoke of the technicians he wanted to have with him: his nephew Claude as cameraman, and "for the sound, my old friend Jo de Bretagne." He also spoke about color film, which is "more commercial than black and white," and said he was forced to shoot an English and a French version although he was opposed to it on principle.

After the Venice Festival, Jean and Dido went to Paris. As usual, their young friends surrounded them and greeted them warmly. Jean's stature with the public was well known, and he was chosen to introduce Orson Welles' latest film, *An Immortal Story*, on TV. He did so in his usual offhand way. He spoke evocatively of the world of Orson Welles:

> A world in which people have special faces, walk in a certain way, move around in a certain way, are illuminated in a certain way, and, especially this, use props and sets that are not everyone's props and sets. They are Orson Welles's props and sets. I believe it is the mark of genius to create a little world like that, in which you make your characters act, and those characters are more or less yourself. In Orson Welles' case, it's flagrant; an Orson Welles film is a little like a self-portrait.[39]

As he knew well, the same was true for him and his films. He said as much elsewhere: ultimately, a painter only paints one picture, a director makes one film. He may feel ready to make many other films that will always be his one film. In fact, he had a precise project involving Jeanne Moreau, the lead in *An Immortal Story*. What he said so lightheartedly about Orson Welles on TV must have cost him some pain, since it reflected his own situation.

◆

The purpose of their trip to Paris was not funny either. It was because of a lawsuit brought by Richard Guino against the Renoir estate. On the recommendation of Maillol in 1916, Guino had worked at Cagnes under the direction of Auguste Renoir. On his own, Auguste had also sculpted a bust of Coco, his youngest son (Claude), in particular, but the state of his hands prevented him from working the clay, and Guino's help was precious to him. In the fifty years since then, Guino had authenticated the casts of twelve statues as being Renoirs, but he had also kept some plaster casts that the master himself had rejected and that he should have destroyed or restored to Auguste's heirs when the painter died. In 1959, he sold these flawed casts to an American who was sure that he could get authorization to make

[39] Dido Renoir archive.

copies. Understandably, Jean and Claude Renoir refused to grant it. This American, a Mr. Bond, made threats to Guino, to whom he had paid ten million old francs ($20,000). A son of his, Michel Guino, started a press campaign to prove that his father had been more than a practitioner, and he had a letter from Pierre Renoir that mentioned him working with Auguste. The Renoirs lost the suit; the court allowed the statues to be signed Guino-Renoir. Some casts were redone, and it will be a long time before those statues are in the public domain.

Dido went back to Los Angeles: Bessie Smith was no longer there to take care of the garden. She had remained in England ever since she had become ill. Dido's intuition was that Jean had nothing to hope for; she wanted to bring him home, where life was less tiring for him and where he would have an easier time accepting, so she thought, that the time had come to do something else. Writing seemed to her to be his salvation. She believed it more and more. But Jean still wanted to try his hand: he felt he shouldn't leave Paris, that he should stay and fight.

The disappointment of the lawsuit, on top of the disappointments already inflicted upon him by producers, left scars. François Truffaut told me that at the end of 1968, when he saw his friend arriving for the first time by car and not on foot—they were going together to have lunch at Jeanne Moreau's house—he was suddenly struck with the feeling that he had grown old. For the first time he thought to himself, "But he's seventy-four!" Jeanne Moreau hadn't given up hope of making *Julienne*. She had confidence in him; their friends at *Cahiers* encouraged them both. It would be a film as strong as *Grand Illusion*, with all the charm of the world before World War I. Jeanne Moreau would be fantastic in that extraordinarily poetic setting. Jean Renoir loved the story of the young prostitute who gets kidnapped from her brothel by a rich young man because he is an insomniac who can only fall asleep by her side. She loves him and pays the price with her life when he gets tired of her and leaves. Jean let himself get carried away by the enthusiasm of his friends, but underneath he wasn't so sure. He soon learned that the producers thought Jeanne Moreau was too old, too. . . . There is no way you can talk with people like that! And they are the same everywhere, in France or the United States.

On December 19, he wrote to Jean Slade:

I miss you very much. More so, since my stay in Paris has been getting longer. I think I'm going to make the TV film that Dido must have talked to you about. If I see that the end of my labors is way off in the distance, I'll jump on a plane to join you at Leona Drive. Best wishes for the New Year. I hear that you're spending Christmas with Dido. I wish I were there with you. All my love.

With Guilio Macchi's help, he was concentrating on the sketches for TV; some he revised, and he added others, like "The Little Apple." [40]

In February 1969, the Los Angeles County Museum of Art put on the largest retrospective of the work of Jean Renoir ever seen in the United States. Philip Chamberlain, curator of the film department of the museum, was in contact with Langlois and the Cinémathèque. He had started with a series called "The Treasures of the Cinémathèque" that was a big success in November 1968. The Renoir retrospective was attended by a lot of friends. Dido was at the premier, accompanied by Nicholas Frangakis. Jean wrote to him afterwards to thank him and said: "I'm very busy getting my TV show ready, and I hope that in the fall I'll be able to shoot my film, *Julienne.*" [41] He was still in Paris, wavering between hope and disappointment. Henri Langlois was preparing to show some excerpts from his films at the Cannes Festival. Since it was also the fiftieth anniversary of the death of Renoir the painter, the festival issued a small volume with the portrait of Mademoiselle Diéterlé on the cover. Jean wrote a short blurb for the volume that describes the superb Mademoiselle Diéterlé at the time. He also speaks of his memories of Cannes, "of the beautiful women I used to watch in the summertime, riding around on the Croisette in victorias." [42]

On March 31, he went back to Beverly Hills, but not for long. To get his mind off things, he agreed to play himself in a short called *The Christian Licorice Store*, directed by James Frawley. The movie wasn't distributed commercially, and in fact no one knows if it was ever really completed. Meanwhile, Jean had to prepare his film for French and Italian television, and he wanted to try to sell *Julienne* one more time. So he left again, with Dido, on April 24. But the following month, Dido returned to Beverly Hills.

◆

Finally, the film had a title: *Le Petit Théâtre de Jean Renoir*, and it was clear which sketches it would consist of: *Le Dernier Reveillon (The Last*

---

[40] Jean Renoir, *Oeuvres inédites*, 399–408.
[41] Letter dated February 26, 1969, provided by Nicholas Frangakis.
[42] Jean Renoir, *Ecrits*, 31–32.

Christmas Eve Party), a story that Alain told him; *La Cireuse électrique* (*The Electric Floorpolisher*), a tale that makes use of Grandmother Charigot's obsession with cleaning floors; and *Le Roi d'Yvetot* (*The King of Yvetot*), a ménage à trois in Provence in which each of the lovers is happy. The director himself introduces each sketch standing next to a miniature theater, where the scenes are supposed to unfold. After *La Cireuse électrique*, Jeanne Moreau stands in front of a painted scrim on an empty caf'conc' stage and sings the 1900 waltz entitled "Quand l'amour meurt" ("When Love Dies"), which Marlene Dietrich used to hum in New York during the war.

Taken up with the preparations for this film, Jean Renoir could not attend the presentation of his films at Cannes. On May 20, he sent a message expressing his regrets:

> I am very happy to know that Henri Langlois has decided to present some excerpts from my films at the Cannes Festival this year. I am all the more pleased in that I am in the midst of resuming my cinematic activities and that his overview of my work helps give me my bearings (ibid., p. 218).

Shooting *Le Petit Théâtre de Jean Renoir* took longer than expected. They started in June and were not done until September, a few days before the author's seventy-fifth birthday.

Jean Renoir shot the film near Versailles, in an apartment that consisted of five small rooms in high seventeenth-century style. The windows were kept closed because of the noise, and that summer the heat was suffocating. "He was still in great shape," as Anne de Saint-Phalle told me. "After working all day long, he'd suggest that we take a look at the day's work that night." When they were filming exteriors at Saint-Rémy-de-Provence and on the outskirts of Aix, he was always there to look at the rushes at night, after days when the heat was unbearable. And he would have liked to do the editing right on the spot. Françoise Arnoul's memories of filming in the south of France echo Anne de Saint-Phalle's, but she insists that Jean's leg was giving him a lot of trouble. He went out rarely, except to shoot. Everyone was lodged in Saint-Rémy, and they all met for breakfast in the morning before going to the spot they had decided on the night before. Françoise Arnoul and Jean Carmet used to tell everyone what they had done the night before, a dinner at Avignon, say. It reminded Jean of Gabrielle. "When I was little, one day I went out for a walk with Gabrielle on the Pont d'Avignon. Since the mistral was blowing, Gabrielle put her arms around me and held me to her tightly to protect me from the wind." Françoise Arnoul also said: "We tried to find ways to force him to sit down during the day. We had to be tricky! His energy amazed us all."

He had to go to Rome to negotiate with the agents of the RAI (Italian National Radio and Television). In an interview he gave to the correspondent of *La Tribune de Genève*, he still maintained that he was preparing a film called *Julienne et son amour*. But one month later, on October 8, he let it be known that he had not found anyone to finance his project, whose "estimated budget" had risen to about six million francs.[43]

Jean's brother Claude had just died at Cagnes, where he was still living, although Les Collettes no longer belonged to him. The town had purchased the estate. He was buried at Essoyes, alongside his mother, who loved him so, and his brother Pierre. Jean attended the funeral. He saw all the townspeople again; they were almost his relatives. He promised them he would come back, which he wanted very much to do, but would he? In the time since he had been returning more often to France, he made only short stops at Essoyes, once to bring Dido there, another time, without her, to get some documents about a story that he was thinking of writing. He never forgot his childhood friends. During the war and thereafter, he kept up a correspondance with the Suriot family, their daughter Ginette Guénin, and Louise Chevalier. But the town had no place in the life he was then leading, between two worlds. He never had time to rest, as his old friends from the town suggested he do.

Jean was tired. He was eager to finish editing *Le Petit Théâtre de Jean Renoir*. As soon as he finished the job, he went home to Dido. That November, *La vie est à nous*, which had never been shown in a commercial theater since it had never received a censor's visa, was finally screened and was very well received. It was certain, if anyone still doubted it, that this work had finally found an echo. But Jean was not about to wait around for the revival of this film, which had been shot at a time that now seemed distant indeed. He left Paris on October 26 without knowing it was his last visit.

[43] Jean Renoir, *Julienne et son amour*, 13.

THE FRENCHMAN

OF BEVERLY HILLS

♦

T ill now, I've been preoccupied with my checkup. I had it at the
Scripps Clinic in La Jolla, about 120 miles away. They looked me
over inside and out and said I needed a rest. So I'm going to rest, and
then I hope I'll be able to walk as usual." Jean wrote these words
about a month after coming back from Paris.[1] He did not take care of
himself during the shooting of *Le Petit Théâtre*. In his joy at being able
to work, he went too far without realizing it. "He had even consid
ered himself for the role of the King of Yvetot, which eventually went
to Fernand Sardou," as Dido Renoir recalled. Show business was his
passion: acting, getting others to act, making up stories and telling
them to an audience, telling people what he thought and what he believed, what he had learned in life by watching other people, but say
ing it without delivering a message, almost without people knowing
that he was saying it. When his father painted a rose, he was not
aware that his rose portrayed himself as clearly as a self-portrait. But
Gabrielle understood that. In a word, Jean Renoir was not ready to
quit just yet.

He had not forgotten the film with Jeanne Moreau. "I'm thinking
of the two songs that Jeanne asked me for," he wrote in the same letter to François Truffaut. And in another letter, one year later, "When
you see Jeanne Moreau, tell her how much my wife and I are de-

[1] Letter dated November 22, 1969, provided by François Truffaut.

lighted to know her. She has a genuineness that's pretty rare in the history of relations between human beings; almost all people wear masks, but not her." Then he adds: "We're hoping to see you and her this summer. Meetings like that make the trip worthwhile." The subject of work does not come up, but the beginning of the letter speaks volumes about what he was thinking:

> Dear François Truffaut, Your letter is like the morning dew. It banishes the evening's nightmares. I won't go so far as to say that it restores my health, but it helps me get out of this strange stagnation that comes from not being able to overcome some unpleasant dizzy spells. Even so, I think that I'm coming to the end of my woes, that I'll be able to look at life and take part in it instead of resigning myself to standing on the sidelines, which is always a depressing place to be.[2]

Nightmares, stagnation, the life in which he does not take part, all that comes from not making movies any more. He was constitutionally unable to get the rest the doctors advised for him. In his head, he was still constructing plans for his next movie. So as not to worry Dido, he pretended that he still had hopes. He joked with everyone, played with the two dachshunds, Tambeau and Nénette. His dear friend Gabrielle was no longer next door, but her son was not far off, and he bubbled with friendliness and wit. He was full of stories about a past that he had not known himself but which he had lived out in another way, through the wonderful stories that his mother and Jean used to tell.

♦

Again like his father, Jean Renoir always seemed to be in good spirits. For his neighbors in Benedict Canyon, for the Hollywood film world, he was *the* Frenchman of Beverly Hills, the one who made them want to love the country from which he came. He was affable, talkative, easy to understand even though his accent was funny, and people loved him. You could run into him at certain Hollywood parties or at the Farmers' Market or at the huge Schwab's drugstore at the intersection of La Cienega and Beverly Hills boulevards. But he spent less and less time among those baskets of produce worthy of the land of plenty or in that store that had fascinated him for so many years, because he was less and less able to walk. He was glad to do without the parties, since he had never been interested in socializing for its own sake, and

---

[2]Letter dated December 29, 1970, provided by François Truffaut.

Dido didn't push him to go—she did not much care for going out either.

They were both well acclimated to American life. What is still rarer, they understood Americans, since they took the trouble to see each one they met in his or her ethnic and religious context. The preface Jean wrote to the French translation of Jessica Ryan's *City of Angels* reveals the extent of his understanding in just a few pages:

> Jessica's book brings home the great danger that threatens Hollywood: isolation. This suburb, or rather this environment, has real powers of absorption. Soon enough any newcomer gets caught up in a little world that limits one's intellectual activity to eating up rumors that make the rounds at certain swimming pools. When you leave Hollywood, you only go to one of its branch offices, like Palm Springs. It's a town 180 miles off into the desert, and lots of stars, producers, and directors have houses there. Life goes on there just as it does around Sunset Boulevard. This type of isolation is really tragic, since Hollywood is a mushroom that just sprang up out of the ground. There are towns in the Northeast that fold back on themselves this way, but they are still nourished by the great Puritan tradition. The South can still find some identity in its memories of aristocratic splendor. But Hollywood's traditions hardly deserve the name. They're still as fragile as a child's dreams. With a little bit of luck, maybe they'll grow ripe and strong. All the talented people who have passed through here must have left some kind of mark. Among all the members of this voracious community, there are some whose disinterest is beyond doubt. From their urgent efforts something will maybe emerge that is better than the tacky junk that has stopped Hollywood's progress; it makes you think of a little girl wearing so much cheap jewelry that she can hardly move her arms and it's stunted her growth. Let's not forget that before it became self-conscious, Hollywood's films were the best in the world. Precocious success is what it has to struggle against.[3]

He had not forgotten that the films of those days, when Hollywood's were the best in the world, still haunted him. In the airplane that brought him there in 1940, "I saw myself in a dream, in paradise, beside Griffith, Charlie Chaplin, Lubitsch, and all the saints of the worldwide cult of films."[4] It seemed normal to him to choose to live there, but in his habits, his tastes, as well as in his language and manners, he remained French. Dido had figured out how to recreate a little Provençale and Parisian enclave that suited him perfectly. After

---

[3] Jessica Ryan, *La Cité des Anges* (Paris, 1986), preface.
[4] Jean Renoir, *Ma vie et mes films* (Paris, 1974), 171.

all, she, too, had spent many years in Paris. She was educated in France rather than in her birthplace, Brazil, which her parents had left when she was only a few months old. She says that she was almost born in Japan and that she lived in Chile. When she was in the Dupanloup boarding school, her parents were already living in Liverpool. Her father died there, and her mother refused to move even during the Blitz. Dido is one of those faithful and devoted wives; thanks to her, there was always something happening at Leona Drive to distract Jean.

After five o'clock, their friends knew that they were welcome.

> Maybe it's Leslie Caron, like a daughter to them since *Orvet*, or Chuck who sells autographs of Zola or Napoleon in a little shop on Canyon Drive, or maybe the ideal couple, Jeanne and Robert Weymers, two Belgians who were teaching Americans how to light buildings. There was Jeannot Slade's daily visit, Gabrielle's son, . . . the weekly visit of Professor Alexander Sesonske, who taught film at the University of California at Santa Barbara and who was in the process of writing the fattest book ever devoted to the auteur of the *Golden Coach*.[5]

Beginning in 1971, Jean Renoir's health began to decline. His wounded leg always had been the first thing to start hurting. It got infected, and the wound had to be drained. Nicholas Frangakis says that already in those days, they couldn't diminish or even stabilize the infection. He had become a family member by this time, and Dido and Jean called him Nick. Jean was interested in the films he was making for the ABC TV network, and Nick went with him to the showing of *Petit Théâtre* on May 15, 1970, at the Los Angeles County Museum. It was the first time the film was shown. Unfortunately, the print had not been subtitled. Jean Renoir was so disappointed that he tried to call off the screening, but they got around him and the print even made it to New York, where it was shown at the Metropolitan Museum of Art in the fall. All this was way before the film was seen in Paris, where the French Channel 2 put it on its program for December 15, 1970. There were several previews in the Cinémathèque française, the Ciné-club des Invisibles, and at the Institute of Art and Archaeology.[6]

According to the contracts between the television station and the commercial distributors, the film could not be distributed in Paris un-

---

[5] François Truffaut, "Jean Renoir, 1273 Leona Drive. . ." December 15, 1975, in *Jean Renoir cinéaste* (Lyon, 1976).

[6] *L'Avant-Scène cinéma*, "Spécial Renoir," 251–52, July 1–15, 1980, 165.

til after October 15, 1975. But its New York premier took place in May 1972, and it was a terrific success. You can still see it now and then on American television. Jean Renoir, who usually charmed the French with his presence on the screen, did not interest them. He is standing there, bent over a bit in front of his little cardboard castle introducing each sketch, but the magic doesn't work. The film does not resonate. Still, it is exciting to see how this seventy-five-year-old remained free in spirit before life's big questions. Yet he treated them with such subtlety that he was misunderstood once again. The stories, so well staged, betray an independent, discerning mind that goes beyond their apparent simplicity. But the reception accorded *Petit Théâtre* did not affect him. He was far away, and a film that is finished interested him no more. He was always thinking of the next one. But from now on, there was no next one. Even the film with Jeanne Moreau, *Julienne et son amour*, which he was so eager to shoot—he knew well that he would never get it done. His plan now was to change the screen version into a novel. He was so disappointed about all this that the manuscript remained incomplete for a very long time. Yet Dido never stopped urging him to write. Writing screenplays or writing books, what's the difference, especially when you are so talented and it comes so easily? Jean knew that a director's trade is not the same as a writer's. He spoke about it to Nick, who was all ears and ready to help, as was Dido.

On May 7, 1971, Orson Welles wrote Jean Renoir that he wanted to do a short film with him, a series of interviews about directing. For the first time, Jean refused a project that must have been tempting. He explained that he was too sick. It was not an easy decision; giving up was not his strong suit. He hated not being able to move. He had always been restless, not just active.

Sometimes he blew his top: "These people think I'm dead!" The people he was thinking of were producers. They knew very well that he was alive, but they did not think he was a moneymaker. In fact, he might as well have been dead as far as they were concerned. "Most of the time, Jean succeeded in hiding how sad he felt. He wanted to spare his family and friends, above all his wife, but also Norman Lloyd, Peter Bogdanovich, and me," says Nicholas Frangakis. "He became more and more meditative. His religious feelings were deep and highly personal, and his work was also his religion. His creative gift was part of that." It was very important for him to share experiences with friends. He had never been a loner, and, in part, that is what scared him about becoming a writer. Dido understood that, and urged him to work with a secretary, so as to create at least a semblance of the setting he was used to.

They had set things up to watch movies at home even before it became a necessity. In the living room, there was a screen that you could roll down on a wall between two sliding doors that opened on the backyard. On the opposite wall, you only had to take down a picture to reveal a hole with an old sixteen-millimeter army projector sticking out of it. It was on a shelf in a closet in the hall behind. Friends from UCLA or the Academy of Motion Pictures would bring him movies, old ones or new ones, that Jean would look at whenever he felt like it. That was how, after twenty years, around the end of 1971, he saw *The River.*

> Seeing it again reinforced an idea that was in the back of my head when I was making it, namely, that the Indians, especially those miserable ones who die of hunger in the streets, are in the process of conquering the world. . . . The destructive power of the ideas from India comes from the way they make plain to millions of us Westerners the vanity of our acts. For people of my generation, God was action. Work was the most popular form of act, and modern society is based on the notion of work. You've got to move, buy and sell, and produce. Among adults, meditation is something that is almost unknown. But I know a lot of young people who meditate. It's very dangerous for the stability of our economic life. . . . Maybe the public will figure out that the fishermen I show them on the riverboats, the coolies who are always running back and forth in the factories, the crowds that mill around in the bazaar, and all those groups of people who nap on the steps of temples are unconscious authors of the decline of the world erected by Western technology.[7]

The student revolt, life in communes, the Black Panthers, the campus demonstrations against the war in Vietnam—all that could make you think that the postmodern age would be a kind of return to nature, dominated by spiritual quests instead of the hunt for bucks. Young people seemed more open and more oriented to idealism.

◆

Dido and Jean knew how to surround themselves with interesting young people who were delighted to be able to visit with them: students, children of friends, young foreign visitors who were interested in the world of movies. It was a little like the painters who came to

---

[7]Letter dated December 4, 1971, published in *Ecran 72,* 1, January 1972, and reprinted in Jean Renoir, *Ecrits, 1926–1971,* ed. C. Gauteur (Paris, 1974), 271–72.

Les Collettes after a long trip in the hopes of laying eyes on Auguste Renoir. The son's spirit was as alert as his father's had been, but his body became just as handicapped; but unlike his father, Jean couldn't pursue his profession until his very last day. François Truffaut told me that in 1973, after he made *La Nuit américaine* (*Day for Night*), he got into the habit of going to visit the Renoirs at the conclusion of each of his films, and from 1973 on, Jean didn't talk about making movies any more.

New visitors who arrived ready to talk about their interests, their plans, and their lives masked, at least for a while, the loss of old friends. In 1972, Jean and Dido decided to give up their apartment on the avenue Frochot. Why keep it when they could not use it? Until then, they had refused to even pose the question. But that was a hard year where friendships are concerned: their dear friend Bessie Smith, who had been with Dido all her life, died, and there was no one left to call Jean "mon frangin" ("my little brother"), when in October it was Renée Cézanne's turn to pass on.

The next year, Norman Lloyd directed *Carola* for PBS with Leslie Caron in the lead role and Mel Ferrer playing the German general, her ex-lover. Lloyd cut the play the way it had been cut by Jean himself a few years earlier at Berkeley. Jean was consulted and approved the changes. He also wrote a foreword to the French edition: "Before it became a play, *Carola* was a vow cleverly formulated by Kipling when his hero, Mowgli, jumped behind an old ruin that was inhabited by a family of cobras: 'We're the same blood, you and I,' he said to them. Moved by his good manners, the snakes put down their hoods.

"My great wish in life is that the snakes will realize that other creatures have the same blood as they do."[8] According to him, that is what the play is about. In the person of Carola, Jean is on familiar ground: she is like Camilla in *The Golden Coach* or Nini in *French Can-can*. The show is the only thing that is real to them. Life, love, and ideas are not part of their world. Jean belonged to that family.

◆

Little by little, by structuring another kind of life for him, Dido gently led Jean into the kind of fixed daily routine that writers have. She found him a secretary who came mornings and afternoons. He even got in the habit of dictating his texts instead of writing them down first. The tremendous facility that he had had when he was preparing

---

[8] *L'Avant-Scène théâtre*, 587, November 1, 1976, 6.

a movie came back to him quickly. He conversed with the secretary as he had been in the habit of doing with his assistants. Talking was important for him, as Dido knew well. That way he kept the spark alive and his imagination active.

He charmed the young people who came to the house to take care of his leg. Several of them took turns; they were students, either registered nurses or not, depending on the time of year. They had never seen a patient like him, who made them laugh and who always seemed cheerful.

> I keep on deluding myself about my sickness. It seems to me that sickness is a well-defined kingdom, with its own frontiers, its own customs, and even its own language. When you're sick, you become a little infantile; you get into the habit of people around you doing things for you, especially in my case, where I'm forbidden to use a leg. I'm having a hard time getting used to being dependent on others. What's more, I'm the last word in cowardice: I hate suffering, and when it hurts, I like to be able to yell. However, it seems to me that our civilization does not approve of such yelling; the only noise it approves of is mechanical noise. But the microphone that makes it possible for singers to get away with a murmur also makes them forget the beauty in the vocal efforts of opera singers, especially female opera singers. When it rains and I feel deprived, I think of Florence Mills, a black singer who belonged to a group called The Blackbirds, around 1920. She had a high-pitched, almost a piercing voice, like a nightingale in the forest, and she died of tuberculosis. I also was crazy about Carola Neher, who sang the songs of Brecht and Kurt Weill, and she, too, died of tuberculosis.[9]

The letter shows how he tried to distance himself from his suffering by calling up the past. A man who, as a filmmaker, never repeated the same experiment twice, Jean mingled memories and invention in what he wrote. His reader has a hard time separating the autobiographical parts from the fiction. In 1974, his first book after *The Diaries of Captain Georges* appeared: *Ma vie et mes films* (*My Life and My Films*), which was published simultaneously in French and in an English translation by Norman Denny. His memories are packed with films, director friends, actors, and producers. Like the book on Auguste Renoir, it gives us a living portrait of its author. In reading it again, a remark of Nicholas Frangakis' kept coming back to me:

> You could sense a great compassion for people in Jean Renoir. He never tried to belittle anyone. Yet he wasn't sanctimonious or blind. But if

[9] Letter dated November 19, 1974, provided by François Truffaut.

338

someone made him laugh, he was ready to see him every day, even if he knew that that person was far from being a trustworthy friend. He hated people who were pretentious. His suffering hadn't changed him, but it was awful to see him fighting against physical conditions that did nothing but grow worse.

Yet even when you close this book, which ends with the strange phrase that I cited above, "Wait for me, Gabrielle," you are blown away by the talent and the power with which he conjures up his whole life, and you forget that the man who wrote it was eighty years old.

◆

For his eightieth birthday, a program was dedicated to him on September 19 in the *Grand Ecran* series on French television (Channel 1). It included a broadcast of *Grand Illusion* and an homage to him written by Jean-André Fieschi, read and acted by Françoise Arnoul, Claude Brasseur, Marcel Dalio, and Jean Carmet. Jean wrote an article that appeared in *Le Monde* and *The New York Times*, in which he remarked:

> Even at this stage of my life, I'm still incapable of following a party line. I feel like a bird . . . a fat bird who pecks haphazardly at fruits from the wildest collection of orchards. I have often stated my distrust for programs, and even though I'm free to talk about whatever interests me, I let myself go off into a kind of literary anarchy. That's why my greatest joy these last few years was orchestrating the disorder in my film *Le Petit Théâtre de Jean Renoir*. Fortunately for me, there are actually people who like such things[10]

The once-over he gave himself had not lost its clarity.

That same year, Marcel Pagnol died, the man whose friendship had made it possible for Jean to make *Toni*. Such happy memories! Pagnol had quit movies long since, and in the meantime his were rediscovered and appreciated anew by the team at *Cahiers du cinéma*. The public premier of *Le Petit Théâtre de Jean Renoir* took place in New York in May, and Claude Gauteur published a large volume called *Ecrits* in which he brought together "the articles written from 1926 to 1971 by the greatest French filmmaker," as he says in his preface. In 1975, from February 3 to March 30, the largest and most complete retrospective of Jean Renoir's films yet held anywhere took place at the National Film Theater in London. On April 8, in Hollywood, Ingrid Bergman read this brief homage to him: "He loves humanity in

---

[10] *Le Monde*, September 15–16, 1974.

all its nobility and despite its foolishness. Throughout the world, he is known as the best of men, and in the world of the movies, he is a living god." Since he could not get around, she accepted an Oscar in his name from the Academy of Motion Picture Arts and Sciences, "a special honorary award for exceptionally distinguished service to the art of motion pictures."

He knew how to keep in touch even with the most distant friends, and he was interested in what they loved. So on July 15, 1975, he wrote this to Henri Cartier-Bresson, who had announced to him his decision to give up photography in order to devote himself to drawing:

> Your picture of Martine and Melanie makes me want to see them in person. I know that the pictures you have sent me represent the last stage before physically authentic reproduction: you even succeed in giving an idea of the sound of their voices, but I have no regrets that you are quitting photography. You've gotten all that can be gotten from optical devices. You have made us remember what's essential in human beings. But at your age, you can take up a new type of conversation. You have all my best wishes in such a bold experiment.

It was a wonderful way to encourage what certainly was a "bold" undertaking, and it came from someone who understood it as well as anyone did. Jean still had that same acute way of expressing himself: what he perceived and expressed about Henri Cartier-Bresson's art is amazingly appropriate and concise.

◆

At the same time, he had become a prisoner of his body, which refused to obey him. Every year, in peach season, the monks from the little desert monastery brought him a crate of them, but he could never return to visit them. Several came regularly. Jean especially liked Father Yang, a Chinese Buddhist who converted to Catholicism at Louvain and had been ordained at St. André of Bruges. They got along very well, talking and laughing together. The happiness of this Benedictine friend made him forget for a moment that he was nailed to his armchair. It also befell him to have to spend long months in bed. Despite the advent of Parkinson's disease, which made everything still worse, he kept his mischievous sense of humor: Nick Frangakis remembers a quote from Victor Hugo that he cited to him in October 1975:

> Tout cela pour des altesses
> Qui vous à peine enterré

Se feront des politesses
Tandis que vous pourrirez.

All that for their highnesses;
But before the dust has settled on your grave
They will be exchanging pleasantries
While you will be rotting away. [*Trans.*]

He kept up his spirits by watching comedy shows on TV. Nick
Frangakis, Alexander Sesonske, and Norman Lloyd all told me of his
taste for the *Three Stooges,* a series of slapstick sketches inspired by
the great silent-comedy comics. Jean Renoir had a young man with
him, a student at UCLA who had been a nurse in Vietnam. Greg took
care of him, helped him take his bath, drove him in his car, and was
strong enough to sit him down in his wheelchair. He also read to him
and showed him films. He even helped Dido out, going shopping or
painting one thing or another. He became indispensable, was completely devoted to Jean, and his presence was never heavy.

At the end of that year, 1975, the fiftieth gala of the Union of Artists moved to Los Angeles. Jean-Claude Brialy organized the recep-
tions, where Jean was reunited with some of his old actors and many
of his friends who had made the trip to see him again: Valentine
Tessier, Paulette Dubost, Françoise Arnoul, Catherine Rouvel, Jean
Marais, Anne de Saint-Phalle, Sophie Renoir, his grandniece who
was not yet an actress but who was already hoping to become one,
and her mother, Évangèle, the wife of Claude Renoir. Claude himself
was unable to attend because he was working as a cameraman. A big
celebration was planned for December 27 in honor of Jean's promo-
tion to officer of the Legion of Honor. He received the insignia from
Françoise Giroud, secretary of state for culture, who asked him: "Do
you remember me? I am the young girl to whom you said one day,
long ago: "You have talent, you'd better first learn how to waste it."
She also said to him: "Since they came into being, movies have provided few giants, and you're one of them. Today, people recite your
sequences the way others recite from Victor Hugo or Mallarmé." His
friends applauded, but they had the feeling that once the celebration
was over, they would get on their planes and never again see someone whom they already missed very much. They could not keep
themselves from feeling very sad.

In fact, it was the last time that Jean Renoir appeared in public.
He no longer had the strength for it. Dido protected him as much as
she could, but in a way that their friends understood and appreciated.
She did not try to cut him off from the world, quite the contrary. She

encouraged people to visit him individually. One of Denise Tual's sons, Christian, was cultural attaché to the French consulate in Los Angeles. She invited him very often, since she knew that his conversation stimulated Jean and made him laugh. They soon became great friends. Louis Malle remembers spending a lot of time with the Renoirs in 1976–77. "At the time, he was considered the great French movie director. . . . He was very happy (in Los Angeles). He kept on telling me: 'Stay here, Louis, it'll be fantastic for you. The people—the producers and the studios—will drive you nuts, but it's a great country.'"

Indeed he was happy, as happy as you could be under such sad circumstances. "I'm still on wheels. I'm getting pretty good at it," he wrote on December 23, 1976.[11] The woman he had loved for forty years was there. For his sake, she had learned how to cook, and she took care of their garden with great affection.

> In my yard in California, near the kitchen door, there's an orange tree. I look at it and I breathe in deeply. It's covered with flowers. I can't look at an orange tree in flower without thinking of Cagnes. Thinking of Cagnes immediately evokes the image of my father. . . . The shadow cast by the olive trees is often deep purple, and it is always moving around, sparkling, full of gaiety and life. It I let myself go, it seems that Renoir is still there, and that all of a sudden I'm going to hear him singing to himself while he winks at his canvas. He's part of the landscape. You don't need a lot of imagination to see him there, with his white canvas hat posed jauntily on that long noggin of his. His emaciated face is expressing some affectionate joke.[12]

Jean's face was also emaciated, and it, too, was often "expressing some affectionate joke." These lines written about his father fifteen years earlier remained true for him. His father was always present to mind, as a model for his whole life and even for his old age, in which he suffered just as his father had.

Medicine gave him no relief. Dido felt great hidden rage over that. But her good humor in comforting him was unflappable. Everyone who was near them during those difficult times agrees that he was lucid until the end, that he maintained throughout his vibrant intelligence, his spirit of good fun, and his taste for laughter. During those years, he wrote relentlessly, dictating every day for hours on end. He went through several secretaries. Real life took them from him. There was the young Eve Lotar, then Luli Barzman, who, in March 1976, asked to be replaced by her brother, Paulo; they were the

---

[11] Letter provided by François Truffaut.
[12] *Renoir par Jean Renoir,* 31–32 *Renoir, My Father,* 33.

children of the famous screenwriter Ben Barzman, who had been driven out of Hollywood by McCarthyism. They were bilingual, having lived in Mougins, where Paulo was born in 1957. Paulo's arrival at Leona Drive was an event. Usually, Jean worked with young women, and Paulo had never had a job before. He was supposed to stay for three months. Jean Renoir was writing a book called *Le Coeur à l'aise* (*Heart at Ease*). "There already was a first draft that was supposed to become a fictional autobiography consisting of several stories loosely linked to each other.

"His energy and his will remained intact, but he had to fight physical reality," Paulo Barzman told me. "He was very patient, very friendly. We often had wild laughing fits over what he was writing." Jean Renoir loved jokes, usually off-color ones. He had acquired a taste for them when he was young, and Americans resisted them. But young Barzman, who had grown up in France, was immediately at home. He also told me what Jean Renoir used to say to him: "'What I'm doing doesn't mean a damn next to what's going on.' As detached as he was from the world around him, he was simple and he was always thinking about what was happening to other people. At the same time, sometimes his look went blank because of the pain he was feeling. If there were people around him, he would say nothing for a long time, a half-hour, or an hour, and then, suddenly, he would come up with a phrase that summed everything up. He was a person who wanted to bring out the best in other people." For Paulo, the few years he spent at Leona Drive were very important personally. In the morning, Jean Renoir dictated to him, and in the afternoon, he would read back and correct what they had done that morning.

◆

In March 1976, just when young Paulo Barzman appeared, news came of the death of a friend whose memory was dear to both Dido and Jean, since he had shown them Rome for the first time. Luchino Visconti had remained a loyal friend ever since. He said: "Jean Renoir taught me my trade without teaching me. . . . You had to watch him live and work to understand his work. . . . I was coming from fascism, and in France, thanks to Jean Renoir, I understood, and I went back to Italy and made an antifascist film. . . . Jean Renoir is my idol. He is my master and my god. There is no other." [13]

Jean never got used to the loss of his friends; he could not stand

[13] *Radioscopie*, "Luchino Visconti," program by Jacques Chancel broadcast January 30, 1970.

their absence. The following year was marked by the heartrending disappearance of yet another one, Roberto Rossellini, who had been a really intimate friend of Jean's. When they no longer lived on the same continent, the bonds between them only apparently loosened. In 1963, Jean Renoir gave this account of him: "In Rossellini's films, the actors are part of the crowd, they are even part of the landscape, and that's because Rossellini himself is part of the crowd and the landscape. He isn't an observer of life, he's living it." [14] Jacques Prévert, who had been his collaborator in the past and his friend during his relationship with Marguerite, died that same year. And on Christmas day, Jean learned of the death of Charlie Chaplin, his idol as a young man, his friend as an adult.

Death was carrying off his friends and could not be far away from him; how could he not think about it? Nick Frangakis said: "He dreaded death like a child, and then, little by little, he was overtaken by a kind of resignation. His physical suffering seems to have been responsible." Nick Frangakis observed his old friend with as much affection as admiration. Jean Renoir, who had so often and so vociferously claimed that he was a "born coward," was making his way toward death with dignity.

But he needed to feel friendship around him more than ever. He was careful to stay in touch with the people who were near and dear to him. On March 16, 1978, he wrote to François Truffaut, "Your letter made me so happy that I laughed by myself as I read it over. Thanks." A few months later, on August 11: "I'm writing this note for no practical purpose. You know my affection, and I know yours. I'm telling you out loud because it gives me pleasure. It's like a little farewell on the platform of a train station. It's missing the smell of sweat in Victoria Station. You don't need anyone to take your friends to a world whose inhabitants are true knights. The New Wave is like those barons at a round table." [15] This token of friendship is addressed to his "dear François" and his friends of *Cahiers du cinéma*, and it shows how much he still thought about them, how much his mind was still focused on the craft he had served so well.

◆

Writing did not preoccupy him as deeply as his films had. He worked at it relentlessly because there was no other way he could express himself and because he had a taste for work that was well done. What

---

[14] In Mario Verdone, *Roberto Rossellini* (Paris, 1963), 198–99.
[15] From letters provided by François Truffaut.

is striking in his narratives is his extraordinary eye, his way of bringing out the right detail to illuminate a character or a situation. His
books are full of expressions that stick in your head.

During the year 1978, he published *Le Coeur à l'aise*, which he finally decided to call a novel. And in Paris, the same Claude Gauteur,
with appropriate admiration and great devotion to the task, was preparing and writing an introduction to the screenplay of *Julienne et son
amour* followed by a synopsis of *En avant, Rosalie!* (*Forward March,
Rosalie!*). These were the two films that Jean Renoir had so wanted to
make with Jeanne Moreau, because "she is an actress whom I admire
very much. Probably the one whom I admire most, and I would like
to give her a surprise."[16] Jean wrote a little introduction to the
screenplay in which he notes: "This kind of film is largely based on
details. . . . Henri's automobile is a Delaunay-Belleville or a valve-
less Panhard. The headlights are acetylene, which is turned on by a
handle."[17] These films were never made, but at least, thanks to
Claude Gauteur, we can dream of what they might have been. The
book was ready for publication in the beginning of 1979. *Le Crime de
l'Anglais* (*The Englishman's Crime*) was also complete by then. It is a
slim volume that also bears the word *novel* on its cover, like *Le Coeur à
l'aise*. It is the story of an event that took place at the end of the nineteenth century in the neighborhood of Essoyes. Gabrielle had told
him the story. On one of his last stays in France, Jean had returned to
the village of his mother and Gabrielle to ask questions of some old
peasants who still remembered the event. He also went to the scene
of the crime. His tale is lively and well polished. Jean had the knack of
putting what he imagined or what he saw into words that are as striking and direct as the images he created in his films. Interestingly, he
always situates what he wrote in the past, perhaps because he lived in
Beverly Hills and had the feeling he had lost contact with what was
happening in Paris, Cagnes, or Essoyes; or perhaps it was merely a
consequence of his aging.

He had dictated this particular book to Paulo Barzman, who had
to learn how to proofread. Jean's physical pains did not stop growing
worse. The wound on his leg got infected again in a worrisome way,
and the Parkinson's disease continued to rack him despite medica-
tion. But he did not give up struggling. He tried to forget his ills by

---

[16] *Combat*, November 25, 1967, cited by Claude Gauteur in Jean Renoir, *Julienne et son
amour*, 11.

[17] *Combat*, November 25, 1967, cited by Claude Gauteur in Jean Renoir, *Julienne et son
amour*, 20.

working, and everyone helped him as best they could. He dictated another book, he forced himself to read it, he corrected it. The animals were a joy to him, and the yard beneath the windows of his bedroom, which he now hardly ever left. Greg, the student who took care of him, loved him like a father. Jean got interested in his communication studies, and they discussed them together. "None of us realized the extent of their friendship before Jean's death." [18]

At Christmastime in 1978, Dido knew that Jean's health was deteriorating irreversibly, so she asked Nick to get the monks from Vallermo to come "to prepare Jean for what seemed imminent at the time. Then Dido, Dulce, her sister, and I went together to see Jean in the living room, and Dido asked him: 'Would you like Father Yang and Father Werner to visit you?'"

Father Yang, whom she also liked very much, and Father Werner, who was a sculptor and who sometimes spoke with Jean, both came. They celebrated mass at the dining-room table. "Jean was very moved, and he took communion," in the presence of Dido, her sister Dulce, Zenaida, a Costa Rican maid, and Nick Frangakis. He said nothing, as was his habit; for a man who was very talkative with his friends, he never said a word about his religious feelings.

◆

Year's end came peacefully. Jean was not concerned about the way his books were received in Paris. He was completely detached from all that. François Truffaut spent Christmas at Leona Drive. Jean was too weak to have his grandchildren; they had grown into youngsters who needed too much space for a house with an invalid in it. In the week between Christmas and New Year's, Alexander Sesonske and his wife Sally paid them a visit. Jean felt tired and, with Greg's help, he went to bed. François Truffaut followed him to his room and sat in silence for a while beside him. Alexander Sesonske was impressed by the attitude of the two men toward each other and the warm affection they radiated. In India, Jean Renoir had been struck by the silent relationships between people whose feelings were expressed simply by their motionless presence and a state of concentration that allowed them to grasp each other's souls at the deepest level. That evening, it was surely a farewell that those friends were exchanging.

Dido had had the feeling that the end was near, but when Jean wasn't suffering too much, she was almost happy, since he kept "all

---

[18] Letter dated February 9, 1986, from Nicholas Frangakis to the author.

of his magnificent intelligence" and remained as alert and attentive as before. Unfortunately, there were pains that nothing could get rid of completely, and his strength was diminishing from one day to the next. Yet, still following his father's example, he kept on inventing and dictating. With the help of Paulo Barzman, he composed *Geneviève*, a strange tale about a young invalid girl confined to a wheelchair who dies of the wild passion inspired in her by a schoolboy, the story's narrator.

On February 12, 1979, he had finished *Geneviève*, and that morning he spoke to Dido about a new project. It was a novel that he was going to begin to write and whose subject he refused to reveal to her. Greg was there, preparing him for the day, and Jean was waiting for Paulo. He was eager to begin to dictate the first pages of the draft to him. He died later that morning, peacefully. Greg, overwhelmed with grief, ran off. Dido telephoned Alain and Nick, who took charge of the funeral.

Dido did not feel lonely. The man whom she loved had gone to his death serenely. That was the only thing that mattered for her.

◆

Five-part Gregorian chants accompanied the funeral mass celebrated by Fathers Yang and Werner. There was not a large audience in the Church of the Good Shepherd, which was the way Dido wanted it. After the mass, she followed the coffin to the hearse with Alain, François Truffaut, and Nick Frangakis; then she went to the main entrance of the church on Santa Monica Boulevard, where their friends greeted her. Greg, whose face reflected the depth of his grief, appeared during the office but disappeared right afterwards. He refused to go with Dido and the family and friends to the Hotel Bel Air, where Dido had ordered lunch.

That lunch resembled a sequence from one of Jean's films, as Dido and Alain remember it. The two monks told a story about the communion wine being stolen at their monastery and how Father Werner had caught the culprit, who turned out to be a postulant. Father Werner had surprised him drinking the stolen wine with his friends from the village. The story went on and on. Then the time came to pay the bill, and no one had any money. Dido and Alain had forgotten their credit cards and their checkbooks. "Jean would have really enjoyed Father Werner's story, and he would have laughed so hard at all of us standing there with no way to pay the bill," added Dido.

There was a spate of articles about him in the press. The one in the *Los Angeles Times* was signed by Orson Welles, and its headline read, "Jean Renoir, the Greatest of All Directors." The article was as intelligent as its author, and it ended with this quote from Jean: "Art is 'making.' The art of poetry is the art of making poetry. The art of love is the art of making love. . . . My father never talked to me about art. He couldn't bear the word."[19] There was a long article in the *New York Times* and another in the *Washington Post.* America acknowledged the passing of the Frenchman of Beverly Hills.

◆

Two weeks later there was a memorial service for Jean at UCLA, and no one foresaw that so many students would attend. Royce Hall, which had two thousand seats, was full, and four or five hundred students were unable to get in. François Truffaut, Christian Tual, and John Huston all spoke. George Cukor told an anecdote that had nothing whatever to do with the occasion. It was about Katherine Hepburn, whom he had invited to his home; she was living in a bungalow for guests and had to attend a dinner somewhere else. It was a story that had neither a head nor a tail, and it would have made Jean burst out laughing his resounding laugh, which lives on in his son. Dido did not attend this homage to Jean. It concluded with a showing of *The Golden Coach.*

A few days later, Dido left for France with Alain. They went to carry out Jean Renoir's wish that he be buried at Essoyes, alongside his parents and his brothers.

His death had been announced in France as well, where there was an outpouring of articles in the press. The one by Jean-Louis Barrault, who acted for him in *Dr Cordelier,* deserves to be cited in its entirety:

> Of good artistic stock, he did not like to reveal his inner concerns; on the contrary, he wrapped himself up in good humor and unforgettable courtesy. The man was a charmer. All smiles, and with a bagful of cunning tricks, he got his actors to catch fire by making them believe in their own genius. . . . In reality, it was his own genius that he inoculated them with. . . . Today it seems to me that, in his everyday life, Jean was able to be relaxed and impish, with a bad boy's obstinate streak in him; the only reason he got away with it was that his whole being was built on the foundations of a great poet, with roots as deep as an oak's.[20]

[19] *Los Angeles Times,* February 16, 1979.
[20] *Le Figaro,* February 14, 1979.

Dido, Alain, and their friends had a hard time avoiding an official funeral. As Jean had wished, there was a religious service in the church at Essoyes. The village pastor's homily retraced all of Jean's career. It was touchingly naïve. Then the coffin joined the family tombs in the village cemetery. Janine Bazin told me that all of Essoyes escorted the hearse along the road lined with linden trees that leads to the cemetery. The linden trees were as old as the ones that Jean had looked at not long before from his windows in avenue Frochot. Children were bawling in their mothers' arms. "It was one of their own whom the villagers were burying. Jean would've loved the whole thing," she concluded.

FILMOGRAPHY

♦

1924

Catherine ou Une vie sans joie / Catherine, or A Life without Joy

Screenplay: Jean Renoir, adapted by Jean Renoir and Pierre Lestringuez
Director: Albert Dieudonné
Photography: Jean Bachelet and Alphonse Gibory
Shot at: Gaumont Studios, Paris, and on location at Cagnes, St.-Paul-de-Vence, March–May, 1924
Production: Films Jean Renoir, and from 1927 on, Pierre Braunberger
Length: 1,800 meters
Cast:

Catherine Ferrand	Catherine Hessling
Maurice Laisné	Albert Dieudonné
Madame Laisné	Eugène Naud
Georges Mallet	Louis Gauthier
Madame Mallet	Maud Richard
The Mallets' son	Pierre Champagne
Adolphe, the pimp	Pierre Philippe (a.k.a. Pierre Lestringuez)

Plot: The misadventures of a young servant girl, the victim of women's jealousy and men's lust.

La Fille de l'eau / The Water Girl

Screenplay: Pierre Lestringuez, adapted by Jean Renoir
Assistant Director: Pierre Champagne
Photography: Jean Bachelet and Alphonse Gibory
Set Design: Jean Renoir
Shot at: G. M. Films and on location at La Nicotière and the café Au Bon Coin in Marlotte, June and July, 1924
Producer: Jean Renoir
Distributor: Maurice Routhier; subsequently, Pierre Braunberger

Length: 70 minutes
Cast:

Gudule Rosaert	Catherine Hessling
Uncle Jef	Pierre Philippe
Justin Crepoix	Pierre Champagne
Georges Raynal	Van Doren or Harold Livingston
A peasant	Pierre Renoir
Proprietor of Au Bon Coin	André Derain

Plot: A young girl living on her uncle's river barge runs away with some gypsies. Eventually a handsome young man sets her free from her sadistic uncle and from being unjustly accused of setting fire to a farm.

1926

Nana

Screenplay: Pierre Lestringuez, based on the Zola novel; adapted by Jean Renoir
Captions: Denise Leblond-Zola
Director: Jean Renoir
Assistant Directors: André Cerf and Pierre Lestringuez
Photography: Edmond Crown and Jean Bachelet
Cameramen: Charles Ralleigh and Alphonse Gibory
Set Designer: Claude Autant-Laura
Set Builder: Robert-Jules Garnier
Costumes: Claude Autant-Laura
Editing: Jean Renoir
Shot at: Gaumont Studios, Paris, Grünewald Studios, Berlin, and on location at Montigny, from October 1925 to February 1926
Producers: Films Jean Renoir
Distributors: Aubert, Pierre Braunberger
Original Length: 2,700 meters
Cast:

Nana	Catherine Hessling
Count de Vandeuvres	Jean Angelo
Count Muffat	Werner Krauss
Zoé, Nana's maid	Valeska Gert
Bordenavel	Pierre Philippe
Fauchery	Claude Autant-Lara
La Faloise	Pierre Champagne

"Le Tigre," Nana's stable boy	André Cerf
Spectators in the balcony of the music hall	Pierre Braunberger
	Raymond Turgy

Plot: Zola revised by Jean Renoir. The novel's realism is set aside in favor of a fantasy in which the director plays on the contrast between Nana, whom Catherine Hessling mimes rather than acts, and Count Muffat, the Emperor's chamberlain, played by Werner Krauss. Krauss was a great star of German expressionist theater. Nana, a poverty-stricken actress turned high-class prostitute, is kept by Muffat, whom she treats like a dog. She leads a life of luxury and debauchery. Another of her lovers, Count de Vandeuvres, she drives to suicide. Finally, wasted by smallpox, Nana dies in agony.

Charleston or Sur un air de Charleston

Screenplay: Pierre Lestringuez, based on an idea by André Cerf
Director: Jean Renoir
Assistant Director: André Cerf
Director of Photography: Jean Bachelet
Original Musical Score: Clément Doucet
Shot at: Epinay Studios, a few days in the fall of 1926
Producer and distributor: Néo-Film (Pierre Braunberger)
Length: 21 minutes
Cast:

The dancer	Catherine Hessling
The black explorer	Johnny Huggins
Four angels	Pierre Braunberger, André Cerf,
	Pierre Lestringuez, and Jean Renoir

Plot: A scantily clad dance number. Catherine Hessling, survivor of a catastrophic glacier that has destroyed the earth, uses her skills as a dancer to seduce a black explorer who carries her off with him in a balloon headed for some faraway world.

1927

Marquitta

Screenplay: Pierre Lestringuez, adapted by Jean Renoir
Director: Jean Renoir
Photography: Jean Bachelet and Raymond Agnel
Set Design: Robert-Jules Garnier

Shot at: Gaumont Studios (Buttes-Chaumont), on location in Nice (on the coast road along the cliffs, la moyenne Corniche)
Producers: Aristes Réunis
Distributor: Jean de Merly
Length: 2,400 meters
Cast:

Marquitta	Marie-Louise Iribe
Prince Vlasco	Jean Angelo
Casino owner	Pierre Philippe
Taxi driver	Pierre Champagne
Extra	Simone Cerdan

Plot: A Street-singer seduces a prince. After several ups and downs, Marquitta is a great success, but her benefactor becomes a target of the Revolution. She saves him in turn.

1928

La Petite Marchande d'allumettes / The Little Match Girl

Screenplay: Jean Renoir, after the Andersen fairy tale
Co-Directors: Jean Renoir and Jean Tedesco
Assistant Directors: Claude Heymann and Simone Hamiguet
Director of Photography: Jean Bachelet
Set Design: Erik Aaes
Shot at: Vieux-Colombier Theater Studios, and on location at Marly (on a sandy desert), from August 1927 to January 1928
Producers: Jean Renoir and Jean Tedesco
Distributors: Sofar
Current Length: 29 minutes
Cast:

Karen	Catherine Hessling
The handsome officer	Jean Storm
The policeman and the hussar of Death	Manuel Raabi
Amy Wells, the mechanical doll	Aimée Tedesco
A passer-by	Catherine Hessling's mother, Mrs. Heuschling

Plot: A little girl sells matches to wealthy passers-by on New Year's Eve. They hardly notice her, and she falls asleep in the snow. She dreams of the toys she has seen in the store windows: wooden soldiers who obey the orders of a handsome lieutenant leading her around on horseback over the clouds; he ultimately turns into the hussar of Death. After the fantasy, reality returns: the little match girl dies of cold.

Tire au flanc / Shirker

Screenplay: Jean Renoir, Claude Heymann, and Alberto Cavalcanti, based on a vaudeville skit by André Mouezy-Eon and A. Sylvane
Captions and Drawings: André Rigaud
Director: Jean Renoir
Assistant Directors: André Cerf and Lola Markovitch
Director of Photography: Jean Bachelet
Set Design: Erik Aaes
Production Assistant: Armand Pascal
Shot at: Billancourt Studios, and on location at the "Cent Gardes" barracks in Saint-Cloud and the bois de Saint-Cloud
Producers: Armor-Film (Pierre Braunberger)
Distributors: Armor-Film
Length: 2,200 meters
Cast:

Jean Dubois d'Ombelles	Georges Pomiès
Joseph Turlot	Michel Simon
Georgette	Fridette Fatou
Colonel Brochard	Félix Oudart
Solange Blandin	Jeanne Helbling
Teacher in the park and girl in the barracks	Catherine Hessling
New recruit	André Cerf

Plot: A silent comedy! A young man of good family enters military service at the same time as his servant. Pomiès, a dancer by trade, adds a poetic touch to this farce, which Renoir and Heymann filled to overflowing with standard army jokes.

Le Tournoi or Le Tournoi dans la cité / The Tournament

Screenplay: Henri Dupuy-Mazuel and Andre Jaeger-Schmidt, adapted by Jean Renoir
Director: Jean Renoir
Assistant Director: André Cerf
Technical Consultant: Colonel Wemaere (on the cavalry)
Photography: Marcel Lucien and Maurice Desfassiaux
Cameraman: Joseph-Louis Mundwiller
Set Design: Robert Mallet-Stevens
Costumes: Georges Barbier
Editing: André Cerf

Shot at: Saint-Maurice Studios and on location at Carcassonne
Producers: Société des films historiques (Henry Dupuy-Mazuel)
Distributors: Jean de Merly and Fernand Weil
Length: 2,400 meters
Cast:

François de Baynes	Aldo Nadi
Isabelle Ginori	Jackie Monnier
Henri de Rogier	Enrique Rivero
Catherine de' Medici	Blanche Bernis
Countess de Baynes	Suzanne Desprès
Count Ginori	Manuel Raabi
Charles IX	Gérald Mock
The great riding master	William Aguet

With the added participation of Albert Rancy
and the Cadre Noir de Saumur

Plot: At the time of the religious wars, in the reign of Catherine de' Medici, a decadent and bloodthirsty nobleman falls in love with an innocent young maid who has been secretly promised to another. The nobleman is a Protestant, the last survivor of a great family that has been decimated by the wars; he is the despair of his mother. His rival is a Catholic who is as pure and virtuous as his beloved. A jousting match is set to decide their fates.

1929

Le Bled / Inside Algeria

Screenplay: Henry Dupuy-Mazuel and André Jaeger-Schmidt
Captions: André Rigaud
Director: Jean Renoir
Assistant Directors: André Cerf and René Arcy-Hennery
Master Falconer: M. Martin
Photography: Marchel Lucien and Léon Morizet
Cameramen: Brissy and André Bac
Set Design: William Aguet
Editing: Joinville
Shot at: On location in Algeria, in the towns of Ferruch, Biskra, Boufarik, and Staouéli
Producers: Société des films historiques, with additional support from the French government
Distributors: Mappemonde Film

Length: 2,400 meters
Cast:

Claude Duvernet	Jackie Monnier
His cousin, Diane Duvernet	Diana Hart
Pierre Hoffer	Enrique Rivero
His uncle, Christian Hoffer	Alexandre Arquillière
Manuel Duvernet	Manuel Raabi
Marie-Jeanne	Renée Rozier
A farm worker	Jacques Becker

Plot: This film was produced for the one hundredth anniversary of the conquest of Algeria. It tells the story of a pair of young French settlers, newly arrived in North Africa, who meet and fall in love amid various hardships.

1931

On purge bébé / Baby Takes a Laxative

Screenplay: Jean Renoir, based on the comedy by Georges Feydeau
Director: Jean Renoir
Assistant Directors: Claude Heymann and Pierre Schwab
Photography: Théodore Sparkhul and Roger Hubert
Still Photographer: Roger Forster
Cameraman: Roger Forster
Set Design: Gabriel Scognamillo
Sound: D. F. Scanlon
Music: Paul Misraki
Recording: Western Electric
Editing: Jean Mamy
Shot at: Billancourt Studios, end of March 1931
Producers: Braunberger-Richebé
Length: 1,700 meters
Cast:

Bastien Follavoine	Jacques Louvigny
His wife, Julie Follavoine	Marguerite Pierry
Their son, Toto	Sacha Taride
Chouilloux	Michel Simon
His wife, Clémence Chouilloux	Olga Valéry
Their cousin, Horace Truchet	Fernandel

Plot: A play on film, with theatrical actors; doesn't stray too far from the original. The story revolves around a laxative that little Toto refuses to take. The same day, Toto's father entertains an important businessman who offers to go into business with him selling unbreakable chamberpots to the army. The horrible child's atrocious behavior offends the businessman (played by Michel Simon), as well as his wife and their cousin (played by Fernandel), all of them high-class folks.

La Chienne / The Bitch

Screenplay: Jean Renoir and André Girard, based on the novel by Georges de La Fourchardière and the play based on it by André Mouezy-Eon
Director: Jean Renoir
Assistant Directors: Pierre Schwab and Pierre Prévert
Continuity: Suzanne de Troye
Director of Photography: Théodore Sparkhul
Cameraman: Roger Hubert
Set Design: Gabriel Scognamillo
Sound: Hotchkiss, Bell
Music: Songs by Eugénie Buffet, *La Sérénade du pavé*, and Toselli, *Sérénade*, as well as *Marlborough s'en va-t-en guerre* and tunes on a player piano
Editing: first cut: Denise Batcheff, assisted by Paul Fejos; final: Jean Renoir, Marguerite Houllé
Shot at: Billancourt Studios, summer of 1931, on location in Montmartre, in place Emile-Goudeau and the streets nearby, avenue Matignon
Producers: Pierre Braunberger; subsequently, Braunberger-Richebé and their silent partner, Marcel Monteux
Distributors: Braunberger-Richebé and Films de la Pléiade
Length: 2,900 meters
Cast:

Maurice Legrand	Michel Simon
Lucienne Pelletier, called Lulu	Janie Marèze
André-Etienne Joguin, called Dédé	Georges Flamant
Adèle Legrand	Magdelaine Bérubet
Alexis Godart	Pierre Gaillard
Dugodet	Jean Gehret
Hector Langelarde	Alexandre Rignault
Walstein	Lucien Mancini
Henriot	Romain Bouquet
Bernard	Max Dalban

Gustave Brocheton	Pierre Desty
The concierge	Jane Pierson

Plot: This is the first example of a kind of film Jean Renoir later called "drame gai" ["comic drama"]. It is the story of a naive lower-middle-class man in the throes of a midlife crisis who falls in love with a prostitute. Maurice Legrand sets her up in housekeeping, and life is his oyster. But when Lulu relentlessly expresses her disgust with him and her love for Dédé, the pimp who wouldn't leave, he kills her. Dédé is convicted of the crime, and Legrand, who gets caught stealing from the till and is fired from his job, becomes a tramp.

1932

La Nuit du carrefour / Maigret at the Crossroads

Screenplay: Jean Renoir, based on the novel by Georges Simenon
Director: Jean Renoir
Assistant Directors: Jacques Becker, Maurice Blondeau, and Roger Gaillard
Photography: Marcel Lucien and Georges Asselin
Cameramen: Paul Fabian, assisted by Claude Renoir
Continuity: Mimi Champagne
Sound: Dugnon, Joseph de Bretagne
Sound Recording: Western Electric
Editing: Marguerite Renoir, assisted by Suzanne de Troye and Walter Ruttmann
Shot at: Billancourt Studios, and on location at La Croix Verte in Bouffémont, January and March, 1932
Producer: Jacques Becker, for Europa Film
Distributors: Comptoir français cinématographique
Length: 2,000 meters
Cast:

Inspector Maigret	Pierre Renoir
Lucas, his assistant	Georges Térol
Else Andersen	Winna Winfried
Carl, her brother	Georges Koudria
Emile Michonnet	Jean Gehret
His wife	Jane Pierson
Jojo, the garage hand	Michel Duran

Arsène	Jean Mitry
The doctor	Max Dalban
The butcher	Roger Gaillard

Plot: The first filmed version of a Simenon novel. In a bizarre, typically Simenonian place, in the midst of a network of roads shrouded in fog and glistening with rain, a Dutch diamond merchant and his wife are murdered. There are too many suspects, but Maigret knows how to discover the guilty ones. Despite the loss of a reel, the film is bewitching. The characters created by Simenon and Renoir are murky and disturbing, their behavior strangely fascinating. A very poetic film.

Boudu sauvé des eaux / Boudu Saved from Drowning

Screenplay: Jean Renoir, based on the play by René Fauchois
Director: Jean Renoir
Assistant Directors: Jacques Becker and Georges Darnoux
Director of Photography: Marcel Lucien
Cameraman: Georges Asselin
Continuity: Suzanne de Troye
Set Design: Jean Castanier and Hugues Laurent
Sound: Igor B. Kalinowski
Sound Recording: Tobis Klangfilm
Editing: Marguerite Renoir and Suzanne de Troye
Shot at: Epinay Studios and on location at Chennevières and Paris (on the banks of the Seine and the Pont des Arts), Summer 1932
Producers: Jean Gehret and Marcel Pelletier for Société Sirius (Films Michel Simon)
Distributors: Jacques Haik
Length: 83 minutes
Cast:

Boudu	Michel Simon
Edouard Lestingois	Charles Granval
His wife, Emma	Marcelle Hainia
Anne-Marie	Séverine Lerczinska
The student	Jean Dasté
Godin	Max Dalban
Vigour	Jean Gehret
Poet sitting on a bench	Jacques Becker
A wedding-guest	Georges Darnoux

Plot: A tale of the triumph of nonconformity. Jean Renoir completely transforms the playwright's original message. Boudu, Renoir's hero and stand-in, is a tramp who loses his dog and decides to throw himself into the Seine to end it all. A generous and free-thinking bookseller saves him. But he gets no thanks from Boudu, who is always at odds with social convention. He wipes his nose with the drapes, rips up books, and seduces the maid/mistress and then the wife of his benefactor. He ends up letting himself go and resuming his life as a tramp on the day of his wedding to the pretty maid.

Chotard et cie / Chotard & Co.

Screenplay: Jean Renoir, based on the play by Roger Ferdinand
Dialogue: Roger Ferdinand
Director: Jean Renoir
Assistant Director: Jacques Becker
Technical Director: Charles Ralleigh
Director of Photography: Joseph-Louis Mundwiller
Cameramen: René Ribault, assisted by Claude Renoir
Continuity: Suzanne de Troye
Set Design: Jean Castanier
Sound: Igor B. Kalinowski
Sound Recording: Tobis Klangfilm
Editing: Marguerite Renoir and Suzanne de Troye
Shot at: Joinville Studios, November–December 1932
Producers: Films Roger Ferdinand
Distributors: Carl Laemmle, for Universal
Length: 2,125 meters
Cast:

François Chotard	Fernand Charpin
His wife, Marie	Jeanne Lory
Their daughter, Reine, wife of Collinet	Jeanne Boitel
Julien Collinet	Georges Pommiès
Emile, grocery boy	Max Dalban
Edmond Ducasse, Police captain	Louis Seigner
Parpaillon	Dignimont
Grocery-store worker	Georges Darnoux
Guests at the masked ball	Fabien Loris and Jacques Becker

Plot: Roger Ferdinand wrote the play, produced the film, and wrote the dialogue, so Jean Renoir had to stick to his text. Only Pomiès, the dancer who plays the wholesale grocer's son-in-law, is a recognizably Renoirian character. He is a novelist who wins the Prix Goncourt but eventually turns to the grocery business, while M. Chotard himself abandons his trade to devote himself to the joys of literary life in the provinces.

1933

Madame Bovary

Screenplay: Jean Renoir, based on the novel by Gustave Flaubert; adapted by Jean Renoir, with the assistance of Anne Mauclair (a.k.a. Mme. Estournelles de Constant) and Karl Koch

Director: Jean Renoir

Assistant Director: Pierre Desouches

Director of Photography: Jean Bachelet

Cameramen: Alphonse Gibory, assisted by Claude Renoir

Set Design: Robert Bys, assisted by Georges Wakhevitch

Sound: Marcel Courmes

Music: Darius Milhaud, *Le Printemps dans la plaine;* hurdy-gurdy music; excerpts from Donizetti's *Lucia di Lammermoor*

Editing: Marguerite Renoir

Shot at: Billancourt Studios, and on location in Normandy, at Rouen, Rys, Lyons-la-Forêt, and environs, fall 1933

Producer: Robert Aron for NSF

Distributor: CID; subsequently, Télédis

Original Length: 3,200 meters

Current Length: 120 minutes

Cast:

Charles Bovary	Pierre Renoir
His mother	Alice Tissot
Emma Bovary	Valentine Tessier
Héloïse, the first Madame Bovary	Héléna Manson
Mr. Homais, the pharmacist	Max Dearly
Léon Dupuis	Daniel Lecourtois
Rodolphe Boulanger	Fernand Fabre
The prefect	Léon Larive
Hippolyte Tautain, the clubfoot	Pierre Laquey
Father Bournisien, the abbot	Louis Florencie
Mr. Guillaumin, the notary	Romain Bouquet
Lheureux, a fabric seller	Robert Le Vigan
Father Rouault	Georges Cahuzac
Dr. Larivière	Alain Dhurtal

Plot: By choosing theatrical rather than movie actors for this film, Jean Renoir doesn't just pictorialize the tale of Emma Bovary, the romantic and vacuous wife of a provincial doctor whose ambitions lead her to debt, disappointment (in her supposedly "brilliant" lovers), and, finally, suicide. Elaborately reconstructing her epoch, Renoir exposes the image Emma Bovary had of herself. She sees herself going through life exactly as Flaubert presented her. Sadly, the film suffers from disastrous cuts.

1934

Toni

Screenplay: Jean Renoir and Carl Einstein
Dialogue: Carl Einstein and Jean Renoir
Director: Jean Renoir
Assistant Directors: Georges Darnoux and Antonio Canor
Director of Photography: Claude Renoir
Set Design: Léon Bourrely
Set Builder: Marius Brouquier
Sound: Bardisbanian, with the assistance of René Sarrazin
Sound Recording: RCA sound truck from Pathé-Nathan Studios
Continuity: Suzanne de Troye
Editing: Marguerite Renoir and Suzanne de Troye
Shot at: Marcel Pagnol Studios, Marseille, and on location at Martigues, summer 1934
Producers: Pierre Gaut, for Films d'aujourd'hui
Development and Printing: Usine Marcel Pagnol, Marseille
Distributors: Films Marcel Pagnol; subsequently, Télédis
Length: 2,600 meters/100 minutes
Cast:

Antonio Canova, called Toni	Charles Blavette
Marie	Jenny Hélia
Josefa	Célia Montalvan
Albert	Max Dalban
Fernand	Edouard Delmont
Gabi	Andrex
Uncle Sébastien	André Kovachevitch

With help from the local police

Plot: A film that is said to have inspired the Italian neorealists. Shot at Martigues, it retells the story of a minor crime relating to the problem of migrant workers, Italians or Spaniards, who come periodically to Southern France or who live there and are scarcely acknowledged by the surrounding population. Toni, an Italian quarry worker, is slain by a local man after the death of a sadistic foreman. The foreman was killed during a domestic quarrel by the beautiful Josefa, a young Spanish woman forced to marry him. Toni is in love with her. Although not to blame for the crime, he is ready to sacrifice himself to save the woman he loves.

1935

Le Crime de Monsieur Lange / The Crime of M. Lange

Screenplay: Jacques Prévert and Jean Renoir, from an idea by Jean Castanier
Director: Jean Renoir
Assistant Directors: Georges Darnoux and Jean Castanier
Artistic Director: Marcel Blondeau
Director of Photography: Jean Bachelet
Still Photographer: Dora Maar
Assistant Cameraman: Champion
Continuity: Marguerite Renoir
Sound: Guy Moreau, Louis Bogé, Roger Loisel, and Robert Teisseire
Sound Recording: Marconi sound truck from Vaison and Moreau
Set Design: Jean Castanier and Robert Gys, assisted by Roger Blin
Music: Jean Wiener; song by Joseph Kosma, "Au jour le jour, à la nuit, la nuit," to lyrics by Jacques Prévert; orchestra lead by Roger Desormières
Editing: Marguerite Renoir
Shot at: Billancourt Studios and on location in Paris (Champs-Elysées, place de la Bastille, Bois de Boulogne) and Le Tréport, October–November 1935
Producer: Geneviève Blondeau for Obéron (André Halley des Fontaines)
Length: 90 minutes
Cast:

Paul Batala	Jules Berry
Amédée Lange	René Lefèvre
Valentine Cardès	Florelle
Estelle	Nadia Sibirskaïa
Edith	Sylvia Bataille
Meunier's son	Henri Guisol
Mr. Beznard, the concierge	Marcel Levesque
His wife, also the concierge	Odette Talazac
Their son, Charles	Maurice Baquet
Bather	Jacques Brunius

Foreman	Marcel Duhamel
Dick, the model maker	Jean Dasté
Louis, a typographer	Paul Grimault
Workers in the publishing company	Guy Decomble,
	Henri Saint-Isles, and Fabien Loris
Whore	Claire Gérard
Parish priest on the train	Edmond Beauchamp
Inspector Juliani, Batala's cousin	Sylvain Itkine
Customer at the inn on the border	René Génin
A worker	Janine Loris

And others, including Jean Brémand, Pierre Huchet, Charbonnier, Marcel Lupovici, Michel Duran, and Dora Maar

Plot: Monsieur Lange is the author of *Arizona Jim,* a serial that appears in a little magazine put out by the printing company where he works. After the boss of the company, a real swindler and a gigolo, disappears, the printing house is managed by the employees, who form a cooperative. Its fantastic success is a source of joy and prosperity to all the people on the block. Sadly, one day the wicked boss resurfaces. As sinister and manipulative as ever, he threatens the group's harmony. Yet he is gunned down by the timid Monsieur Lange, who suddenly identifies with his own hero, a great righter of wrongs.

1936

La Vie est à nous / It's Our Life

Screenplay: Jean Renoir, Paul Vaillant-Coturier, Jean-Paul Le Chanois, and André Zwobada

Directors: Jean Renoir, André Zwobada, Jacques Becker, and Jean-Paul Le Chanois

Assistant Directors: Henri Cartier-Bresson, Marc Maurette, Jacques B. Brunius, Pierre Unik, and Maurice Lime

Photography: Louis Page, Jean-Serge Bourgoin, Jean Isnard, Alain Douarinou, Claude Renoir, Nicolas Hayer

Continuity: Renée Vavasseur

Sound: Robert Teisseire

Shot at: Marlotte and the porte de Montreuil

Producer: French Communist Party

Distributor: from 1969, *l'Avant-Scène cinéma;* then Uni-Ci-Té

Length: 66 minutes

Cast:

The teacher	Jean Dasté
The president of the Administrative Council	Jacques B. Brunius
Marcel Cachin's secretary	Pierre Unik
Brochard "The Stopwatch"	Max Dalban
A factory worker	Madeleine Sologne
A worker	Fabien Loris
Old Gustave Bertin	Emile Drain
Tonin	Charles Blavette
Café owner	Jean Renoir
Secretary at meeting	Madeleine Dax
Metal worker	Roger Blin
Accountant	Sylvain Itkine
Factory head	Georges Spanelly
A secretary	Fernand Bercher
Bailiff	Eddy Debray
René, out of work engineer	Julien Bertheau
Ninette, his friend	Nadia Sibirskaïa
Garage owner	Marcel Lesieur
Mohammed, the North African janitor	O'Brady
M. Moutet, army volunteer	Marcel Duhamel
Young unemployed worker	Jacques Becker
A middle-class woman on the street	Claire Gérard
Little Louis	Jean-Paul Le Chanois
Singers in a dance-hall	Charles Charras and Francis Lemarque

Appearing as themselves: Marcel Cachin, André Marty,
Paul Vaillant-Couturier, Renaud Jean, Martha Destrumeaux,
Marcel Guitton, Jacques Duclos, Maurice Thorez, and
trick photographs of Colonel de La Rocque.

Plot: The French Communist Party never requested a permit to show this film in public; it was not distributed commercially until 1969, in the aftermath of the events of May 1968. A series of sketches, it was intended to convince people to vote Communist in the legislative elections of 1936. Jean Renoir supervised the production and himself directed the parade of the people, an echo of Soviet cinema, that concludes the film.

Une Partie de campagne / A Day in the Country

Screenplay: Jean Renoir, based on the short story by Guy de Maupassant

Director: Jean Renoir

Assistant Directors: Yves Allégret, Jacques Becker, Jacques B. Brunius, Henri Cartier-Bresson, Claude Heymann, and Luchino Visconti
Director of Photography: Claude Renoir
Cameramen: Jean-Serge Bourgoin, assisted by Albert Viguier and Eli Lotar
Set Design: Robert Gys
Sound: Marcel Courmes and Joseph de Bretagne
Sound Recording: RCA
Editing: Marguerite Renoir (final edit: Marinette Cadix and Marcel Cravenne, under the supervision of Marguerite Renoir)
Music: Joseph Kosma, a song hummed by Germaine Montero; orchestra lead by Roger Desormières
Shot: on location at pont de Sorques, the vicinity of Marlotte and Montigny-sur-Loing, July and August 1939
Producers: Roger Woog and Jacques B. Brunius for Pierre Braunberger
Distributors: Films du Panthéon
Length: 40 minutes
Cast:

Henriette Dufour	Sylvia Bataille
Her mother, Juliette	Jane Marken
Her father, Cyprien	Gabriello
Henri	Georges Darnoux
Rodolphe	Jacques B. Brunius
Anatole	Paul Temps
The grandmother	Gabrielle Fontan
Papa Poulain, the innkeeper	Jean Renoir
Servant	Marguerite Renoir
The old parish priest	Pierre Lestringuez
A young fisherman	Alain Renoir

Plot: Jean Renoir and Pierre Braunberger picked out Maupassant's short story as a vehicle for Sylvia Bataille. Jean was delighted by her sensual beauty and the charm of the landscape along the Loing that his father had once loved so well. The Dufour family, Parisian hardware store owners, set out to spend Sunday in the country. Henriette, their daughter, is engaged to Anatole, a drab fellow who works at the store. At the inn where they stop for lunch, mother and daughter, lulled by the spring air, agree to an outing with two friendly young rowers, who immediately begin courting them. A thunderstorm breaks out and cuts short the idyllic relationship between Henriette and her suitor. That afternoon will remain in her memory as the sole moment of love in her life. The film that has come down to us is incomplete, but perfect: Sylvia Bataille's face vividly reflects the blossoming of passion, and, in turn, the most heartrending resignation.

Les Bas Fonds / The Lower Depths

Screenplay: Eugene Zamiatin, Jacques Companeez, based on the play by Maxim Gorky; adaptation and dialogue by Charles Spaak and Jean Renoir
Director: Jean Renoir
Assistant Directors: Jacques Becker and Joseph Soiffer
Photography: Fedoze Bourgassoff and Jean Bachelet
Cameraman: Jacques Mercanton
Music: Jean Wiener
Set Manager: Koura
Sound: Robert Ivonnet
Set Design: Eugène Lourié and Hugues Laurent
Editing: Marguerite Renoir
Shot at: Eclair Studios (Epinay) and on location on the banks of the Seine between Epinay and Saint-Denis, 24 August to October 1936
Producers: Alexander Kamenka and Vladimir Zederbaum for Albatros
Distributors: Les Distributeurs Français, S.A.
Length: 90 minutes
Cast:

The Baron	Louis Jouvet
Pépel	Jean Gabin
Vassilissa	Suzy Prim
Kostileff	Vladimir Sokoloff
Natasha	Junie Astor
The actor	Robert Le Vigan
The inspector	Gabriello
The Count	Camille Bert
Félix, the Baron's butler	Léon Larive
The superintendent	Fernand Bercher
Luka	René Génin
Aliocha, the accordeon player	Maurice Baquet
Nastia, the prostitute	Jany Holt
Satine, the telegraph operator	Paul Temps

This film was the first to win the "Prix Louis Delluc" in 1936.
Plot: A ruined baron takes up residence in Kostileff's shelter along with the thief, Pépel, who has become his friend. He adapts

quickly to this closed world, which is also inhabited by Vassilissa, who is Kostileff's wife and Pépel's mistress; Vassilissa's sister, Natasha, whom Pépel is in love with, an actor, and a series of other characters, one more wretched than the next. They detest Kostileff, who manipulates them and ends up getting himself killed in a brawl. After his murder, Pépel runs off with Natacha, his hopes still high. Although the characters in the film bear Russian names, Jean Renoir made no effect to put them in a Russian context.

1937

La Grande Illusion / Grand Illusion

Screenplay: Charles Spaak and Jean Renoir
Director: Jean Renoir
Assistant Directors: Jacques Becker and Robert Rips
Technical Adviser: Karl Koch
Director of Photography: Christian Matras
Cameramen: Claude Renoir, assisted by Ernest Bourreaud and Jean-Serge Bourgoin
Still Photographer: Sam Levin
Continuity: Gourdji (Françoise Giroud)
Sound: Joseph de Bretagne
Set Design: Eugène Lourié
Music: Joseph Kosma
Editing: Marguerite Renoir, assisted by Marthe Huguet
Shot at: Eclair Studios (Billancourt), and on location at Neuf-Brisach (Upper Rhine) and the barracks at Colmar
Producers: Raymond Blondy, for Réalisation d'art cinématographique (Frank Rollmer and Albert Pinkevitch)
Distributors: RIC, then Cinédis, Filmsonor-Gaumont and les Grands Films Classiques
Length: 113 minutes
Cast:

Captain von Rauffenstein	Erich von Stroheim
Lieutenant Maréchal	Jean Gabin
Captain de Boeldieu	Pierre Fresnay
Rosenthal	Marcel Dalio
Traquet, the actor	Julien Carette
A civil engineer	Gaston Modot

A teacher	Jean Dasté
Cartier, a soldier	Georges Péclet
A British officer	Jacques Becker
Demolder	Sylvain Itkine
Elsa, the peasant woman	Dita Parlo
Krantz	Werner Florian
Ringis	Claude Sainval

And others including Karl Heil, Michel Salina, and Karl Koch
This film won the prize for the best overall work of art in the
Venice Biennale of 1937 and the prize for the best foreign film in
New York 1938, and it was the first French film to receive a
citation in the international competition at Brussels in 1958.

Plot: World War I, 1916: A fighter plane manned by Lieutenant Maréchal and Captain de Boeldieu is shot down behind German lines. The two officers are taken prisoner. In their cell block, prison life has not eradicated social barriers, but friendship and a willingness to help survive nonetheless. Their attempt to escape fails. Transferred to a fortress, Maréchal and Boeldieu meet up with Rosenthal, whose generosity they already knew and appreciated. The commandant of the fortress speaks immediately of his own affinities with Boeldieu: their birth and education are the same. Boeldieu, too, is conscious of it, but that doesn't prevent him from sacrificing his own life so that his two friends can make good their escape this time. Beneath the uniforms and the harshness of their circumstance, Jean Renoir shows us human beings in all their complexity. He did not like war movies, and his is a far cry from typical examples of the genre.

La Marseillaise

Screenplay: Jean Renoir, with the help of Karl Koch and Nina Martel-Dreyfus

Director: Jean Renoir

Assistant Directors: Jacques Becker, Claude Renoir (Jean's brother), Jean-Paul Dreyfus, Louis Demazure, Marc Maurette, Antoine (Tony) and Francine Corteggiani. Lotte Reiniger was responsible for the shadow puppets.

Photography: Jean-Serge Bourgoin, Alain Douarinou, Jean-Marie Maillols, Jean-Paul Alphen, and Jean Louis

Still Photographer: Sam Levin

Set Design: Georges Wakhevitch and Jean Périer

Costumes: L. Granier; Coco Chanel (Marie-Antoinette's dress)

Music: Lalande, Grétry, Mozart, J. S. Bach, Rouget de l'Isle, Joseph Kosma, and Sauveplane
Sound: Joseph de Bretagne, Jean-Roger Bertrand, and J. Demède
Sound Recording: Western Electric
Grips: CGT Régisseurs technical workers group (Edouard Lepage, Raymond Pillon, Barnathan, Veuillard, Henri Lepage, Renée Decrais, Deffras)
Editing: Marguerite Renoir, with help from Marthe Huguet
Shot at: Billancourt Studios, and on location at Fontainebleau, Alsace, Antibe, Haute-Provence, Paris (place du Panthéon), summer–fall 1937
Producers: André Zwobada and A. Seigneur, for the CGT; later, Louis Joly for Société de production et d'exploitation du film *La Marseillaise*
Distributors: RAC, then Compagnie Jean Renoir
Length: 135 minutes
Cast:

THE COURT:

Louis XVI	Pierre Renoir
Marie-Antoinette	Lise Delamare
Picard, the King's valet	Léon Larive
La Rochefoucauld-Liancourt	William Aguet
Madame de Lamballe	Elisa Ruis
Madame Elisabeth	Germaine Lefébure
The Dauphin	Marie-Pierre Sordet-Dantès
The Dauphine	Yveline Auriol
Two attendants	Pamela Stirling, Genia Vaury

CIVIL AND MILITARY AUTHORITIES:

Roederer, the public prosecutor	Louis Jouvet
The mayor of the village	Jean Aquistapace
La Chesnaye	Georges Spanelly
Dubouchage	Pierre Nay
Captain Langlade	Jaque-Catelain
Leroux	Edmond Castel
Westerman	Werner Florian-Zach

THE ARISTOCRATS:

Monsieur de Saint-Laurent	Aimé Clariond
The lord of the village	Maurice Escande
Monsieur de Saint-Méry	André Zibral

Monsieur de Fougerolles	Jean Ayme
Madame de Saint-Laurent	Irène Joachim

PEOPLE FROM MARSEILLE:

Honoré Arnaud	Andrex
Jean-Joseph Bomier	Charles Blavette and Edmond Ardisson
Javel	Paul Dullac
Moissan	Jean-Louis Allibert
Fernand Flament	Ardisson

THE PEOPLE:

Louison	Nadia Sibirskaïa
The interrogator	Jenny Hélia
Two volunteers	Gaston Modot and Julien Carette
A peasant woman	Séverine Lerczinska
Bomier's mother	Marthe Marty
Thérèse	Odette Cazau
The parish priest	Edmond Beauchamp
Clémence	Blanche Destournelles

Plot: Jean Renoir wanted to show, in his own words, that "the Revolution was brought about by normal, intelligent, and pleasant people." The first sequence of *La Marseillaise* takes place in a scrub forest in Provence where three men have gone to escape the injustice that is everywhere; then the scene switches to the story of a batallion of confederates from Marseille who arrive in Paris the day that Louis XVI signed the Brunswick Manifesto. After the bloody riots that result, the King himself is forced to make good his escape. The film has several facets: we see what life was like for Louis XVI, who could well be counted among the "normal, intelligent, and pleasant people." Other scenes give us a close-up of the nobility who fled to Germany, the "emigrés of Coblenz"; they seem more deserving of pity than hatred, which is remarkable in itself, since the film was apparently conceived in the spirit of the Popular Front.

1938

La Bête humaine / The Beast in Man

Screenplay: Jean Renoir, based on the novel by Emile Zola
Director: Jean Renoir
Assistant Directors: Claude Renoir (Jean's brother) and Suzanne de Troye

Director of Photography: Curt Courant
Cameramen: Claude Renoir and Jacques Natteau, assisted by Maurice
  Pecqueux, Guy Ferrier, and Alain Renoir (a trainee)
Still Photographer: Sam Levin
Sound: Robert Tesseire
Sound Recording: RCA
Music: Joseph Kosma
Set Design: Eugène Lourié
Editing: Marguerite Renoir; for the railroad scenes, Suzanne de Troye
Shot at: Billancourt Studios, and on location at the gare Saint-Lazare,
  Evreux, Le Havre, and the vicinity of Bréauté-Beuzeville, Au-
  gust–September 1938
Producer: Roland Tual, for Paris Film Production (Robert Hakim)
Distributors: Paris Film
Length: 105 minutes
Cast:

Jacques Lantier	Jean Gabin
Séverine	Simone Simon
Roubaud, her husband	Fernand Ledoux
Pecqueux	Julien Carette
Victoire, his wife	Colette Régis
Philomène Sauvagnat	Jenny Hélia
Henri Dauvergne	Gérard Landry
Grandmorin	Jacques Berlioz
His butler	Léon Larive
Camy-Lamothe, the secretary	Georges Spanelly
Cabuche, the poacher	Jean Renoir
Two farmhands	Emile Genevois and Jacques B. Brunius
A maintenance man	Marcel Pérès
Flore	Blanchette Brunoy
A traveler	Claire Gérard
Dabadie, section head	Tony Corteggiani
Misard, a level-crossing keeper	Guy Decomble
Aunt Phasie, the godmother	Charlotte Clasis
Singer at the Trainmen's Ball	Marcel Veyran

Plot: So that the trains and costumes of another era would not distract
his audience, Jean Renoir situated his adaptation of Zola's novel
in 1938. He wanted to make it a true tragedy. The hero, Jacques
Lantier, is haunted by the curse of alcoholism, and the action
from start to finish has a driving intensity that Zola would not
have disavowed. Lantier burns with passion for Séverine, a
strange little creature whose callowness results in a kind of non-

chalance bordering on frigidity. She is the accomplice of her jealous husband and passively assists in the murder of her old benefactor and lover. Lantier catches them in the act, but out of love for her says nothing. He is unable to kill her husband, as she asks him to, and he ends up strangling her in a fit of passion. Mad with grief, he kills himself, which is not the way Zola ended the novel. Right before his suicide comes one of the most beautiful moments in film, the justly famous Trainmen's Ball.

1939

La Règle du jeu / The Rules of the Game

Screenplay: Jean Renoir, assisted by Karl Koch
Director: Jean Renoir
Assistant Directors: Karl Koch, André Zwobada, Henri Cartier-Bresson, and Raymond Pillon
Technical Consultant: Tony Corteggiani, for the hunting scenes
Director of Photography: Jean Bachelet
Cameramen: Jacques Lemare, assisted by Jean-Paul Alphen and Alain Renoir
Sound: Joseph de Bretagne
Sound Recording: Western Electric
Continuity: Dido Freire
Set Design: Eugène Lourié, assisted by Max Douy
Costumes: Coco Chanel
Editing: Marguerite Renoir, assisted by Marthe Huguet
Shot at: Joinville Studios and on location at La Motte-Beuvron, the Castle of La Ferté-St. Aubin, Aubigny, and the vicinity of Brinon-sur-Sauldre, February–April 1939
Producers: Claude Renoir (Jean's brother), for NEF (Nouvelles Editions Françaises)
Distributors: NEF (1939); Gaumont (1948); Les Grands Films Classiques (since 1965, in a restored and complete version)
Length: (165 version) 112 minutes
Cast:

Robert de La Chesnaye, a marquis	Marcel Dalio
Christine, his wife	Nora Gregor
André Jurieux	Roland Toutain
Octave	Jean Renoir
Geneviève de Marras	Mila Parély

Charlotte de La Plante	Odette Talazac
The General	Pierre Magnier
Saint-Aubin	Pierre Nay
Jackie	Anne Mayen
M. La Bruyère	Richard Francoeur
His wife	Claire Gérard
Berthelin	Tony Corteggiani
Effeminate guest	Géo Forster
The South American	Nicolas Amato
Lisette, the maid	Paulette Dubost
Her husband, Edouard Schumacher, the gamekeeper	Gaston Modot
Marceau, the poacher	Julien Carette
Corneille, the majordomo	Eddy Debray
The head cook	Léon Larive
A serving girl	Jenny Hélia
Radio reporter at the airport	Lise Elina
Engineer from Caudron Aircraft	André Zwobada
The radio announcer	Camille François
The British manservant	Henri Cartier-Bresson

Plot: La Chesnaye, a rich marquis whose mother was a Jewess and whose wife is the daughter of a great Viennese musician, has invited some friends to their castle in the Sologne. An evening of theater and a masked ball are in the offing, along with the murder of a naive man, a record-breaking aviator in love with the marquess, who does not know how to bend to the rules of the game. The life of the servants reflects that of their masters: that is, their amorous adventures are the same, but they are more costly since servants are more stringent about respectability. Their snobbism and even racism make this "drame gai" a trenchant critique of society dressed up as elegant banter. The characters reveal, sometimes despite themselves, their real sources of anguish; the film is unique for its psychological depth and clarity.

1941

Swamp Water

Screenplay: Dudley Nichols, based on a story by Vereen Bell
Director: Jean Renoir
Photography: Peverell Marley and Lucien Ballard

Music: David Rudolph
Set Design: Thomas Little
Artistic Director: Richard Day
Editing: Walter Thompson
Shot at: Waycross, Georgia, and the Okefenokee Swamp
Producer: Irving Pichell, for Twentieth Century–Fox
Distributors: Twentieth Century–Fox
Length: 86 minutes
Cast:

Ben Ragan	Dana Andrews
Thursday Ragan	Walter Huston
Jesse Wick	John Carradine
Sheriff Jeb MacKane	Eugene Pallette
Jim Dorson	Ward Bond
Bud Dorson	Guinn Williams
Julie	Ann Baxter
Mabel Mackenzie	Virginia Gilmore
Tom Keefer	Walter Brennan
Hannah	Mary Howard
Marty McCord	Russell Simpson
Hardy Ragan	Joseph Sawyer
Tulle Mackenzie	Paul Burns
The barber	Dave Morris
Fred Ulm	Frank Austin
Miles Tonkin	Matt Williams

Plot: While hunting one day, Ben Ragan loses his dog and sets off to
find him. He happens on the hideout of Tom Keefer, who has
been living for several years in the wild swamps of southern
Georgia because he was accused of a crime he didn't commit. Ben
decides to prove him innocent and to call those really responsible
to account. He succeeds, and one of the guilty ones disappears in
quicksand, while the other gets himself lost in the swamp. Ben's
reward for his courage is the love of Tom's daughter.

1943

This Land is Mine

Screenplay: Dudley Nichols and Jean Renoir
Director: Jean Renoir
Assistant Director: Edward Donohue

Director of Photography: Frank Redman
Special Effects: Vernon L. Walker
Sound: Terry Kellum and James Stewart
Music: Lothar Perl
Set Design: Albert d'Agostino
Shot at: Hollywood
Editing: Frederic Knudtsen
Producer: Jean Renoir and Dudley Nichols, for RKO
Associate Producer: Eugène Lourié
Distributors: RKO
Length: 103 minutes
Cast:

Albert Lory	Charles Laughton
Paul Martin	Kent Smith
Louise Martin, his sister	Maureen O'Hara
George Lambert	George Sanders
Major von Keller	Walter Slezack
Mrs. Lory, Albert's mother	Una O'Connor
Professor Sorel	Philip Merivale
Julie Grant	Nancy Gates
Henry Manville, the mayor	Thurston Hall
The judge	Ivan Simpson
The public prosecutor	George Coulouris
Mr. Lorraine	Wheaton Chambers
Edmund Lorraine	John Donnat
Lt. Schwartz	Frank Allen
Little Man	Leo Bulgakov
Mrs. Lorraine	Cecile Wetson

Plot: A film that addresses the issue of collaboration. In a city occupied by Nazis (there is nothing to show that it is in France), Lory, a teacher, is hired against his will. He is secretly in love with Louise, his colleague, and he is taken hostage by the Germans when Paul, Louise's brother, who is a member of the resistance, throws a bomb at the commandant's car. Paul is denounced by Louise's fiancé, a collaborator, who later kills himself in a fit of remorse, and also by Lory's mother, who wants to save her own son. Paul is executed and Lory released, but he glorifies the spirit of the resistance by reading the Declaration of the Rights of Man aloud to his class. This prompts his second arrest, but as he is led away, Louise takes up the reading where he left off.

1944

Salute to France / Salut à la France

Screenplay: Philip Dunne, Jean Renoir, and Burgess Meredith
Director: Jean Renoir
Photography: Army Pictorial Service
Music: Kurt Weill
Shot at: New York
Editing: under the supervision of Helen Van Dongen
Producer: Office of War Information
Distributors: Associated Artists
Length: 540 meters
Cast:

Tommy	Burgess Meredith
Joe	Garson Kanin
Jacques, the narrator	Claude Dauphin, who also plays various

      other roles, including the soldier, the peasant, the worker, etc.

Plot: A short film that was distributed right after the liberation. Its goal was to show American soldiers what the country they were landing in was like, and to give the French a sense of what GIs were like.

1945

The Southerner / L'Homme du sud

Screenplay: Jean Renoir, based on the novel by George Perry Sessions, *Hold Autumn in Your Hand* (New York, 1950), adapted by Hugo Butler, with dialogue by Jean Renoir
Director: Jean Renoir
Assistant Director: Robert Aldrich
Director of Photography: Lucien Andriot
Sound: Frank Webster
Music: Werner Janssen
Set Design: Eugène Lourié
Shot at: Hollywood
Editing: Gregg Tallas
Producers: David L. Loew and Robert Hakim
Distributors: Associated Artists
Length: 92 minutes

Cast:

Sam Tucker	Zachary Scott
Nora, his wife	Betty Field
Jottie, their son	Jay Gilpin
The grandmother	Beulah Bondi
Devers	J. Carroll Nash
Harmie Jenkins	Percy Killbride
Momma	Blanche Yurka
Tim	Charles Kemper
Finlay Hewitt	Norman Lloyd
Lizzie	Estelle Taylor
Becky	Noreen Nash
The doctor	Jack Norworth

This film won best film at the Venice Biennale of 1946, as well as Best Director from the National Board of Review.

Plot: Before the war, a family of farmers in Tennessee decides to rebuild a miserable farm left in ruins and to plant the land around it. But Mother Nature is wild and harsh, and the family has a very hard time. Yet they accept their terrible ordeals and ascribe them to the will of God. They have terrible relations with a hateful neighbor who prefers to give milk to his pigs instead of to their little boy, who comes down with scurvy. A violent thunderstorm sweeps down on their fields just when the harvest looks promising. They lose everything, even the cow they finally succeeded in buying. Yet they decide to continue, their faith unquenched.

1946

The Diary of a Chambermaid / Le Journal d'une femme de chambre

Screenplay: Jean Renoir and Burgess Meredith, based on a play by André Heuzé, André de Lorde, and Thielly Nores, which was in turn based on the novel by Octave Mirbeau

Director: Jean Renoir

Assistant Directors: Joseph Depew

Director of Photography: Lucien Andriot

Special Effects: Lee Zavitz

Sound: William Lynch

Music: Michel Michelet

Set Design: Eugène Lourié; sets built by J. Héron

Costumes: Barbara Karinska

Shot at: General Services Studios, Hollywood
Editing: James Smith
Producers: Benedict Bogeaus and Burgess Meredith
Associate Producers: Corley Harriman and Arthur M. Landau
Distributor: United Artists
Length: 91 minutes
Cast:

Célestine	Paulette Goddard
Captain Mauger	Burgess Meredith
George Lanlaire	Kurt Hatfield
Mr. Lanlaire	Reginald Owen
Mrs. Lanlaire	Judith Anderson
Joseph	Francis Lederer
Rose	Florence Bates
Louise	Irene Ryan
Marianne	Almira Sessions

Plot: Jean Renoir and Burgess Meredith took liberties with Mirbeau. To begin with, being in Hollywood, Jean had no desire to reconstruct French provincial life at the beginning of the century. He shot absolutely everything in the studio, so as to be unequivocal: all was strictly artificial. As for the story, they changed it a lot. In 1946, moralizing was still fashionable in American films. You had to be careful. Burgess Meredith, who gave himself the role of Captain Mauger, made him into a fantastic, utterly burlesque character. Célestine is not taken with Joseph: she distrusts him and will not go near him until she is rejected by George, the master's son, who thinks he is about to die of tuberculosis. Joseph is a dishonest man who steals from his masters and won't stop even at killing Captain Mauger in order to get his nest egg. George intervenes, and he is strong enough to defend himself. He wants to save Célestine, whom he loves. The evildoer Joseph gets lynched by the villagers, and George and Célestine are able to live together.

The Woman on the Beach / La Femme sur la plage

Screenplay: Jean Renoir, Frank Davis, and J. R. Michael Hogan, based
    on the novel by Mitchell Wilson, *None So Blind*
Director: Jean Renoir
Assistant Director: James Casey
Artistic Directors: Albert S. d'Agostino and Walter E. Keller
Photography: Harry Wild and Leo Tover
Sound: John L. Speak and Clem Portman

Music: Hans Eisler
Set Design: Darrell Silvera and John Sturtevant
Shot at: Hollywood
Editing: Roland Gross and Lyle Boyer
Producer: Jack L. Gross, for RKO
Associate Producer: Will Price
Length: 71 minutes
Cast:

Peggy Butler	Joan Bennett
Her husband, Tod Butler	Charles Bickford
Lt. Scott Burnett	Robert Ryan
Eve Deddes	Nan Leslie
Vernecke	Walter Sande
Mrs. Vernecke	Irene Ryan
Kirk	Glenn Vernon
Lars	Frank Doren
Jimmy	Jay Norris

Plot: Lt. Burnett, a Coast Guard officer, happens upon the lovely and mysterious Peggy Butler, who is gathering driftwood on the beach. A world divides them: she is married to Tod Butler, a blind painter with whom she has a love/hate relationship. As for the lieutenant, who suffers from shellshock, he is a simple creature engaged to a nice, pure young thing. It is clear that the attraction Peggy has for both men is purely sexual, even though Renoir does not put a single gesture of affection between them and her on the screen. Burnett is so confused that he goes so far as to make Butler walk along a cliff because he doubts his blindness (and also because he wishes he were dead). The end of the film is strange and beautiful, as is the allusive narrative style of the whole. After his dangerous walk, Tod Butler sets fire to his canvases. Peggy calls Burnett for help, but the house cannot be saved, and it, along with all the painter's work, perishes in the flames. Peggy then goes off with her husband, and Burnett, set free, returns to the simple life he had before.

1950

The River / Le Fleuve

Screenplay: Rumer Godden and Jean Renoir, based on Rumer Godden's novel of the same name
Director: Jean Renoir

Assistant Director: Forrest Judd
Director of Photography: Claude Renoir (Technicolor)
Cameraman: Romananda Sen Gupta
Sound: Charles Paulton and Charles Knott, with the help of Harishad-
     nan J. das Gupta, Sukhano y Sen, and Bansi Ashe
Music: Indian folk music and Weber's *Invitation to the Dance*
Set Design: Eugène Lourié and Bansi Chandra Gupta
Editing: George Gale
Shot at: Calcutta, on the banks of the Ganges
Producers: Kenneth McEldowney, Kalyan Gupta, and J. Renoir for Ori-
     ental International Films (with the support of the Theater Guild)
Distributors: Associated Artists
Length: 99 minutes
Cast:

The mother	Nora Swinburne
The father	Esmond Knight
Mr. John	Arthur Shields
Captain John	Thomas E. Breen
Melanie	Radha Shri Ram
Nan	Suprova Mukerjee
Harriet	Patricia Walters
Valery	Adrienne Corri
Bogey	Richard Foster
Elizabeth	Penelope Wilkinson
Muffie	Jane Harris
Mouse	Jennifer Harris
Victoria	Cecily Wood
Shajin Singh	Ram Singh
Kanu	Nimai Barik
Anil	Trilak Jetley
Narrator	June Hillman

This film won first prize in the International Competition
in the Venice Biennale of 1951.

Plot: India, not from the perspective of an Indian, but of a British family. The father works in a jute factory; his oldest daughter is an
adolescent who wants to become a writer. She has two girlfriends,
one of them Eurasian, the other British, like herself. The three
young women are excited by the arrival of a young American,
Captain John, who has lost a leg in the war and wonders what
the future holds for him. The Englishwomen throw themselves at
his feet. As for Melanie, the Eurasian, she speaks to him like a
Hindu woman, poetically and with wisdom, but she is in love

with him no less than the others. While the girls are sorting out their passions and jealousies, the narrator's younger brother dies of snakebite, the American leaves, alone as ever, and the Ganges, the holy river, continues flowing, like the ceaseless stream of life. "The world is one." The images of Jean Renoir's first color film express more than the beauty of the countryside or the native population; they create a serene harmony.

1952

La Carrosse d'or / The Golden Coach

Screenplay: Jean Renoir, Renzo Avenzo, Giulio Macchi, Jack Kirland, and Ginette Doynel, based on the play by Prosper Mérimée, *le Carrosse du Saint-Sacrement*
Director: Jean Renoir
Assistant Directors: Marc Maurette, Giulio Macchi, and Franco Palagi
Photography: Claude Renoir and Ronald Hill; assisting with the Technicolor film: Ernest Tiley and Hubert Salisbury
Cameraman: Rodolfo Lombardi
Continuity: Ginette Doynel
Sound: Joseph de Bretagne and Olidio del Grande
Sound Recording: Western Electric
Music: Antonio Vivaldi, Arcangelo Corelli, and Olivier Mettra
Set Design: Mario Chiari
Costumes: Mario de Matteis
Editing: Mario Serandrei and David Hawkins
Shot at: Cinecittà Studios, starting February 4, 1952
Producers: A French/Italian coproduction: Valentino Brosio and Giuseppe Bardogni for Panaria Films (Francesco Alliata) and Hoche Productions (Ray Ventura)
Distributors: Corona
Length: 100 minutes
Cast:

Camilla	Anna Magnani
Ferdinand, the viceroy	Duncan Lamont
Don Antonio, head of the troupe	Odoardo Spadaro
Ramon, the bullfighter	Riccardo Rioli
Felipe Aquierre	Paul Campbell
Isabelle	Nada Fiorelli
Martinez	George Higgins
Arlequin	Dante

Dr. Balanzon	Rino
Irene Altamirano, the marquess	Gisela Mathews
The old actress	Lina Marengo
The Duke of Castro	Ralph Truman
The Duchess of Castro	Elena Altieri
Captain Fracasse	Renato Chiantoni

Plot: Camilla, the star of a *commedia dell' arte* troupe, seduces the viceroy of a baroque Latin American country along with Ramon, its most famous bullfighter. Within her troupe, Felipe is madly in love with her. But whom does she love? Felipe and Ramon fight an inconclusive duel. Meanwhile, the viceroy really hopes to win her, although his mistress and the whole court hardly appreciate her presence. The courtiers are vying with each other for a splendid golden coach that their sovereign has sent from Italy. As a symbol of his power, the viceroy offers it to Camilla, thinking that he will in one stroke guarantee himself her heart and dispossess the envious courtiers. But mutinous grumbling breaks out in the palace as a result. Camilla ends up providing the unexpected solution: she gives the golden coach to the bishop and resumes her position in the troupe. Her one true love is the theater.

1954

French Cancan

Screenplay: Jean Renoir, based on an idea by André-Paul Antoine
Director: Jean Renoir
Assistant Directors: Serge Vallin, Pierre Kast, Jacques Rivette, Paul Seban, and Lucien Lippens
Director of Photography: Michel Kelber (Technicolor)
Still Photographer: Serge Beauvarlet
Cameramen: Henri Tiquet, assisted by Vladimir Lang and Georges Barsky
Choreography: Georges Grandjean
Sound: Antoine Petitjean
Sound Recording: Western Electric
Music: Georges Van Parys; lyrics to "La Complainte de la Butte" by Jean Renoir; includes a medley of tunes from the caf'conc' of 1900
Set Design: Max Douy, assisted by Jacques Saulnier
Interiors: Vigneau
Costumes: Rosine Delamare, designer; Coquatrix and Karinska, makers

Continuity: Ginette Doynel
Editing: Boris Lewin
Shot at: Joinville Studios, October 4–December 20, 1954
Producer: Louis Wipf, for Franco London Films/Jolly Films
Assistant to the Producer: Simone Clément
Distributors: Gaumont
Length: 97 minutes
Cast:

Danglard	Jean Gabin
Lola di Castro, a.k.a. "La Belle Abbesse"	Maria Felix
Nini	Françoise Arnoul
Baron Walter	Jean-Roger Caussimon
Prince Alexandre	Gianni Esposito
Casimir	Philippe Clay
Valorgueil	Michel Piccoli
Coudrier	Jean Parédès
Barjolin	Albert Rémy
Guibole	Lydia Johnson
Proprietor of La Reine Blanche	Max Dalban
Bison	Jacques Jouanneau
Savate	Jean-Marc Tennberg
Madame Olympe, Nini's mother	Valentine Tessier
Isidore, the café waiter	Hubert Deschamps
Paulo, the baker	Franco Pastorino
Génisse	Dora Doll
Thérèse	Annick Morice
Bigoudi	Michèle Nadal
Ester Georges	Anna Amendola (with the voice of Cora Vaucaire)
Paquita	Anne-Marie Mersen
Titine	Sylvine Delannoy
Mimi Prunelle	Pâquerette
The Commandant	Léo Campion
Oscar, the piano player	Gaston Gabaroche
The minister	Jacque-Catelain
The bailiff	Pierre Moncorbier
The hotel manager	Jean Mortier
The neighbor	André Numès, fils
The elevator operator	Robert Auboyneau
The Pygmy	Laurence Bataille
Pierrot siffleur	Pierre Olaf
Two young snobs	Jacques Ciron and Claude Arnay

Police inspector	R. J. Chauffard
Béatrix	France Roche
Eléonore	Michèle Philippe
Danglard's manservant	Gaston Modot
The doctor	Jacques Hilling
Yvette Guilbert	Patachou
Eugénie Buffet	Edith Piaf
Paul Delmet	André Claveau
Paulus	Jean Raymond

Plot: A studio reconstruction, with a painter's choice of colors, of life in a caf'conc' in Montmartre in 1900, complete with Toulouse-Lautrec's models and other characters associated with the impressionists (it was a milieu that Jean had learned to love at a very tender age). The story ennobles those who loved their art, while the greedy producers who were actually enemies of the art they pretended to defend get their just desserts. Danglade the Great, having already launched some very famous caf'conc's and having no illusions about the risks involved, wants to put together a review whose star will be Nini, a young laundress whom he thinks has the makings of a dancer. No small undertaking: "La Belle Abbesse," in theory his mistress, is jealous of Nini, and the silent partners take her side. But thanks to Danglade's pertinacity, to the money of a nice prince in love with Nini, and to her talents, Danglade and Nini are triumphant. Her Pygmalion teaches Nini that she must devote herself to her art and not waste time crying over faithless lovers.

1956

Eléna et les Hommes / Eléna and Her Men

Screenplay: Jean Renoir, adapted by Jean Serge and Jean Renoir
Director: Jean Renoir
Assistant Director: Serge Vallin and Lucien Lippens
Director of Photography: Claude Renoir (Eastmancolor)
Sound: William Sivel
Music: Joseph Kosma, with arrangements of period songs by Georges Van Parys
Continuity: Ginette Doynel
Set Design: Jean-André, assisted by Jacques Saulnier
Costumes: Rosine Delamare and Monique Plotin

Editing: Boris Lewin
Shot at: Saint-Maurice Studios and on location at the parc d'Ermenon-
ville and the bois St. Cloud, December 1, 1955–March 17, 1956
Producers: Franco London Films, les Films Gibé, and Electra Com-
pania Cinematografica
Distributors: Cinédis
Length: 96 minutes
Cast:

Princess Eléna Sorokovska	Ingrid Bergman
General François Rollan	Jean Marais
Henri de Chevincourt	Mel Ferrer
Hector Chaillol, the orderly	Jean Richard
Lolotte, the maid	Magali Noël
Miarka, the gipsy	Juliette Greco
Martin-Michaud	Pierre Bertin
Lionel Villaret, the composer	Jean Claudio
Isnard	Jean Castanier
Paulette Escoffier	Elina Labourdette
Rosa la Rose	Dora Doll
Godin	Frédéric Duvallès
His son, Eugène	Jacques Jouanneau
Marbeau	Mirko Ellis
Lisbonne	Jacques Hilling
Fleury	Renaud Mary
The head of the Romanies	Gaston Modot
Duchêne	Jacques Morel
Denise	Michèle Nadal
Buchez	Albert Rémy
Olga	Olga Valéry
Singer in the street	Marjane

Plot: Eléna, a Polish princess living in France in the 1880s, is an extravagant widow. She believes she has the power to help men achieve
exceptional success. After helping a composer with his career,
she attaches herself to a general whom the government wants to
get rid of; he is not unlike General Boulanger. One of the general's friends, the Viscount de Chevincourt, is in love with Eléna.
Martin-Michaud, a wealthy industrialist, is also in love with her
and wants to marry her. Everyone meets in the country in his
castle. There Eléna is forced to rethink her strategy: the general
prefers to run away with his mistress instead of acquiring power.
She consoles herself in the arms of Chevincourt, who teaches her

the joys of doing nothing. The film makes a fine art of its lightness, but there is an underlying element of tragedy even so.

1959

Le Testament du Docteur Cordelier / The Testament of Dr. Cordelier

Screenplay: Jean Renoir, based on the Robert Louis Stevenson story, "Doctor Jekyll and Mr. Hyde"
Director: Jean Renoir
Assistant Directors: Maurice Bechey and Jean-Pierre Spiero
Artistic Assistant: Jean Serge
Technical Assistant: Yves-André Hubert
Director of Photography: Georges Leclerc
Cameramen: Bernard Giraux, Jean Graglia, Pierre Guégen, Pierre Lebon, Gilbert Perrot-Minot, Arthur Raymond, and Gilbert Sandoz
Continuity: Andrée Gauthey and Marinette Pesquet
Sound: Joseph Richard
Music: Joseph Kosma
Set Design: Marcel-Louis Dielot
Costumes: Monique Dunand
Editing: Renée Lichtig
Shot at: RTF Studios, and on location in Paris (Montmartre, avenue Paul-Doumer) and Marnes-la-Coquette, January 1959
Producers: Albert Hollebecke for RTF Sofirad and Compagnie Jean Renoir
Distributors: Consortium Pathé
Length: 100 minutes
Cast:

Doctor Cordelier and Opale	Jean-Louis Barrault
Mr. Joly	Teddy Bilis
Doctor Lucien Séverin	Michel Vitold
Désiré, the majordomo	Jean Topart
Marguerite	Micheline Gary
Inspector Salbris	André Certes
Superintendent Lardaut	Jacques Dannoville
Manager of the sleazy hotel	Jean-Pierre Granval
Blaise, the gardener	Gaston Modot
Alberte	Jacqueline Morane
Suzy	Ghislaine Dumont
Juliette	Madeleine Marion

Mary	Primerose Perret
Georges	Didier d'Yd
The ambassador	Jacque-Catelain
His wife	Régine Blaess
The invalid	Raymond Jourdan
The little girl	Sylviane Margolle
A girl	Céline Salles
Madame des Essarts	Raymone

Plot: Jean Renoir, using the still new techniques of television, shoots whole scenes with several cameras instead of the usual succession of shots. His film scarcely resembles the Stevenson tale that inspired it. Doctor Cordelier, who lives alone and has no family, asks his notary that a certain Mr. Opale be named his sole heir. Mr. Opale is a dreaded personage in the residential neighborhood where Cordelier lives, and everyone knows that his sadistic behavior verges on criminality. So the good doctor's decision is surprising to his friend the notary. Yet the doctor insists on it. Opale is indispensable for his research, which attempts to show that human behavior can be modified at will. Cordelier does not admit that Opale is his double. He knows only too well that the doses of medicine he must take to transform himself into Opale keep increasing and that, in the end, they will be fatal, but he will not abandon his research. The virtuous Cordelier, completely devoted to his science, lacks the strange radiance of Opale, who has a kind of innocence and inner joy. The contrast is pure Renoir. His tale is not meant for the edification of children. Cordelier-Opale suffers a horrible, agonizing death.

Le Dejeuner sur l'herbe / *Picnic on the Grass*

Screenplay: Jean Renoir
Director: Jean Renoir
Assistant Directors: Maurice Beuchey, Francis Morane, Jean-Pierre Spiero, Hedy Naka, and Jean de Nesles
Technical Assistant: Yves-André Hubert
Director of Photography: Georges Leclerc (Eastmancolor)
Cameramen: Ribaud, Jean-Louis Picavet, Andreas Winding, and Pierre Guégen
Sound: Joseph de Bretagne
Music: Joseph Kosma
Set Design: Marcel-Louis Dieulot, assisted by André Piltan and Pierre Cadiou
Costumes: Monique Dunand

Continuity: Andrée Gauthey and Marinette Pasquet
Special Effects: Marcel Jaffredo
Gaffer: André Moindrat
Electricians: Georges Gandart and Henri Prat
Editing: Renée Lichtig, assisted by Françoise London
Shot at: Francoeur Studios and on location at "Les Collettes" and in
    the vicinity of Cagnes, July–August 1959
Producer: Ginette Doynel, for Compagnie Jean Renoir
Distributors: Consortium Pathé
Length: 92 minutes
Cast:

Professor Etienne Alexis	Paul Meurisse
Antoinette, called Nénette	Catherine Rouvel
Nino, her father	Fernand Sardou
Titine, older sister of Nénette	Jacqueline Morane
Ritou, her husband	Jean-Pierre Granval
Laurent	Robert Chandeau
His wife, Madeleine	Micheline Gary
Rudolf	Frédéric O'Brady
His wife, Magda	Gislaine Dumont
Marie-Charlotte	Ingrid Nordine
The old parish priest	André Brunot
Isabelle, the secretary	Hélène Duc
Rousseau, the majordomo	Jean Claudio
Paignant	Jacques Dannoville
His wife	Marguerite Cassan
Gaspard, the old shepherd	Charles Blavette
Mademoiselle Forestier,	
the switchboard operator	Paulette Dubost

Four announcers playing themselves: Michel Péricard,
Roland Thierry, Dupraz, and Lucas

Plot: Professor Etienne Alexis is a candidate for president of the
    United States of Europe. It is 1959, and his outstanding biological
    research has made him a proponent of artificial insemination. A
    pompous fellow, very sure of himself, he is about to celebrate his
    engagement to a countess with a picnic on the grass of a country
    estate. Nénette, a young peasant girl who would like to have a
    child but dreads marriage, gets herself hired as a maid in the pro-
    fessor's household and is ready to be used as a guinea pig. In-
    stead the child that she will bear is conceived naturally: thanks to
    a severe thunderstorm that breaks out during the picnic, the pro-

fessor, who turns out to be more human than he looks, is moved by the beauty of the young girl bathing naked in a stream. He will not leave her side thereafter, and he learns the joys of peaceful domesticity. He becomes a father, and she, president of the United States of Europe.

1962

Le Caporal epinglé / *The Elusive Corporal*

Screenplay: Jean Renoir and Guy Lefranc, based on the novel by Jacques Perret
Director: Jean Renoir, assisted by Guy Lefranc
Assistant Directors: Marc Maurette, J. E. Kieffer
Director of Photography: Georges Leclerc
Cameramen: Jean-Louis Picavet, Gilbert Chain, Antoine Georgakis, and Robert Fraisse
Sound: Antoine Petitjean, assisted by Jacques Bissière, Gaston Demède, and Jacques Gérardo
Special Effects: Eugène Herrly
Gaffer: André Moindrot
Continuity: Charlotte Lefcbvre-Vuattoux
Music: Joseph Kosma
Editing: Renée Lichtig, assisted by Madeleine Lacompère
Shot at: Studios in Vienna and on location in Vienna and vicinity and Paris (pont de Tolbiac), Winter, 1961–62
Producer: René G. Vuattoux for Films du Cyclope (G. W. Byer)
Associate Producer: Georges Glass
Administrative Assistant: Yvonne Tourmayeff
Press agent: Marianne Frey
Distributors: : Pathé
Length: 105 minutes
Cast:

The corporal	Jean-Pierre Cassell
Pater	Claude Brasseur
Adrien Ballochet	Claude Rich
The drunken passenger in the train	O. E. Hasse
Guillaume	Jean Carmet
Penche-à-gauche	Jacques Jouanneau
Erika Schmidt	Cornelia Froboess
Caruso	Mario David

The electrician	Philippe Costelli
Hippolyte Dupieu, the adjutant	Raymond Jourdan
The stutterer	Guy Bedos
The shifty character	Gérard Darrieu
The transvestite fugitive	Sacha Briquet
Worker in the train station	Lucien Raimbourg
Peasant	François Darbon
A guard	Bill Kearns

This film was selected for projection at the Berlin Festival
of 1962 and presented at the inaugural session of the
London Film Festival that same year.

Plot: Jean Renoir's idea was to make a series of sketches in black and
white retelling the attempted escapes of a group of friends who
became prisoners of war in 1940. He warned the producers ahead
of time that it would not be *Grand Illusion* revisited. World War II
was nothing like World War I, and the era of the Prussian aristocrat was over and done with, and the same was probably true of
men like Boeldieu; in any case, Jacques Perret's characters are
really different. Jean Renoir was inspired by them, but he set
aside the parts of the book that take place in Berlin at a time he
did not know and could not well imagine. The sketches are reminiscent of silent films and are often slapsticky. Only one is tragic:
a prisoner decides to escape on his own, without the least chance
of succeeding. So one night he goes out and gets shot and killed
like a rabbit. This episode gives an inkling of the danger lurking
in the background of the movie. It is hard to feel it otherwise,
since the producers cut out the newsreels that Jean Renoir put
in to give a context to the whole film. Like Jean Renoir's other
works, this one has an extraordinary and profound human quality
that belies its lightness of tone.

1969

Le Petit théâtre de Jean Renoir / Jean Renoir's Miniature Theater

Screenplay: Jean Renoir
Director: Jean Renoir
Assistant Director: Denis Epstein
Director of Photography: Georges Leclerc, assisted by Antoine Georgakis
and Georges Liron (for the colors)
Cameramen: Henri Martin and Claude Amiot

Sound: Guy Rolphe, assisted by Jean Bareille
Sound Effects: De Vaivre
Mixing: Alex Pront
Continuity: Charlotte Lefevre
Set Design: Gilbert Margerie
Assistant to the director (studios): Daniel Messère
Assistant to the director (on location): Jean Boulet and Maurice Jumeau
Music: Jean Wiener, for "Le Dernier Réveillon," "Le Roi d'Yvetot"; Joseph Kosma for "La Cireuse électrique"; Octave Crémieux for "Quand l'amour meurt," with lyrics by G. Millandy
Shot at: Paris-Studios Cinéma for "Quand l'amour meurt"; Saint-Maurice for the three others, and on location at Versailles, Résidence "Grand Siècle" (for "La Cireuse électrique); around Aix-en-Provence and Saint-Rémy for "Le Roi d'Yvetot"
Producers: A film/television coproduction: for film, Pierre Long for Société Son et Lumière; for television, Robert Paillardon for RAI, Bavaria, ORTF
Cast:

1. "LE DERNIER RÉVEILLON"

The hobo	Nino Formicola
The female hobo	Milly-Monti
Max Wialle	Roger Trapp
The maître d'	Robert Lombard
Gontran	Roland Bertin
Another tramp	Paul Bisciglia

2. "LA CIREUSE ÉLECTRIQUE"

Emilie	Marguerite Cassan
Gustave, her husband	Pierre Olaf
Jules, her second husband	Jacques Dynam
The lovers	Denis de Gunsburg and Claude Guillaume
The traveling salesman	Jean-Louis Tristan

3. "QUAND L'AMOUR MEURT"

The singer	Jeanne Moreau

4. "LE ROI D'YVETOT"

Duvallier	Fernand Sardou
Isabelle, his wife	Françoise Arnoul
Dr. Féraud	Jean Carmet
Paulette, the maid	Dominique Labourier
César, the tramp	Edmond Ardisson

Plot: Jean Renoir himself introduces each of the four sketches:

1. "Le Dernier Réveillon" ["The Last Christmas Eve Party"]: On the banks of the Seine, an old hobo and his girlfriend celebrate Christmas by dining on leftovers retrieved from a great restaurant. They imagine themselves young and handsome, dancing in evening dress, and then they fall asleep in each other's arms. During the night, they die of cold.

2. "La Cireuse électrique" ["The Electric Floorpolisher"]: A woman obsessed with cleanliness shines her floor so well that her husband slips on it and kills himself. Her second husband, who can't stand the noise of the floor polisher, throws the damn thing out the window. In despair, his wife does the same with herself.

3. "Quand l'amour meurt" ["When Love Dies"]: A famous song from the year 1900 sung by a motionless Jean Moreau on an empty stage in front of a painted scrim from a caf'conc' of the Gay Nineties.

4. "Le Roi d'Yvetot" ["The King of Yvetot"]: A couple live peacefully on an estate in Provence. The woman, who is much younger than her husband, has occasional bouts of melancholy. One day her dog is injured, and she ends up becoming the veterinarian's mistress. He is a decent guy who gets along well with everyone in the household. So all three are content, but the local gossips go on the attack. However, the generous and kindly husband quiets them all by being the first to laugh at their situation. His good humor soon becomes general.

At the end of the film, the actors take a bow before the curtain falls for the last time, as in the theater.

BIBLIOGRAPHY

◆

Screenplays

The Rules of the Game, trans. John McGrath and Maureen Teitelbaum (New York, 1970; rev. ed., London, 1984).
La Grande Illusion (Paris, 1971).
Julienne et son amour, suivi d'En avant Rosalie! intr. Claude Gauteur (Paris, 1979).
Oeuvres de cinéma inédites. Textes réunis et presentés par Claude Gauteur (Paris, 1981).

Plays

Orvet (Paris, 1955)
Carola, in *L'Avant-Scène théâtre*, 597, 1 Nov. 1976 (see also *Les Cahiers du cinéma*, 78, Christmas, 1957)

Biography

Renoir (Paris, 1962); repr. 1981 under the title *Pierre-Auguste Renoir, mon père;* = *Renoir, My Father*, trans. Randolph and Dorothy Weaver (Boston, 1962)

Novels

Les Cahiers du capitaine Georges (Paris, 1966) = *The Notebooks of Captain Georges*, trans. Norman Denny (Boston, 1966)
Le Coeur à l'aise (Paris, 1978)
Le Crime de l'Anglais (Paris, 1979)
Geneviève (Paris, 1979)

Memoirs

Ma vie et mes films (Paris, 1974), repr. 1987 = *My Life and Films*, trans. Norman Denny (New York, 1974)

BIBLIOGRAPHY

Miscellaneous

Ecrits 1926–1971 (Paris, 1974)

Entretiens et propos, Paris, 1979 = *Renoir on Renoir: Interviews, Essays, and Remarks*, trans. Carol Volk (New York, 1989)

Lettres d'Amérique, pres. Dido Renoir & Alexander Sesonske, ed. Alexander Sesonske (Paris, 1984)

Le Passé vivant, edition établie par Claude Gauteur (Paris, 1989)

INDEX

◆